D0906434

EUROPEAN HISTORICAL DICTIONARIES
Edited by Jon Woronoff

1. *Portugal,* by Douglas L. Wheeler. 1993
2. *Turkey,* by Metin Heper. 1994
3. *Poland,* by George Sanford and Adriana Gozdecka-Sanford. 1994
4. *Germany,* by Wayne C. Thompson, Susan L. Thompson, and Juliet S. Thompson. 1994
5. *Greece,* by Thanos M. Veremis and Mark Dragoumis. 1995
6. *Cyprus,* by Stavros Panteli. 1995
7. *Sweden,* by Irene Scobbie. 1995
8. *Finland,* by George Maude. 1995
9. *Croatia,* by Robert Stallaerts and Jeannine Laurens. 1995
10. *Malta,* by Warren G. Berg. 1995
11. *Spain,* by Angel Smith. 1996
12. *Albania,* by Raymond Hutchings. 1996
13. *Slovenia,* by Leopoldina Plut-Pregelj and Carole Rogel. 1996
14. *Luxembourg,* by Harry C. Barteau. 1996
15. *Romania,* by Kurt W. Treptow and Marcel Popa. 1996
16. *Bulgaria,* by Raymond Detrez. 1997
17. *United Kingdom: Volume 1, England and the United Kingdom,* by Kenneth J. Panton and Keith A. Cowlard. 1997
18. *Hungary,* by Steven Béla Várdy. 1997
19. *Latvia,* by Andrejs Plakans. 1997
20. *Ireland,* by Colin Thomas and Avril Thomas. 1997
21. *Lithuania*, by Saulius Sužiedėlis. 1997
22. *Macedonia,* by Valentina Georgieva and Sasa Konechni. 1997
23. *Czech Republic,* by Jiri Hochman. 1997
24. *Iceland,* by Guðmundur Hálfdanarson. 1997
25. *Bosnia and Herzegovina,* by Ante Čuvalo. 1997
26. *Russia*, by Boris Raymond and Paul Duffy. 1998

Historical Dictionary of Bosnia and Herzegovina

Ante Čuvalo

European Historical Dictionaries, No. 25

The Scarecrow Press, Inc.
Lanham, Md., & London
1997

SCARECROW PRESS, INC.

Published in the United States of America
by Scarecrow Press, Inc.
4720 Boston Way
Lanham, Maryland 20706

British Library Cataloguing in Publication Information Available

Library of Congress Cataloging-in-Publication Data

Cuvalo, Ante.
Historical dictionary of Bosnia and Herzegovina / by Ante Čuvalo
p. cm. — (European historical dictionaries ; no. 25)
Includes bibliographical references.
ISBN 0-8108-3344-1 (cloth ; alk. paper)
1. Bosnia and Hercegovina—History—Dictionaries. I. Title. II. Series.
DR1675-5.C88 1997
949.742—dc21 97-14417
CIP

ISBN 0-8108-3344-1 (cloth : alk. paper)

∞™ The paper used in this publication meets the minimum requirements of American National Standard for Information Sciences—Permanence of Paper for Printed Library Materials, ANSI Z39.48–1984.
Manufactured in the United States of America.

This book is dedicated to all the innocent victims of the recent war in Croatia and Bosnia-Herzegovina, to my late father who was himself an innocent victim of the "Revolution" after World War II, and to my mother who, despite all the misfortunes, remained a believer in humanity.

CONTENTS

EDITOR'S FOREWORD

Few states have had a more painful birth than Bosnia and Herzegovina. Hopefully conceived as a home for much of the Muslim population and a haven of multiethnic harmony, it was nearly torn apart during years of hostilities that pitted domestic groups and their external supporters against one another. For some time, it looked as if even remnants of the Bosnian state would not survive despite international support. Even now, it is hard to be sanguine about the future of a still fragmented country, with terribly complex political institutions and many remaining impediments to economic development. Yet, despite all this, Bosnia is reviving, Bosnians are getting used to living with one another again, and the news is finally better than expected or, at least, better than had been feared.

Events during the birth of this nation showed that what happens in Bosnia is not only important for the Bosnians. It concerns the neighboring states, European and Muslim countries, the United States, and the United Nations. This only enhances the importance of obtaining useful information such as is provided in this *Historical Dictionary of Bosnia and Herzegovina*. Obviously, here as in other works, there is considerable emphasis on the current situation and recent past. Significant leaders are presented, crucial events are described, and political institutions are analyzed. More broadly, here are entries on the economy, society, culture and religions. But they only make sense when read in conjunction with other entries delving into earlier periods, entries, for example, on Tito's Yugoslavia, previous kingdoms, the Ottoman occupation, and still older units. Attitudes throughout the region have very deep roots, and the chronology and introduction allow the reader to follow their development through time. Further information can be derived from the books cited in the bibliography.

The author of this volume, Ante Čuvalo, was born in Bosnia-Herzegovina and received his elementary, his secondary, and parts of his college education there and in Croatia. His further studies were in the United States, where he majored in Eastern European history. He has taught at Ohio State University and Joliet Jr. College. Dr. Čuvalo has both lectured and written extensively on former Yugoslavia and Croatia. This present volume provides an informative and illuminating view of Bosnia and Herzegovina, where he grew up and which he knows very well.

Jon Woronoff
Series Editor

ACKNOWLEDGMENTS

In the preparation of this dictionary I received help from a number of friends and I thank all of them. Special thanks go to my wife Ivana for her support and professional help, to Concordia Hoffmann and Krešimir Šego for their professional assistance and suggestions, and to the library staff of Joliet Jr. College, especially Barbara Wilson for her patience and cooperation.

Ante Čuvalo

NOTE ON SPELLING

Three languages are in use in today's Bosnia and Herzegovina: Croatian, Serbian, and Bosniac. Croatian and Bosniac use the Latin, and Serbian the Cyrillic script.

Some letters in the Latin script, however, marked by diacritical signs or composed of two letters, indicate specific sounds. The same sounds can be found in the Cyrillic alphabet and they can be easily transcribed into the Latin alphabet.

The original spelling is retained in domestic names and concepts. The following pronunciation key for English-speaking readers will be helpful.

C c	*ts* as in *nuts*
Ć ć	*ch* as in *cheap*
Č č	*ch* as in *chair*
Đ đ	*j* as in *joke*
Dž dž	*j* as in *joke* but harder
J j	*y* as in *yes*
Lj lj	*li* as in *million*
Nj nj	*ny* as in *canyon*
Š š	*sh* as in *shell*
Ž ž	*zh* as in *seizure*

In alphabetizing the dictionary the diacritical signs have been ignored.

ACRONYMS

ABiH	Armija Bosne i Hercegovine—Army of Bosnia and Herzegovina
ANUBiH	Akademija Nauka i Umjetnosti Bosne i Hercegovine—Academy of Sciences and Arts of Bosnia and Herzegovina
AVNOJ	Antifašističko Vijeće Narodnog Oslobođenja Jugoslavije—Anti-Fascist Council of the National Liberation of Yugoslavia
CSCE	Conference on Security and Co-operation in Europe
DNZ	Demokratska Narodna Zajednica—Democratic People's Union
DSS	Demokratska Stranka Socijalista—Democratic Party of Socialists
DSZ	Demokratska Liga Zelenih—Democratic League of Greens
EC	European Community
EU	European Union
HABENA	Herceg-Bosna Novinska Agencija—Herceg-Bosna News Agency
HDS	Hrvatska Demokratska Stranka—Croatian Democratic Party

HDZ	Hrvatska Demokratska Zajednica—Croatian Democratic Union
HMDZ	Hrvatska Muslimanska Demokratska Stranka—Croatian Muslim Democratic Party
HOS	Hrvatske Oružane Snage—Croat Armed Forces
HSP	Hrvatska Stranka Prava—Croatian Party of Right
HSS	Hrvatska Seljačka Stranka—Croatian Peasant Party. From 1918-1925, Croatian Republican Peasant Party (HRSS).
HVO	Hrvatsko Vijeće Obrane—Croat Defense Council
IFOR	Implementation Force
IMRO	Internal Macedonian Revolutionary Organization
ICFY	International Conference on Former Yugoslavia
JMO	Jugoslavenska Muslimanska Organizacija—Yugoslav Muslim Organization
JNA	Jugoslavenska Narodna Armija—Yugoslav People's Army
KOS	Kontra Obavještajna Služba—Counter-intelligence Service
LCY	League of Communists of Yugoslavia
LS	Liberalna Stranka—Liberal Party
MBO	Muslimanska Bošnjačka Organizacija—Muslim Bosniac Organization
MDS	Muslimanska Demokratska Stranka—Muslim Democratic Party
MOS	Muslimanske Oružane Snage—Muslim Armed Forces
NATO	North Atlantic Treaty Organization
NDH	Nezavisna Država Hrvatska—Independent State of Croatia
OSCE	Organization for Security and Cooperation in Europe
RBH	Radio Bosne i Hercegovine—Radio of Bosnia and Herzegovina
RRF	Rapid Reaction Force
RS	Republikanska Stranka—Republican Party

RTVBH	Radio-Televizija Bosne i Hercegovine—Radio-Televison of Bosnia and Herzegovina
SBiH	Stranka za Bosnu i Hercegovinu—Party for Bosnia and Herzegovina
SCC	Serb Civic Council—Srpsko Građansko Vijeće
SDA	Stranka Demokratske Akcije—Party of Democratic Action
SDG	Srpska Dobrovoljačka Garda—Serbian Volunteer Guard
SDP	Socijalistička Demokratska Partija—Social Democratic Party
SDS	Srpska Demokratska Stranka—Serbian Democratic Party
SFRJ	Socijalistička Federativna Republika Jugoslavija—Socialist Federative Republic of Yugoslavia
SFRY	Socialist Federative Republic of Yugoslavia
SGV	Srpsko Građansko Vijeće—Serb Civic Council
SIDRA	Savez Islamskih Derviških Redova Alijje—Alliance of Islamic Dervish Orders Allijja
SKSDP	Savez Komunista, Stranka Demokratskih Promjena—League of Communists, Party for Democratic Change
SMPSR	Savez za Mir i Progres (Republika Srpska) —Union for Peace and Progress (Serb Republic)
SNO	Srpska Narodna Obnova—Serbian People Renewal (Party)
SPRS	Socijalistička Partija (Republika Srpska)—Socialist Party (Serb Republic)
SPAS	Srpska Patriotska Stranka—Serb Patriotic Party (Serb Republic)
SPO	Srpski Pokret Obnove—Serbian Renewal Movement
SPS	Socijalistička Partija Srbije—Socialist Party of Serbia
SRJ	Savezna Republika Jugoslavija—Federal Republic of Yugoslavia

SRNA	Srpska Republika Novinska Agencija—Serb Republic News Agency
SRS	Srpska Radikalna Stranka—Serb Radical Party
SRSJ	Savez Reformskih Snaga Jugoslavije—Alliance of Reform Forces of Yugoslavia
SRSBiH	Savez Reformskih Snaga Bosne i Hercegovine—Alliance of Reform Forces of Bosnia and Herzegovina
SRT	Srpska Radio-Televizija—Serb Radio-Television
SSK	Srpska Stranka Krajine—Serb Party of Krajina
TVBH	Televizija Bosne i Hercegovine—Televison of Bosnia and Herzegovina
TVSA	Televizija Sarajevo—Sarajevo Television
UDBA	Uprava Državne Bezbjednosti—Directorate of State Security
UN	United Nations
UNPROFOR	United Nations Protection Force
UNSC	United Nations Security Council
US/USA	United States of America
VRS	Vojska Republike Srpske—Army of the Serb Republic
ZAVNOBiH	Zemaljsko Antifašističko Vijeće Narodnog Oslobođenja Bosne i Hercegovine—The Territorial Anti-Fascist Council of the National Liberation of Bosnia and Herzegovina
ZIDRA	Zajednica Islamskih Derviških Redova Alijje—Community of Islamic Dervish Orders Allijja
ZLBiH	Združena Lista Bosne i Hercegovine—United List for Bosnia and Herzegovina.

CHRONOLOGY

Neolithic epoch	Distinctive culture present in regions of today's Bosnia-Herzegovina. Butmir (near Sarajevo) is best finding from the period.
Bronze age	A number of human settlements present.
ca. 1100 BC	Indo-European Illyrians settle in Balkans from Macedonia to the Alps.
ca. 359 BC	Celts invade the Balkans.
229 BC	Long struggle between Illyrians and Romans starts.
AD 9	Finally, Romans crush Illyrian resistance. A year later Caesar Augustus divides Roman province of Illyricum into two provinces, Pannonia and Dalmatia. Today's northern Bosnia belongs to Pannonia, and the rest to Dalmatia.
395	Permanent division of the Roman Empire into Eastern and Western halves. Present border

	between Serbia and Bosnia-Herzegovina becomes a permanent boundary between East and West.
ca. 600	First Slavic migration to the Balkan region takes place, together with or perhaps in service of the invading Avars.
626-635	Croats from White Croatia, a state around today's city of Cracow in Poland, fight Avars and settle eastern shores of the Adriatic. Present lands of Bosnia and Herzegovina become mostly a part of the Croat domain.
ca. 635	Serbs from today's southeastern Germany migrate to today's southern Serbia.
877	First known reference to Bosnian Catholic diocese under the Archdiocese of Split.
925	First Croatian king, Tomislav, is crowned in today's Bosnian town of Tomislavgrad.
949-960	Original Bosnian territory is under Serbian ruler Časlav.
960-990	Bosnia is under rule of Croatian kings again.
990	A short Bulgarian rule in Bosnia.
1018-1040	Bosnia is under Byzantium.
1040-1087	Bosnia is part of Croatian rule again.
1060	Catholic diocese of Vrhbosna is established.
1087-1102	Bosnia under Duklja (Dioclea).

1154-1163	First known Bosnian ruler, *ban* Borić.
1164?-1204	Rule of Kulin *ban* in Bosnia.
1203	Renunciation of heresy at Bilino Polje by *ban* Kulin and local church leaders.
1222	First Hungarian "Crusade" against Bosnian "heretics." The country comes under direct Hungarian rule.
1225-ca. 1253	Matija Ninoslav *ban* of Bosnia.
1254-1287	*Ban* Stipan Prijezda (Kotroman).
1287-1302	Stipan I Kotromanić *ban* of Bosnia.
1290	Croatian *ban*, Pavao I Šubić, invades Bosnia.
1291	Franciscan friars arrive in Bosnia as missionaries.
1302	Mladen Šubić, brother of Pavao Šubić, occupies Bosnia. *Ban* Stipan I Kotromanić on the run. Mladen is assassinated in Bosnia 1304.
1304-1318	Mladen II Šubić, oldest son of *ban* Pavao I Šubić, ruler of Bosnia.
1312-1353	Stipan II Kotromanić *ban* of Bosnia.
1322	Stipan II begins expanding Bosnia's borders to west and south, including region of Hum.
1339/40	Franciscans establish Bosnian Vicariate.
1350	Ruler of Serbia, Stevan Dušan, invades Bosnia but is not able to keep it.

1353-1391	Reign of *ban* and then King Stipan Tvrtko I Kotromanić
1365/67	Bosnian *kr'stjans* rebel against Tvrtko.
1373	Tvrtko I captures Podrinje from Serbs.
1377	Tvrtko I declares himself king.
1385-1390	Tvrtko I gains the town of Kotor and recaptures Tropolje (Duvno, Livno, Glamoč), Hum, and parts of southern Croatia.
1386	First Turkish incursion into Bosnian kingdom.
1391-1395	Rule of King Stipan Dabiša.
1393	Dabiša recognizes suzerainty of Hungarian-Croatian king Sigismund and promises him Bosnian crown after his own death.
1395-1398	Jelena, Dabiša's wife, rules Bosnia.
1398-1404	Ostoja king of Bosnia and again in 1408-1418.
1404-1408	Tvrtko II ruler of Bosnia and again in 1420-1443.
1419-1420	King Stipan Ostojić.
1444-1461	King Stipan Tomaš.
1448	Stipan Vukčić Kosača, ruler of Hum, takes title of *Herceg* (duke). Later, the land becomes known as Herzegovina or Herzeg's land.
1461-1463	King Stipan Tomašević—last king of Bosnia.

1463 End of medieval Bosnian state. Bosnia becomes a victim of Ottoman expansionism in Europe. Turks make Bosnia a military district (*sandžak*). Parts of the land are temporarily recovered by Hungarian-Croatian king and Herzeg Stipan.

1470 Turks make Herzegovina a separate military district (*sandžak*).

1482 Last remnant of Herzeg's land (Herzegovina) falls to the Turks.

1527 Fall of town of Jajce to the Turks.

1580 Bosnia becomes an Ottoman province (*beylerbeylik*, *eyalet*, or better known as *pašaluk*). It includes *sandžak* of Herzegovina and newly established *sandžak*s in Croatia.

1592 Town of Bihać falls to the Turks.

1699 The Treaty of Karlowitz (Srijemski Karlovici) ends Habsburg-Ottoman war (1683-1699). Ottomans start retreating from Europe.

1718 Republic of Dubrovnik grants Ottomans in Bosnia-Herzegovina two exits to the Adriatic Sea, Neum-Klek in the north and Suturina to the south of its territory.

1826 As a part of Ottoman reforms, Janissary corps are abolished. Great dissatisfaction in Bosnia with reforms.

1831 Open Muslim revolt in Bosnia, under charismatic leadership of *Kapetan* Husejin

	Gradaščević, known as "Dragon of Bosnia." Revolt is crushed a year later.
1832	Herzegovina becomes an independent Ottoman province (*eyalet*).
1835	*Kapetanije* in Bosnia-Herzegovina are abolished.
1849	One of biggest Muslim anti-reform revolts in Bosnia crushed by Omer-pasha Latas in 1850.
1851	Major revolt of Christians in Bosnia. They demand equality under the law. Christians revolt again in 1857-58 for similar reasons.
1864	A capable governor, Topal Osman-pasha, implements provincial reforms in Bosnia. Bosnia and Herzegovina are united once again into a single Ottoman administrative province *(vilayet)*.
1875	Rebellion of Croatian and Serbian peasants against Muslim landlords starts a crisis that brings an end to Ottoman rule in Bosnia.
1876	Serbia and Montenegro declare war on Ottoman Empire. Ottomans win the war.
1877-1878	Successful Russian intervention in the Balkans. The Ottomans suffer a major defeat.
1878	Congress of Berlin revises Russian dictated Treaty of San Stefano and, among other provisions, entrusts Bosnia and Herzegovina to Austria-Hungary to "occupy and administer." On July 29, 1878, Habsburg forces march into Bosnia-Herzegovina and by end of October take full control over the country. Bosnia-

	Herzegovina remains a separate province under a shared rule of Austria and Hungary.
1882	Benjamin Kállay becomes Joint Imperial Finance Minister and ex officio in control of Bosnian affairs till 1903.
1908	Austro-Hungary annexes Bosnia-Herzegovina.
1910	Constitution for Bosnia-Herzegovina is promulgated. Limited base franchise elections to Parliament take place.
1912-1913	First and Second Balkan Wars.
1914 Jun 28	Assassination of Archduke Francis Ferdinand in Sarajevo. First World War follows (1914-1918).
1918 Dec 1	Formation of Kingdom of Serbs, Croats, and Slovenes (known as Yugoslavia after 1929) under Serbia's Karađorđević dynasty.
1919	Yugoslav Muslim Organization (JMO) is established.
1928 Jun 20	Assassination of Croatian parliamentary leaders in Belgrade's Parliament.
1929 Jan 6	King Aleksandar Karađorđević outlaws all "tribal" parties, declares personal dictatorship, and renames the country Yugoslavia. Ante Pavelić, a member of Parliament, establishes *ustaša* revolutionary movement shortly after.

1939	Croat-Serbian Agreement (*Sporazum*). Croatia becomes an autonomous banate (*banovina)* that includes parts of Bosnia-Herzegovina.
	Beginnings of "Young Muslims" movement in Bosnia.
1941	Yugoslavia disintegrates. Independent State of Croatia declared (1941-1945). Bosnia-Herzegovina is part of Croatia.
1943 Nov 29	Second Session of Anti-Fascist Council of the National Liberation of Yugoslavia (AVNOJ) takes place. It proclaims second Yugoslavia based on federalist principles under leadership of Josip Broz Tito and Yugoslav Communist Party.
1946 Jan 31	New Yugoslav Constitution is proclaimed. Bosnia-Herzegovina becomes one of six republics in socialist Yugoslavia.
1948 Jun 28	Soviet-lead Cominform expels Yugoslav Communist Party from its ranks. Soviet-Yugoslav split ensues.
1952	Yugoslav "road to socialism" is introduced, including idea of "self-management." Communist Party of Yugoslavia is renamed into League of Communists of Yugoslavia.
1965	Yugoslav economic reforms start.
1966	Fall of unitarist Serbian leader Aleksandar Ranković who opposed reforms.

1971 Dec 1	End of "Croatian Spring." Many students and intellectuals are jailed and Party in Croatia is purged of "rotten liberalism."
1974	New Yugoslav Constitution is promulgated. It enhances power of the six Republics and two Autonomous Provinces. Tito is confirmed as president for life. Principle of rotating collective presidency is established.
1980 May 4	Josip Broz Tito, President of Yugoslavia dies.
1983 Jul-Aug	Trial of 13 prominent Muslims in Bosnia, including Alija Izetbegović.
1986	*Memorandum* issued by Serbian Academy of Sciences and Arts exposes growing nationalism among Serbs. Document considered an ideological blueprint for events that followed among Serbs.
1987	Slobodan Milošević gains power in Serbia and the issue of Kosovo becomes rallying cry of Serbian nationalism.
	Financial scandal in well-known business enterprise (Agrokomerc) shakes Muslim ruling establishment in Bosnia-Herzegovina.
1990 Jan	League of Communists of Yugoslavia disintegrates. Slovene Party officials walk out of Fourteenth, and last, Party Congress.

Nov 18	Multi-party elections in Bosnia-Herzegovina. Muslim, Serb, and Croat nationalist parties victorious. Runoff elections Dec. 2.
1991	
May 15	Serbian and Montenegrin representatives in federal collective presidency of Yugoslavia block Stipe Mesić of Croatia from assuming Presidency.
Jun 25	Croatia and Slovenia declare independence.
Jun 26	"Ten Day War" between Slovene Defense Forces and Yugoslav Peoples Army (JNA). Within a few months JNA pulls out of Slovenia.
Jul-Dec	War in Croatia between Croatian Territorial Forces on one side and local Serbian rebels, paramilitary forces from Serbia, backed by JNA on the other. Serbs consolidate their control over one-third of Croatia.
Sep 29	Serb and Montenegrin forces attack Croat village of Ravno in Herzegovina. Destruction and massacre follow.
Oct 15	Memorandum of Sovereignty is adopted by parliament of Bosnia-Herzegovina; 73 Serb deputies walk out in protest.
Dec 20	Bosnia-Herzegovina asks EC for recognition of its independence.
1992	
Jan 2	UN envoy, former U.S. secretary of state Cyrus Vance, negotiates agreement between Croatia and Serbs according to which United Nations Protection Force (UNPROFOR) will separate

	belligerents and JNA will pull out of Croatia. Eventually JNA moves most of its troops from Croatia to Bosnia-Herzegovina.
Jan 15	EC and several individual countries formally recognize Slovene and Croatian independence.
Feb 21	UN Security Council establishes United Nations Protection Force (UNPROFOR) to facilitate peace implementation in Croatia.
Feb 29 & Mar 1	Bosnia holds referendum on independence, as required by European Community. Over 99 percent of participants vote for independence from Yugoslavia. Most of Bosnian Serbs do not participate in vote.
Feb-Mar	European Community sponsors talks in Lisbon, Portugal, on future of Bosnia and Herzegovina. EC plan proposes national cantons within federal Bosnian state. Provisions for central government are so weak that Radovan Karadžić, leader of Bosnian Serbs, endorses plan. President Izetbegović at first accepts plan, than changes his mind and rejects it.
Mar 3	President Izetbegović announces independence of Bosnia and Herzegovina and calls on all armed groups to disarm.
Mar 27	Radovan Karadžić proclaims "Serbian Republic in Bosnia-Herzegovina" with Banja Luka as its temporary capital, and declares that Republic's loyalty is to "all-Serbian State of Yugoslavia."
Apr 6	Serb irregulars start massive war campaign. Shelling of Sarajevo starts. Yugoslav Peoples

	Army (JNA) directly involved in attacks on Muslim and Croat areas of country.
1992	
Apr 6 & 7	Bosnia-Herzegovina is recognized by European Community and United States, respectively. U.S. also recognizes Croatia and Slovenia.
Apr 27	Federal Republic of Yugoslavia, composed of Serbia and Montenegro, is proclaimed in Belgrade.
May 30	UNSC imposes mandatory sanctions against Serbia and Montenegro.
Jun 29	UNSC votes to immediately deploy additional elements of UNPROFOR to ensure security of Sarajevo airport and delivery of humanitarian assistance.
Aug 6	News team from British TV network ITN visits concentration camps of Omarska and Trnopolje. First pictures documenting ethnic cleansing and confirming existence of Serb concentration camps are exposed to the world.
Aug 26	A multilateral conference on war in Bosnia, sponsored by the EC and UN, takes place in London. John Major and Boutros Boutros-Ghali preside.
Sep 3	First session of UN-sponsored talks in Geneva begins. Cyrus Vance and David Owen act as mediators of the UN and EC.
Sep 14	UNSC authorizes (Resolution 776) the enlargement of UNPROFOR's mandate and

	strength in Bosnia-Herzegovina from approximately 1,500 to up to 6,000 ground troops to protect humanitarian mission.
Sep 22	UN General Assembly expels Yugoslavia from UN for its role in war in Bosnia-Herzegovina.
Oct 9	UNSC establishes ban on military flights in airspace over Bosnia-Herzegovina.
Oct 21	Sporadic fighting between Muslims and Croats in central Bosnia is reported. It escalates into serious conflict during 1993.
Oct 27	Two mediators, Cyrus Vance and Lord Owen, present a peace plan that would divide Bosnia-Herzegovina into 10 semiautonomous, mostly ethnic cantons with common central government.
Nov 9	Radovan Karadžić, president of "Serb Republic of Bosnia-Herzegovina," announces that his republic and "Serbian Republic of Krajina" in Croatia have established a confederation.
Nov 16	UNSC authorizes a naval blockade against Serbia and Montenegro.
Nov 29	First UN aid convoy comes to besieged town of Srebrenica; first outside assistance since war began.
1993	
Jan 2	New round of peace talks opens in Geneva, Switzerland. Lord Owen and Cyrus Vance offer various proposals that would split Bosnia into 10 semiindependent cantons. Croat leadership

accepts deal on January 4. Muslim leaders endorse it reluctantly in March. Serbs reject deal in May 1993 referendum.

1993

Feb 22 UNSC (Resolution 808) approves creation of an International War Tribunal to try war crimes committed during war in Croatia and Bosnia-Herzegovina.

Feb 28 U.S. Air Force begins parachuting humanitarian relief supplies to Muslim towns under siege by Serb forces in eastern Bosnia.

Apr 2 Cyrus Vance resigns as UN mediator and is replaced by Thorvald Stoltenberg, Norwegian Foreign Minister.

Apr 16 UNSC (Resolution 819) declares Srebrenica "safe area," and then extends it to Sarajevo.

Apr 27 Serb forces attack Bihać enclave.

May 6 UNSC (Resolution 824) declares four more Muslim strongholds (Bihać, Goražde, Tuzla, and Žepa) UN "safe areas."

May 30 Intensive shelling of Sarajevo by Serbs starts. At least 20 people killed and more than 150 wounded. Other Bosnian towns are shelled too.

Jun Muslim forces initiate an offensive in central Bosnia against Croats.

Jun 23 Talks in Geneva on a peace plan that would divide Bosnia-Herzegovina into three ethnic federated states with a powerless central

government. Owen and Stoltenberg recommend plan as only "realistic alternative."

Aug 5 Bosnian peace talks are suspended due to Serbian seizure of strategic positions on Mount Bjelašnica and Mount Igman. Izetbegović refuses to compromise at peace talks in Geneva.

Aug 28 Croat leadership accepts Owen-Stoltenberg peace plan and proclaims "Croat Republic of Herceg-Bosna." Muslim-controlled parliament of Bosnia-Herzegovina rejects offer and puts forward new demands.

Sep 27 Fikret Abdić, leading Muslim politician and member of Bosnian collective presidency from Bihać region, dissociates himself from Sarajevo government. His local "assembly" votes to create Autonomous Province of Western Bosnia. Fight with Army of Bosnia-Herzegovina (government forces) over control of Bihać pocket follows.

Sep 29 Muslim dominated Bosnian parliament rejects Owen-Stoltenberg peace plan of three ethnic ministates under the name of Union of the Republics of Bosnia-Herzegovina. By October 15, negotiators concede that peace efforts have failed.

Nov 17 War Crimes Tribunal for former Yugoslavia opens in The Hague.

1994

Jan 26 Lieutenant General Sir Michael Rose of Britain takes command of UN forces in Bosnia, replacing Lt. Gen. Francis Briquemont of Belgium.

1994

Feb 5	Serbian bombardment of a crowded, open market in Sarajevo leaves 68 people dead and over 200 wounded.
Feb 8	Mate Boban, leader of Croat Republic of Herceg-Bosna, resigns.
Feb 9	NATO gives Bosnian Serb forces besieging Sarajevo 10 days to pull back heavy guns from Sarajevo exclusion zone (a radius of 20 km or 12 miles from center of the city) or place their heavy weapons into the hands of UNPROFOR, or face air strikes. But air strikes to take place only at UN's request.
Feb 28	Four Serb military jets are shot down by NATO fighters moments after Serb jets bomb a hospital and two military targets around Travnik. This is first NATO military action in its history. On same day Karadžić goes to Moscow.
Mar 18	Constitution on Muslim-Croat Federation of Bosnia and Herzegovina and Declaration on Confederation with Croatia is signed in the presence of President Clinton and other U.S. high officials in Washington.
Mar 29	Serb forces start major assault on UN "safe area" of Goražde, where about 65,000 people are besieged.
Apr 10	Two NATO (U.S.) jets carry out very limited air strike against Serb positions near Goražde.
Apr 14-17	A number of UN troops abducted by Serbs near Sarajevo; movement of UN troops restricted;

Serbs shell a UN observation post, Tuzla airport, and town centers.

Apr 16 British reconnaissance plane shot down by Serb surface-to-air missile near Goražde.

Apr 19 Serbs take back 18 antiaircraft guns from UN collection points around Sarajevo that were taken earlier as part of creating a Sarajevo "exclusion zone."

Apr 22 NATO alliance issues two sets of demands. First, it requires Serbs to pull back 3 km from the center of Goražde, which would coincide with cease-fire and free access to the town by medical workers and UN peacekeepers. Second, removal of all Serb artillery from 20 km in the radius of exclusion zone around the town. A day later, General Michael Rose, commander of UN forces in Bosnia, precludes the use of NATO air strikes.

Apr 23 NATO resolution on "exclusion zone" and air power umbrella issued on Goražde is extended to four other "safe areas," Bihać, Tuzla, Srebrenica, and Žepa.

Apr 25 U.S. and Russia join UN and EU in agreeing to establish Balkan Contact Group to coordinate international efforts to bring about end of war in Bosnia-Herzegovina. Group consists of U.S., England, France, Germany, and Russia.

Apr 27 UNSC approves dispatch of another 6,550 peacekeepers to Bosnia. This raises total number of peacekeepers in former Yugoslavia to 44,870, of which over 23,000 are in Bosnia-Herzegovina. Sending additional 150 observers and 275 policemen is also approved.

1994

May 13	Five Members of Contact Group unveil joint Bosnian peace plan in Geneva according to which Bosnia-Herzegovina is to be divided into two parts. Serbs would get 49 percent and Muslim-Croat Federation 51 percent of country's territory.
May 31	Newly formed constitutional Assembly of Muslim-Croatian Federation elects Krešimir Zubak (Croat) as Federation president and Ejup Ganić (Muslim) as vice president.
Jul 8	UNSC names Richard J. Goldstone from South Africa to be chief prosecutor for war crimes committed in Bosnia-Herzegovina and Croatia.
Jul 18	Bosnian government accepts Contact Group peace plan by parliamentary vote.
Jul 20	Serb leadership rejects Contact Group peace plan that gives them 49 percent of the land in Bosnia-Herzegovina.
Jul 21	Shelling and sniper attacks in Sarajevo resume.
Jul 30	Contact Group countries decide to tighten economic sanctions against Serbia and Montenegro, after Bosnian Serbs reject peace plan.
Aug 3-11	Bosnian government forces make considerable gains on three fronts, most of all in western Bosnia.

Sep 5	Two U.S. A-10 fighters hit antitank weapon near Sarajevo, after Serbs took heavy guns from UN-guarded depot.
Sep 6	Pope cancels his planned visit to Sarajevo, scheduled for September 8. UN officials state they could not guarantee his safety in the city.
Sep 19	Gen. Rose threatens Muslim-dominated Bosnian forces around Sarajevo with air strikes. Some Western officials are appalled by his threats.
Sep 22	NATO jets bomb Serb tank in response to their attack on French UN contingent near Sarajevo and for Serb refusal to remove heavy weapons violating "exclusion zone" around the city.
Sep 23	UNSC votes to lift some of sanctions against Yugoslavia. The resolution reopens Yugoslavia to international civil air traffic and allows its participation in international sporting and cultural activities.
Oct 25	Bosnian parliament calls for removal of General Rose as commander of UN forces in Bosnia.
Oct 26-Nov 3	Bosnian Croat forces join Army of Bosnia-Herzegovina in an offensive against Serbs and make gains on several fronts.
Nov 1	Serb forces from Croatia enter western Bosnia to fight Muslims and Croats.
Nov 3	Croat forces take control of town of Kupres, taken by Serbs in April 1992.

	UN General Assembly adopts resolution to ask UN Security Council to lift arms embargo against Bosnian government.
1994	
Nov 7	Yugoslav War Crimes Tribunal in The Hague, the Netherlands, makes its first indictment, charging Dragan Nikolić, former commander of Bosnian Serb-operated Sušica detention camp with war crimes against humanity. Nikolić had been arrested in Germany in February 1994.
Nov 12	U.S. unilaterally withdraws from enforcing UN imposed arms embargo against Bosnia-Herzegovina and Croatia.
Nov 14	Serb forces retake much of territory lost to government troops in Bihać area two weeks earlier.
Nov 21	NATO planes bomb Udbina air base in Croatia used for Serb attacks on UN "safe area" of Bihać.
Nov 21-30	Serbs hold close to 500 UN peacekeepers as hostages in order to prevent NATO air strikes.
Nov 22	Serb missiles attack two British planes on NATO patrol mission over Bosnia.
Nov 23	NATO jets bomb two Serb surface-to-air missile sites near Bihać.
Nov 28	NATO and UN paralyzed over question of bombing Serb positions.

Nov 30	Serbs surround Muslim held enclave of Bihać. International community "unable" to stop assault on this "safe area."
Dec 3	Boutros Boutros-Ghali says that UN and NATO are preparing for possible withdrawal of UN troops from Bosnia.
Dec 4	More than 2,000 U.S. marines on way to the Adriatic Sea to assist in possible evacuation of UN forces from Bosnia-Herzegovina.
Dec 5-6	Conference on Security and Co-operation in Europe (CSCE) meets in Budapest. It only issues declaration calling for a cease-fire in order to allow passage of humanitarian aid to Bihać pocket. Russia blocks CSCE's other efforts concerning crisis in Bosnia.
Dec 8	Clinton administration indicates that it is willing to pledge 25,000 troops to aid possible evacuation of UN forces from Bosnia-Herzegovina.
Dec 18	Former U.S. president Jimmy Carter arrives in Sarajevo. After three days of meetings, he announces cease-fire agreement between Muslim-led government and Serbs in Pale to begin on January 1 and to last four months. Croats join accord on January 2, 1995. Fikret Abdić's troops and Serbs from Croatia do not join truce. Fighting around Bihać area continues.
1995	
Jan 26	Lt. Gen. Rupert Smith of Britain arrives in Sarajevo to assume his post as new commander of UN forces in Bosnia-Herzegovina.

1995

Feb 19	Milošević rejects proposal by five-nation Contact Group to recognize Bosnia-Herzegovina and Croatia in their internationally recognized borders.
Mar 20-30	Bosnian government army launches offensive against Serbs and takes about 35 square miles of territory, including Majevica TV tower. Serbs respond by attacking government installations and by shelling Tuzla, Goražde, Sarajevo, and other towns.
Mar 31	UNSC votes to renew, until November 30, peacekeeping mission in former Yugoslavia, hours before mandate expired. UN forces in Bosnia-Herzegovina to retain UNPROFOR name, those in Croatia to be called UN Confidence Restoration Operation (UNCRO), and troops in Macedonia to be named UN Prevention Deployment Force (UNPDF).
Apr 11	Contact Group members visit Belgrade. Milošević rejects their peace proposals again. As a result, U.S. and Germany want to limit UN relief on sanctions against Yugoslavia while Britain, France, and Russia urge keeping ease on the sanction.
Apr 24	UN-sponsored Yugoslav War Crimes Tribunal names Serb leader Radovan Karadžić, Gen Ratko Mladić, commander of the Bosnian Serb army, and Mićo Stanišić, former chief of the Bosnian Serb secret police, as suspects in war crimes.

Apr 30	Bosnian government and Bosnian Serbs refuse to extend four-month cease-fire that expires May 1, 1995.
May 17	Major fighting around Sarajevo. The city is heavily shelled.
May 23	Serbs defy UN-ultimatum by seizing heavy weapons near Sarajevo from UN-guarded depots. Next day, UN orders Serbs to return weapons to UN control and remove all heavy weapons around Sarajevo.
May 25	Serbs ignore UN orders. NATO military jets hit Serb ammunition arsenal near Pale. Serbs respond by shelling "safe areas" including Tuzla, where 71 young people are killed while sitting in a cafe and over 150 are injured.
May 26	NATO fighter jets attack more ammunition depots. Serbs take 370 UN peacekeepers as hostages and threaten to kill them if air strikes do not cease. Some of hostages are used as human shields. UN personnel abandoning many of their posts.
May 28	Ifran Ljubijankić, Bosnian foreign minister, and six others killed when their helicopter is shot down by Serb guns near Cetingrad in Serb-held Croatian territory.
May 30	Seven U.S. ships, a nuclear submarine, and 12,000 marines and sailors sail into the Adriatic Sea.
Jun 1	David Owen announces his resignation from peace-seeking efforts in the former Yugoslavia.

	He is replaced by Carl Bildt, former Swedish premier, as EC's new mediator.
1995	
Jun 2	Serbs shoot down American F-16 fighter jet near Serb stronghold of Banja Luka. The pilot, U.S. Air Force Capt. Scott F. O'Grady, is rescued early June 8 by U.S. marines.
Jun 3-4	NATO defense chiefs meet in Paris and establish a 10,000-strong Rapid Reaction Force in order to strengthen UN mission in Bosnia. U.S. to provide the force with AC-130 attack gunships, attack helicopters, and cargo aircraft.
Jun 15	Bosnian Serbs assembly votes to unify Serb-held territory in Bosnia with Serb-held territory in Croatia.
	Bosnian government forces begin an offensive in order to break the siege of Sarajevo, but attack is halted a few days later. Serbs step up shelling of "safe areas."
Jul 2	UNPROFOR headquarters in Sarajevo shelled by Serbs.
Jul 8	Serbs attack Dutch UN peacekeepers observation posts near Srebrenica. Dutch soldiers taken as hostages and one is killed.
Jul 11	Bosnian Serb forces capture town of Srebrenica, so-called safe area for about 40,000 Muslims. After two NATO air strikes, UN calls the strikes off because of hostages. Thousands of refugees are on the run. Mass executions of thousands of Muslim

men; also other means of "ethnic cleansing" are implemented.

Jul 16 High military officials from U.S., Britain and France meet in London to discuss response to Serb assaults on "safe areas," but fail to reach an agreement.

Jul 20 Serbs begin new offensive against Bihać area. Serbs from occupied parts of Croatia join the action.

Jul 21 Western allies meet in London and 16 nations promise "decisive and substantial" air strikes to protect "safe areas," particularly Goražde and a timely use of Rapid Reaction Force. NATO authority increased to commence air strikes without asking permission from UN bureaucrats.

Jul 22 Military alliance between Croatia and Bosnia-Herzegovina signed.

Jul 23 Serbs kill two French peacekeepers. In response, France is suspected of bombing Pale in a secret mission on the same day.

Rapid Reaction Force is deployed for the first time on the road to Sarajevo over Mount Igman to protect relief convoys.

Organization of Islamic Conference declares arms embargo on Bosnia-Herzegovina "invalid."

Jul 25 "Safe area" of Žepa falls to the Serbs. About 15,000 civilians run from the region. Men ages 16-55 are taken as prisoners of war, but most of them are executed.

	International War Crimes Tribunal in The Hague indicts Karadžić and Mladić for genocide and crimes against humanity.
1995	
Jul 25-31	Bihać region is under attack from three sides: Bosnian Serbs, Serbs from Croatia, and Fikret Abdić's troops.
Jul 26	U.S. Senate votes to lift arms embargo against Bosnian government. Bill sponsored by Senate Majority Leader Bob Dole and Senator Joseph I. Lieberman.
	General Bernard Javier, French commander of UNPROFOR and the Rapid Reaction Force, is given veto power over calling NATO strikes in Bosnia. Boutros Boutros-Ghali agrees to take this power from Yasushi Akashi. NATO threats become more credible.
Jul 27	Tadeusz Mazowiecki, UN's human-rights investigator in the former Yugoslavia, resigns in disgust over international community's "hypocrisy" and inaction after Serbs attack Srebrenica and Žepa.
Jul 28	Bosnian Croat and troops from Croatia capture Grahovo and Glamoč, key positions in western Bosnia.
Aug 1	U.S. House of Representatives passes bill that would require U.S. president Clinton to end American participation in international arms embargo against Bosnia-Herzegovina.

Aug 4	Croatian troops start successful blitz operation to liberate Serb-controlled Krajina region. U.S. government expresses support for Croatian action. Serb military forces and civilians on the run from Croatia. NATO warplanes fire missiles at Serb radar site in Croatia, after being threatened by surface-to-air missiles.
	Karadžić dismisses Mladić as commander of Bosnian Serb forces but Mladić, who has backing of Serb military establishment and Milošević, refuses to step down.
Aug 10	U.S. reveals photographs as evidence of mass graves of executed Bosnian Muslims after the fall of Srebrenica and calls upon War Crimes Tribunal to investigate.
Aug 11	President Clinton vetoes bill passed by the House and Senate to end U.S. participation in arms embargo on Bosnia-Herzegovina.
Aug 12	Croat and Bosnian government forces launch new offensive in Bosnia-Herzegovina.
Aug 13	Russian Duma passes resolution to lift international trade sanctions against Yugoslavia.
Aug 14	U.S. launches new diplomatic offensive in order to reach peace in Bosnia. Croat and Bosnian government military successes seen as new opportunity for peace. U.S. shuttle diplomacy in the Balkans begins. UN personnel pulled out of Goražde.
Aug 19	Three key diplomats from U.S. peace-searching team, Robert Frasure, Joseph Kruzel, and Nelson

	Drew, killed on the way to Sarajevo, when armored personnel carrier they were riding in slipped off Mount Igman road.
1995	
Aug 28	Two Serb-fired mortar shells kill 37 civilians and injure many in a busy Sarajevo marketplace. UN secretly pulls out last peacekeepers from Goražde enclave.
Aug 30	NATO fighter jets, supported by UN Rapid Reaction Force, launch massive air strikes to silence Serb guns around Sarajevo. The largest action by NATO force in its history starts. Croat and Muslim offensive continues in northwestern Bosnia. Serbs losing ground.
Sep 5	Russia condemns NATO bombings.
Sep 8	Croatian, Bosnian, and Yugoslav (Serbian) foreign ministers in Geneva agree to a U.S.-brokered peace plan that would divide Bosnia-Herzegovina into two entities within a single state, Muslim-Croat Federation and Serbian Republic. Milošević government acting on behalf of Bosnian Serbs.
Sep 10	U.S. warship USS *Normandy* under NATO command fires 13 self-propelled *Tomahawk* cruise missiles at Serb military targets near Banja Luka.
Sep 11	Croats and Muslims launch an offensive in western Bosnia. Serb army and civilian population on the run.

Sep 19	West pressures Croats and Muslims to stop their successful offensive by which they took control of more than 50 percent of the country's territory.
Sep 20	NATO and UN announce halt to air strikes after Serbs complied with UN-NATO demands.
Sep 26	Agreement to establish collective presidency and common parliament is reached by Bosnian Muslims, Croats, and Serbs under the assistance of U.S. Assistant Secretary of State Richard C. Holbrooke.
Oct 4	NATO forces bomb Serb targets after Serb surface-to-air missile sites locked their radar on NATO planes flying over Bosnia.
Oct 10	It is announced that Yasushi Akashi will be recalled as special UN envoy to the former Yugoslavia effective Nov. 1, 1995, and replaced by UN Undersecretary General Kofi Annan.
	UN reports that Serbs expelled about 10,000 Muslims and Croats from Banja Luka region. Paramilitary forces of Željko Ražnjatović-Arkan involved in this latest ethnic cleansing.
Oct 12	A 60-day cease-fire agreement goes into effect.
Oct 27	Russian defense minister Pavel S. Grachev and U.S. secretary of defense William J. Perry, in joint news conference, announce that Russian troops would take part in implementing peace agreement in Bosnia.

1995

Nov 1	U.S.-sponsored peace talks open at Wright-Patterson Air Base outside Dayton, Ohio. Presidents of Bosnia-Herzegovina, Croatia, and Serbia are there to hammer out a peace settlement after four years of war. Besides U.S. participation, negotiations include EC, Russia, Britain, France, and Germany. Secretary of State Warren M. Christopher opens the talks.
Nov 16	International War Crimes Tribunal indicts Karadžić and Mladić on war crimes for the second time for the July massacre of civilians at Srebrenica region.
Nov 21	Presidents of Bosnia-Herzegovina, Croatia, and Serbia agree to a comprehensive settlement in Bosnia-Herzegovina and to end a nearly four-year-long war that claimed about 250,000 human lives and forced 2.7 million people from their homes. The agreement is to be implemented by UN-NATO 60,000-strong Implementation Force, out of which 20,000 will be U.S. troops.
Nov 22	UNSC votes to suspend its economic sanctions against Serbia and also to lift arms embargo against all former Yugoslav republics commencing in March 1996.
Nov 29	UN issues a report on atrocities in Bosnia and Herzegovina in which Secretary General Boutros Boutros-Ghali states Bosnian Serbs have engaged in "a consistent pattern of summary execution, rapes, mass executions, arbitrary detentions, forced labor and large-scale disappearances."

Dec 4 A contingent of NATO troops arrives in Bosnia to prepare for deployment of nearly 60,000 NATO-led international force to come to Bosnia to enforce the Dayton peace accords.

Dec 13 U.S. Senate votes to support U.S. troops in Bosnia and Herzegovina but limits their deployment to approximately one year.

Dec 14 Presidents Alija Izetbegović, Franjo Tuđman, and Slobodan Milošević, in the presence of President Clinton of U.S.A., President Jacques Chirac of France, Chancellor Helmut Kohl of Germany, Prime Minister John Major of Britain, and Prime Minister Viktor Chernomyrdin of Russia, sign in Paris agreement initialed in Dayton, Ohio, on November 21, 1995. Presidents Tuđman and Izetbegović also sign Agreement on Establishment of Joint Cooperation Council between Croatia and Bosnia-Herzegovina.

Dec 20 UN officially hands over peacekeeping duties in Bosnia and Herzegovina to NATO.

1996

Jan 1 Clashes between Croats and Muslims in Mostar.

Jan 3 U.S. defense secretary, William J. Parry, U.S. Army Gen. George Joulwan, NATO's supreme commander, and chairman of the U.S. Joint Chiefs of Staff, Gen. John Shalikashvili, are visiting Sarajevo and Tuzla.

Jan 7 It is reported that Serbs are exhuming bodies from mass graves in northwest Bosnia and

	destroying them in the iron-mine pits near Ljubija.
1996	
Jan 13	President Clinton visits U.S. troops in Bosnia. Clinton also makes a stop in Zagreb.
Jan 15	Bosnian government announces it is not going to take part in exchange of prisoners until Serbs disclose whereabouts of more than 24,000 Bosnian Muslims that have been missing.
Jan 19	Opposing military forces in Bosnia and Herzegovina are completing their withdrawal of their heavy weapons and most of their troops from 2.5-mile-wide "zone of separation," as compelled by Dayton agreement.
Jan 21	Bosnian premier Haris Silajdžić announces his resignation.
	U.S. assistant secretary of state John Shattuck inspects a number of sites near Srebrenica where it is believed thousands of Muslim men perished after fall of Srebrenica in July of 1995.
Jan 30	Hasan Muratović appointed as Premier of Bosnia and Herzegovina.
	Two senior Serb officers, Gen. Đorđe Đukić and Col. Aleksa Krsmanović, arrested by Bosnian government forces.
Feb 2	Carl Bildt, head of the international civilian peace effort in Bosnia, makes a deal with Serbs according to which their officials could retain

power in Sarajevo suburbs till late March 1996 in order to avert mass exodus from city.

Feb 3-4 U.S. secretary of state Warren Christopher tours Balkan states.

Feb 15 French troops in Bosnia discover an alleged terrorist-training camp in central Bosnia and detain two Iranians and eight others under suspicion of preparing terrorist acts.

Feb 18 A two-day conference, that includes the presidents of Bosnia, Croatia, Serbia, and various international representatives, ends in Rome. Fulfillment of the Dayton treaty is reaffirmed. Croat-Muslim disagreement over fate of city of Mostar is settled. Role of Richard C. Holbrooke as a Balkan peace negotiator ends. He resigns his position as assistant secretary of state on February 21.

Feb 22 UN secretary general Boutros Boutros-Ghali appoints Louise Arbour, a judge of the Ontario provincial Court of Appeals in Canada, to succeed Richard J. Goldstone as head of the War Crimes Tribunal of the former Yugoslavia and Rwanda in October of 1996.

Feb 26 Bosnian Muslims take control of Vogošća, suburb of Sarajevo. Many return to their homes for the first time in four years. Most of Serbs flee the area.

Feb 27 UNSC lifts sanctions against Bosnian Serbs as reward for their compliance with Dayton agreement.

1996

Feb 29	Bosnian government announces that siege of Sarajevo is officially over.
Mar 22	Madeleine Albright, U.S. ambassador to the UN, while visiting suspected mass grave sites in eastern Bosnia, releases spy satellite photographs that indicate mass graves of Muslims who had been executed by Serbs in July 1995.
Mar 24-25	Hillary Rodham Clinton, U.S. first lady, visits U.S. troops in Bosnia and Herzegovina.
Apr 3	U.S. commerce secretary Ronald H. Brown and 32 other Americans and two Croatians are killed in plane crash near Dubrovnik. Secretary Brown and a number of American leading business executives were touring Croatia and Bosnia-Herzegovina in an effort to help rebuild the two countries after the U.S. helped to bring peace in the region.
May 15	Radovan Karadžić, Bosnian Serb leader, dismisses Rajko Kasagić, moderate premier of the self-styled Serb Republic. Kasagić is replaced by Gojko Kličković, an ally of Karadžić.
May 18	Biljana Plavšić, a biology professor who was elected to Bosnian collective presidency in 1991, is named Karadžić's spokesperson because international community will not deal with an indicted war criminal.
Jun 2	U.S. secretary of state Warren Christopher meets in Geneva with presidents of Bosnia and Herzegovina, Croatia, and Serbia and puts

pressure on all sides to implement Dayton peace agreement.

Jun 27 International War Crimes Tribunal in The Hague defines rape as war crime and on the same day indicts eight Bosnian Serbs on rape charges.

Jun 29 Serbian Democratic Party (SDS) in Bosnia and Herzegovina reelects Radovan Karadžić as its chairman for four more years. Next day Karadžić delegates his presidential powers to his deputy, Biljana Plavšić, known as "Iron Lady of the Bosnian Serbs."

Jun 30 Municipal elections take place in the city of Mostar. Muslim-dominated List of Citizens for a United Mostar wins 48.9 percent and Croat Democratic Union (HDZ) list receives 45.8 percent of vote. Croat side refuses to accept results alleging election fraud on the part of the Muslims.

Jul 3 Biljana Plavšić is nominated as SDS candidate for president of the Serb Republic and Momčilo Krajišnik, speaker of the Bosnian Serb parliament, SDS candidate for the presidency of Bosnia and Herzegovina in the September elections.

Jul 11 United Nations International Criminal Tribunal in The Hague issues international arrest warrants for Bosnian Serb political and military leaders, Radovan Karadžić and Ratko Mladić.

Jul 16 U.S. and Muslim-Croat Federation sign an agreement that will secure military aid to the Federation worth up to $360 million, in order to establish military balance between the Federation and the Serb Republic in Bosnia.

1996

Jul 17-19	Richard Holbrooke, former U.S. assistant secretary of state, negotiates with Serbia's president Slobodan Milošević the resignation of Radovan Karadžić as president of Serb Republic and head of ruling Serb party (SDS) in Bosnia. Karadžić signs agreement, but remains man of influence in the Serb republic.
Jul 23-24	An official delegation from the Muslim-Croat Federation, led by vice president Ejup Ganić, visits Serbia's capital, Belgrade. This is first such visit since war began in 1992. Serbia and Bosnian Federation agree to restore telephone, rail, bus, and air links.
Aug 6	Bosniac and Croat sides reach an agreement on joint administration of the city of Mostar.
Aug 15	Sarajevo airport, closed to civil air traffic since 1992, opens for commercial flights.
Sep 14	Elections for three-member presidency, national parliament, and separate legislatures for Muslim-Croat Federation and the Serb Republic take place in Bosnia-Herzegovina. Municipal elections were postponed earlier because of loophole in Dayton agreement regarding voter registration rules. Regardless of widespread criticism of election irregularities, the Organization for Security and Cooperation in Europe (OSCE), which organized and supervised the voting, declared elections valid at the end of September.

Sept 30	Newly elected three members of the Bosnian presidency, Alija Izetbegović, Krešimir Zubak, and Momčilo Krajišnik, meet for the first time. Krajišnik promises to cooperate with newly elected Sarajevo leadership.
	Judge Louise Arbour becomes the new chief prosecutor for the International War Crimes Tribunal in The Hague.
Oct 3	Presidents of Bosnia and Serbia, Izetbegović and Milošević, after a one-day meeting in Paris, agree to establish full diplomatic relations between two countries.
Oct 5	Newly elected Bosnian Serb representatives boycott inaugural meeting of the national assembly and multiethnic presidency.
Oct 15	U.S. Army troops start arriving in Bosnia-Herzegovina.
Oct 22	Second full meeting of the Bosnian presidency in Sarajevo National Museum. Momčilo Krajišnik promises to uphold and defend constitution of Bosnia and Herzegovina.
	Municipal elections, scheduled to take place on November 23-24, postponed by Provisional Election Commission. They should take place "as soon as possible" in 1997.
Nov 9	Gen. Ratko Mladić, the leader of the Bosnian Serb army and an indicted war criminal, is fired by Biljana Plavšić, president of the Serb Republic.

1996	
Dec 12	The UNSC approves an 18-month mandate a for 31,000-strong Stabilization Force (SFOR) to replace IFOR.
Dec 20	The Stabilization Force (SFOR) is deployed in Bosnia and Herzegovina under the command of the North Atlantic Treaty Organization (NATO).
1997	
Jan 3	The Bosnia-Herzegovina's parliament, elected in September 1996, meets for the first time.
Jan 25	After shooting himself in the head nine days earlier, Nikola Koljević, former vice president of the self-proclaimed Serb republic, dies.
Feb 12	Roberts Owen, U.S. arbitrator in Bosnia-Herzegovina, announces that the Serb-controlled strategically located town of Brčko will remain under international supervision until March 1998.

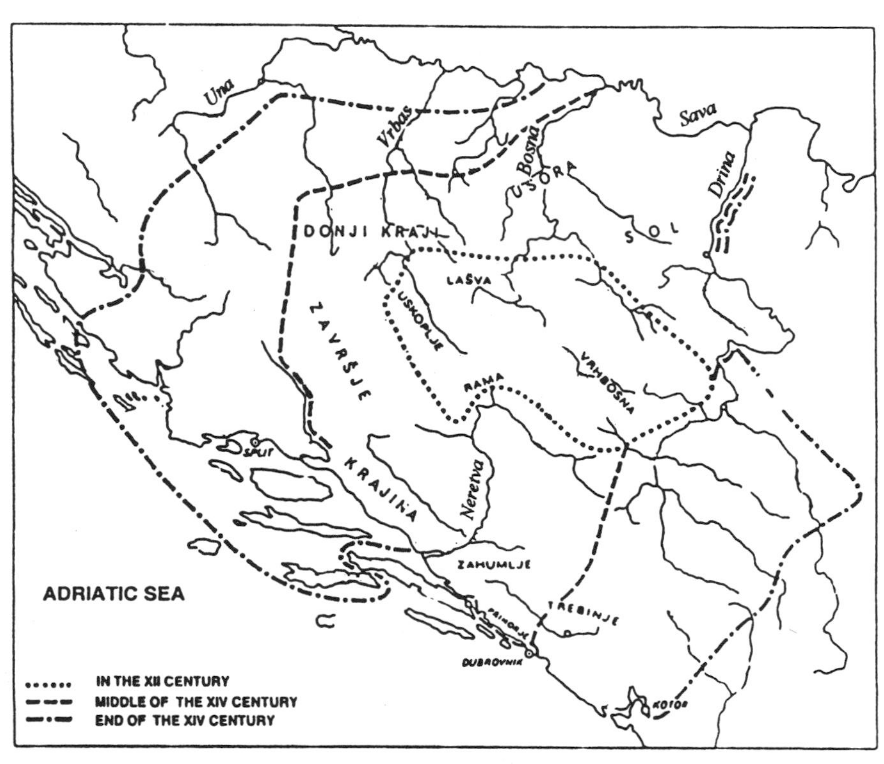

MEDIEVAL BOSNIA

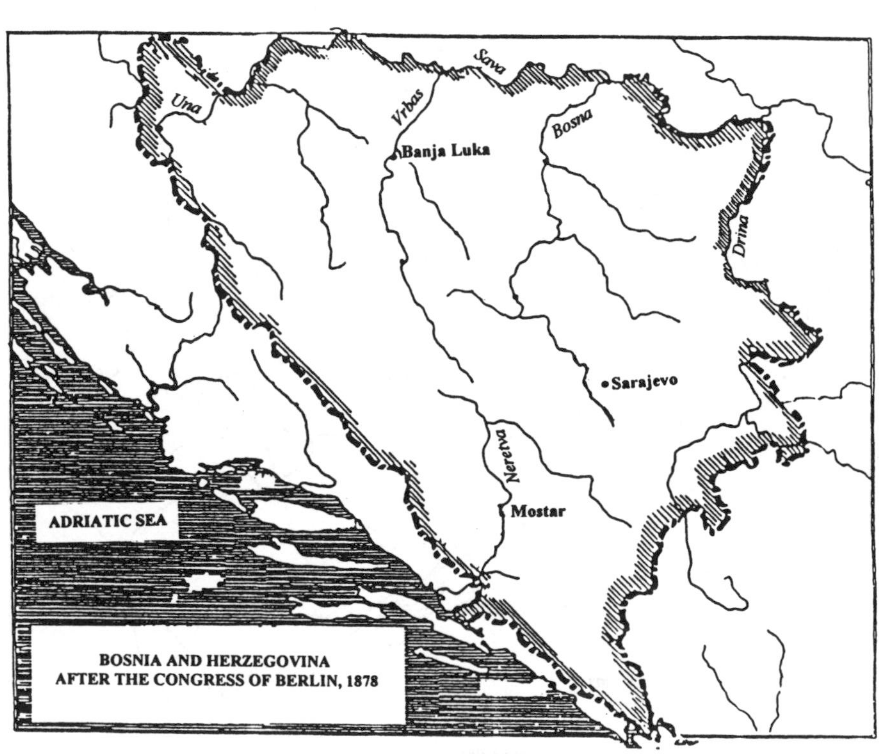

BOSNIA AND HERZEGOVINA
AFTER THE CONGRESS OF BERLIN, 1878

BOSNIA AND HERZEGOVINA AFTER 1945

BOSNIA AND HERZEGOVINA
AFTER THE DAYTON PEACE ACCORD, NOVEMBER 1995

INTRODUCTION

Diversity has been at the heart of Bosnia and Herzegovina's character. Even its "dualistic" name and physical geography display a particular heterogeneity. The medieval Bosnian state never enjoyed lasting political and ideological unity. Its rifts were feudal, regional, and religious in nature, and sometimes a combination of all three. Because of its location and by a quirk of history, three major world religious and cultural traditions (Catholicism, Islam, and Orthodoxy) became cohabitants in this small Balkan country. The recent birth of its statehood, however, has been exceptionally bloody and its diversity has been shaken. At the present time, it is hard to say if this new European country is in the process of remaking or breaking itself.

TERRITORY, POPULATION, AND NAME

Bosnia-Herzegovina is located in the northwestern part of the Balkan Peninsula and the southeastern end of the Alpine region. The northern parts of Bosnia are at the same time the southern boundaries of the Pannonian plains.

This triangle-shaped country is embraced by Croatia from two sides. The border demarcation in the north is the river Sava. The Una River, the spurs of the mountains Zrinski and Petrova Gora, the river Korana, the mountains Plješevica and Dinara separate it from Croatia in the west and southwest. In the southeast, Bosnia and Herzegovina is separated from Montenegro by a mountain range and the river Tara. In the east, its natural border with Serbia is the river Drina. Near the town of Neum, the country has a narrow exit to the Adriatic Sea. Presently, Bosnia-Herzegovina includes most but not all of the territories consolidated in the middle ages and also regions in the northwest that were gained during the Ottoman conquest.

Today's confines of Bosnia-Herzegovina are approximately those of 1878, the time when the Habsburg monarchy took over the land from the failing Ottoman Empire in accordance with the mandates of the Berlin Congress of 1878. The country comprises 51,129 square kilometers (19,741 square miles). Out of that, 20.9 percent of the land is arable, 10.4 percent is pasture, and 46 percent forests.

In 1991 Bosnia had 4,364,574 inhabitants. Bosnian Muslims had a relative majority of 43.6 percent; the Serbs 31.4 percent; the Croats 17.3 percent; the "Yugoslavs" 5.5 percent, and other minorities 2.2 percent.

The word *Bosnia* as a geopolitical term is found for the first time in the middle of the eighth century. The original Bosnian territory, however, consisted only of the area around the upper flow of the river Bosna, the region from Ivan Mountain in the south to Zavidovići in the north, Vlašić and Vranica Mountains in the west to the Drina River in the east.

The southeastern part of the country was known as Hum or Zahumlje in the Middle Ages. But after the Ottoman conquest in the 15th century the region became known as Herzegovina (Herzeg's land). It was named after a well-known local ruler, Herzeg (Duke) Stipan, who ruled on the eve of the Turkish onslaught.

The medieval feudal districts of the Lower Regions (Donji kraji), Usora, Soli, Hum or Zahumlje (Herzegovina), Završje or Western Regions (Zapadni kraji), Travunja and some other parts of neighboring lands originally were not part of Bosnia. These regions were incorporated into the Bosnian medieval state during the 13th and 14th centuries.

PHYSICAL FEATURES

Bosnia and Herzegovina is mainly a mountainous land. The lowlands, located in the northern regions along the Sava River (Posavina), make up only about 5 percent of the total territory. These northern Pannonian lowlands gradually rise up to about 2,000 meters above sea level along a mountain chain that separates Bosnia from Herzegovina through the middle of the country. From that point, contours slowly decline toward the Adriatic Sea. For that reason, the gateway into Bosnia is from the northern (Pannonian) and into Herzegovina from the southern (Adriatic) perimeter. Western Bosnia and almost all of Herzegovina, about 29 percent of the country, is made up of an arid limestone, known as karst. In this region, the only lands suitable for cultivation are small depressions, karst fields, between barren mountains.

The two principal regions in the country, Bosnia and Herzegovina, are separated by a chain of mountains. The two parts are connected by the pass at Ivan Mountain. This is a natural junction between the valley of the river Bosna and the canyon of the Neretva River, and the only gateway that links the northern Pannonian plains and the southern Adriatic parts of the country. The most important communication line between the north and the south has been along the rivers Bosna and Neretva since ancient times. Both Sarajevo, the capital, and Mostar, the main city in Herzegovina, are located on this important route.

Rivers and Lakes

Because of the high mountains in the middle of the country, the waters of Bosnia and Herzegovina flow either into the river Sava in the north, then via the Danube River into the Black Sea, or into the Adriatic Sea in the south. Generally speaking, the Bosnian rivers belong to the Black Sea, and the Herzegovinian to the Adriatic confluence. Exceptions are the underground rivers in southwest Bosnia and small rivers in northeast Herzegovina.

The main rivers in Bosnia are: Una (213 km/132.2 mi.), Vrbas (253 km/157.1 mi.), Ukrina (129 km/80.1 mi.), Bosna (308 km/191.2 mi.), and Drina (339 km/210.5 mi.). Other less known rivers in the region are: Vrbaska, Tolisa, Tinja, and Brka. The largest river in Herzegovina is Neretva (228 km/141.5 mi.), which springs at the foot of Mount Grdelj and flows into the Adriatic Sea. A number of underground rivers flow through the karst regions in the south and southwestern parts of the country.

All of the rivers in Bosnia and Herzegovina flow through picturesque canyons and gorges. Some of them create beautiful cataracts, torrents, rapids, and waterfalls. For the most part these rivers are not suitable for navigation, except in the Pannonian region, but are, however, a very important source of hydroelectric power. Moreover, most of the main roads in the country are built along the rivers and in that way the rivers provide accessibility to all parts of the country.

While Bosnia and Herzegovina is blessed with rivers, the land has only a few lakes. Worth mentioning are the Boračko Lake near the town of Konjic; Jablaničko Lake (artificially accumulated for a hydroelectric power plant); Deransko Lake in Hutovo Blato; and a number of mountain lakes in the central part of the country.

Mountains

Bosnia and Herzegovina has numerous mountains that are well known for their magnificence and contrasts, consisting from very high snowy peaks, thick forests, and gentle pastures to sheer rocks. These mountains are rich in natural resources, especially those that are closer to the Pannonian lowlands, while those that stretch toward the sea are rugged and less friendly.

The highest mountains in the country are: Maglić (2,387 m/7,830 ft.), Čvrsnica (2,228 m/7,308 ft.), Prenj (2,123 m/6,964 ft.), Vranica (2,107 m/6,911 ft.), Treskavica (2,088 m/6,849 ft.), Vran (2,074 m/6,803 ft.), Bjelašnica (2,067 m/6,780 ft.), Lelija (2,032 m/6,665 ft.), and Zelengora (2,016 m/6,613 ft).

Climate

Two main types of climate, continental and Mediterranean, clash on the territory of Bosnia and Herzegovina. The northern part of the country is on the periphery of the Pannonian continental zone, and has moderately cold winters and hot summers. On the other hand, the southern part is under Mediterranean climatic influences and has very hot and long summers and mild winters.

Temperatures can reach as high as 50° C/122° F in the Mostar region. The high mountain range in the middle of the land, however, has the attributes of alpine climate, very long and cold winters, a large amount of snow fall, and short cool summers. Temperature as low as -40° C/-40° F was recorded at Veliko Polje on Igman Mountain.

HISTORY

Ancient

The first evidence of human dwellings in today's Bosnia and Herzegovina dates from the period of the Paleolithic Age (before 7000 BC). During the Neolithic (7000-3000 BC), however, the territory of Bosnia-Herzegovina had numerous settlements. The best-known Neolithic culture in the region is found at Butmir near Sarajevo. To what branch of human family these and other dwellers in the area belonged, will, in all probability, remain unknown. But they do attest to highly developed stone culture in this part of Europe. New and higher cultural development is noticed with the introduction of copper in the area around 2500 BC, and of bronze about 2000-1800 BC.

The first known state-making inhabitants in today's Bosnia and Herzegovina were Illyrians, an Indo-European people who migrated to the Balkan region in the 11th century BC. In the fourth century BC, Celts from the Alpine zone invaded the territory of today's Croatia and western Bosnia. Their sojourn resulted in a blend of Illyrian and Celtic cultures. Illyrian tribes, especially the ones living in today's Herzegovina, also came (after

600 BC) under Greek cultural and economic influence. It would be, however, under the Romans that the Illyrian kingdom, culture, and people would fade away.

Roman armies began to attack the Illyrian lands in the third century BC (229 BC), but it took them over two centuries to subdue the fierce Illyrian resistance. The final Illyrian rebellion was crushed (AD 9) by Emperor Augustus. The conquest was followed by the establishment of Roman cities, administrative units, and Romanization of the indigenous people. The Illyrians entered into higher echelons of the Roman world mainly through the military service, and a number of them became Roman emperors, including Diocletian (AD 284-305) and Constantine (AD 306-337).

In the occupied Illyrian territories, the Romans established the province of Illyricum (ca. 80 BC) In order to have better control over the rebellious region, Augustus divided the Illyricum into two provinces (AD 10), Pannonia and Dalmatia. The lowlands of today's northern Bosnia-Herzegovina belonged to Pannonia, and the rest of the country belonged to mountainous Dalmatia in the south.

The emperor Diocletian in his administrative reforms (AD 297) separated the land east of the river Drina (today's Serbia) from Dalmatia and created a new Roman province (Praevalis). In AD 395, the Roman Empire was permanently divided into Eastern and Western halves. The regions of today's Bosnia-Herzegovina were allotted to the Latin West, while the land east of the Drina River, came under Byzantine or Eastern rule. That ancient boundary between East and West became a European political and cultural faultline that has a significance even today.

The Germanic Goths, Monogolo-Turkic Huns, and other invaders passed through the Balkans during the fourth and fifth centuries. Another wave of invaders, Turkic Avars and Indo-European Slavs, appeared in southeastern Europe in the sixth century. But while the Avars, consisting mostly of raiding hordes, were able to maintain their power in the region for a relatively short time, the Slav immigrants came there to stay. The Slavic presence in the Balkans, however, was strengthened at the beginning of the seventh century, when Croats from the White Croatia in the trans-Carpathian region (as the allies of Byzantium in the struggle with the Avars) settled on the eastern shores of the Adriatic. The Serbs, too, migrated from the north to the eastern Balkans soon after the Croats.

Medieval Period

Very little is known about the history of Bosnia from the time of the Slavic migrations in the sixth and seventh centuries to the beginning of Bosnian autonomy in the 12th century. Early church affiliation, spoken idiom, art form, political association, and terminology attest that during the second Slavic migration (seventh century), most of Bosnia was settled by the Croats, or at least that the newly arrived Croats imposed their reign over the previous settlers and indigenous peoples. We also know that the territory around the upper flow of the Bosna River (the original Bosnia) changed hands a number of times before it became an autonomous state. It was a part of the Croatian kingdom till the middle of the 10th century. Bosnia's local ruler (*ban*) was one of the electors of the Croatian kings. The province came under the control of Serbia (949-960), of Croatia again (960-990), of Bulgaria (990), of Byzantium (1018-1040), of Croatia (1040-1087), and of the kingdom Dioclea (Duklja) (1087-1102). Only after the decline of the regional powers, Croatia in the West and Duklja in the Southeast, did Bosnia begin to assert its autonomy. But even then, the country was compelled to recognize the suzerainty of the Hungarian-Croatian kings for most of its autonomous life.

Before Bosnia became a kingdom in 1377, its rulers were called *ban*, a title also held by the Croatian governors. The first known autonomous *bans* in Bosnia were Borić (1154-63) and Kulin (1164?-ca. 1204). For his wise, long, and noble rule, Kulin became nearly a mythical figure among the people of Bosnia. This "great *ban*," as he is called in a papal document of 1180, successfully used the conflict between the two competing regional powers, Byzantium and Hungary (the latter holding nominal sovereignty over Bosnia) and advanced his autonomy, expanded the original

Bosnian territory to the north (Usora, Soli, and Donji Kraji) and to the south (Neretva region). He laid the foundations for the future Bosnian statehood.

The rise of Bosnian independence, however, was constantly challenged by the Hungarian-Croatian sovereigns, who, a number of times, used religious justifications for attacking the Bosnian state. Under the pretext of combating the spread of an unorthodox and/or heretical Christian teaching, Hungarian armies marched the first time into Bosnia in 1222 and the country came under direct Hungarian rule. However, the capable *ban* Ninoslav (1225-ca. 1253), while recognizing Hungarian suzerainty, exploited the Mongol attack on Hungary (1241) and enhanced Bosnian power and self-rule.

Other important *bans* who enhanced Bosnian power and self-rule were the *bans* of the Kotromanić dynasty. It seems that the *ban* Stipan Prijezda (1254-1287) was the ruler who took the name Kotroman, and thus, he is considered to be the founder of the Kotromanić lineage. The rule of his son, *ban* Stipan I Kotromanić (1287-1302) was cut short, however, because Croatia's *ban* Pavao I Šubić invaded Bosnia (1302) in response to the Bosnian support of Venice, Croatia's traditional enemy. Because of this invasion, the Croatian Šubić family had an overlordship over Bosnia till 1318.

In contrast to Stipan I Kotromanić's short reign, the long reign of *ban* Stipan II Kotromanić (1312-1353) was exceptionally successful. In the struggle between the Hungarian king and Croatian nobility, Stipan supported the king in order to advance his expansionist aims at the expense of the neighboring Croatian nobility, mainly of his Šubić cousins. Hum (later known as Herzegovina), Krajina (coastal region between Hum and the river Cetina in today's western Herzegovina and southern Croatia), and Završje or Tropolje (region around the town Livno) recognized at that time the Bosnian *ban* as their ruler. In 1350, the Serbian ruler Stevan Dušan (1331-1355) invaded Bosnian territories, but Stipan II was able to free his lands from a short Serbian incursion. This able ruler signed treaties with Dubrovnik (1334) and Venice (1335); while having the support of the independent Bosnian

Church, invited Franciscans to Bosnia in 1340; coined the first Bosnian money; extended the borders of his realm from the Sava River to the Adriatic Sea and from the Cetina River in the West to the Drina in the East. It was Stipan II who set the stage for the rise of the Bosnian kingdom.

Religious and Cultural Orientation

Since the division of the Roman Empire into Western and Eastern parts (395), the present-day territory of Bosnia and Herzegovina was on the periphery of the Roman Church and of Western civilization. The Drina River, today's border between Bosnia and Serbia, was traditionally the boundary between the Roman and Byzantine worlds.

The Roman form of Christianity was brought to medieval Bosnia from the cities along Croatia's sea coast. While the religion spread much earlier, the first known reference of a local Bosnian Catholic diocese dates back to 1089, under the jurisdiction of the Archdiocese of Split. The clergy in Bosnia used the Roman rite, the Old Slavonic language, and Glagolitic script in church practices, as did the rest of southern Croatia.

For various reasons, however, the Catholic institutions in Bosnia remained weak and neglected. The native bishop was replaced (1232) by a foreigner. Even the diocesan seat was moved (1252) from Bosnia to Đakovo, a town in northern Croatia, from where the bishops seldom, if ever, ventured into Bosnia. These and other factors precipitated diverse unorthodox religious practices and beliefs, and even the appearance of a heretical Bosnian Church, whose adherents were known as the "Bosnian Christians" (they were also referred to as Bogomils and Patarens). The first accusations of heretical practices against Bosnian rulers date from 1199.

This Bosnian Church was similar to the neo-Manichean (dualistic) heresy that appeared in a number of European countries at the time. The best-known such groups were the Albigensians in France, Cathars or Patarens in Italy, and Bogomils in Bulgaria. There is, however, still much debate among scholars about the nature and strength of the Bosnian Church. It seems that the lines between the "native," and most probably deluded, Roman Catholicism, and the Bosnian Christians were very blurred. It will probably remain impossible to determine whether there was a clear line of division between the two.

For political and expansionist reasons, the Hungarian kings undertook "crusades" against the schismatic and/or heretical believers in Bosnia. With the coming of the Franciscans in the middle of the 14th century, however, the Catholic institutions were strengthened, and by the end of Bosnian independence most of the people adhered to the Roman Catholic Church. There was an exceptional religious toleration in medieval Bosnia. Toward the end of Bosnia's independence, however, the remaining Bosnian Christians were under strong pressure to embrace Catholicism. Faced with lurking Ottoman threats, Bosnian rulers wished to have a unified country and to make a better case in their quest for help in the Catholic West.

Besides Roman Catholicism and the Bosnian Church, Greek Orthodoxy appeared in present day Bosnia and Herzegovina at the beginning of the 13th century. At this time, an intrusive Serbian political authority crossed into present-day Montenegro and eastern Herzegovina, which threatened the traditional political and religious boundaries. This Serbian expansion, however, was checked and rolled back by the rising power of Bosnia and by the republic of Dubrovnik (Ragusa). However, when the first Bosnian king Tvrtko occupied the Lim and Drina valleys in 1376, the Orthodox presence became visible in the Bosnian state again. But only after the Turkish invasions (1463), did Orthodoxy, along with Islam, significantly spread to Bosnia. It came with the major waves of migrations from the southeastern Balkans to the deserted regions of Bosnia and Croatia.

Summit and Fall

Bosnia reached the apex of its medieval power under the rule of Stipan Tvrtko I Kotromanić (1353-1391), son of Stipan II's brother Vladislav and Jelena Šubić. At the beginning of his reign, the youthful Tvrtko lost parts of his realm to the Hungarian-Croatian king Louis I (1357). In spite of his initial war successes against Louis I, he had to recognize the king's suzerainty, and even found refuge at Louis's court in 1365. Some Bosnian nobles, supported by the adherents of the Bosnian Church, forced Tvrtko and his mother out of the country and recognized his brother Vuk as their king.

With the help of King Louis I, Tvrtko overpowered his opponents (1367), consolidated his power, and then began to expand Bosnian borders. First, capitalizing on the Serbian aristocratic feuds, he occupied southwestern parts of Raša (Serbia) and in 1377 proclaimed himself king of Bosnia and the Serbs. Then he conquered the coastal regions of Zeta (Montenegro) and Croatia (from the Bay of Kotor to the region of Zadar) and in 1390 proclaimed himself also the king of Dalmatia, Croatia, and the Littoral. His royal seat was at the town of Bobovac.

Along with his successful territorial expansionism, Tvrtko also set the stage for the Bosnian political instability that emerged after his death. The newly acquired feudal principalities were never solidified into a stable state. Moreover, ominous events for the Bosnian kingdom appeared even during his reign: the Ottoman Turks were already well established in the eastern part of the Balkans and Tvrtko's realm came under Ottoman attack for the first time in 1386.

The new king, Stipan Dabiša (1391-1395), Tvrtko's half-brother, was an incompetent ruler. Besides the Turkish threat, the newly acquired coastal cities in Croatia and some other parts of the kingdom broke away. Feudal lords began to assert their autonomy and the Bosnian kings were constantly caught up in a web of regional power struggle. Dabiša also recognized the suzerainty of the Hungarian-Croatian king and had to pledge (1393) the Bosnian crown to King Sigismund. In order to evade this agreement, however, Dabiša's wife Jelena (1395-1398), and not the oldest male member of the ruling family, became his successor.

Jelena's reign was challenged by a number of noblemen, the most powerful among them were Sandalj Hranić and Hrvoje

Vukčić Hrvatinić. This noble faction recognized Ostoja (1398-1404), another illegitimate brother of Tvrtko I. But his political ambitions got him in trouble with the high nobility, and he had to run from the country. Tvrtko II (1404-1408), son of Tvrtko I, was proclaimed the new king of Bosnia. After losing a war with Hungary (1408), Tvrtko II also was removed by the aristocracy and Ostoja came to power again (1408-1418). But Ostoja had to run for his life (1416) one more time because of his disputes with some of the magnates, who turned to the Turks for help in their struggle with Ostoja. Ostoja's son, 17-year-old Stipan Ostojić (1419-1420), succeeded his father to the throne. He received the support of most of the Bosnian nobility until the next major crisis.

Turkish forces raided eastern Bosnia (1420) under the pretext of punishing the local Pavlović family for their disloyalty. Namely, the Pavlovićes had attempted to rebuff Turkish suzerainty which they had acknowledged in return for Turkish help they received at the time of the family's struggle with the former king Ostoja. This Turkish assault sparked a new round of political crisis in the country that resulted in the election of Tvrtko II (1420-1443) to the royal throne for the second time. After a short period of peace, however, some of the nobility with the Turkish acquiescence endorsed Radivoj, an illegitimate son of the late king Ostoja, and declared him King of Bosnia in 1432. Despite obvious external dangers, the Bosnian nobility was unable to unite around the royal throne, and the feudal kings lacked competence to unify and lead the country. On the contrary, internal political and religious disunity, Ottoman incursions, and Hungarian-Turkish regional rivalry were tearing the country apart.

The legitimate successor of Tvrtko II was another illegitimate son of the late King Ostoja, Stipan Tomaš (1444-1461). While he was recognized as the ruler by most of the Bosnian nobility, Radivoj, the pretender to the throne, continued to serve (till 1447) the interests of the centrifugal feudal forces in the country and of the Turks. Moreover, King Tomaš's foremost enemy and his father-in-law, Stipan Vukčić Kosača (ruler of Hum), in order to emphasize his independence from king Tomaš, took the title of *Herceg* (from the German *Herzog* - duke) in 1448. He asserted his independence from the Bosnian king but became a vassal to the Turks. His lands are known today as Herzegovina, or the Herzog's land. But his aggressive and expansionist policies got him in trouble with the neighbors, his own son, and the Turks.

While the Bosnian rulers and nobility were bickering among themselves, the Ottomans were laying the ground for their decisive assault on Bosnia. They were raiding the country frequently, establishing a permanent foothold in 1448 in the vicinity of today's Sarajevo, and fostering political and religious strife inside the country. In order to prevent the Ottoman aggression, Stipan Tomaš turned to the pope for understanding and help. He also suppressed the schismatic, or as some think, heretical Bosnian Church, recognized the suzerainty of the Hungarian-Croatian king Vladislav, and relied on his assistance. But even in such a difficult situation, the Bosnian king did have ambitions to regain the territories that were lost after the death of Tvrtko I. But such ambitions and unsuccessful attempts to fulfill them only increased the number of Bosnian enemies.

King Tomaš was succeeded by his son, Stipan Tomašević (1461-1463). Faced with the immediate danger of an Ottoman onslaught, the new king turned entirely to the West in his political and ideological orientation. He was rewarded by being crowned king in the town of Jajce in 1461 with the crown sent to him by the pope. Even Herceg Stephen Kosača pledged his support and allegiance to the new king. Bosnia clearly was now in the West's political sphere. Moreover, the king refused to pay the imposed tribute to the Turks. These factors and the Ottoman hatred of the West clearly set the stage for the Turkish decisive strike against Bosnia.

Realizing the immediate threat from the East, the Bosnian king asked for a 15-year truce with Istanbul. After giving a positive but deceitful answer, Mehmet II with a large Turkish army invaded Bosnia in the spring of 1463. The country fell to the Turks without much resistance. The last Bosnian king was captured in the fortress of Ključ, and, despite the Grand Vezir's written promise to spare his life, Stephen Tomašević was beheaded near the town of Jajce. In the same year, the original medieval Bosnia became a Turkish military district (*sancak* or *sandžak*).

The main force of the invading Turkish army withdrew from Bosnia and Herzegovina in the autumn of 1463. A counter-offensive, led by the Hungarian-Croatian king Mathias, Venice, and Herceg Stipan, began immediately after the departure of the principal Ottoman military forces. Mathias liberated the northern half of the country and established there two banates (*banovine*), Jajce and Srebrenica. He even installed one of his men, Nikola of Ilok, as the "king" of Bosnia (1471). The banates did serve for a few decades as a line of defense in the Croatian-Hungarian efforts to slow down Turkish expansionism to the West. Herceg Stephen and his sons, on the other hand, were able to reestablish their control of the southern part of the Bosnian kingdom, at least for a short while.

A new Turkish offensive a year later to reconquer the rest of Bosnia did not bring the desired results. For reasons of political expediency, the Ottomans also paraded a "king of Bosnia" of their own (1465). The Turkish "Bosnian kingdom" was abolished in 1476, after the "king" asked for an official Hungarian recognition of his title. The Turkish struggle with Herceg Stephen (died in 1466) and his sons continued till 1482. In that year, the last of Herceg's military holdouts, Novi, fell under the Turks. This marked the end of the medieval Bosnian kingdom and the land was ruled by the Ottomans till 1878.

Under the Ottomans (1463-1878)

There are no indications that en masse conversion took place in Bosnia after the Turkish occupation. A considerable percentage of the native higher class, however, and a smaller proportion of the peasantry did accept Islam. By becoming Muslims, members of the Christian aristocracy in many cases saved not only their heads but their hereditary possessions and privileges too. At the beginning of the Turkish rule, some noblemen entered the sultan's service as feudal cavalry *(sipahis)* while remaining Christians, but with the passing of time all of them became converts or died out.

The most intensive Islamization of Bosnia-Herzegovina took place mainly during the first hundred years of Ottoman rule, while the empire was still exuberant and expanding, but conversion was initially inspired more by economic and social incentives than by religious zeal. The process was also linked to the beginning of urbanization, sparse as it was. The converted or Muslim-born administrative and commercial class settled around the new business centers *(čaršija)* and the Christian peasants remained in the countryside.

The Bosnian administrative and military elite, during the entire Ottoman period, came mostly from such Islamized population. Moreover, a large number of high dignitaries in the Ottoman Empire came from Christian families in Bosnia and Herzegovina. Most of these ascended through the system of boy-tribute, known as *devşirme* (collection). About 3,000 young men were levied from the Balkans annually and, after their conversion to Islam, they were trained in military or administrative skills. Most of the enslaved young men became the *Jeni Çeri* or Janissaries, the regular infantry troops. The brightest ones were placed at the sultan's administrative service. Some of these were fully Ottomanized and served in the highest offices of the government (the Sublime Porte).

The levy of Christian boys was abolished in the middle of the 17th century. The Janissary fighting zeal and discipline weakened during the time of the imperial decline; they were permitted to marry, and the service became hereditary. Moreover, these former elite troops became obsolete and a major obstacle to the necessary military reforms in the empire. For that reason the Janissaries were abolished in 1826.

With the Turkish invasion, the traditional European feudal relations in Bosnia and Herzegovina, officially at least, disintegrated. The land legally became the sultan's possession; the military and bureaucratic aristocracies were directly responsible to the executive offices (the Sublime Porte) in Istanbul. In the eyes of the Ottomans, following the Middle Eastern tradition of state craft, society was divided into two basic categories: The ruling class (the military, administrative, judicial, and educational elite), and the subjects or *raya* (flock), which consisted of all (non-Muslims and Muslims) who, by their work, sustained the state. The sultan, with his military and bureaucratic servants, had an obligation to accumulate and protect the wealth that was his patrimony, keep law and order, ensure security and justice for his subjects, and promote Islam. In return, the sole duty of the *raya* was to provide material support for the state, the ruling class, and the sultan.

The socioeconomic relations in Ottoman Bosnia were initially founded on the ruling class and the *raya* structure of society. The native Muslims and converts, and also a number of Christian nobles who remained in the country, became the sultan's feudal cavalry (*sipahis*). Their hereditary lands were converted into fiefs (*timars*) in return for their military or other services to the state. These former Bosnian nobles became Turkish lower military aristocracy.

There were three categories of land holdings: *timar*, *zeamet*, and *hass*. The smallest was *timar* and the largest *hass*. In Bosnia-Herzegovina, *timars* were given not only to the feudal cavalry (*sipahis)*, but also to the defenders of the frontier fortresses. Because of the constant warfare in the region, *timars* exchanged hands quite often. But at the end of the 16th century, the process of *timar* privatization began and the number of small holdings multiplied while the number of larger ones decreased.

Some peasants in Bosnia and Herzegovina were freeholders and owned small plots of land. These were mainly Muslims. Others, mainly Christian peasants, were sharecroppers or customary tenants(*kmets*), similar to serfs in the West . Generally speaking, during the first hundred years of Ottoman rule, the life of the peasant, Christian and Muslim, was relatively stable and secure. However, as the Turkish power and the military fortunes of the Bosnian feudal aristocracy began to dwindle so did the living conditions of the peasants, especially of the Christians. While originally many were leaseholders, the Christian peasants became overwhelmingly sharecroppers (*kmets*) to the local Muslim feudal lords, who gradually appropriated the state lands and made them hereditary. While the *sipahi* once was the sultan's reliable soldier and an efficient treasury agent, his military skills became outdated. He became a liability to the state and a despotic landlord to the peasant. Tax collection was entrusted more often to tax farmers, who became hereditary owners of the sultan's land (*çifliks*), and to local nonmilitary notables. The peasants' fortunes slipped from the ostensible security of the Islamic Law (*Şeriat)* into the hands of the corrupt state bureaucrats who were trying to retain their economic and social position by exploiting the *raya*, as well as defrauding the state. Besides paying the land and poll tax to the sultan, the Christian peasants' assessments increased from one-tenth to one-third, even to a half, of the annual yield. Labor obligations and numerous other assessments were increased or newly imposed. The declining status of the peasant in turn resulted in revolts, brigandage, and an increase of religious intolerance.

After the Turks occupied the central and southern parts of today's Bosnia and Herzegovina, they kept the basic local administrative divisions found at the time of the conquest. Two military districts (*sandžaks)*, however, were established in the former kingdom: Bosnian in 1463 and Herzegovinian in 1470. Both *sandžaks* belonged to the Rumeli (Rumelian) province (*beylerbeylik)* that included all of the occupied Balkan lands at the time.

The Bosnian lands that were not occupied in 1463, as well as Croatia and parts of Hungary, became a defensive line against Turkish expansion into Central Europe. Those defenses, however, began to disintegrate at the beginning of the 16th century, especially after the fall of Belgrade (1521) and the battle of Mohacz (1526).

As the Ottomans expanded their possessions to the north and west, they established more districts (*sandžaks)* in the region and, as a result, Bosnia became an Ottoman province (*beylerbeylik, eyalet*, or better known as *pašaluk*) in 1580. At the apex of the Ottoman power, the Bosnian *pašaluk* had eight military districts (*sandžaks)*: Bosnia, Herzegovina, Zvornik, Klis, Pakrac-Cernik, Krk-Lika, Bihać, and Požega. Districts were divided into judicial and administrative districts *(kazas* or *kadiluks)* in which the judges *(kadis)* dispensed the holy law of Islam or the *Şeriat.*

As the power and stamina of the Ottoman Empire began to decline in the 17th century, so did the borders of the Bosnian province *(pašaluk)*. After the liberation of Ottoman Hungary and parts of occupied Croatia from the Turks in 1699, the Bosnian *pašaluk* lost large portions of its northern and western territory. Thus, at the beginning of the 18th century, its territory consisted of four districts (*sandžaks)*: Bosnia, Herzegovina, Klis, and Bihać. This administrative division lasted till the time of the Ottoman reforms in the middle of the 19th century.

The seats of the chief Turkish administrators (*beglerbeg/ beylerbey*) in Bosnia were at first in Sarajevo; then Banja Luka (1554-1638); Sarajevo again (1639-1697); Travnik (1697-1850); and since that time, Sarajevo has remained as the center of political power in Bosnia to the present time.

There was a peculiar local military and administrative structure that evolved in Bosnia from the Ottoman *timar* (state service) system. In the border zones, mainly in and around the military forts, officials known as *kapetans* or *kapudans* (captains) performed a mix of military, administrative, and border police duties. They also went to war when the sultan called upon them. The districts they controlled were known as *kapetanije* (captainies). While at the end of the 17th century there were 12 of such districts, all of them along the borders, a hundred years later there were 39 *kapetanije* throughout Bosnia and Herzegovina.

While the imperial powers were formidable, the *kapetans* were kept in check by the central government. During the 16th and 17th centuries, however, the *kapetans* were able to convert the land into private holdings, make their office hereditary, treat the local peasants as they pleased, diminish the power of the governor (*beglerbeg*), and make Bosnia a state within the state.

Ottoman Reforms in Bosnia

The destiny of Ottoman Bosnia, from the outset to the end of its existence, was to be an Ottoman borderland. During the expansionist phase, it served as a staging ground for continuous onslaught into central Europe. During the time of decline (17th and 18th centuries), Bosnia became a defensive outpost against the Western powers (the Habsburgs and Venice). In the 19th century, however, during the time of Ottoman reforms, Bosnia's fate was entangled in a number of difficulties which, instead of making it a politically viable unit, turned the province into a playground of various combating forces. Some of them were an imperialistic power struggle between Russia and the Habsburgs, revolts and liberation of the neighboring Christian peoples, aspirations and revolts of its own Christian subjects, pressures of the central government to reassert its power in the province, and the struggle of the Bosnian ruling class for survival and protection of its privileges. These and similar forces were detrimental in shaping the history of Bosnia in the last two centuries.

Being far away from the capital of the empire (Istanbul), its mountainous geography, its lack of communications, and the power structure that evolved during the two centuries of Ottoman decline, all helped Bosnia to become a semiautonomous country. However, the Turkish retreat from central Europe was a great disappointment for the Bosnian elites. They began to see themselves as defenders of Islam from the Christian West. The reforms of Sultan Muhamed II (1808-1839), emulating the Western states, were perceived by the Bosnian feudal lords as a betrayal of Islam and a grave threat to their political and economic power. Resistance to change and religious conservatism prevailed in Bosnia. The central government in Istanbul had to undertake seven military campaigns in order to implement its reforms and to break the power of the Bosnian landed aristocracy.

From the first violent clash between the newly appointed governor and the Bosnian aristocracy in 1813, to the Austrian occupation of Bosnia and Herzegovina in 1878, there were numerous uprisings and violent disturbances in the province by both Muslims and Christians. While the Christian rebellions were directed mostly against the burdensome obligations of taxes and assessments, the semi-independent landlords in turn revolted in defense of their local autonomy and against the imposition of the central government's reforms and obligations.

A grave discontent erupted with Sultan Mahmud II's decision in 1826 to abolish the Janissaries, by this time more a privileged layer of society than an army. Bosnians also refused to enlist in the sultan's new-style army. Their opposition to the military changes and to the reforms in general escalated to an open revolt in 1831. Under the charismatic leadership of Captain Husejin Gradaščević, known as the Dragon of Bosnia, the Bosnians were initially successful in their military campaign. Their army marched as far as Kosovo, where a similar Albanian rebellion was taking place. Bosnian forces wanted to extort from the Grand Vezir guarantees of self-rule and prevent the intended modernization. It seemed that the rebels were on the verge of political victory, but the Ottomans were able to entice the landlords of Herzegovina to abandon the cause and their Bosnian brothers. Because of the split, the rebellion was crushed in 1832. Herzegovina became an independent province (*elayet*), Husejin Gradaščević ended in exile, and the sultan was able to impose limited reforms in the region. The most important was the abolishment of the *kapetanije* in 1835. Many of the former *kapetans*, however, and other feudal lords, were appointed as local representatives of the governor or *musselims*.

The second major period of insurrections of the Muslims in Bosnia came after the promulgation of Sultan Abdülmecid's famous Noble Rescript of the Rose Chamber (*Hatt-i Şerif of Gülhane*) on November 3, 1839. The decree proclaimed liberal principles of security of life, honor, and property; equality under the law; public trials; the abolishment of tax-farming; better methods of recruitment into the armed forces; and an end of abuses by the landlords. This edict and a similar one issued in 1856 (*Hatt-i Humayun*) is collectively known as the Reorganization or *Tanzimat* period in Ottoman history. These reforms, however, were either ignored or circumvented in Bosnia and Herzegovina.

After several antireform revolts in the 1840s, the one in 1849 was especially remembered for the man who crushed it in 1850.

Omer-pasha Latas, an Islamized former sergeant in the Austrian army, came with a large military force from Istanbul and defeated the local Muslim forces. Some Muslim notables were executed and many others exiled to Anatolia. Bosnia-Herzegovina was divided into nine new districts under the command of governor's representatives or *kajmaks*. Latas finally crushed the political power of the Bosnian landed aristocracy.

The high hopes of the Christian peasants, however, were not fulfilled. Latas was not kind to them either. Although the Muslim elites were subjugated, most of their privileges were still assured. The burdens of the peasants became even greater. This resulted in Christian revolts in 1851 and again in 1857-58. Among other demands, they wanted equality under the law (officially guaranteed in 1839) and abrogation of the poll-tax. In 1855 the tax was eliminated, but, instead, the Christians were to pay a new tax for not serving in the Ottoman armed forces. These and other changes did not in reality alleviate the burdens on the peasantry. In the 1860s, however, the life conditions of the peasants (*kmets)* did slightly improve.

The man responsible for implementing progressive changes in Bosnia and Herzegovina was Topal Osman-pasha, who served as governor from 1861 to 1869. Through the provincial reform law of 1864, he made administrative, judicial, and military changes in Bosnia. Two provinces, Herzegovina and Bosnia, were joined again into one, now called Bosnian *vilayet*. The governor (*valiya*), was nominated by the central government in Istanbul. An elected 28-member council met once a year and served as the advisory body. The unified province was divided into seven districts *(sandžaks* or *lives*). In addition to the Islamic courts, civil courts were introduced in the province. With some minor changes, this legal and administrative setting remained till the end of the Ottoman rule in Bosnia and Herzegovina. The duration of Topal Pasha's service in Bosnia was known as the "period of peace and work," but after his departure the situation sharply deteriorated. Neither the provincial nor the imperial leadership was competent to resolve the internal and external complexities that evolved in Bosnia by the second half of the last century.

In the last nine years of the de facto Ottoman rule in Bosnia, 15 governors served in the province. There were new revolts caused by social, economic, and ethnic grievances and aspirations. National consciousness of the Christian population steadily intensified; Serbian nationalism was growing among the Orthodox, and Croatian nationalism among the Catholic population. Each side desired to be unified with their co-nationalists in Serbia or Croatia, and claimed Bosnia and Herzegovina to be their land. As Serbia and Montenegro were strengthening their autonomy in the second half of the century, they were increasingly active in instigating revolts among their co-religionists in Bosnia. There were also sporadic incursions from Montenegro into Herzegovina in order to "liberate" the land. In turn, the Muslims became steadily suspicious of the Christians and their activities, and the ethnic discontent and differentiation were continuously exacerbated.

As it became clear that the Ottoman reforms would not animate the empire, the European powers, specifically Russia and Austria, were eager to fill the power vacuum that was growing in the Balkan region. Under the pretext of protecting the Christian subjects, they were meddling in Ottoman affairs and projecting their influences among the peoples in the empire. It seemed that Russia's great project of assembling a large "sister" Orthodox state in the Balkans and getting the Straits would finally be realized. Austria, on the other hand, after losing the contest for the primacy among the Germans, turned to the Balkans to secure its interests.

The rebellion of Croatian and Serbian peasants in 1875 inaugurated a crisis that brought an end to the Ottoman rule in Bosnia. It started in Herzegovina in response to the brutal tax collections regardless of a disastrous harvest failure a year earlier. The revolt spread to other regions of the province. Volunteers from various Christian countries came to assist the rebels. But the rebellion was ruthlessly quelled during the winter months of the following year by the Muslim forces. The peasants paid a heavy price in life and property. Estimates are that about 5,000 peasants were killed and over 100,000 became refugees.

The events in Bosnia and Herzegovina were only a part of the immense predicaments facing the Ottomans domestically and on the international scene. Bulgarians also rose against the Turks in 1875. Serbia and Montenegro declared war on the Turks in June of 1876, in the hope of acquiring Bosnia and Herzegovina, respectively. But they were badly beaten by the Ottomans and their hopes of procuring Bosnia and Herzegovina were shattered. Only the Russian intervention saved them from a complete disaster. A year later Russia declared war on the Ottoman Empire, with an understanding that Austria-Hungary would remain neutral and, in return, Russia would recognize the Habsburgs' right to occupy Bosnia and Herzegovina. Alarmed by the Russian victory and the San Stefano treaty that procured a large Bulgarian state, the European powers at their meeting at the Congress of Berlin in July 1878 prevented Russia from projecting its power into the Eastern Mediterranean and blocked the Bulgarians from fulfilling their dream of an independent Greater Bulgaria. The Berlin Congress also recognized the full independence of Serbia, Montenegro, and Romania. Bosnia and Herzegovina, while still under the sultan's suzerainty, was to be administered by the Dual Monarchy (Austria-Hungary). On July 29, 1878, Austrian army units crossed the Bosnian borders, crushed a weak Muslim and partial Orthodox resistance, took Sarajevo on August 19, and subdued all of Bosnia by October of that year.

Under the Dual Monarchy (1878-1918)

The new Bosnian and Herzegovinian rulers from the outset were faced with three major difficulties regarding the administration of the land. First, there was the question of which of the two imperial partners, Austria or Hungary, would attach the occupied land. The second concern was how to govern three already quarrelsome religious groups in an underdeveloped and neglected former Ottoman province. The third and more delicate issue was how to establish a workable governing relationship between a European Christian empire, which for centuries had been a bulwark against Islam, with the ruling Muslim elites in the provinces.

After pacifying Muslim and some Orthodox armed resistance, and crushing local brigandage, the first problem was resolved by making Bosnia and Herzegovina neither an Austrian nor a Hungarian possession, but the crown land administered by the Joint Imperial Finance Ministry. The resolution of the second and third predicaments, to govern a land with three diverse peoples and religions with conflicting political aspirations, and to bring about the Muslim community to accept the rule of a Christian power, was entrusted to a Hungarian official of noble descent, Benjamin Kállay. After seven years in Belgrade as an Austro-Hungarian diplomat, he was named Joint Imperial Finance Minister from 1882 to 1903. Kállay effectively controlled the fate of Bosnia for over 20 years.

The Dual Monarchy kept the Ottoman administrative divisions in the land, except the terminology changed: *sandžak* became *Kreise* (regions) and *kadiluks* were named *Bezirke* (districts). The *Şeriat* (Muslim religious) courts were kept along the civil justice system. The provincial administration was headed by a general, the commander-in-chief of the Fifteenth Army Corps in Sarajevo. He was aided by a deputy for civil affairs and four directors in charge of political, judicial, financial, and economic matters.

Although there were no major institutional changes in Bosnia-Herzegovina after the occupation, Kállay, however, did aspire to bring the administrative practices in the provinces to the existing imperial level. That is why the Austrian period in the country is the best remembered for its large and relatively efficient bureaucracy that drastically improved the old Ottoman administrative practices. Through the efforts of ardent public servants, Bosnia-Herzegovina became, in relation to the periods before and after Habsburg rule, a good example of an efficient government and conscientious public service. The main Austro-Hungarian (that is, Kállay's) policies in Bosnia-Herzegovina were administrative efficiency, economic and educational improvements, reduction of Serbian and Croatian national influences, and, in turn, affirmation of the Bosnian identity as a separate political and ethnic unit.

Along with a fervent building of new roads and some railroads, economic initiatives were undertaken in order to industrialize and link Bosnia-Herzegovina with the rest of the empire. Initiatives were also made to improve the agricultural production. There were, however, some major problems with the economic transformation. First, major capital investments from other parts of the empire never took place. Second, in order to gain the loyalty of the Muslim landlords, the government hesitated to carry out a meaningful land reform. Furthermore, lack of technology and peasants' resistance to new ideas prevented any significant increases in agricultural production.

As part of an effort to bring about economic and social changes, the government also encouraged settlers from other regions of the empire to move to Bosnia and Herzegovina. Economic stimuli were provided to a few thousand settlers that did come to live and work in the provinces. Furthermore, attempts were made to establish educational institutions in order to lower a very high illiteracy rate in Bosnia-Herzegovina. A few hundred primary and some secondary schools were founded, as well as a technical school, a teachers' training college, and some other cultural institutions. Although much of the Austro-Hungarian efforts in Bosnia and Herzegovina were motivated by geopolitical interests, the fact is that substantial advancements were made in the country's infrastructure, education, and public services. The long-range economic efforts, however, had mixed results.

The national awakenings of the 19th century caught Bosnia and Herzegovina in a crossfire among Serbian, Croatian, and Muslim identities. The European civilization fault-line which separated the Latin West and Byzantine worlds for centuries became visible in Bosnia-Herzegovina once again. The Orthodox population, which either migrated to Bosnia-Herzegovina or was converted after the Turkish occupation, embraced Serbian nationalism. Catholics, who lived in Bosnia-Herzegovina before the Ottoman conquest, linked their revival to Bosnian medieval history and to the national movement in Croatia. The Muslim population, also mostly indigenous to the region, was in a perplexed situation regarding their ethnic identity. Their previous imperial Ottoman pride was becoming irrelevant. Rising Turkish nationalism was not an option because they were not of Turkish origin. Furthermore, the Muslim concept that Islam is all inclusive (*Umma Muslima*) was an ideal and not a political reality. This situation resulted in uncertainty and confusion.

By the beginning of this century, a considerable number of Bosnian Muslim intellectuals identified themselves as Croats, a smaller number as Serbs, but most of the people remained ambiguous regarding their national orientations. To them Islam, and not ethnicity, remained as the main identifying mark. While the Croats and the Serbs wanted to be unified with their "mother" countries, among the Muslims there was no urge to unify either with Serbia or Croatia, or into a larger Slav state. Their main goal was to retain Bosnia-Herzegovina as a separate political unit in which they could preserve their Islamic tradition and hopefully maintain their privileged status.

The Serbian national ideologists claimed not only that the Orthodox were Serbs, but that all three groups in Bosnia-Herzegovina were actually Serbs. Therefore, according to them, Bosnia and Herzegovina, as well as most of Croatia, should be united with Serbia. The Croatians also claimed Bosnia-Herzegovina as their land on historical principles, as well as that the Muslims were Islamized former Croats. The concept of Yugoslavism, an attempt to create a new and supranational identity with a program of unifying all of the South Slavs in a single state, complicated the ethnic relations even more.

The idea of unifying Bosnia-Herzegovina with Croatia and making the two an equal partner to Hungary and Austria under the Habsburgs, known as trialism, was circulating as a possibility. This would have provided a balance among the German, Hungarian, and Slavic segments of the empire. But it was unacceptable to the Hungarians, Serbs, and most of the Muslims. The Hungarians did not want to strengthen Slav power in their realm. For the Serbs it would end the dream of unifying Bosnia with Serbia. And in the eyes of the Muslims, trialism would threaten their Islamic tradition and their privileged status.

Because of such a variety of nationalist aspirations and political speculations, Minister Kállay wanted to make Bosnia-Herzegovina a separate entity (*corpus separatum*) within the monarchy and isolate it from other Balkan political and ethnic predicaments. His main project was to cultivate a separate Bosnian ethnicity that would melt all the citizens of Bosnia-Herzegovina into a new nationality.

In order to assure the cooperation of the religious leaders, especially Muslim and Orthodox, the new rulers fully respected freedom of religion and subsidized Christian and Muslim schools. However, the imperial authority gained ultimate control of all institutions in the province, including the power to appoint the bishops of the Catholic and Orthodox dioceses, and the religious head of the Muslim community (*reis ul-ulema*) and a four-man Muslim council (*mejlis al-ulema*). As Catholic rulers, the Habsburgs were especially careful to avoid making Catholic co-religionists a privileged group in the province.

To advance the Bosnian or Bosniak identity, Kállay banned political and even cultural activities under national names. His efforts, however, did not bring about the desired results. Even the Muslims, who remained cool to Croatian or Serbian nationalism, did not think in terms of an all-inclusive Bosniak national character. They saw themselves as a separate entity. Besides the religious exclusiveness, however, one should not forget the socioeconomic differences that for centuries separated the Muslim elites from the Christian peasantry. Religious and economic differences, plus the already developed national consciousness of the Serbs and the Croats, were detrimental to integration processes.

The legitimacy of a Christian monarchy to rule Bosnia-Herzegovina was constantly resisted by the Muslim community in Bosnia-Herzegovina. It was seen as a temporary setback and not as a permanent solution. A dream remained that either the Ottoman Empire would do something to alleviate their dissatisfaction or a solution would be found in which Bosnia-

Herzegovina would remain an Islamic region of Europe. The sultan's sovereignty in Bosnia-Herzegovina till 1908, although on paper only, gave a ray of hope to the Muslims that better times might yet come.

Because the new rulers retained the old structures, the Muslims worked at first through the traditional religious and cultural institutions. Petitions and grievances concerning religious matters were constantly raised in order to protect their interests. The question of conversion of some Muslim members to Christianity became a mobilizing issue for all segments of Muslim society. While, in the eyes of Vienna, conversions were a private matter, this was portrayed by the Muslims as a matter essential for their survival. However, such issues became the means through which they put pressure on the government in order to achieve a better political status.

In 1881, Bosnian military units from the Ottoman period were merged with the Austro-Hungarian imperial armed forces and a general conscription was ordered in Bosnia-Herzegovina. There were strong objections by the Muslims to the service in a Christian army. This, along with some other grievances, resulted in a short-lived Muslim revolt in the Mostar region.

Muslims also fought the government over control of the charitable religious land foundations (*vakufs* or *vakifs*). By the end of the Ottoman rule, the use of the *vakufs* deteriorated so much that they were little more than tax-free family possessions. The Dual Monarchy made major reforms in this area, but the question of *vakuf* control became a political issue. Finally, in 1909 control of these institutions was given to Muslim leadership. This victory contributed greatly to the Muslim political and nationalist aims.

The end of the 19th and the beginning of the 20th centuries, in the Balkans and in Europe, witnessed a series of political crises and shifting alliances. The demise of the Alliance of the Three Emperors (Germany, Russia, and Austria), formation of the Triple Alliance (Germany, Austria, and Italy) and of the Triple Entente (England, France, and Russia), and growing tensions among the old and the new European colonial powers, greatly affected the fate of the Balkan region. Suspicions among the former allies, the Russians and the Habsburgs, were growing and hostile activities in the Balkans were intensified. Events in Serbia and Croatia, and ensuing Balkan wars all had an impact on Bosnia-Herzegovina.

In Serbia, a group of zealous Serbian nationalist officers eliminated the ruling Obrenović dynasty and installed the Austrophobe Karađorđevićs to the Serbian royal throne. They also organized and sponsored secret societies (Unification or Death, better known as the Black Hand) and paramilitary groups like the *četniks* in order to carry out the Serbian nationalist program formulated in three sentences: "Serbia is wherever the Serbs live. All the Serbs must live in Serbia. Serbia for the Serbs." Serbian foreign policy, because of the shared culture and common expansionist interests, shifted openly to the Russian sphere of influence. Furthermore, both Bulgaria and Serbia were competing for Macedonia. And Serbia relied on Russian help.

In Croatia, a hated *ban* (viceroy), Kuen Hedervary (1883-1903), used the Serbian minority in an attempt to keep Croatia in his firm grip and to deprive it of political autonomy and cultural identity. This contributed greatly to Serbian-Croatian tensions. Serbs were seen as a minority willing to be used by Hungarians against Croatian interests. In 1903, however, a political coalition was formed in Croatia between the Croatian and Serbian political forces, and among the intellectuals the idea of Yugoslavism was fostered. But the two peoples had different, and in many ways incompatible, visions of their national futures. Developments in Bosnia-Herzegovina were also growing more complex, especially after Kállay's death in 1903. His successor, Stephen Burián (1903-1912), realized that Kállay's ethnic policies were not working, and he opened the door to organizational structures under ethnic labels. A significant religious autonomy for the Orthodox Church was secured in 1905. It officially became known as the Serbian-Orthodox Church. This greatly stimulated Serbian nationalism and provided it with an organizational instrument. From that point on, all three groups, Muslim, Serb, and Croat, established ethnic institutions that shaped and sharpened their national goals and programs.

The first crisis of significant proportions erupted when Austro-Hungary, prompted by the 1908 revolution of the Young Turks, decided to annex Bosnia-Herzegovina. Within less than a year the matter was resolved with the Turkish government. The Turks were given monetary compensation for the provinces, the sandžak of Novi Pazar (also known just as Sandžak) was left in Turkish hands, and Bosnian Muslims were guaranteed freedom of religion. The tensions between Austria and Serbia, however, grew to the breaking point. If the Russians had not suffered defeat in the war with Japan in 1905, most probably Serbia would have kindled a war with the Habsburgs in 1908 over the annexation of Bosnia.

The First Balkan War erupted less than four years later. The Serbs, Montenegrins, Bulgarians, and Greeks made an alliance and wanted to drive the Turks from the Balkans. They defeated the Turks in the war of 1912. The victory, however, brought about another war among the allies over the spoils. In the Second Balkan War (1913), Serbia, Montenegro, and Greece, joined by Romania, defeated Bulgaria, depriving it of sizable territories. Victory in both Balkan wars and more than doubling the size of its territory encouraged Serbia to pursue its expansionist policy. While the pro-Yugoslavs among the Croat and Muslim intelligentsia in Bosnia-Herzegovina looked toward Serbia as the Piedmont of the South Slavs, the others saw it as an aggressor and wished to achieve their national aspirations within the Habsburg Empire.

The Serbian nationalist forces, however, were eager to provoke a conflict over Bosnia and Herzegovina and enlarge its territory. Their efforts and desires were fulfilled on June 28, 1914, when a young Serb nationalist, Gavrilo Princip, shot the Archduke Francis Ferdinand in Sarajevo. This ignited the First World War in which Bosnia and Herzegovina found itself on the side of the Dual Monarchy. At the end of the war, the dissolution of the Austro-Hungarian Empire placed Bosnia-Herzegovina into a newly created South Slavic state.

From 1918 to 1992

The creation of the South Slav state in 1918 (the Kingdom of the Serbs, Croats, and Slovenes, known as Yugoslavia after 1929) was more a calculated result of the post-World War I peacemakers than a yearning of the people who became a part of it. It was stitched together from parts of the former Austria-Hungary (Slovenia, Croatia, Vojvodina, and Bosnia-Herzegovina), and the kingdoms of Serbia and Montenegro.

Various peoples that made up the new country had antithetical national and political visions, and perceptions of what the new state should be. To the Croatians and their Slovene and Bosnian Muslim neighbors, the common state was to be a loose union of equal partners. To the Serbs, the new state was a substitution for a Greater Serbia, their paramount dream that dissipated with the fall of their champion, Imperial Russia. To the Western peacemakers, the newly created state was to serve as a link in a chain of new states designated to be a buffer zone against the spread of the Bolshevik revolution. This creation of the Versailles Treaty (1918) was a quick fix to a very complex and unstable region of Europe. The forced union of various peoples with different cultures and religions was from the very outset susceptible to failure.

During World War I, the future of Bosnia and Herzegovina was envisioned by some in Vienna and by leading Muslim politicians as either an autonomous entity directly under the Hungarian crown, or indirectly through an affinity with Croatia. But as soon as some Slovene and Croatian politicians established a National Council for the unification of the South Slavs (October 5, 1918), a branch of the same National Council was constituted in Bosnia and Herzegovina. The Governor of the province, Baron Sarkotić, handed over the power to the members of the Council on November 1, 1918. Two days later, the First National Government of Bosnia and Herzegovina was formed. Serbian and Montenegrin armies moved into Bosnia and Herzegovina a few days later, and violence erupted in many places.

As in the past, the politics in Bosnia-Herzegovina continued to follow mostly ethnic lines. The Bosnian Serbs were strong supporters of the Serbian controlled central government in Belgrade. They voted exclusively for the Serbian political parties. They were free now to orient their cultural and economic activities toward Belgrade. To belong to the ruling nationality in the country definitely had its tangible rewards and the Serbs from the former Habsburg regions utilized that advantage to the fullest. The Croats of Bosnia-Herzegovina were of federalist political orientation and strongly opposed Serbian unitarism. Most of them were followers of the Croatian (Republican) Peasant Party. Culturally and economically they were Zagreb-oriented. The Muslim leadership, meanwhile, maneuvered between the two camps. Although there were some pro-Serb enthusiasts, the overwhelming majority of the Muslim population was in the federalist camp with the Croats and Slovenes.

The Yugoslav Muslim Organization (JMO) established in 1919 became the largest Muslim political formation. It politicized the Muslim masses and attempted to protect their interests in the new South Slavic state. At the beginning of the new country, the JMO leadership was pro-Serb oriented. By collaborating with the ruling Serbian party, the Muslims attempted to secure Bosnia's territorial unity, to retain Muslim unity, to have freedom in Muslim religious and educational institutions, and to diminish the impact of the impending land reforms on the Muslim landlords. In return, the JMO, with its Muslim allies from Kosovo, Sandžak, and Macedonia, voted for the unitarist constitution that was promulgated on June 28, 1921, the day of the Kosovo battle (1389) and of the Sarajevo assassination (1914).

Whereas the constitution stated that "Bosnia and Herzegovina would be divided into districts within her present [1921] borders," in actuality Bosnian administrative integrity was only an appearance. It did not have political or ethnic significance. Pan-Serbian policies also caused a split among the Bosnian Muslims. A small and older group of politicians remained faithful to Belgrade, while the majority, under the leadership of Mehmed Spaho, moved close to the federalist Croatian camp. All the

Muslim deputies to the Belgrade parliament from this faction, except Spaho, went so far as to declare themselves in 1924 to be of Croatian nationality. Spaho, who resigned from the Belgrade government in 1922, claimed to be a "Yugoslav." There was a strong pro-Croatian wing in the JMO and in the mid-1920s, a number of Muslims voted for the Croatian Peasant Party.

After the 1923 elections, Croatian, Slovene, and Bosnian Muslim main political parties formed a Federalist bloc. A year later, the Serbian Democratic party joined the Federalists and together they formed an Opposition bloc. This contributed to the fall of the Serbian Radicals and to the formation of a new coalition government under the leadership of Serbian Democrats. During this short-lived government (July 1924 - October 1924), the Bosnian Muslims (JMO) enjoyed considerable power. But with the increase of their power in Belgrade came Serbian anti-Muslim (and anti-Croatian) violence in the Bosnian countryside.

Regardless of the Bosnian central location in the country and a strong Serbian unitarist force in it, and despite a relatively cooperative Muslim leadership, the region underwent economic and cultural stagnation in the interwar period. The Belgrade regime chose oppression and exploitation rather than magnanimity as its overall policy in the newly consolidated lands.

In 1927, Spaho joined the unitarist Serbian Radical government and remained faithful to it even after the assassination of the Croatian political leadership in the Belgrade Parliament (1928). King Aleksandar, however, outlawed all "tribal" parties in January of 1929, declared a personal dictatorship, renamed the country into Yugoslavia, and, under the disguise of official Yugoslavism, continued to advance the Serbian cause.

In the same year, the administrative boundaries of the country were redrawn. Instead of the existing (more than 30) districts, nine banates (*banovine*) were created. Traditional administrative districts in Bosnia-Herzegovina were divided up and consolidated with neighboring regions in such a way that a Serbian majority could be assured in all of them except one, which had a Croatian majority. Even the pretense of Bosnian integrity retained in 1921 vanished in 1929. Furthermore, the king's appointments to his personal cabinet indicated that he favored JMO renegades and pro-Serb Muslims. Genuine Muslim or Croatian political representatives were excluded from power. Such policies only contributed to the radicalization of the Croatian and Muslim politics and masses in the 1930s. Out of such despotic rule a revolutionary (ustaša) movement rose among the Croatians and began to advocate the breakup of Yugoslavia by any means. This movement had sympathy among the Bosnian Muslims and some joined it.

After King Alexander's assassination (1934) by Croat and Macedonian separatists from revolutionary groups (ustaše and IMRO), the JMO joined the ruling Yugoslav Radical Union under the leadership of Prince Pavle's regency and it remained a part of the regime till 1939. Spaho died in June of that year and in August the regent struck an agreement (*Sporazum*) with Vladko Maček, leader of the Croatian Peasant Party, by which Croatia became an autonomous banate (*banovina)*. The Croatian Banovina, however, included parts of Bosnia and Herzegovina.

The interests of the Bosnian Muslims and their goals to safeguard the unity of Bosnia and Herzegovina were ignored by the Serb-Croat deal. The agreement, however, was vehemently opposed by Serbian nationalist forces, and as Spaho's successor, Dr. Džafer-beg Kulenović, predicted, the Banovina was only a temporary arrangement. In April of 1941, the Yugoslav state disintegrated. It became a victim of its own Serbian despotism and of German and Italian aggression.

During the Second World War, Bosnia and Herzegovina became an integral part of the Independent State of Croatia (1941-1945), a state that was established by the ustaša revolutionaries under the "protection" of fascist Italy and Nazi Germany. The unification of Bosnia-Herzegovina with Croatia was justified by the claim that those were Croatian historic lands and also by an ideology that the Muslims were Croats of Islamic religion.

Persecutions of the non-Serbs in the interwar period and the Serbian struggle against the Croat state led to mutual retaliations and slaughters among the Serbs, Croats, and Muslims. Persecutions of Jews in Croatia and Bosnia-Herzegovina began in

June of 1941, as well as in Serbia. Most of the Croats of Bosnia and Herzegovina welcomed the disintegration of Yugoslavia and the unification with Croatia, and many of them joined the ustaše forces. Numerous Bosnian Muslims supported the Independent State of Croatia while others simply accepted reality and adjusted to the new situation. Even many sympathizers of the state, however, were not pleased with the policies of the ustaše regime and attempted to distance themselves from it. Leading Muslims complained about their under-proportionate representation in the state offices and military ranks. There were also moves on their part to make Bosnia-Herzegovina an autonomous province within the German political configurations in the region. This proposal did not go through, but the Germans did organize a separate volunteer Muslim military division in 1943. At the end of April 1944, a group of leading Muslims in Sarajevo openly protested to the Zagreb government against the ustaša policies and demanded "equality for everyone, justice for all, and the rule of law above everything."

There were mainly three antagonistic local forces operating in Bosnia-Herzegovina during the war. They became a lethal triangle of shifting combinations and retaliations that cost an enormous number of human lives in the country during the Second World War. The Croatian regulars and ustaše volunteers fought the Serbian četniks and the Communist-led partisans. The četniks stood for the restoration of Serbian-controlled royalist Yugoslavia and a homogeneous Greater Serbia and fought the Croats and Muslims. The third force, the partisans, stood for a new and socialist Yugoslavia. Their promises of freedom, federalism, and national equality attracted a considerable following from various ethnic backgrounds. All three turned to mass killings in order to achieve their goals. The partisans, however, by the support of the Allies, emerged as the winners at the end of the war.

The Yugoslav Communists were not consistent in their pronouncements regarding the national question in the country. Being faithful to the Comintern, their teaching on this issue followed the interests of the Soviet Union. Thus, in the mid-1920s, they advocated the dissolution of Yugoslavia but by the end of the 1930s they championed a federalist cause. Furthermore, they were not sure on the question of Bosnian Muslim identity. Although there was an understanding among the Communists before and during the war that the Muslims were not a nation, they remained vague in defining their ethnic status.

Toward the end of the war, the Communist leadership had a heated debate on the status of Bosnia and Herzegovina in the new state. Forces from Serbia demanded that Bosnia-Herzegovina be absorbed into their republic, but the Bosnian forces with the help of Tito, the head of the Party and Communist government, were able to prevent this, and they secured for Bosnia-Herzegovina the status of a federal republic.

The post-war period brought terror and new reprisals throughout the whole country. It was the duty of the state secret police, controlled by the Communist Party, to destroy the "enemies of the people" and force everyone to appreciate the new regime. Thousands were executed and many more jailed. Ethnic cultural institutions were banned and their property nationalized, religious activities were curtailed, and no independent activities of any kind were tolerated.

The situation in Bosnia and Herzegovina was even worse than in other republics. Most of the war operations took place on its territory that resulted in major destruction and population losses. There was a great distrust of the Croatians and Muslims, and the Serbs were given a dominant role in the republic. It was openly admitted in the late 1960s that post-war development of some regions, like western Herzegovina, was neglected as a part of collective punishment. The Muslims were given "equal status" to the others in the country, but they were denied a chance to declare themselves as a separate national entity. It was expected that in time the Serbian identity would prevail among them. From the end of the war till the end of the 1960s, the leading Muslims declared themselves as either Serbs or "Yugoslavs," and a few as Croatians, but the majority of the Muslim populace remained ethnically "undeclared."

After the Serbian hard-liners were subdued (1966) and Croatian nationalist voices silenced (1967 and 1971), Tito began to favor the affirmation of Bosnian Muslims as a new political base. Under the Communist leadership they finally gained full national status in 1971. On the census form of that year they were allowed to declare themselves as "ethnic Muslims." During that decade they also became the most influential group in the republic. Furthermore, a number of Bosnian Muslims became a part of Tito's inner circle. The best-known among them was Džemal Bijedić, the Prime Minister of Yugoslavia from 1971 to his death in a plane crash in 1977. Many claimed that his death was not an accident, but the work of his opponents in Belgrade. Whether an accident or not, it was a symbolic indication of a growing feeling among Serbian forces that the Muslims were getting too much power. Croatians were also not pleased with their situation in the republic, or the country. They complained that their political and economic position in the republic was growing more and more negligible in relation to the Serbs and Muslims. They were under-represented in every level of state institutions and the primary road of their social and economic advancement was to find a job in Western Europe.

In the 1970s, the Yugoslav state system underwent two opposing processes. One was centripetal in nature—the Communist Party discipline and its control of society were tightened. The other was centrifugal—the new constitution of 1974 permitted greater self-rule in the republics and in the autonomous provinces of Kosovo and Vojvodina. This was also the period when Yugoslavia borrowed billions of dollars from the West in order to prove to citizens and to the world its economic and political viability. Bosnia and Herzegovina, after being neglected for a few decades, enjoyed a fresh infusion of economic growth as well as political importance.

After Tito's death in 1981, however, besides acute economic difficulties, the Yugoslav republics began to move in two opposite directions: the Serbs pushed for recentralization, and the non-Serbs, primarily Croatia and Slovenia, championed further decentralization. The intranational relations in the country deteriorated rapidly during that decade. The cracks that had always been there began to surface. While Croatians were relatively quiet at the time, Albanian ethnic disturbances took place in Kosovo, as Slovenes began to demand greater autonomy and personal liberties. A group of Muslim intellectuals in Bosnia-Herzegovina, headed by Alija Izetbegović, undermined the position of their secular Muslim leaders by publishing an *Islamic Declaration*. In it, the group indicated its displeasure with Muslim secularism, stressed the superiority of Islam over Christianity and Communism, and called for a return to the basic teaching of the Koran in order to achieve a true Islamic society. The supporters of the *Declaration* were tried in 1983 and sentenced to long years of imprisonment. The leading members of the group once belonged to the Young Muslim organization, that was condemned as an antistate organization in 1946 and 1949. This fact indicated that a quest for a Muslim religious orientation and identity was simmering under the surface even under Communist rule.

Another blow to the Bosnian Muslim influence in Yugoslav politics came in the late 1980s. A financial scandal that involved a well-known business enterprise in western Bosnia (Agrokomerc) and its boss, Fikret Abdić, was identified as a sign of Muslim misuse of power. Abdić was a member of the Bosnian Central Committee and too close to the all-powerful Pozderac family. While economic embezzlements were common practice in Yugoslavia, many believed that the Agrokomerc affair was used by the Serbian forces to push the Muslims from political prominence. As a result of this affair, Hamdija Pozderac, the vice president of Yugoslavia, in line to become the president in May of 1988, was pressured to resign the position.

The most powerful nationalist tide in the 1980s, however, came from the Serbs. While the Yugoslav constitution of 1974 promoted decentralization, Serbian political and nationalist forces began to advocate a "strong Serbia in a strong Yugoslavia." The blueprint for the revived Serbian nationalism was drawn in the 1986 *Memorandum*, written by leading members of the Serbian Academy of Sciences and Arts in Belgrade. It accused Tito and the non-Serb Yugoslav leaders of anti-Serbian conspiracy. It was a call for the defense of Serbian culture and national interests "wherever Serbs live," especially in Kosovo, Bosnia-Herzegovina, and Croatia.

At first, the "protection" of the Kosovo province from the Albanians, who made up 90 percent of the local population, became the rallying point for the Serbs. This coincided with the 600th anniversary of the Battle of Kosovo (1389), where the Serbs and their allies were defeated by the Ottoman Turks. The leader of the Communist Party in Serbia, Slobodan Milošević, took the struggle for "Serbia and all the Serbs" to the masses in 1989. His populism was a new type of politics in a Communist country. In the atmosphere of triumphalism, militarism, and a general nationalist euphoria, Milošević crushed the provincial governments in Vojvodina and Kosovo. Through his proxies he also took control of Montenegro, and exported his movement into Croatia and Bosnia-Herzegovina. The cry was the "unification of all Serbian lands." This was the prelude to the war in Slovenia (June 1991) that quickly spread to Croatia (June-December 1991), and then to Bosnia-Herzegovina (April 1992). These were also the final moments of the Yugoslav state.

Road to Independence and War for Survival

Besides the cult of Tito, president of socialist Yugoslavia, there were two vital institutions that were holding the South Slavic state together, the League of Communists of Yugoslavia - LCY (the Communist Party) and the Yugoslav Peoples Army (Jugoslavenska narodna armija - JNA). The Party had been cracking along the national lines ever since Tito's death (1980) and the demise of its central hub in Belgrade finally came in January of 1990. The army, on the other hand, did not disintegrate but merely transformed itself into an all-Serb military force in 1991.

Once the Communists gave up the monopoly of power (1990), new ethnocentric parties were quickly organized and they easily defeated the "reformed Communists" in the first post-Communist elections in all of the former Yugoslav republics except in Serbia and Montenegro. In the last two, the Communists were already at the forefront of the nationalist movement.

Forty-one registered parties and associations in Bosnia-Herzegovina were formed, and 1,551 candidates from 18 different parties ran for the National Assembly in the first free elections (November 1990). The three ethnic parties, (Muslim) Party of Democratic Action (SDA), Serbian Democratic Party (SDS), and Croatian Democratic Union (HDZ), became the most important political formations in Bosnia. After the November-December 1990 elections, there were 99 Muslims, 85 Serbs, 49 Croats, and seven "Yugoslavs" in the 240-seat bicameral legislature (Chamber of Citizens 130 seats and a Chamber of Municipalities 110 seats). The leader of the SDA, Alija Izetbegović, became the president of the nine-member multi-ethnic collective presidency. A principle of ethnic parity was to be maintained in all branches of government.

Although the new government was formed from all three political and ethnic groups, it became clear from the outset that Serb-dominated municipalities in the republic refused to recognize Sarajevo's preeminence. At the same time, Serb representatives in the Assembly declined to cooperate in anything that would increase Bosnia's self-rule, claiming that a sovereign Bosnia would become an Islamic state. Already in October 1990, the Serbs set up a Serbian National Council in the city of Banja Luka, soon to become a Serb nationalist stronghold. This led to the formation of a Serb Community of Municipalities of Bosnian Krajina (April 1991) and the signing of a "treaty of cooperation" (June 1991) with the self-proclaimed Serbian Autonomous Region of Krajina in Croatia. The two entities even announced a "declaration of unification." In fact, by November 1991, Bosnian Serbs proclaimed six *krajinas*, Serbian autonomous regions, in Bosnia-Herzegovina that claimed to be parts of a "Greater Serbia." It was clear that such moves were not the work of the Bosnian Serbs alone, but a component of a larger plan concocted by the Serbian national leaders in Belgrade.

The Muslim leadership in Sarajevo was caught in the middle between Serbian centralism and the Slovene and Croatian drive for independence. In the fall of 1991, President Izetbegović, together with the Macedonians, made a last-ditch effort to stop the

Croatian and Slovene move to independence, and promoted Yugoslav confederalism. But this was a dead issue. Thus, conscious of the consequences if Bosnia remained a part of truncated Yugoslavia, the Muslim leaders with the help of the Croats finally began to move toward the independence of Bosnia-Herzegovina.

On October 15, 1991, the (Muslim) Party of Democratic Action (SDA) and the Croatian Democratic Union (HDZ) adopted a memorandum on the sovereignty and neutrality of Bosnia and Herzegovina without declaring independence. The Serb representatives rejected the move and walked out of the Assembly. A referendum on independence, however, followed in February 1992. Over 64 percent of the eligible voters participated and 99.7 percent of them answered affirmatively to the question "Do you support a sovereign and independent Bosnia-Herzegovina?" Thus, the country was proclaimed independent and the international recognition by the European Community and the United States followed on April 6 and 7, 1992, respectively.

The Serbian leadership rejected the referendum as illegal and immediately turned to military operations in order to consolidate territories already declared autonomous and to occupy other parts of the country they claimed to be theirs. The previously local violent "incidents" turned now into a full-fledged war of Serbian rebellion-cum-aggression against Bosnia-Herzegovina.

It is often perceived that the EC recognition of Slovenia and Croatia, and then of Bosnia-Herzegovina, as independent states precipitated the outbreak of war in Bosnia. The fact is, however, that Bosnia-Herzegovina was involved in a war from the time the JNA attacked Slovenia and Croatia in June 1991. The republic became a staging post for the Yugoslav army, its factories were producing arms for the Serbian forces, a number of Bosnian Serb and Muslim officers participated in the JNA units on various fronts in Croatia, and many Serb and Croat volunteers from the republic were fighting on their co-nationalists sides. Also, the Serbian Democratic Party (SDA) was getting ready for a war by organizing and arming its paramilitary units, while the JNA disarmed the Bosnian Territorial-Defense force by the November

1991 elections and left the Muslims and Croats helpless. Furthermore, major Serb attacks, especially against Croat villages in eastern Herzegovina, began to take place in the fall of 1991. Moreover, by creating autonomous *krajinas* the Serbs had already divided the country, except for Sarajevo, before the end of 1991. However, the Sarajevo leadership and the media ignored these events. Nothing was done to prepare the country for war till the brutal attacks by Serbian paramilitary forces on Muslim settlements in northeastern Bosnia began on April 2, 1992, and till the mask of calm in Sarajevo was shattered by Serbian heavy artillery a few days later. The recognition of Bosnia-Herzegovina (April 6, 1992) was only an excuse for the Serbs to sever ties with the rest of Bosnia and declare an independent Serb Republic of their own.

Possessing an overwhelming superiority in military might, the Serbs within a month took control of more than two-thirds of Bosnia-Herzegovina. After accomplishing this, their leadership engaged in a waiting game in which, they hoped, the international community would coerce the Sarajevo government to concede capitulation and would legitimize the creation of a "Greater Serbia." The conquest of land, however, was not enough. By mid-summer 1992, it became clear that the Serbs were engaged in systematic "ethnic cleansing" of the non-Serbs, namely Muslims and Croats, in the regions under their control. Besides expulsion of people from their homes, villages, and towns, numerous concentration and rape camps were operated as a part of warfare. The war in Bosnia essentially was a war against civilians in order to create "pure" ethnic areas.

By the end of summer 1992, it became clear, however, that the Serbs were not able to conquer the entire country. Despite of a weak and improvised military organization, Croats and Muslims were able to halt the assault. The Croats even pushed the Serb forces from the Mostar region in June 1992. However, it soon became apparent that Bosnia was recognized as a sovereign and independent state but abandoned by the international community. Moreover, while the JNA and the Serbs inherited the entire arsenal of the former Yugoslavia, the leading world powers would not even considered lifting the UN arms embargo imposed (September 1991) on all former Yugoslav republics.

The response of the world, particularly of the European Community (EC) and the United Nations (UN), to the war in Bosnia-Herzegovina was one of ambivalence, impotence, and, some would say, even deceitfulness. The leading European powers never admitted the true nature of the war. For them this was a "civil war" and an eruption of "ancient Balkan feuds," not an aggression on a sovereign state. Only the horrifying pictures from concentration camps and the public outcry that followed their revelation forced the EC and UN leaders to convene the London Conference at the end of August 1992 to address the crisis. The rhetoric at the conference and its framework for stopping the war were encouraging, but no one was willing to do anything about implementing its decisions. Two mediators, Lord Owen and Cyrus Vance, on behalf of the EC and UN, respectively, as a part of the Geneva Conference (a continuation of the London meeting), attempted to find a formula that would preserve the Bosnian state, at least on paper, find the minimum arrangement acceptable to the Serbs, and then pressure the Muslim-led government and the Croats to accept it. The two came with a peace plan (end of 1992) that would divide Bosnia-Herzegovina into 10 semiautonomous cantons, mostly along ethnic lines, with a loose central authority. This, and three more international peace proposals that followed, indicated the apparent willingness of the West to accept "reality," abide by the law of the stronger, and dismantle Bosnia into, by now, "ethnically cleansed" areas. The EC-UN plans did not bring any beneficial results. On the contrary, they greatly helped to push the Croats and Muslims, reluctant allies, into a war over the remaining 30 percent of the land under their control. Their conflict, however, provided a strong argument for those who claimed that this was a civil war and, therefore, the outside world should not get involved in Bosnia.

Already at the end of 1991, Bosnian Croats began to organize a self-defense that proved to be crucial in protecting at least some parts of the country. But as the war was evolving and the

Sarajevo government proved to be impotent, the Bosnian Croats filled the power vacuum in the regions where they constituted the majority, and began to play two political cards. First, if Bosnia survived, they wanted to secure their national equality with the Muslims and Serbs, and possibly gain regional self-rule. Second, if Bosnia collapsed as an independent state, they were ready to take "their part" and unite with Croatia. Among the Croats themselves there were differences as to which option should be at the forefront. The Croats from Bosnia proper stood mostly for the first, and those from Herzegovina for the second option. As the Herzegovinian faction dominated Croat politics, they began to push a separatist plan and proclaimed their own Croat Republic of Herceg-Bosna in August of 1993. The apparent Western willingness to divide the country was an incentive and justification for such moves.

On the other hand, the Muslim leadership desired a unitary state. It perceived the Muslims as the "basic" people in Bosnia, and therefore the only trustworthy "guardians" of the state. Furthermore, as the Croats had Croatia and the Serbs Serbia, the conclusion of the Muslims was that the Bosniacs (Bosnian Muslims) should have Bosnia as their nation-state. This, sometimes explicit but more often implicit, integralist message contributed to the mistrust and the growing gap between the Muslims and Croats and others who remained willing to support the independence of Bosnia on the basis of ethnic equality. Realizing the (in)actions of the EC and UN, and the seeming willingness of the world to accept the result of military conquest, the Muslims began to grab the land held by the Croats (1993) and were even on the verge of proclaiming a separate Bosnian Muslim Republic at the beginning of 1993. Moreover, a leading Bosnian Muslim in Northwestern Bosnia, Fikret Abdić, declared his own Autonomous Region of Western Bosnia in September 1993 and began to fight the Sarajevo government. Thus, by the end of 1993, the situation looked hopeless. The world was staring at the worst human disaster in Europe since World War II and was seemingly helpless to do anything about it.

The United Nations involvement in Bosnia focused mainly on humanitarian needs. Besides some 1,500 UN troops already in Bosnia, in September 1992, the UN Security Council approved to extend the existing 15,000 UN Protection Force (UNPROFOR) in Croatia by 6,000 in order to protect humanitarian aid in Bosnia, including the opening of the Sarajevo airport. By the summer of 1995, there were approximately 23,000 "peacekeepers" from 18 nations in Bosnia-Herzegovina. All the UN Security Council decisions regarding Bosnia, however, were a reaction to some major human disaster (the May 1992 bread-line massacre in Sarajevo, for example) with no meaningful force or willingness to implement them. The resolutions imposing economic sanctions against Serbia and Montenegro (May 1992), creating the no-fly-zone over Bosnia (October 1992), and establishing six UN "safe areas" in Bosnia (May 1993) lacked a clear mechanism of implementation, a well-defined command, or a measure of response to provocations. These and other resolutions were passed to pressure the Serbs to accept a negotiated settlement, while being careful to avoid any direct UN "involvement" in the war. Even after the "discovery" of concentration and rape camps, mass executions, and blatant genocide, the UN and EC did nothing meaningful to stop the Serb onslaught. One has to recognize, however, that the UN and other humanitarian organizations did, with great sacrifices, keep most of the Bosnian population alive and helped to sustain the life of the state itself.

The fate of Bosnia was also complicated by political contentions among the international power players: the UN, United States, EC, NATO, and Russia, to name the main ones. Each one had its own agenda in the Balkans. The UN secretary general, Boutros Boutros-Ghali, wanted to be at the forefront and not bullied by the United States on the Bosnian question. The British and the French demanded that Europe should resolve its own problems and resented American encroachments on "their turf." The Russians remained not only Serb advocates, but used the Bosnian war as a stage for their international visibility. By the agreement with the UN, NATO was authorized to patrol the declared no-fly-zone and use air strikes when called upon. But in order to prevent a more decisive approach to the problem and to lessen the impact of the U.S. leverage, the key command to air strikes was in the hands of the UN civilian chief in the former Yugoslavia till July of 1995. For such reasons, it took the international community almost three years into the war to undertake a direct action against Serb military targets. In February 1994, NATO (U.S.) jets shot down four Serb military planes over Bosnia. Even that, however, was not a turning point of the war but merely a reaction to a Sarajevo market massacre two weeks earlier. It seems that the main concern of the international factors was to contain the war and hopefully choke it off in Bosnia regardless of human suffering, rather than to resolve the Bosnian question in a meaningful manner.

A major shift in the Bosnian quandary came in March 1994 when Presidents Alija Izetbegović of Bosnia-Herzegovina and Franjo Tuđman of Croatia, in the presence of President Clinton, signed an agreement in Washington by which Bosnian Muslims and Croats entered into a common federation, to be linked to Croatia in the future. This not only ended the one-year-long Muslim-Croat war, but most important, indicated a direct American involvement in the region. Furthermore, a month later, a five-nation Contact Group was assembled (United States, Britain, France, Germany, and Russia) with UN and EC approval to revive the Bosnian peace talks, which had temporarily collapsed. But the Contact Group did not have much success. The Bosnian Serbs were not willing to accept anything less than a victory on their terms.

Meanwhile, some major shifts were in the making regarding the Bosnian peace initiative. Slobodan Milošević, the prime mover of the war in the former Yugoslavia, shifted his policy and became an advocate of peace, in order to preserve his hold on power in Serbia and to salvage for the Serbs in Croatia and Bosnia, through peace, what he could not gain through war. At the same time, the United States began to support Croatia in order to attain a balance of power in the region. As a result, by mid-August 1995, the Serbs lost almost all of the territory they held in Croatia and large parts of western Bosnia. Moreover, the Bosnian Serb attacks on the UN "safe areas" in eastern Bosnia (July 1995), that resulted in one of the worst human disasters of the war, and a Sarajevo marketplace massacre (Aug. 28, 1995) prompted massive NATO air raids, under U.S. initiative, against Serb military positions and installations. Thus a combination of the NATO actions, a successful Croat and Muslim ground offensive, and active U.S. diplomatic efforts finally brought some concrete results for the people in Bosnia. Although the leaders of the Bosnian Serbs were not ready to make a deal, it was done for them by the president of Serbia, Slobodan Milošević, and finally the fighting was over.

After some arduous negotiations and a period of shuttle diplomacy by American emissaries, the American peace proposal was initialed by the presidents of Croatia, Bosnia-Herzegovina, and Serbia in Dayton, Ohio, on November 21 and signed by the involved parties in Paris on December 14, 1995. The agreement confirmed the sovereignty and independence of Bosnia-Herzegovina in its internationally recognized borders. It did, however, establish two autonomous political entities in the country, the (Muslim-Croat) Federation of Bosnia and Herzegovina and the Serb Republic. The first controls 51 and the second 49 percent of the total territory. The central government has responsibility over foreign policy and trade, customs, immigration, monetary policy, international law enforcement, communications, transportation, and air traffic control. The accord established a bicameral legislature of 15-person upper and 42-person lower chambers, and a three-member collective presidency. Furthermore, it provided for a common constitutional court and a central bank.

In order to set in motion the peace accord, a 60,000-strong international peace Implementation Force (IFOR), including 20,000 U.S. soldiers, descended on Bosnia to make sure that each side fulfilled its promises. The Dayton agreement also resulted in the UN lifting trade sanctions, with some conditions, against Serbia and Montenegro, and the arms embargo against Bosnia-Herzegovina.

The implementation of the Dayton peace accord was set on two main tracks, military and civilian. The military portion was successfully achieved by the NATO-led Implementation Force (IFOR). It secured the end of the fighting and separated the opposing military forces along the demarcation lines between the two state entities, the Muslim-Croat Federation and the Serbian Republic. However, to avoid any potential long-range entanglement in the Balkans and to preserve political unity among the participating peace enforcing countries, the IFOR leadership interpreted its role in the narrowest sense possible. It was, for example, unwilling to apprehend indicted war criminals, insure the freedom of travel, secure the return of refugees, or enforce any aspect of the agreement that it perceived to be civilian in nature. Many believe that such an IFOR attitude was not helpful in achieving the goals set by the Dayton treaty and that, because of it, the implementation of the civilian part of the agreement is in great doubt.

The main problems in post-Dayton Bosnia and Herzegovina stem from the vague and contradictory nature of the treaty's text, unwillingness of its sponsors to enforce all decisions made in Dayton, reluctance of all three sides to implement the agreement, and disagreements on the part of all relevant protagonists in this tragedy, internal and external, on the ultimate goal in Bosnia and how to achieve it.

Moreover, two fundamental post-Dayton problems are the nature and evolution of the Muslim-Croat Federation, and the future relationship of the two entities in the same state (the Federation of Bosnia and Herzegovina and the Serb Republic). None of the three sides is happy with the idea of a multiethnic state and each side considers the Dayton treaty as a temporary solution. As a result, there has been very little if any movement regarding the pivotal question of the return of refugees. Each side is trying to hold on to the regions it controls. Among the other critical questions are freedom of movement between the two entities, control of media, responsibilities for war crimes, presence of Mujahedeens or their followers in the army of Bosnia and Herzegovina, school curricula, ethnic imbalance in the state institutions and diplomacy, to mention a few. In light of the present situation and the lack of democratic tradition in the country, many doubt that these and other problems can be successfully resolved. On the other hand, others think that the transitional process from wartime to a civil society was successfully put in motion and in time Bosnia and Herzegovina will become a viable state.

One of the provisions of the Dayton peace accord mandated national, regional, and municipal elections in Bosnia and Herzegovina by mid-September 1996, as a significant and symbolic step toward normality. Given the short time since the end of fighting and because of manifold unresolved issues, many believed that the elections should have been postponed. As a result of preelection manipulations, the municipality elections were postponed, but under U.S. pressure the national and regional elections did take place on September 14, 1996. The organization and supervision of the elections were entrusted to the Organization for Security and Cooperation in Europe (OSCE).

The winners were, as expected, the nationalist parties among the three communities, (Muslim) Party of Democratic Action (SDA), Croatian Democratic Union (HDZ), and Serbian Democratic Party (SDS). The other nonnationalist or smaller ethnic opposition parties did not have a chance. The ruling parties controlled all the media and portrayed themselves as the guardians of the true interests of their respective communities. Although the elections might have been a sound symbolic step in the right direction, it is doubtful that they will make a significant contribution to the process of making Bosnia and Herzegovina a viable state if resistance to the implementation of Dayton and other agreements continues.

During the 1990s Bosnia and Herzegovina has been, and probably will for a time remain a testing ground for various political changes locally and internationally. It will be closely watched to see if a multiethnic and multireligious society can (and under what conditions) function in a new state that went through a bitter ethnic war; if neighboring countries with large segments of their co-nationalists in Bosnia and Herzegovina can establish workable lasting relations with that state and with the respective co-nationalists; and if the emergence of Bosniac identity will successfully reconcile religious and secular concepts and be a Western-style nation.

The Bosnian crisis has brought a number of post-Cold War issues to the forefront and it will remain a major stage for clarifying questions such as: What is the future role of the United States in Europe and its relationship with the European partners? Can the EU partners (Germany, Britain, France, Greece, for example) reconcile their foreign policy interests and differences? What is the role of NATO, OSCE, and Orthodox Russia in the post-Cold War era? What influences will Islamic countries, specifically more radical movements in the Middle East, have in Bosnia and Herzegovina and Europe? Will the hope of pluralism, democracy, and prosperity guarantee peace in Bosnia (and the region) or will the balance of arms secure peace till the first opportunity comes to wage a new war? The answers to these and similar questions will depend on all local, regional, and world players.

THE DICTIONARY

ABDIĆ, FIKRET (1934-). For 20 years (1967-1987), a popular manager-director of a food processing, transportation, and tourism conglomerate (Agrokomerc) in Velika Kladuša in northwestern Bosnia. He was known in the region as the Babo (Daddy). The Agrokomerc was established in 1963, but it reached its zenith under Abdić's leadership, and then its downfall. In the mid-1980s the company was one of the largest enterprises in Yugoslavia (q.v.), employing over 12,000 workers. In July 1986, the federal presidency awarded Abdić the "Order of the Red Flag" for his successes in Velika Kladuša. In 1987, however, the company went bankrupt, with a debt of over $900 million. After an investigation, it was determined that leaders of the Agrokomerc were involved in major financial irregularities and Abdić was jailed for his part in the scandal.

The Agrokomerc affair had a major ripple effect in Bosnian and Yugoslav politics. Many Communist Party members were removed from their positions for being involved in the scandal. The leading Bosnian Muslim (q.v.) political power holders became targets of the investigation. Among those investigated was Hamdija Pozderac (q.v.), Abdić's patron and vice president of the federal presidency at the time. Although Pozderac was waiting to become president of the rotating federal presidency on May 15, 1988, he was forced to leave this highest political body in September 1987. The Agrokomerc scandal put a major strain on the entire political leadership of the republic, especially those of Muslim background. Abdić and others implicated in the affair argued, however, that Agrokomerc's financial dealings were not different from practices of other economic enterprises in the country. According to them, the affair was concocted by the Serb political forces in order to curb the growing power of the Bosnian Muslims (q.v.) in Yugoslav politics. On the local level, the affair caused the collapse of the Bihać (q.v.) Bank, the Agrokomerc disintegrated, and the workers lost their jobs. Abdić, however, retained his popularity in the region. In the 1990 elections, he received more votes than any other Bosnian Muslim politician and became a member of the presidency of Bosnia and Herzegovina.

After the war broke out in 1992 , Abdić gained full control of his native "Bihać Pocket." In contrast to the Bosnian government, he supported the Vance-Owen (qq.v.) peace plan, challenged the political leadership in Sarajevo (q.v.), and, together with his followers, gathered in a Constitutional Assembly in Velika Kladuša, near Bihać, on September 27, 1993, where he proclaimed the "Autonomous Province of Western Bosnia." His militia fought the Sarajevo government in order to keep the Bihać region under his control. Beside his personal ambitions, perhaps he hoped to spare the lives of the Muslim people in the region by cooperating with the Serbs (q.v.). But his fortunes ran out with the collapse of the Serbian controlled Krajina region in Croatia in August 1995. With the help of Croatia and the local Croat troops, regular Bosnian military forces took command of Abdić's fiefdom. While he saw himself as an advocate of a pluralistic Bosnia and an opponent to more radical Islamic forces in the country, his adversaries considered him a traitor to the Bosnian cause, and a Bosnian court indicted him for war crimes in August 1996. Abdić's new political party (Democratic People's Union) ran in the September 1996 elections. He was a candidate for the presidency of Bosnia and Herzegovina and received about 3 percent of the vote in the Muslim-Croat Federation. Since August 1995, he has lived in Croatia.

ACADEMY OF SCIENCES AND ARTS OF BOSNIA AND HERZEGOVINA/AKADEMIJA NAUKA I UMJETNOSTI BOSNE I HERCEGOVINE (ANUBiH). The academy is the highest learning institution in the country. Its headquarters are in Sarajevo. The ANUBiH was founded on June 22, 1966, when by state law the Scientific Society of Bosnia and Herzegovina, established in 1951, was raised to the level of academy.

The academy is divided into sections, centers, and committees. Its six sections are: social sciences, medicine, natural sciences and mathematics, technology, language and literature, and art. At the present time, the academy has 16 regular members, 15 correspondent members, and 20 members from outside Bosnia and Herzegovina. During the 1992-1995 war, the number of working members in the academy decreased from 52 to 20. Its regular publications before the war were *Radovi, Godišnjak, Djela, Posebna izdanja, Gradja,* and *Ljetopis.*

The ANUBiH has two main purposes. First, by accepting its members it recognizes and rewards their scholarly and artistic achievements and, second, it promotes research and excellence in various fields of arts and sciences.

AGOVIĆ, MEHMED. The leader of the nine-member committee of journalists of various nationalities appointed by the Bosnian government in April 1992 to run the Sarajevo television station (TVSA). Although he was a Muslim, he did not belong to the ruling party and was therefore removed at the end of 1992.

AKASHI, YASUSHI (1931-). A Japanese diplomat who served in various UN positions since 1957 and also as the Japanese ambassador to the United Nations (1974-79). In January 1994, he was appointed as a special UN envoy to the former Yugoslavia (q.v.) and as head of the entire UN mission in the

Balkan region. Akashi was often criticized for his reluctance to use NATO air power to protect UN peacekeepers and the so-called safe areas in Bosnia. He was declared persona non grata by the Bosnian government, and Sarajevo officials refused to deal with him after the fall of two "safe areas," Srebrenica and Žepa (qq.v.), in July 1995. As a result, Akashi was removed from Bosnian affairs on July 14, 1995, but he retained his title of UN envoy to the former Yugoslavia until November of the same year, when he was replaced by the UN Undersecretary General Kofi Annan from Ghana.

In the Bosnian conflict, Akashi was perceived by many as a pro-Serb "realist" who respected power more than any other principle. He is now a senior advisor to UN secretary general.

Akashi was born in Akita. Graduated from the University of Tokyo, he completed his master's degree at the University of Virigina as a Fulbright scholar. He also studied at the Fletcher School of Law and Diplomacy and at Columbia University. He has published several books dealing with the United Nations.

ALIĆ, FERID (1956-). Appointed minister of social policies, displaced persons and refugees of the Federation of Bosnia and Herzegovina in January 1966. Bosniac by nationality, he was born in Zenica (q.v.) and finished higher education in dentistry.

ALKALAJ, SVEN (1948-). The first ambassador of the Republic of Bosnia and Herzegovina to the United States. Born to a well-known Jewish family in Sarajevo (q.v.). He received his bachelor of science degree in mechanical engineering (1974) and master's degree in international economy (1987) from the University of Sarajevo.

After working for an engineering company, Petrolinvest, Alkalaj earned his master's degree and began to work for the largest engineering and exporting company in the former Yugoslavia (q.v.), Energoinvest. First he became regional manager for the Middle East and Far East regions. In 1988, he became managing director of Energoinvest in its Bangkok, Thailand, branch office. For his achievements he was awarded a medal in 1990.

In November 1993, Alkalaj became charge d'affaires of the newly opened Embassy of the Republic of Bosnia and Herzegovina in Washington, D.C. In June 1994, he was appointed ambassador extraordinary and plenipotentiary. As an ambassador, Alkalaj was very successful in representing his war-torn country and in laying a solid foundation for future Bosnian diplomatic efforts in Washington.

ALPHA SPECIAL FORCES. Also known as Captain Dragan's Red Berets. A Serbian terrorist commando group led by Captain Dragan, whose full name is believed to be Dragan Vasiljković or Daniel Sneden. In 1991, he was described by the leading Serbian weekly *NIN* as a "military variant of Saint Sava" (founder of the Serbian Orthodox Church [q.v.]). Vasiljković was born in 1954 and emigrated with his parents to Australia in 1969, where he became a small-time gambler, brothel operator, and petty criminal. In 1991, he returned to Serbia, joined the war in Croatia and then in Bosnia, and earned himself a reputation as a Serbian Rambo. His group committed major atrocities against the Croat and Bosnian Muslim civilians in both countries.

ANDRIĆ, IVO (1892-1975). A poet, novelist, short-story writer, and the best-known man of letters from Bosnia-Herzegovina. He was born to an artisan Croatian family in the village of Dolac, near the town of Travnik. Because of his father's early death, his mother took him to live with an aunt near the town of Višegrad (q.v.). Andrić finished his primary education in Višegrad and gymnasium (high school) in Sarajevo (q.v.). He studied philology, literature, and history at the Universities of Zagreb, Vienna, and Cracow. In 1924 he received a Ph.D. at the University of Graz. While at the secondary school in Sarajevo, he joined the revolutionary "Yugoslav" nationalist movement and opposed Austro-Hungarian rule in his native land. Because of his political orientation and activities he was jailed during most of World War I. The prison years, however, provided him time to read and study various literary works, especially the writings of his two favorite authors, Fedor Dostoevsky and Danish philosopher Søren Kierkegaard. After a general amnesty in 1917, he moved to Zagreb where he began his literary career.

Two books of poetry are his best-known works from this early period, *Ex Ponto* (From the Sea, 1918) and *Nemiri* (Anxieties, 1920). From 1920 to 1941, Andrić was in diplomatic service. As a regime loyalist, he served in various Yugoslav consulates in Europe (the Vatican, Bucharest, Madrid, Geneva, and Berlin, among others) till the country collapsed in April of 1941. When the war began, he returned from Berlin to Belgrade and turned to writing full time.

By the end of World War II, Andrić had written three novels, known as the Bosnian Trilogy: *The Bridge on the Drina*, *Travnik Chronicle* (better known in English as Bosnian Chronicle or Bosnian Story), and *The Woman from Sarajevo*. The three novels deal with life in Bosnia during the Ottoman period and are considered his most important literary works. His novel *Devil's Yard* is also acclaimed as a superb literary achievement. In 1961, he was awarded the Nobel Prize for Literature.

Although immediately after World War II Andrić joined the Communist Party and was a member of the Assembly of Bosnia-Herzegovina and of the Federal Assembly in Belgrade (1946), he stayed away from active politics and dedicated himself to writing. Besides the Noble Prize, he received various cultural honors and awards in Yugoslavia (q.v.) and in other countries for his literary works.

ARKAN (real name Željko Ražnjatović) (1952-). A baby-faced Serbian political leader well-known for his acts of ethnic cleansing (q.v.). He commands the Serbian Volunteer Guard (SDG-Srpska Dobrovoljačka Garda), an ultranationalist paramilitary organization set up, trained, and armed by the

Minister of the Interior in Belgrade, Mihalj Kertes, in early 1991. He also received major help from the Serbian Orthodox Church (q.v.) in financing his militia.

Arkan's followers are also known as Arkanovci (Arkan's men) and "Tigers." He and his men were responsible for mass killings of Croatian civilians and looting of occupied territories in northeastern Croatia, especially in the Vukovar region (1991). In March 1992, Arkan and his troops moved to eastern Bosnia to mobilize and train the local Serbs (q.v.). Shortly thereafter they began to terrorize the Muslim population in the region. On April 4, 1992, Arkanovci opened fire on Muslims (q.v.) on the way to a mosque in Bijeljina, killing many of them. In a few days they took over the town and death and destruction across eastern Bosnia followed. They also operated in Banja Luka (q.v.) and other Serbian strongholds (Zvornik, Bratunac, Prijedor, Foča, and Srebrenica [q.v.]) implementing the policy of "ethnic cleansing" of the Serbian held regions of Bosnia. He and his Tigers are considered by various international observers of the war in the former Yugoslavia (q.v.) as greatly responsible for inciting the war and committing war crimes.

In December 1992, the U.S. secretary of state at the time, Lawrence Eagleburger, named Arkan, among others, as a war criminal. Serbia's president Slobodan Milošević (q.v.) gave him a seat in the Serbian parliament, as a reward for Arkan's services, and his support in the December 1993 elections.

Arkan was born in the town of Brežice, Slovenia, where his father was stationed as a Yugoslav Air Force officer. Arkan emigrated to the West because of a criminal record at home and became a Yugoslav secret service hit-man in Western Europe. He is wanted by the Interpol for bank robbery, murder, and a prison break while living in the West. Presently he lives in Belgrade. Besides being president of the Party of Serbian Unity, he owns a chain of ice-cream parlors and a number of shady business enterprises. He is a leading figure among the new Serbian political and business circles.

ARMS EMBARGO. From the very beginning of the war of Yugoslav disintegration (summer 1991), the imbalance of firepower was overwhelming. The Serb side inherited all of the military might of the former Yugoslavia (q.v.), including the federal army (JNA [q.v.]). All of that power was used for the purpose of creating a Greater Serbia. The non-Serbs in the country were left defenseless. The United Nations (UN) ensured the imbalance of power by banning arms sales to any party in the conflict and imposing an arms embargo on the former Yugoslavia on September 25, 1991 (UNSC Resolution 713). The European Community (EC) made a similar decision in July, 1991.

Although it was declared that the reason for the embargo was to "contain the conflict," the decision secured the Serbs' (q.v.) preponderance of power, made it harder for others to defend their territories and population, and, in reality, prolonged the war with the imbalance of power. Although various pressures were made to remove it, including non-binding votes in the U.S. Congress and the U.S. withdrawal from its enforcment at the end of 1994, the imposition of the embargo remained. This, however, did not prevent the illegal sale of arms to the region.

ARMY OF BOSNIA-HERZEGOVINA/ARMIJA BOSNE I HERCEGOVINE (ABiH). The main military force under the Muslim-led Sarajevo government. It originated in the summer of 1992, after the country came under the Serb and Yugoslav People's Army (JNA) (q.v.) attack in April 1992. The ABiH was formed out of various paramilitary organizations (the Territorial Defense, Green Berets [q.v.], MOS, SDA [qq.v.] militia, antiterrorist police force, etc.). Its officer cadres were mainly Muslim and a few Serb and Croat professional officers who left the JNA after Bosnia was assailed. The estimates are that the ABiH is around 150,000 men strong today. It has five corps: Sarajevo, Tuzla, Zenica, Mostar, and Bihać. Despite its numbers, it was not able to mount a major offensive to lift the siege of Sarajevo (q.v.) or to liberate the country. Although the

ABiH claims to be multiethnic and apolitical in nature, it is dominated by Bosnian Muslims (q.v.) and some of its top officers are among the top functionaries of the ruling Party of Democratic Action.

ARMY OF THE SERB REPUBLIC/VOJSKA REPUBLIKE SRPSKE (VRS). The Serbian forces in Bosnia and Herzegovina after the old JNA (q.v.) forces were divided between the Federal Republic of Yugoslavia (Serbia and Montenegro) and Bosnian Serbs in May 1992. Lieutenant-General Ratko Mladić became its commanding officer. The VRS inherited from the JNA about 300 tanks, 200-300 armored personnel carriers, about 1,000 artillery pieces, 35 aircraft, 21 helicopters, an S-S missile system, and air defense rockets. It was regularly supplied and reinforced by troops from Serbia and Montenegro. The VRS is divided into five corps: First Krajina, Second Krajina, East-Bosnian, Sarajevo-Romania, Drina, and Herzegovina.

AVARS. A people of Asiatic origin. As nomads and warriors, they were constantly on the move, invading and pillaging East Central Europe numerous times from the mid-sixth to the beginning of the seventh century. In 626, they threatened Constantinople itself. The Avars established themselves for a while at the Pannonian plains, in today's Hungary. They contributed their share in forcing other peoples in the region to migrate. Under Avar pressure the Germanic Lombards moved to northern Italy and Slavic tribes, as the Avar allies or vassals, settled in the Roman provinces of Pannonia and Dalmatia. In need of a military alliance, the Croats were invited by the Byzantine emperor to fight the Avars and take control of the western Balkans (q.v.), including today's Bosnia-Herzegovina.

AVAZ. Full title *Dnevni avaz* (Daily Voice). A sensationalist Sarajevo (q.v.) newspaper. It claims to be the "voice of independent public" in Bosnia-Herzegovina. The word *avaz,* which is a Turkish word and is used by Bosnian Muslims (q.v.), indicates that the paper is close to the Muslim tradition.

The publication assumed the legacy of the pre-war Sarajevo tabloid *As*.

AVNOJ. (ANTIFAŠISTIČKO VIJEĆE NARODNOG OSLOBOĐENJA JUGOSLAVIJE/ANTI-FASCIST COUNCIL OF THE NATIONAL LIBERATION OF YUGOSLAVIA). Delegates from various regions and peoples in the former Yugoslavia (q.v.) gathered in Bihać (q.v.), a town in western Bosnia, on November 26th and 27th, 1942, and formed the AVNOJ. The First Session was opened by the leader of the Yugoslav Communist Party, Josip Broz Tito (q.v.). Dr. Ivo Ribar, a Croatian left-wing politician, was named president of the executive council of AVNOJ. On November 29, 1943, during its second session at the town of Jajce, central Bosnia, the AVNOJ was proclaimed the highest legislative and executive body for the new Yugoslavia. Tito was proclaimed marshal. The government of the first Yugoslavia in exile was stripped of its legitimacy. The Council declared the formation of the second Yugoslavia, a federation of six republics: Slovenia, Croatia, Bosnia-Herzegovina, Serbia, Montenegro, and Macedonia. From that time till the collapse of the country in 1991, November 29th was celebrated as the Yugoslav independence day. Every republic and some regions established their own branches of AVNOJ. In Bosnia-Herzegovina, the ZAVNOBiH - The Territorial Anti-Fascist Council of the National Liberation of Bosnia and Herzegovina was constituted on November 26, 1943, in the town of Mrkonjić-grad.

-B-

BADINTER COMMISSION. The arbitration committee created by the European Community (EC) in November 1991 to work within the framework of the Peace Conference on the former Yugoslavia (q.v.). It consisted of the presidents of the constitutional courts of five West European countries and was headed by Robert Badinter, a former French justice minister.

After analyzing the events in the former Yugoslavia, it concluded (December 1991) that the country was dissolving and, because of that, it set the standards and the deadline (December 23, 1991) for the former Yugoslav republics to apply for EC recognition of their independence. Slovenia, Croatia, Bosnia-Herzegovina, and Macedonia submitted their application on time. The committee, however, did not recommend that Bosnia-Herzegovina be recognized as an independent state because the Serbs (q.v.) in the republic objected to such a move. As a result, the committee recommended that Bosnia hold a referendum on independence under the supervision of the international community. Such a referendum was held on February 29 and March 1, 1992, and the overwhelming majority of the voters declared themselves for independence.

BALKAN LEAGUE. Formed by Bulgaria, Serbia, Greece, and Montenegro in 1912. Originally it was to be an anti-Austrian alliance, but it turned its efforts against the Ottomans, which led to the Balkan Wars (q.v).

BALKAN WARS. There were two successive wars in the Balkan region at the beginning of this century. The First Balkan War was instigated by the Balkan League over the issue of Macedonia. October 8, 1912, Montenegro declared war on Turkey. The allies (Greece, Bulgaria, Serbia, and Montenegro) expelled the Turks from the Balkans (q.v.), except from Istanbul and vicinity. The alliance collapsed, however, after the victors could not agree on the division of the spoils. This led to the Second Balkan War, which began on June 29, 1913. Serbia, Greece, and Montenegro, joined by Romania, quickly defeated Bulgaria. A peace treaty was signed on August 10, 1913, by which Serbia gained most of Macedonia. World War I, more specifically its initial stage, is often regarded as the Third Balkan war.

BALKANS. The name *Balkans* has been used since the last century to refer to the peninsula in southeastern Europe that is confined by the rivers Danube and Sava (north), the Black Sea (east), the Aegean Sea (southeast), the Mediterranean Sea (south), and the Ionian and Adriatic Seas (southwest). The modern states of Greece, Albania, the Yugoslav Federation, Bulgaria, Romania, Bosnia-Herzegovina, partially Croatia, and the European part of Turkey are located in the Balkans. The name *Balkan* comes from Turkish for "mountain," referring to the Stara Planina (Old Mountain) in Bulgaria. Because of the great mix of peoples and cultures in this small part of Europe, the region became a symbol of disunity and the word *balkanization* is often used to denote fragmentation.

BAN. Croatian term for a viceroy. According to some historians, the title is of Persian origin. The title and power of the *ban* existed not only in Croatia but also in Bosnia-Herzegovina. *Bans* were the heads of medieval Bosnian principalities before *ban* Stipan Tvrtko I (q.v.) declared himself king in 1377.

BANJA LUKA. Bosnian city located 160 m (525 ft) above sea level in the northern part of Bosnia and Herzegovina, on the banks of the river Vrbas and the southern edges of Pannonian flat lands. Its name is derived from two words meaning the *ban*'s (q.v.) field (*banova luka*). *Ban* was the Croatian term for a viceroy and *luka* meant field along the river. In 1994, the county of Banja Luka had 195,692 inhabitants. Out of that number, Serbs made up 54.6 percent, Croats 14.8 percent, and Muslims 14.6 percent (qq.v.). The city is an important communications link in northern Bosnia. It has a strong economic and industrial base. Its university was established in 1975.

The roots of the settlement go back to Roman times. The earliest mention of the town under the name of Banja Luka, however, comes from the 15th century (1494). It was a well-fortified place with a Franciscan monastery and a big marketplace at the time. After the Turks occupied the eastern parts of Bosnia, Banja Luka became an important part of the defensive system established by Croatian-Hungarian rulers.

In 1527, Banja Luka fell under the Turks and, as an already important town, it began to expand even more rapidly. Its best years during the Ottoman era were from 1554 to 1638, the time when Banja Luka became the seat of the Bosnian province (*pašaluk*). It became the core of the Ottoman military and political organization in their expansionist efforts. This factor influenced the city's rapid expansion and economic growth. It is estimated that in the middle of the 17th century the city had over 300 shops and close to 4,000 houses.

Another result of the Turkish invasions was a major shift in religious and ethnic balance in this part of today's Bosnia and Herzegovina. Many indigenous Croatians converted to Islam (q.v.) or ran in front of the Ottoman invaders, while, as a part of Turkish military and economic needs, Orthodox Vlach and Serb immigrants from the eastern Balkans (q.v.) were brought to the frontier regions to settle the abandoned lands. Eventually, the Orthodox became the most numerous of the three religious segments in northwestern Bosnia.

Banja Luka's fortunes began to dwindle with the decline of the Ottoman Empire at the end of the 17th century. In 1688 it was captured and held for a short time by a Habsburg army. Several fires, plagues, and floods also contributed to its deterioration. Like other Bosnian towns, its revival began in the middle of the 19th century with the reluctant imposition of Ottoman reforms and the Austro-Hungarian occupation.

The Banja Luka region suffered a major earthquake in 1969. With major foreign aid, the city went through a rapid reconstruction and economic development after this disaster. Because of the population increase, its ethnic balance also changed.

Among its many historical monuments two stood out because of their beauty and magnificence: the Ferhad-Pasha Mosque - Ferhadija (1583), endowed by the Bosnian governor (*beyler-bey*) Ferhad-Pasha, and the Arnaudija Mosque (1587), bequeathed by Hassan-effendi, treasurer of Bosnia at the time, who was of Albanian origin. Both mosques, among many other religious and cultural monuments, were destroyed by the Serbs in 1993.

In the post-Yugoslav period, Banja Luka became the center of Serbian nationalist forces, the "capital" of their self-proclaimed republic, and practically "ethnically cleansed" of all non-Serbs.

BANOVINA. In 1929, king Aleksandar Karađorđević (q.v.) changed the name of the Kingdom of Serbs, Croats, and Slovenes into Yugoslavia (q.v.), declared a personal dictatorship, and created nine banovine (banates) as the new administrative units in the country. Bosnia-Herzegovina's territory was divided among the following banates: Vrbaska, Drinska, Zetska, and Primorska. This ended the administrative unity of Bosnia-Herzegovina since none of the banates was fully on its territory. An autonomous Croatian Banovina was established by the Serb-Croat agreement of 1939 that included parts of today's Bosnia and Herzegovina.

BAŠAGIĆ, SAFVET-BEG (1870-1934). A well-known scholar, poet, and politician. He was born in the Herzegovinian (q.v.) town of Nevesinje, but from his youth lived in Sarajevo (q.v.). After finishing high school in Sarajevo and higher education in Oriental languages at Vienna University (1895-1899), where he later also received a Ph.D. in Oriental studies, Bašagić returned to Sarajevo. Besides being a teacher, he was also an activist in cultural and political fields. In 1910, he was elected member of the *sabor* (assembly) of Bosnia-Herzegovina and was its president soon after his election till World War I. Bašagić's poetry was greatly influenced by Islamic literary classics, his political orientation was Western, and his national orientation was Croatian. He was proud of his Bosnian Muslim (q.v.) religious and cultural heritage and of Bosnians who became famous in the service of sultans, but for him these elements were parts of the Croatian history and heritage. His best-known work is *Bosniacs* (q.v.) *and Herzegovinians in Islamic Literature.*

BENAC, ALOJZ (1914-1992). A well-known archaeologist and historian, specializing in archaic and medieval history of Bosnia and Herzegovina. Born in Plehan, near the town of Derventa. After finishing his higher education at the University of Belgrade in archaeology, he was director of the Land Museum in Sarajevo, professor of history at the University of Sarajevo, founder of the Center for Balkan Studies, and a distinguished member of the Academy of Sciences and Arts of Bosnia and Herzegovina (q.v.).

BENEVOLENCIA, LA. A Jewish (q.v.) cultural, educational, and humanitarian society in Bosnia and Herzegovina established in 1892. Its initial goal was to support the schooling of talented Jewish students who were not able to afford it. On its 100th anniversary in 1992, however, the society's only aim was to help the needy citizens of Sarajevo (q.v.) and Bosnia and Herzegovina to survive the war. La Benevolencia has established numerous offices in Europe and Israel in its efforts to solicit humanitarian aid and direct it to the needy people in Bosnia.

For its humanitarian work during the 1992-1995 war in Bosnia, La Benevolencia received the International League for Human Rights in Berlin Award, the Carl von Ossietzky Medal for 1995. The medal was given for the first time in 1962.

BERLIN, CONGRESS OF (June 13—July 13, 1878). The 1875 widespread nationalist rebellions in the European part of the Ottoman Empire had led to a major Russo-Turkish war (1877-1878). In March 1878, the defeated Turks were compelled to sign the humiliating Treaty of San Stefano, which provided for a major expansion of Russian influence in southeastern Europe and threatened the interest of other European powers, mainly Austria-Hungary and Britain. Leaders of major European powers met in Berlin to defuse the international tension created by the Ottoman defeat. The Treaty of San Stefano was replaced by the Treaty of Berlin. Russia's attempts to project its power toward the eastern Mediterranean were limited. The Ottoman Empire retained a part of its European holdings and thereby remained a Europan power. The Austro-Hungarian Empire was given the right to "occupy and administer" Bosnia and Herzegovina. Serbia and Romania were recognized as independent countries, and the boundaries of Bulgaria were greatly reduced and the land was granted local autonomy. Bosnia and Herzegovina was a part of the Habsburg empire until the end of World War I.

BIHAĆ. A town located in the northwestern part of the country 231 m (760 ft) above sea level. In 1991, the county of Bihać had close to 71,000 inhabitants. Out of that 66 percent were Muslims, 17.8 percent Serbs, 7.7 percent Croats (qq.v.), and 6 percent "Yugoslavs." Its strategic location in the Una River valley has been a mixed blessing. The town guards one of the very important gates in and out of Bosnia, and passage from the Pannonian flatland in the north to the mountainous regions along the Adriatic Sea in the south.

Although the settlement has existed from ancient times, according to an old chronicle the town was established in 1205. The Hungarian-Croatian king Bela IV running from the Tartars found refuge in Bihać (1262), and on that occasion made the town a free municipality. Thus the town was governed by a freely elected judge and 12 councilors. King Louis (1342-1382) stayed with his army in Bihać (1345) for an extended period of time. The town for a while belonged to Hrvoje Vukčić Hrvatinić (q.v.) at the end of the 14th century. King Sigismund (1387-1437), after a stay in the town (1412), entrusted it to the Croatian noble Frankopan family. In 1527, however, it passed to the Jurišić family. After the fall of Bosnia to the Turks (1463), Bihać became a very important military base in the Croatian-Hungarian defensive system against Turkish invasions. In a surprise attack in 1592, however, the town fell to the stronger Ottoman forces and became a vital Ottoman outpost, first, in an offensive and, later, in a defensive struggle against the West.

Out of the preserved historical monuments from the Ottoman era, the best known is the Fethija (captured) Mosque. Originally it was St. Anthony's Catholic Church, a Gothic building erected most probably in the 12th century. It was turned into a mosque after the town fell to the Ottomans. The old church steeple served as a minaret till 1863. Bihać remained under Ottoman rule till 1878, when Austro-Hungary occupied Bosnia and Herzegovina.

Besides serving as a garrison, Bihać was an important trading and administrative center in the region. During the Ottoman period for a while it was the seat of a separate *sandžak* (military district) and at the times of Austrian rule, it served as an administrative center for one of the six districts in Bosnia-Herzegovina. The town lost its significance after the creation of the First Yugoslavia (q.v.), but gained it again after 1945.

In the history of socialist Yugoslavia, Bihać had a significant place. The first meeting of AVNOJ (Anti-fascist Council of the National Liberation of Yugoslavia) (q.v.) was held in the town in November of 1942.

In the 1992 war, the Bihać region, better known as the "Bihać pocket," became an island surrounded by Serb military forces. Besides that, a regional Bosnian Muslim (q.v.) leader, Fikret Abdić (q.v.), rebelled against the Sarajevo government and declared (September 1993) the "pocket" an "Autonomous Republic of Western Bosnia." The pocket was one of the six "safe areas" established in May 1993 for the Bosnian Muslim refugees to be protected by the international community. Although the region suffered great hardship, forces loyal to the Sarajevo government, with the help of Croat troops, were able to break the isolation and free the region from Serbian attacks and crush Abdić's (q.v.) insurrection in August 1995.

BIJEDIĆ, DŽEMAL (1917-1977). A leading Bosnian politician in the post-World War II period. He was born in Mostar (q.v.). While studying law at the University of Belgrade, he came under Communist influence, became a member of the Communist Party in 1939, and held various positions in the party during and after the Second World War. Among other functions, he was a member of the Central Committee of the Communist Party of Bosnia-Herzegovina and Yugoslavia (q.v.). He was delegate to the Federal Assembly a number of times and also a member of the Federal Executive Committee. In 1970, Bijedić was elected president of the Assembly of Bosnia-Herzegovina. From 1971 till his death in 1977 he was president of the Federal Executive Committee, and a member of Tito's (q.v.) ruling inner circle. It was during his tenure that Bosnian Muslims (q.v.) began to assert themselves more vividly on the Yugoslav scene. Bijedić also helped to promote a close cooperation between Yugoslavia and the Muslim world. He died on January 18, 1977, in an airplane crash near Kreševo in central Bosnia. Speculations persisted that the crash was not an accident but a work of anti-Bosnian forces in Belgrade.

BILANDŽIJA, DRAGO (1949-). Became Deputy Prime Minister and Finance Minister of the Federation of Bosnia and Herzegovina (q.v.) in January 1996. He was born in Travnik of Croat nationality and finished higher education in economics.

BILDT, CARL (1949-). A former Swedish Premier who was named European Community negotiator in peace-seeking efforts dealing with the war in Bosnia-Herzegovina and Croatia after David Owen (q.v.) resigned on June 1, 1995. His "equalizing" approach to the peace making in Bosnia was similar to that of David Owen. Both were ready to reward the Serbian aggression in one form or another in the name of realism.

After the signing of the Dayton peace accord (q.v.), Bildt became the international high representative to facilitate civilian aspects of implementation of the peace agreement.

Bildt became a member of the Swedish Parliament in 1979, and served as Prime Minister from 1991 to 1994.

BLEIBURG. A town in Austria, near the Austrian-Slovene border, where massacres of thousands of Croatian soldiers and civilians began in May 1945. After the demise of the *ustaša* (q.v.) regime at the end of the war, a mass evacuation from Croatia took place. Civilians and soldiers who were drafted into regular armed forces (Domobrans), along with *ustaša* volunteers, surrendered to the British forces in the region. Although promised protection, most of them were forcibly returned to Yugoslavia (q.v.) by the British. Mass executions and death marches began in the Bleiburg region and ended in Macedonia. Many of the killed were Croatian Catholics and Muslims (qq.v.) from Bosnia and Herzegovina.

BOBAN, MATE (1940-). Former president of the Croatian Republic of Herceg-Bosna (q.v.), and former head of the Croatian Democratic Union (HDZ) (q.v.) in Bosnia and Herzegovina. Boban was born in the village of Sovići, western Herzegovina (q.v.). He became a member of the Communist Party when he was 18 years old, received higher education in economics, and held important positions in various state enterprises and local Communist Party functions. He did, however, get in trouble with the regime. According to some, for embezzlement, but according to him, because of his Croat nationalism. In 1991, Boban was cofounder of the Croatian Community of Herceg-Bosna, with headquarters in the town of Grude. With the blessing of the political leadership in Croatia, he replaced Stjepan Kljuić (q.v.) as leader of the Croatian Democratic Union (HDZ) in Bosnia-Herzegovina in January 1992. Kljuić was seen as too moderate in implementing the party's policies. In August 1993, the Croatian Republic of Herceg-Bosna was officially declared by Boban who was eager to consolidate Croat territories that responded to the objectives of the Owen-Stoltenberg (qq.v.) peace plan. In that plan Bosnia-Herzegovina was to be divided into three autonomous ethnic states. These proposals contributed to a clash between the Muslim and Croat forces in Herzegovina and central regions of Bosnia. Under U.S.

pressure, not only did the Croat-Muslim conflict end but the two formed the Federation of Bosnia and Herzegovina (q.v.) in early 1994. Because of this policy shift Boban was removed from the political scene (February 1994) and given a lucrative position in one of the largest enterprises in Zagreb, Croatia.

BORAČKO LAKE/BORAČKO JEZERO. This small but beautiful mountain lake is located on the northeastern side of the Prenj Mountain about 20 km (12.5 mi) from the town of Konjic. It is 405 meters (1,328 ft) above sea level, and is surrounded by dolomitic limestone and thick forests. The stream that flows out of it forms a picturesque 30-meter (100 ft) waterfall. The lake and the surrounding region have become a center for various sport activities and a major recreational spot.

BORIĆ. The first known autonomous *ban* (viceroy) (q.v) in Bosnia (1154-63), appointed by the Hungarian-Croatian king Gejza II (1141-1162). He was a Croatian nobleman from the Požega region in Slavonia. During the struggles between Hungary and Byzantium at the time, *ban* Borić and Bosnia were loyal to the Hungarian kings, which suggests that Bosnia was not coerced to be part of their domain.

In the succession struggle over the Hungarian royal throne between King Gejza II's brothers and his son Stephen III (1162-1172), *ban* Borić found himself supporting the losing side. Because of that he was removed from power and replaced by one of his cousins, most probably *ban* Kulin (q.v.). After his demise in Bosnia, Borić lived and died at his feudal possessions in northern Croatia.

BOSANČICA. A type of Cyrillic alphabet (q.v.), modified from the alphabet ascribed to Saint Cyril, used in Bosnia and Herzegovina, Dalmatian Croatia, and former republic of Dubrovnik from the 10th century to, occasionally, the modern age. At first, *bosančica* was used along with the older Glagolitic script (q.v.) (glagoljica). In Bosnia, however, *bosančica* slowly replaced the glagoljica and became the main script for several centuries. Even after the Turkish occupation (1463), the Bosnian Franciscans (q.v.) and some families among the native Muslim elite continued to use *bosančica*. But eventually, Latin script, which was more universal and adaptable to the printing press, replaced *bosančica*. The same Franciscans, who guarded the native script for a long while, were responsible for the spread of Latin script in Bosnia and Herzegovina.

The oldest known fragment written in *bosančica* is the Humačka ploča (the Humac Tablet) (q.v.) dating from the 10th or 11th century. The script was commonly used for various needs, including epigraphs, liturgical books, royal charters, chronicles, genealogies, and even worldly stories and business transactions. *Bosančica* was also commonly used, along with the Glagolitic and later Latin scripts in southern Croatia, mainly from Zadar to Dubrovnik. Scholars have given various names to this type of Cyrillic script. Among them are *bosančica*, bosanica, Bosnian Cyrillic, Croat-Bosnian Cyrillic, Western Cyrillic, and Croat Cyrillic.

BOSANSKA KRAJINA/BOSNIAN FRONTIER. The region surrounding the flow of the rivers Una, Sana, and Vrbas in northwestern Bosnia. In the Middle Ages, the territory was a part of the Croatian kingdom till the Turkish occupation in the 16th century. After the fall of the town of Jajce (1527), Bihać (q.v.) became the main Croatian stronghold against the Turkish expansion to the northwest. The town, however, fell in 1592, and the territory became an Ottoman staging area for further incursions.

This part of the country, west of the Vrbas River, was commonly known as the Turkish Croatia until the Austrian occupation (1878) when the name was changed to Bosnian Krajina. According to the peace treaties from 1606 and 1625, the river Una was to be the border between the Habsburg and Ottoman domains. The Ottomans, however, fortified many abandoned forts and asserted their presence west of the Una despite the treaties. After several frontier shifts, the present border between Croatia and the Bosnian Krajina was affixed in 1791.

Krajina was a military frontier for centuries. Permanent war zone conditions helped to shape its socioeconomic and cultural life. Even its ethnic makeup was greatly altered by the Turkish invasion. The original Catholic Croatian inhabitants in the area, speaking the *čakavian* dialect, were replaced by the Orthodox Vlach and Serb immigrants from the southeastern Balkans (q.v.). The newcomers colonized the war-devastated territories and were co-opted into the Ottoman service as herdsmen, guards of road passes, or auxiliary Turkish soldiers (*yamaks*), or became sharecroppers to the local Muslim military class dwelling in the fortified towns. Frontier life also helped to shape Krajina's legendary character. People in Krajina are commonly perceived as warriors, rebellious, always ready for combat, and cruel to those under them, but servile to those stronger than them.

A major increase of the Muslim population in the area occurred during the wars of liberation, especially during the Habsburg-Ottoman war of 1683-99. The Muslim population moved into Bosnia from various parts of liberated Habsburg lands.

Bosnian Krajina is rich in mineral resources, water energy, and forestry. In recent times, one of the biggest agricultural giants in the former Yugoslavia (q.v.), Agrokomerc, was located in Velika Kladuša. It was headed by Fikret Abdić (q.v.), infamous Muslim renegade who joined the Serbs (q.v.) against the Sarajevo government during the present-day war.

In April 1991, the Serb Community of Municipalities of Bosnian Krajina was declared by the Bosnian Serbs. This was the first step toward their separation from the rest of the country. They also proclaimed a unification of Bosnian Krajina with the self-proclaimed Serbian Autonomous Region of Krajina in Croatia. The Serbs took full control of the region, except the Bihać pocket, pronouncing the city of Banja Luka (q.v.) its capital and claiming that this part, and most of Bosnia and Herzegovina, was Serbian land that should be united with

Serbia. The Bihać pocket was declared (1993) one of six United Nations "safe areas" in Bosnia for the protection of Bosnian people from Serbian atrocities. But the UN proved to be impotent and the Bihać area remained under constant attacks; its inhabitants found themselves in a concentration camp-like predicament till the siege was broken by Croatian and Bosnian forces in September 1995.

BOSANSKO-HERCEGOVAČKI ZAVOD ZA PROUČAVANJE BALKANA/INSTITUTE FOR BALKAN RESEARCH OF BOSNIA-HERZEGOVINA. This scholarly institution was established in 1908 by Karl Patsch, at the time *Custos* (Director) of the Land Museum in Sarajevo (q.v.). In 1916 the Bosnian government took over the institute. It was, however, abolished by the National Council for Bosnia-Herzegovina after the collapse of the Habsburg Empire in 1918, and consolidated with the Land Museum. This institution and its scholars contributed greatly to the advancement of Balkan studies. It amassed a major collection of important historical documents and manuscripts from the region, especially from Bosnia-Herzegovina, Montenegro, and Albania. It published over 20 scholarly works on the Balkans (q.v.).

BOSNA. A river in north central Bosnia. It is 308 km (192 mi) long and flows from the foot of Igman Mountain near Sarajevo (q.v.) into the Sava River near the town of Bosanski Šamac. In Roman times, the river was called Bosina or Bosona, which probably stems from an Illyrian (q.v.) word *bas,* meaning "flowing water." In the Middle Ages, a small region around the upper flow of the Bosna River became known as Bosnia. Later, as the principality expanded, so did the name *Bosnia.*

BOSNIA-HERZEGOVINA ARMY PRESS CENTER. The official propaganda agency of the Army of Bosnia-Herzegovina (q.v.). Strongly controlled by the Muslim propaganda interests in the army. It considers the Muslims (q.v.) "the fundamental people in Bosnia-Herzegovina."

BOSNIACS. Bosnian Muslims. Bosnia-Herzegovina does not denote a national (ethnic) but a historical and geographic name. There are three main religious and national groups in the country: Serbs, Croats, and Bosnian Muslims (Bosniacs) (qq.v.). While the first two had acquired a strong sense of modern nationalism already in the last and the beginning of this century, the Bosnian Muslims lagged behind in their national identification and assertion. In the last hundred years, their elite oscillated between Croatianism, Serbianism, Yugoslavism, and a general ambiguity in their national orientations, while trying to retain their Islamic religious and cultural heritage as a common bond.

In the post-Second World War period, the Muslims of Bosnia and Herzegovina were classified as having "no national affiliation," and most of them opted to declare themselves as ethnically undecided. In the 1971 Yugoslav census, however, the Muslim nationality was officially promulgated and most of the Muslims in the republic declared themselves as Muslims in the ethnic sense, although many of them were not practical believers. Their Islamic cultural orientation was turned into a nationality. This became a unique case where in the name of a religion was simultaneously an ethnic designation.

With the collapse of Yugoslavia (q.v.) and its Communist system, and after a short period of uncertainty among the Bosnian Muslims themselves, the Bosniac name was adopted to denote Bosnian Muslim ethnicity. On September 27, 1993, a day before the Bosnian Parliament had to accept or reject an internationally proposed plan to divide the country according to ethnic lines, eminent Bosnian Muslim political, cultural, and religious leaders met in an All-Bosniac Congress in the besieged city of Sarajevo (q.v.) and officially inaugurated the Bosniac nationality. The breakup of Yugoslavia and the war that followed had forced them to (re)define themselves in ethnic terms and Bosnian Muslims turned to history in order to support their claims of being a separate nationality.

During the Ottoman Empire, Bosnian Muslims strongly identified with the imperial power and its ruling class. Although many of them belonged to the peasantry (*raya* or flock), their religious affiliation provided them the link to the imperial ruling elite that, in turn, gave them a sense of pride in belonging to a great power and a larger religious community. While during the 19th century modern national homogenization was taking place around them, not only the political fortunes of the Bosnian Muslims but their religious and cultural identities were still tied to the Ottoman Empire. Their rebellions against the imperial center in the middle of the last century were not inspired by nationalism or anti-imperialism, but were attempts to preserve the old system, their local privileges, and the Ottoman concessions to the Balkan Christians. Bosnian Muslims had not gone through a national awakening in the last century as their neighbors had, but the various political pressures in the modern Balkan history have compelled them to seek a national individuality.

Despite their faithfulness to the Ottoman Empire and to Islam (q.v.), for the Bosnian Muslims not all was resolved. Although it is often reiterated that Islam is all-encompassing and above national, ethnic, and social divisions, nationalism and tribalism have been alive and well in Islamic societies. Accordingly, Bosnian Muslims definitely did have a sense of their singularity. They guarded closely their native language and customs, and even their own variant of Islam. But they did remain "Ottomans," perhaps longer than they should have and thereby vacillated in their ethnic identity.

Among various disputes dealing with the Bosnian Muslim ethnogenesis three issues stand out: the pre-Ottoman identity of the people in Bosnia-Herzegovina, the nature of conversions to Islam in Bosnia, and the precise definition of Bosniacism. There is no doubt that most of the Bosnian Muslims are of Slavic origin and not immigrants to the central Balkans (q.v.) during the Ottoman period. There is, however, a debate about their religious and ethnic affiliation in pre-Ottoman times. In their claim of Bosnia-Herzegovina, the Serbs start with the proposition that medieval Bosnia was a Serbian land and that Bosnian medieval Christianity belonged to the Orthodox Church (q.v.). Although there is very little historical evidence for such reasoning, the Serbs traditionally have claimed that the Bosnian Muslims were ethnic Serbs and therefore should either leave the country or convert to their original Orthodox faith. Croatians, on the other hand, claim that the medieval Bosnian population, by its political affiliation to the kingdom of Croatia (later Croatia-Hungary), by its adherence either to Catholicism or to the local Bosnian Church (q.v.) (which disconnected itself from Catholicism in the 13th century), and, by its language, belonged to the Croatian ethnic community. Furthermore, it is only among the Bosnian Croats, specifically the Franciscans (q.v.), that the proud memory of the Bosnian medieval kingdom has been kept. The prevailing attitude among the Croats today, however, is that the Muslims may define themselves any way they like as long as it does not infringe on the national rights of the Croats in Bosnia-Herzegovina. The Bosnian Muslim, or Bosniac, version of medieval history, on the other hand, presupposes that even before the Ottomans they were a separate ethnic community. The Bosniac nationalists emphasize Bosnian political, religious, linguistic, cultural, and ethnic singularity in pre-Ottoman Bosnia. They claim that real Bosniac roots are among the Bosnian Church members *(kr'stjans)* who supposedly welcomed the Ottomans as liberators, converted to Islam, and preserved their ethnic identity which is today being recast into a modern nation.

The beginning of Islam among the people in Bosnia, however, is an issue that has a bearing on Bosniac ethnogenesis. Those who advocate Bosniac nationalism emphasize that there was a relatively large group of adherents to a heretical Bosnian Church at the time of the Ottoman conquest of Bosnia. They presumably recognized a close connection between their Christian beliefs and the teachings of Islam, and, because of the persecutions by the Catholic rulers at the time, the Ottomans were welcomed as deliverers, and they converted to Islam en mass.

Although there is ample evidence that most of the Bosnian *kr'stjans* were back in the Catholic Church (q.v.) before the fall of the Bosnian kingdom and that there was not a mass conversion to Islam at the time of the Ottoman invasion, this presumption is necessary for the "nation makers" to emphasize that Bosniacs are different from Croats or Serbs in more than religion. Furthermore, emphasizing the persecutions of the Bosnian *kr'stjans* and their massive conversions makes it easier for today's Bosnian Muslims to make a connection with a medieval Christian Bosnian state, which is necessary for state building.

A third major issue connected to Bosniac nationalism is the question, who is an ethnic Bosniac? According to the traditional Turkish definition, Bosniacs were all the Muslims living or originating from the territories that more or less made up the former Yugoslavia. The Muslims in Sandžak (q.v.), a province in Serbia, for example, have a strong sense of Bosniac nationalism. Just before the breakup of Yugoslavia, some leading Bosnian Muslims were openly stating or implying that the Muslims in all parts of the former country, except the Albanians, were part of a single community that had more in common than religion. Furthermore, for some Bosniac nationalists, both Catholicism and Orthodoxy were "imports" to Bosnia-Herzegovina, just like Islam (q.v.). But while the Bosnian Catholics and the Orthodox, according to this conjecture, betrayed their Bosniac national heritage and became Croats and Serbs, respectively, the Bosnian Muslims remained the true guardians of Bosniac heritage and identity. For supporters of this theory, the Bosnian Croats and Serbs should, therefore, abandon their "mistaken identity" and become Bosniacs.

The tri-religious Bosniac identity was promoted first by Austro-Hungarian minister Benjamin Kállay (q.v.), the man in charge of Bosnian affairs from 1881 to 1903. He wanted to dull the edges of assertive Serbian and Croatian nationalism in the country by promoting the Bosniac name and individuality. This endeavor, however, did not bring the desired results. Even the Muslims themselves looked for their own separate rights and interests, and most of them did not accept the idea that the other two religious groups could be the same as the Muslims or equal to them.

After a long period of ambivalence concerning their ethnic identity, the breakup of Yugoslavia and an open Serbian attack not only on Bosnia and Herzegovina as an independent state, but on the existence of the Muslim community itself, the Muslims of Bosnia-Herzegovina were compelled to define their ethnicity. The war became a major catalyst in their nation-making process. As a result, the Bosniac identity is emerging as the ethnic name of the Bosnian Muslims. Although many questionable historical arguments and myths are being used in the making of Bosniac national consciousness, obviously the Bosnian Muslims, like anyone else, have the right to decide what they want to be. It will be seen, however, if and what difficulties will arise between Bosniac (secular) nationalism and those who adhere closer to the Islamic precepts. There are indications that Bosniacism might end up in the service of the religion.

BOSNIA-HERZEGOVINA PRESS. An official government news agency founded in April 1992. Its reputation and quality are not held in high esteem by the media either in or outside the country. It is the mouthpiece of the ruling Muslim party (SDA [q.v.]).

BOSNIAN CHURCH/CRKVA BOSANSKA. An independent medieval church in Bosnia that was either a part of or similar to neo-Manichean heresy in Bulgaria (Bogomils) and to the Albigensians or Cathars in the West. Members of the Bosnian Church are often referred to in various documents outside Bosnia or by historians as Bogomils or Patarins, but they simply called themselves Bosnian *kr'stjani* (Christians).

The Christian message was brought to what is present-day Bosnia-Herzegovina in Roman times. But the havoc of various migrations in the early Middle Ages had practically destroyed the church in the region. Christianity was revived in medieval Bosnia by missionaries who came from Croatian coastal towns. Its church was bound administratively to the Archdioceses of Split, Bar, and Dubrovnik. The clergy in Bosnia also followed Croatia in using the old Slavonic language and Glagolitic script (q.v.) in church practices. For political reasons, however, first the jurisdiction over the Catholic Church (q.v.) in Bosnia was transferred to Hungary, then foreigners became its bishops, and, finally, even the seat of the Bosnian diocese was removed to Đakovo (1232), a city in northern Croatia. It is precisely during this time of foreign, mainly Hungarian, encroachment into Bosnian political and church affairs that an independent Bosnian Church appeared (end of the 12th and beginning of the 13th century).

A controversy has been going on for a long time among historians as to the origin, nature, and strength of the Bosnian Church. Some believe that the Bosnian Church belonged to the neo-Manichean movement and that the heresy was brought to Bosnia from Bulgaria. Others argue that the teaching was brought by merchants to the Croatian coastal cities and from there it spread to Bosnia. There is clear evidence that heretics were present in the port cities in Croatia and many of those expelled from the cities found refuge in Bosnia. One major expulsion of heretics from the cities of Split and Trogir took place in 1200. It is probably not an accident that only three years later (1203), the Pope's legate, Johnnnes de Casamaris, came to Bosnia to meet the church leaders and the local ruler, *ban* Kulin (qq.v.), in order to ensure that they adhered to the Catholic Church. There is strong evidence that (at least some) followers of the Bosnian Church, adhered to beliefs that were contrary to neo-Manichean teaching, such as the Trinity, the cross, religious art, and even leaving money to the poor so they would pray for the soul of the deceased. The well-known *Testament of the Gost Rodin* (1466) indicates such religious practices. This evidence has led some historians to conclude that the Bosnian Church was a mixture of a neglected and perhaps rebellious, uncanonical, and even schismatic, Bosnian Catholicism and strains of neo-Manichean heresy brought about by major religious, economic, and social shifts in Europe at the time. It seems, therefore, that the lines between traditional native religious practices and, perhaps deluded, Catholicism, and other heretical beliefs were very much blurred. To foreigners who were eager to absorb Bosnian territory or make its uncommon religious practices conform to the rest of the Catholic Church, these distinctions of religious beliefs and practices were confusing. Political motivations, however, brought about "crusades" against the Bosnian Church and the zeal to bring the real or presumed heretics back to the Catholic fold stimulated the coming of Dominican and then Franciscan friars to Bosnia.

By the end of the Bosnian medieval state, most of the people in Bosnia were back in the Catholic fold, at least officially, due to the work of the Franciscans (q.v.). There was a new missionary zeal in the region, especially after the Great Schism in the Catholic Church was resolved in 1417. Also, a new Catholic diocese was established in Bosnia in 1422. But, after a long tradition of religious toleration, the last two Bosnian kings began to persecute the members of the Bosnian Church in order to obtain Western help in their defense against the encroaching Ottomans.

After the Turkish occupation, most of the remaining Bosnian *kr'stjans* in time converted to Islam (q.v.). Some of their leaders found refuge in Dubrovnik and the Venetian republic. By the mid-16th century the Bosnian *kr'stjans* practically disappeared, but surviving vestiges of the church were noticed in Bosnia-Herzegovina as late as the end of the last century.

BOSNIAN MUSLIMS or MUSLIMS. *See* BOSNIACS

BRČKO. A town in northeast Bosnia 96 meters (315 ft) above sea level. It has always been an important agricultural and trade center because the town is located on the banks of the Sava River and in the rich Posavina flat lands.

According to the 1991 census its municipality had over 87,000 inhabitants, out of which 44.4 percent were Muslims, 25.4 Croats, 20.8 Serbs, 6.4 "Yugoslavs," and 3 percent others. During the 1992-1995 war, the Serbs occupied Brčko, expelled the Muslims and Croats, and settled many Serbs in the town. Because of its strategic military and economic importance the Sarajevo government and the Serb side could not agree on the fate of Brčko at the peace negotiations in Dayton (q.v.) at the end of 1995. According to the Dayton peace accord, the town's future will be decided by the international arbitration before December 14, 1996. For the Serbs, keeping Brčko is essential for protecting the corridor to the western part of the Serb Republic. For the Sarajevo government, the town is a pivotal link of the Federation to the Sava River and international trade. And to many others, leaving Brčko to the Serbs would mean condoning ethnic cleansing (q.v.). The international arbitration has decided to keep Brčko under international supervision until March 1998.

BRIQUEMONT, FRANCIS (1935-). A Belgian lieutenant general who served as the United Nations Protection Force (UNPROFOR) (q.v.) commander in Bosnia from July 7, 1993, to January 24, 1994. He was openly critical of the U.S. advocacy to use air strikes against selected Serb targets in Bosnia. Briquemont was born in Mariembourg. After a long military career, he was promoted to lieutenant general and became commander of the First Belgian Corps and Supreme Commander of the Belgian Armed Forces in Germany in 1993.

BROZ, JOSIP. *See* TITO.

BULIĆ, ŽARKO. Vice president of the Serb Civic Council in Sarajevo (qq.v.). He was president of the Alliance of Legal

Associations of Yugoslavia (q.v.) and president of the Bosnia-Herzegovina Bar Association before the breakup of Yugoslavia.

BUTMIR CULTURE. A Neolithic culture in the central regions of Bosnia, named after the village of Butmir near Sarajevo (q.v.), where its most important settlement was located. Along with many human dwellings, thousands of stone tools for household, hunting, and agricultural needs were found at Butmir and several other excavation sites that belonged to the same culture.

Although the Butmir culture shares in the general aesthetic ideas of the time, unique decorative motifs and original interpretations of borrowed artistic ideas are expressed in pottery drawings that are usually in spiral and geometric patterns. Furthermore, many human-like figurines depicting religious idols bear witness to the fact that Butmir artists reached a high level of realism in their work. Thus, both worldly and religious art speak of a high aesthetic sense of those early Bosnian inhabitants that surpasses other contemporary cultures in the region.

-C-

CARITAS. A Catholic humanitarian organization operating in many countries in Europe and in Bosnia-Herzegovina. Each of the three Catholic dioceses in the country (Sarajevo, Mostar, and Banja Luka [qq.v.]) has its own Caritas branch and through the parish organizations distributes help to the needy. This humanitarian society, among other similar groups, has provided a great service to the destitute during the recent war.

CARRINGTON, LORD [PETER ALEXANDER RUPERT CARINGTON - 6th Baron] (1919-). The European Union (EU) established a Peace Conference on Yugoslavia (q.v.) on September 7, 1991. Lord Carrington, former British Foreign Secretary and Secretary-General of NATO, became its chairman. The Conference's main goal was to contain the war in the former Yugoslavia and find a comprehensive solution to the problems in the region. Carrington, however, was not able (or willing) to pinpoint the real cause of the war. He chose to blame all sides equally. Furthermore, instead of accepting the demise of the country and helping to separate the republics with a minimum of pain, Carrington and the Peace Conference strived to find a formula to keep the Yugoslav pieces together. Thus, the Conference opposed the recognition of Slovenia, Croatia, and Bosnia-Herzegovina. However, once Slovenia and Croatia were recognized by the EU countries, Carrington's solution for Bosnia-Herzegovina was cantonization, dividing the country into three constituent ethnic units. This was tantamount to dismemberment of the republic.

CATHOLIC CHURCH. Christianity came to present-day Bosnia and Herzegovina in Roman times. The northern part of Bosnia (the Sava valley) received Christianity from the Pannonian Christian centers and was under the jurisdiction of the Church of Sirmium (Mitrovica). The rest of the country, however, belonged to the province of Dalmatia and it was Christianized from the towns along the Adriatic Sea.

Archaeological evidence suggests a strong Christian presence at many places throughout Bosnia and Herzegovina in Roman times. Several dioceses existed in the early centuries in the region: Bistue Nove (around Zenica [q.v.]), Martari (near Konjic), Savsenterum (near Mostar [q.v.]), Delminium (Duvno or Tomislavgrad), and Balaie in western Bosnia. Because of the Great Migration and the fall of the Roman Empire, the church was practically wiped out by various pagan peoples that passed through the region.

A second major wave of Christianization on the eastern shores of the Adriatic began with the newly arrived Croatians in 640. The church architecture, the use of Old Slavonic as liturgical language and the Glagolitic script (q.v.), also the church jurisdiction suggests that the rebirth of Christianity in Bosnia and Herzegovina came from Dalmatian towns. Indications are that the renewed Bosnian diocese existed in

877. It was first under the domain of the Metropolitan of Split, then of Bar (1089), of Split again (1137), and a few decades later under the jurisdiction of the archdiocese of Dubrovnik (before 1185). The territory of the Bosnian diocese covered the original Bosnia and the regions of Usora and Soli (qq.v.) in the northeast. As the territory of the Bosnian state expanded, however, other districts were added to the jurisdiction of the Bosnian bishop. The first residence of the local bishop was at the town of Bosna (q.v.) (11th century). Around the year 1238, however, it was moved to Brdo in Vrhbosna, near present-day Sarajevo (q.v.), where a cathedral dedicated to St. Peter was built in 1244.

Besides the Bosnian diocese, eight other church districts existed in present-day Bosnia and Herzegovina in the pre-Ottoman times. The northwest part of the country (west of the Vrbas River) was under the Archdiocese of Zagreb. The Diocese of Knin and Krbava and the Archdiocese of Split had jurisdiction over parts of southwestern Bosnia. The Diocese of Duvno, Makarska, Ston, and Trebinje had administrative control of the central and southern parts of the country.

Because of the territorial and political ambitions of the Hungarian kings and (supposedly) the rise of unorthodox teaching in Bosnia, the jurisdiction over the Catholic Church in Bosnia was transferred to the Vatican (1238), then to Kalocsa in southern Hungary (1247). Even the bishop's residence was moved (1252) from Bosnia to Djakovo, a town in Croatia north of Bosnia. This resulted in a major neglect of the church and strengthened the resolve of the Bosnian religious and political authority to resist outside interference from Hungary in their local affairs. Most probably this was the major cause for the rise of an independent Bosnian *kr'stjan* movement.

In the 13th century Dominican friars appeared in Bosnia. They were squeezed out, however, by the Franciscans (q.v.) who established their Bosnian Vicariate in 1340. Since then, Franciscans have played a major role in the religious and cultural life of the country. The remnants of diocesan priests, known as *glagoljaši,* who used the Glagolitic script and old Slavonic liturgical language, continued to serve the faithful along with the Franciscans. After fading away for a few centuries, they appeared again in Bosnia in the second half of the 17th century and disappeared again in the early 1800s. Being considered less educated than the Franciscans, *glagoljaši* served only as assistants to the Franciscans whose education was on the European level.

The Franciscans obtained from Mehmet II (1463) permission to live and work among the Catholics in Ottoman Bosnia. Because the Catholic powers in the West were in constant warfare with the Ottomans, the Catholics in the empire were treated more harshly than the Orthodox Christians or members of other religious communities. Major persecutions of Catholics in Bosnia, for example, followed the Spanish expulsion of Muslims (and Jews) in 1492. They were also a target of Suleiman the Magnificent's (1520-1566) assaults against Central Europe. Often, especially after the Ottomans began to lose their territory to the Habsburgs, Catholics were suspected of treason, and persecutions followed the accusations.

Emigration of the Catholic population from the war-ravaged border regions, conversion to Islam (q.v.), and pressure from the Orthodox Church (q.v.) leadership on the Catholics to submit to its control, resulted in a sharp decline of the Catholic population in Bosnia and Herzegovina. One such major exodus of Catholics from Bosnia, for example, took place during the Habsburg-Ottoman wars (1683-1699). Thousands of Croatians escaped persecution and moved to the freed lands in northern Croatia.

During the Turkish rule, the Hungarian-Croat kings continued to nominate Bosnian bishops. Although in an unfriendly environment, they operated from Đakovo in Slavonia, which was also under Ottoman rule. After 1699, however, when the Ottomans lost the land north of the Sava River, the Bosnian bishops found themselves outside the Ottoman domain, and they were not allowed to enter Bosnia for pastoral visits. Remaining without customary church leadership, the Vatican found an emergency solution by naming "apostolic vicars" (1735), functioning as bishops, in "Ottoman Bosnia." The Franciscans became vicars and they had full control of the pastoral care in the country. Because Herzegovina (q.v.) became a separate Ottoman province in 1832 and Herzegovinian Franciscans separated from Bosnia in 1846, a separate vicariate was formed in Herzegovina in 1852. On the initiative of the Habsburg monarchy, however, Pope Leo XIII replaced the vicariates by traditional diocesan hierarchy (1881). Accordingly, Bosnia and Herzegovina became a separate church province divided into four dioceses: Vrhbosna (Sarajevo) archdiocese, and Banja Luka (q.v.), Mostar, and Trebinje dioceses. With this change, however, friction between newly organized secular clergy and Franciscans began and is still present in the Catholic Church in Bosnia and Herzegovina.

Besides the Franciscans, other Catholic religious orders were introduced in Bosnia-Herzegovina in modern times. The Society of Jesus (Jesuits) came to the country in 1881. They were involved in education (q.v.). Under pressure from the Communist regime, however, they left Bosnia after the Second World War. The Trappists (or reformed Cistercians) came to Bosnia in 1869. They were known for their work among the orphans. By the end of the 19th century, houses of several women's religious congregations had been established in the country. These nuns were involved in education, as well as in charitable and pastoral work. During the Communist era, however, their activities were greatly curtailed. Although under major restrictions, the religious life and vocations flourished in the post-World War II period.

As a result of the last war and the ethnic cleansing (q.v.) it brought about, two-thirds of the Sarajevo archdiocese has disappeared and the entire Croatian Catholic population in the dioceses of Banja Luka (q.v.) and Trebinje (eastern Herzegovina [q.v.]) is virtually nonexistent today. Catholic churches and monasteries in the Serbian-dominated Bosnian territory have also been destroyed. This war has given a major blow to the Catholic Church in Bosnia and Herzegovina and its recovery will be very slow in the post-war period and, probably, some parts of the country will be lost to the church forever.

Croatian Catholics in Bosnia-Herzegovina pride themselves that the archbishop of Vrhbosna (Sarajevo), Mons. Vinko Puljić (q.v.), was named cardinal of the church in 1994. At the age of 49, he was the youngest member in the college of cardinals.

CATHOLIC CHURCH PUBLICATIONS. Most of the Croat Catholic publishing activities in Bosnia and Herzegovina began after the Communist regime started to relax its grip on society in the late 1960s and 1970s. Currently there are three Catholic monthlies: *Naša ognjišta* (q.v.), *Svjetlo riječi*, and *Crkva na kamenu*. The first two are published by the Franciscans (q.v.) and the third by the Mostar (q.v.) diocese. The *Naša ognjišta* was the first to appear and it suffered major harassment from the regime. Two almanacs are also published, *Kršni zavičaj* and *Kalendar sv. Ante*. Among the scholarly publications are the annuals *Jukić*, *Mladi teolog*, and *Bosna franciscana*, published by the Franciscan theological seminary in Sarajevo (q.v.). *Glas mira* (q.v.) is a voice of the Međugorje (q.v.) Marian shrine. An almanac, *Dobri pastir*, was the first Catholic publication in the post-World War II era in Bosnia and Herzegovina. However, it was published by the regime-sponsored priests' alliance and, therefore, it did not have the blessing of the official church nor support among the faithful.

ĆATIĆ, ĆAZIM MUSA (1878-1915). A leading Bosnian poet. Ćatić was born in Odžak. After significant material hardships and other misfortunes in his youth, he finished the school of Islamic jurisprudence (*Şeriat* school) in Sarajevo (q.v.). His bohemian lifestyle prevented him from working in his profession or even having any steady jobs. He did, however, work for a while for various Bosnian Muslim (q.v.) publications (*Muslimanska sloga*, *Sarajevski list*, *Biser*, and *Muslimanska biblioteka*).

Although Ćatić lived a short and arduous life, his literary accomplishments were significant, especially in lyric poetry. He was also a translator of literary works from Turkish, Arabic, and Persian languages. In his poems, Ćatić contrasts love and anguish, faith and doubt. He interprets human characters and reflects on patriotism and social concerns. He greatly helped to bring the Bosnian Muslim literature (q.v.) closer to the European spirit and standards, and stands out as the best Bosnian Muslim poet till well into the post-World War I period. Ćatić is also included in Croat literature because he considered himself of Croat ethnicity.

ČENGIĆ, HASAN (1957-). Former deputy defense minister of the Federation of Bosnia and Herzegovina. Appointed to the post in January 1996. Born in the village of Odžak near the town of Foča in eastern Bosnia and Herzegovina. After primary education, he was educated at the Gazi Husrevbeg's madresa in Sarajevo and graduated from the Islamic Theological Faculty at the University of Sarajevo in 1982. He served as imam in the town of Stolac till 1983. In March of 1983, Čengić, with 12 other Bosnian Muslims, including Alija Izetbegović (q.v.), was imprisoned and, in August, sentenced to 10 years of prison for antistate activities associated with a group known as the Young Muslims (q.v.). His sentence was later commuted to six years. After release, he served as imam at the mosque in Zagreb, Croatia (1988-1990).

Čengić was one of the founders of the main Muslim political party (SDA) in Bosnia in 1990. He served as Izetbegović's advisor and as a special envoy and plenipotentiary of the Bosnian government. Because of his previous connections in the Muslim world, Čengić became a central figure in channeling money collected in the Middle East for Bosnia and Herzegovina and in procuring illegal arms for the Army of Bosnia-Herzegovina (q.v.). His position became so powerful that he was not accountable to any of Sarajevo's government institutions. He headed a sort of a "private" ministry of defense of the Muslim-led Sarajevo government.

After he became deputy defense minister of the Muslim-Croat Federation, Čengić expected to have total control of the top military institutions. This attempt led to an open clash between him and the chief of staff of the Army of BiH in the summer of 1996.

Under strong American pressure, Čengić was removed from office on November 19, 1996. The United States demanded his dismissal in return for the unloading of $100 million worth of American military hardware to the Federation sitting in Croatia's port of Ploče. He was accused of being too close to the fundamentalist government in Iran. Besides being a symbol of more radical Islamic influences in Bosnia, he was also an impediment to the strengthening of the Federation (q.v.), which is one of the cornerstones of American policy in Bosnia.

CERIĆ, MUSTAFA (1952-). The head *(reis ul-ulema)* of the Bosnian Muslim (q.v.) community since 1993. He was born in Gračanica near the town of Visoko, central Bosnia and finished Islamic studies in Sarajevo (q.v.) and at the El-Azhar University in Egypt (1978). In 1981, he accepted the position of imam at the Islamic Cultural Center in Northbrook near Chicago, Illinois. While in the United States, Cerić received a Ph. D. in Islamic theology at the University of Chicago (1987). After leaving the United States, he became the religious leader of the Muslims in Zagreb, Croatia, and an associate professor of Islamic theology in Sarajevo. He also taught at the International Institute of Islamic Thought and Civilization in Kuala Lumpur, Malaysia.

After the recognition of Bosnia-Herzegovina as an independent country, previously elected *reis ul-ulema* for the entire former Yugoslavia (q.v.), Jakub Selimonski, a Macedonian, was removed from that position and Cerić became the religious leader of the Bosnian Muslim community and a close ally of the ruling Muslim party (SDA [q.v.]) in Bosnia and Herzegovina.

ČETNIK. (plural ČETNICI). Often "Chetniks" in English. A paramilitary nationalist organization established in Serbia in 1903. The Serbian military forces trained the newly formed detachments (*četa*) for terrorist attacks in Macedonia, which was still under the Ottoman rule. The četnik style of warfare, which consisted of hit and run tactics, mainly against civilians, stemmed directly from the tradition of brigandry (*hajdukovanje*) from Ottoman times in the Balkans (q.v.) . The četnik units participated in both Balkan wars (1912-13) (q.v.) and World War I. They were designated to act as commando units and used terrorism in the enemy territory to prepare the way for the regular military forces. Their unshaven faces, a black flag with a skull and bones insignia, and a dagger as their main weapon were supposed to incite fear in the enemy population and make them run from their villages. During the Second World War, the četniks of the Serbian general Draža Mihailović were initially against the German occupiers and had the support of the Western Allies. It became clear, however, that their struggle was not against the German or Italian occupiers but against Communist-led partisans, and Croat and Muslim nationalist forces. Moreover, the četniks collaborated with the occupiers, especially the Italians, and committed major massacres against Muslims (q.v.) and Croat civilians in Bosnia-Herzegovina and Croatia.

The četnik organization was revived among the Serbs (q.v.) before the eruption of the 1991 war in Croatia. Vojislav Šešelj (q.v.), a Serb nationalist from Bosnia, became a četnik "duke" and claimed to be the legitimate successor to general Mihailović. Followers of Vuk Drašković (q.v.) in the Serbian Renewal Movement (q.v.) (Srpski Pokret Obnove) also claimed to be the heirs of the četnik nationalist tradition. Both parties are committed to a greater and ethnically pure Serbia. Šešelj followers were among the first instigators of war in Croatia and Bosnia-Herzegovina and are accused of major atrocities against the civilian population. In December of 1992, Lawrence Eagleburger, the U.S. secretary of state at the time, named Šešelj, among others, as a war criminal.

CONCENTRATION CAMPS. Although intelligence reports about concentration camps in Bosnia-Herzegovina surfaced earlier, they became public in early August 1992. A British ITN TV crew managed to visit Serb-run camps in Omarska, near Banja Luka (q.v.), and another near the town of Prijedor on August 4-5, 1992. They obtained evidence of executions, torture, mass rape, disappearances, and savage treatment of the non-Serbs, mostly Muslims and Croats (qq.v.). This information became an instant reminder of World War II Nazi atrocities. The gruesome TV pictures of the dead and suffering people caused a major outcry across the world that put pressure on Western and UN leaders to "do something." Although the Croats and Muslims had their "detention" camps, they were far outdone by the Serbs. According to a 1994 UN report, the Serbs (q.v.) operated 962 prison camps: 500,000 people were imprisoned, 50,000 tortured, and many thousands raped. It is estimated that there are about 300 mass graves in the regions held by the Serbs during the war, containing from three to 5,000 bodies each.

The most brutal Serb concentration camps were: Omarska, Manjača, Trnopolje, Keraterm (q.v.), Luka, and Foča. Some other camps were Kotor Varoš, Bosanski Novi, Vijak, Bijeljina, Ugljik, Bileća, Ilidža (q.v.), Kula, Bosanski Brod, Doboj, Zvornik, Vogošća, Rogatica, Višegrad (q.v.), Trebinje, and Pale (q.v.). Muslims had camps in Bihać (qq.v.), Cazin, Jajce, Bugojno, Visoko, Hadžići, Tuzla, Zenica (qq.v.), and Konjic. Croat camps were in Dretelj, Mostar (q.v.), Čapljina, Odžak, and Livno.

CROAT DEFENSE COUNCIL/HRVATSKO VIJEĆE OBRANE (HVO). A self-defense military formation among the Croats of Bosnia-Herzegovina established on April 8, 1992. After the foundation of the Croat Union of Herceg-Bosna (q.v.) (Nov. 1992), and later of the Croat Republic of Herceg-Bosna (Aug. 1993), the HVO became the military arm of the main Croat political formation in the country, the Croatian Democratic Union (HDZ) (q.v.). The HVO was recognized by the Dayton agreement (Nov. 1995) (q.v.) as a legitimate military formation in the Federation of Bosnia and Herzegovina (q.v.).

The HVO was organized into four operation zones: South-eastern Herzegovina, North-western Herzegovina, Central Bosnia, and Bosanska Posavina Zone. It had about 40 to 60 tanks, 500 artillery pieces, 150 air-defense portable weapon systems, and 40,000 soldiers.

CROATIAN DEMOCRATIC UNION/HRVATSKA DEMOKRATSKA ZAJEDNICA (HDZ). A national political movement founded in Zagreb in June 1989. Franjo Tuđman, later president of the Republic of Croatia, became its leader and president. The HDZ won the first post-Communist-era elections in Croatia in April 1990 and has held political power there since. The HDZ for Bosnia and Herzegovina was founded in August 1990. It became an offshoot of the main party in Croatia, and as such it became subservient to the Zagreb politics. The first president of HDZ in Bosnia-Herzegovina was Davor Perinović. He was replaced by Stjepan Kljuić (q.v.) in September 1990. Because Kljuić's political stands regarding the future of Bosnia-Herzegovina differed from those of the party bosses in Zagreb, he was forced to resign in January 1992. His successor, Mate Boban (q.v.), represented the so-called Herzegovinian wing of the party and became instrumental in implementing Tudjman's policies toward Bosnia-Herzegovina.

Initially, the HDZ cooperated with the leading Muslim party (SDA [q.v.]) and together they laid the foundations for Bosnia's independence. The HDZ's main goals were to secure individual civil and Croat national rights in order to be equal partners with the Muslims and Serbs (qq.v.). However, the Serbian conquest of 70 percent of the land and peace plans that envisioned a division of Bosnia-Herzegovina on ethnic lines contributed greatly to a year-long Muslim-Croat struggle for the remaining 30 percent of the country. A shift in the HDZ policy toward Muslims and the Bosnian state came when Croats and Muslims under U.S. pressure agreed to create a common Federation (q.v.). This deal was sealed by the Washington Agreement on March 18, 1994. Because Boban was seen as an obstacle to the settlement, he was removed from his position of power and the party began a cautious rapprochement with the ruling Muslim party (SDA [q.v.]).

CROATIAN MUSLIM DEMOCRATIC PARTY/HRVATSKA MUSLIMANSKA DEMOKRATSKA STRANKA (HMDS). A political party of Muslim Croatians formed under the leadership of Mirsad Bakšić in 1991. It opposes the (Muslim) Party of Democratic Action (SDA) (q.v.) and its claims to represent all Muslims (q.v.) that live in or are originally from Bosnia-Herzegovina. Many Bosnian Muslim (Bosniac[q.v.]) nationalists see those who identify as Croats of Islamic faith as traitors.

CROATIAN NATIONAL COUNCIL. A loose political alliance established in February 1994 by some leading Croat intellectuals, church, and cultural leaders mainly from Bosnia who did not agree with the politics of the Croatian Democratic Union (HDZ) (q.v.), the leading Croat political party in Bosnia-Herzegovina and the ruling party in Croatia, regarding the fate of Bosnia and Herzegovina. A major gathering (*sabor*) of prominent Croats (q.v.) was held in Sarajevo (q.v.) on February 6, 1994, and one of the results of the assembly was the formation of the Council. Its achievements, however, did not attain the lofty goals set at the founding meeting.

CROATIAN PARTY OF RIGHT/HRVATSKA STRANKA PRAVA (HSP). A Croatian political party formed in the middle of the last century. It emphasizes the continuity of Croatia's statehood since medieval times and the historical rights of the Croatian people to their independence. Its founder was Ante Starčević (1823-1896), known as the "Father of the Croatian nation."

In the post-Communist era, the party was revived in Croatia and in Bosnia-Herzegovina. Its military arm, the

Croatian Armed Forces (Hrvatske Oružane Snage - HOS), was active in the struggle against the Serbian aggression in Croatia and then in Bosnia-Herzegovina. Besides the Croats (q.v.), HOS attracted many Bosnian Muslim fighters in Bosnia, especially during 1992. Although the Party of Right traditionally claimed that Bosnia-Herzegovina was a historic Croatian land, it stood for preservation of the Bosnian state and for a close alliance between the Croats and the Muslims (qq.v.) against their common enemy. However, the Croatian Democratic Union (HDZ) (q.v.), the ruling party in Croatia and the leading party among the Croats in Bosnia-Herzegovina, could tolerate neither a parallel Croat military force nor the Party of Right's stand on Bosnia-Herzegovina; it, therefore, forced the HOS to disband its military units. The leader of HOS in Bosnia-Herzegovina, Blaž Kraljević and seven of his soldiers, were ambushed and killed by the Croat forces loyal to the HDZ. The end of the HOS and an internal dissension weakened the HSP both in Croatia and in Bosnia-Herzegovina. The party ran in the September 1996 elections and succeeded in gaining two out of 140 seats in the Muslim-Croat Federation Assembly.

CROATIAN PEASANT PARTY/HRVATSKA SELJAČKA STRANKA (HSS). Founded in Croatia (1903) it became the largest Croatian party in the period between the two World Wars. Its leader, Stjepan Radić, and his closest associates were shot in Belgrade's parliament by a Serb colleague in 1928. In 1939, Vlatko Maček, Radić's successor, made an agreement (Sporazum) with the Belgrade regime by which Croatia became a self-governing political unit (*banovina*) within Yugoslavia (qq.v.) . The Croatian banovina included parts of Bosnia-Herzegovina. The HSS was revived in Croatia after the collapse of Communism. A party under the same name was organized in Bosnia-Herzegovina in 1993. Its leader is Ivo Komšić (q.v.), a former member of the Bosnian presidency. In the September 1996 elections, this small party joined a coalition (United List BiH) with four smaller parties in Bosnia.

CROATS. A Slavic people living in present-day Croatia, partly in Bosnia-Herzegovina, and as a minority in a number of countries. While Croatian ethnic communities that live in Austria, Hungary, Slovakia, Serbia (Vojvodina), Romania, and Italy date from the centuries of the Ottoman invasions, the Croats in the United States, Canada, Australia, New Zealand, South America, and a number of countries in Western Europe have immigrated in more recent history.

The origins and name of the Croats are still debatable among scholars. According to the main current hypothesis, the original homeland of the Croats was in ancient Persia where their name (Harauvatiš) is listed among 23 peoples ruled by Emperor Darius the Great (522-486 BC). There are also other political, religious, linguistic, social, and historical indicators that give credence to this theory. Historical evidence suggests that Croats lived in the region of the Black Sea at the beginning of the third century AD and from there migrated in the direction of the Carpathian Mountains, where they absorbed the culture of the indigenous Slavic people. They eventually established their state, known in history as White Croatia in the region of present-day southeastern Poland. Today's city of Cracow was its political center.

A new era of Croat history began when the Croats, as allies of the Byzantine emperor in his efforts to defeat the invading Avars (q.v.), arrived on the eastern shores of the Adriatic Sea at the beginning of the seventh century. At first, they were caught between the two European superpowers, the Frankish and Byzantine empires, but by the ninth century Croats were able to assert their independence. The growth of their own political and religious cohesiveness and the power vacuum that appeared in the region, because of Frankish disunity and Byzantine preoccupation with the Bulgarians, provided the Croats with the opportunity to become an independent medieval nation. They received Christianity in the middle of the seventh century from Rome and came under the Western cultural sphere. Duke Branimir (879-892) was already an independent ruler, but Tomislav became the first Croatian king in 925. In 1102, Croatia entered into a personal union with the Hungarian kingdom, but in 1527 the Croats elected the Habsburgs as their monarchs, as did the Hungarians and a number of other peoples in the region in a common struggle against the invading Ottomans. The union with the Habsburgs lasted till 1918, when the Croats became a part of the Kingdom of the Serbs, Croats, and Slovenes (known as Yugoslavia from 1929) (q.v.), which was ruled by the Karađorđević dynasty of Serbia. Because of the Serbian domination of the country and national inequality, the Croats were soon alienated in the new state and pursued their own national independence.

CYRILLIC ALPHABET. A script named after St. Cyril (826-869), who, together with his brother Methodius (820-885), went from Salonica in Greece to preach the gospel among the Slavs in Moravia. The script is used today by the Orthodox Slavs. Scholars disagree on its medieval origin. Most probably it was introduced in Bulgaria by the disciples of the holy brothers. A version of Cyrillic writing was used in medieval Bosnia, known, among other names, as *bosančica* (q.v.). Serbian Cyrillic is used in modern Bosnia-Herzegovina by the Serbs (q.v.), but during the Yugoslav period the children of other nationalities were required to learn and use the script too.

-D-

DANI/DAYS. An independent news-magazine in Sarajevo (q.v.). It began as *Bosnia-Herzegovina Dani* in late 1992, then *Bosnia-Herzegovina Ratni Dani* (B-H War Days), and finally *Dani*. The financial backing for the publication came from Alija Delimustafić, a former Communist entrepreneur, a leading member of the Party of Democratic Action (SDA) (q.v.) and minister of the interior until 1992. Because of his break with the SDA leadership, he went to live in Austria, but continued to support the publication of the magazine. Its editor in chief is Senad Pečanin. *Dani* is considered the most independent voice in the country.

DAYTON PEACE ACCORD. On November 21, 1995, after three weeks of negotiations, the presidents of Bosnia and Herzegovina, Alija Izetbegović (q.v.), of Croatia, Franjo Tuđman (q.v.), and of Serbia, Slobodan Milošević (q.v.), initialed a peace agreement, with 11 annexes, at the Wright-Patterson Air Force Base in Dayton, Ohio. The agreement marked the end of four years of war in Bosnia and Herzegovina. Milošević negotiated on behalf of the Serbs (q.v.), Tuđman represented the Croats (q.v.), and Izetbegović the Bosnian Muslims (q.v.). The treaty was negotiated under strong pressure from the United States and its chief negotiator in the former Yugoslavia (q.v.), Assistant Secretary of State Richard C. Holbrooke (q.v.).

According to the treaty, Bosnia remains a sovereign state and maintains its internationally recognized borders, but is divided into two entities — the (Muslim-Croat) Federation of Bosnia and Herzegovina (q.v.), with the control of 51 percent of the territory, and the Serb Republic (q.v.), to dominate the remainder. The central government consists of a collective three-person presidency — one elected by direct vote in the Serb Republic and two in the Federation, with a bicameral parliament, consisting of a 15-person upper chamber and a 42-person lower house. The former are to be selected from the assemblies of the districts and the latter by direct elections from the two parts of the country. The central government also includes a constitutional court and a central bank. The responsibilities of the central government include foreign policy, foreign trade, customs, immigration, monetary policy, international law enforcement, communications, transportation, and air traffic control. The two sub-states will have authority over taxation, health, defense, internal affairs, justice, energy and industry, commerce, traffic and internal communications, agriculture, education, city planning, resources, and the environment.

On the land divisions between the two entities, the agreements stipulated that Sarajevo (q.v.) is to be united and be part of the Federation; the Muslim enclave of Goražde is to be linked by a land corridor to the Federation; the final status of the town of Brčko (q.v.), held by the Serbs, is to be determined by arbitration; the Croat forces are to yield Mrkonjić Grad to the Serb Republic, and some other minor territory adjustments were to be made. Bosnian Croats, in a separate agreement with the Muslim-led government, agreed to eliminate the institutions of Herceg-Bosna (q.v.), a Croat political entity established during the war, and to form a joint command between the Muslim and Croat military forces.

The agreement also provided that all foreign forces leave Bosnia and Herzegovina within 30 days, and that the two sides move their forces behind the division lines between the two political entities and a two-kilometer-wide zone of separation established on both sides of the line. All heavy weapons were to be withdrawn to barracks within 120 days after the agreement was initialed. Free elections would take place within six to nine months for all elective offices on the state and local levels. Refugees have the legal right to return to their homes and also have the right to vote in the next election at the place where they lived before the war. Human rights are to be guaranteed and watched over by a Commission on Human Rights, consisting of an Ombudsman and a Human Rights Chamber. Furthermore, war criminals would not be allowed to hold public office, and the parties agreed to cooperate fully with the international investigation and prosecution of war crimes.

The Dayton agreement provided for a deployment of the peace Implementation Force (IFOR) (q.v.), consisting of a 60,000-member NATO-led international force, to keep peace in the country. The IFOR was given authority to arrest indicted war criminals, but its responsibilities did not include tracking them down. In contrast to the limited rules of engagement that regulated the UN peacekeepers' operation in

Bosnia during the war, the IFOR could use decisive force against anyone violating the cease-fire agreement.

The Dayton peace accord was formally signed in Paris on December 14, 1995, in a ceremony attended by, among others, President Clinton of the United States, President Jacques Chirac of France, Chancellor Helmut Kohl of Germany, Prime Minister John Major of Britain, and Prime Minister Viktor Chernomyrdin of Russia.

As the result of the signing of the agreement, the UN Security Council suspended its economic sanctions against Serbia and Montenegro (Nov. 22, 1995) and also voted to lift the arms embargo (q.v) against all former Yugoslav republics, commencing in March of 1996.

The Dayton peace treaty was successful in halting the four years of bloodshed, but in the eyes of many, the agreement, by legitimizing a permanent division of the country and accepting the results of ethnic cleansing (q.v.), might yet prove a failure in the long term.

DERVISH ORDERS. Sunni (traditional) Islam (q.v.) took hold in Bosnia and Herzegovina in the 15th century. But in Bosnia, as well as in other parts of the Ottoman Empire, besides the Sunni *ulema* (orthodox religious/learned leaders) there were a number of heterodox religious organizations. These were dervish orders that stemmed from different mystical movements in the Middle East, known as Sufism. A certain lifestyle, *tariqat* (path of behavior and action) as mandated by the founder of the order, was required from the members so they might gradually achieve a mystical union with the Creator. The human soul separated from its divine origin, according to such teachings, has to return to and be united with its source. Orders had religious centers (*tekke* or *tekija*) headed by spiritual masters (*şeyh, pir,* or *baba*). The founders of the orders were venerated as special friends of God, like Christian saints, and their burial places became centers of very important significance for their followers.

The earliest *tekkes* in Bosnia were established in the middle of the 15th century in today's Sarajevo (q.v.). It is believed that followers of the Naqshibandi order (Nakšibendije), named after its "second founder" Bahaudin Naqshibandi (d.1389) were the first Sufis to come to Bosnia and Herzegovina. Their Bosnian beginnings most probably can be traced to the Naqshibandi *şeyh-gazis*, accompanying and inspiring the Ottoman armies to fight for their faith against the infidels. This order was popularized by Skender-pasha Jurišić (or Juriševič), who participated in the occupation of Bosnia in 1463 and later became one of the most powerful men in the empire. He built a major Naqshibandi *tekke* in Sarajevo at the end of the 15th century and enriched it with a significant religious-charitable foundation *(vakuf* or *vakif)*. Most probably he himself belonged to this order. Besides a few *tekkes* in Sarajevo, other Naqshibandi centers existed in Mostar (q.v.), Fojnica, Visoko, Travnik, Foča, and near Konjic.

Isa-bey Išaković, an Ottoman frontier military leader in the Balkans in the mid-15th century, built the first *tekke* for a popular Turkish Mevlevi order (Mevlevije) or "Whirling Dervishes" in Bosnia. They were the followers of a 13th-century Seljuk mystic poet, Celaluddin Rumi (1207-1273). The remnants of this order survived in Bosnia and Herzegovina till the beginning of this century.

A third major dervish order established in Bosnia and Herzegovina was the Halveti order (Halvetije), founded by Abu Abdulah Sarajudin Omer "Halwat" at the end of the 14th century. The followers of this order emphasized asceticism. Already in the first half of the 16th century, this order appeared in Sarajevo and later in Mostar, Travnik, and other parts of Bosnia-Herzegovina. Gazi Husrev-beg, a well-known governor of the Bosnian *sandžak* (district), who governed several times between 1521 and 1541, built in Sarajevo, along with a mosque and a theology school (*medrese*), a dwelling and education center (*hanekah*) for dervishes. According to his wishes, the head of the center, had to be from the Halveti order. Husrev-beg himself probably belonged to this order. Other Halveti centers were founded in Travnik, Višegrad (q.v.), Rudo, Bijeljina, Tuzla (q.v.), Konjic, Blagaj, and Prusac.

The Kadirije (Qadiriyya) was another major dervish movement that spread in Bosnia and Herzegovina. It was founded by Abdul-Kadir al Gilani, who died in 1166. There were probably some followers of this order in Bosnia from the beginning of the Turkish rule there, but its *tekkes* spread only during the 16th and 17th centuries. Its major centers were in Sarajevo, Travnik, Jajce, and Zvornik.

In the 16th century, a special branch of the Melami order evolved in Bosnia, known as Hamzawi Melami, after its founder Hamza Bali. Shejh Hamza was born in the village of Orlovići, district of Zvornik. He became renowned for his asceticism and religious dedication. However, he came in conflict with the orthodox establishment and was condemned as a heretic. He was executed in Istanbul in 1574 and the Hamzawi order was banned.

These and other dervish orders played a major role in the religious, social, and cultural developments among the Muslim population in Bosnia-Herzegovina. Many of their members were educators, writers, or religious and moral teachers who exerted a lasting influence on Bosnian society and culture.

Although dervish orders were officially banned and the *tekke* closed in Bosnia-Herzegovina in 1952, Islamic mysticism and the orders themselves were not completely crushed. On the contrary, the dervish lifestyle in Bosnia, and in the former Yugoslavia (q.v.) as a whole, began to flourish in the early 1970s. By 1974, the Islamic orders in Yugoslavia felt strong enough to establish the Alliance of Islamic Dervish Orders Alijja in the Socialist Federal Republic of Yugoslavia (or SIDRA - Savez Islamskih Derviških Redova Alijje u SFRJ). In 1978, the name was changed from Alliance into Community of Islamic Dervish Orders Alijja (ZIDRA- Zajednica Iislamskih Derviških Redova Alijje). Twelve recognized dervish orders made up the organization. They published the *Bulletin* as their official voice. The official Muslim authority (Rijaset) in the country was opposed to this parallel religious organization, but, after initial difficulties, the relations were normalized between the two sides. It is estimated that in 1986 there were 50,000 dervish followers in the former Yugoslavia. However, most of them were Albanian Muslims. Out of the existing 70 *tekkes* in the country at the time, 53 were in Kosovo, 10 in Macedonia, and only seven in Bosnia and Herzegovina.

Although most of the *tekkes* in Bosnia-Herzegovina were destroyed during the 1992-1995 war, the interest in Sufism among the Bosnian Muslims (q.v.) is quickly rising. Many dervish orders are being revitalized. The Nakšibendije, Kadirije, and Halvetije are among the most popular, while the others (Bektašije, Mevlevije, Rifaije, Melamije, and Nurije) are also reestablishing their presence in the country.

DESPOTOVIĆ, NEDELJKO (1948-). Appointed minister without portfolio, in the government of the Federation of Bosnia and Herzegovina (q.v.) in January 1996; of Serb nationality; born in Tuzla (q.v.) and finished higher education in law.

DIVJAK, JOVO. General in the Army of Bosnia-Herzegovina (q.v.) and deputy chief of staff of Bosnian Armed Forces of Serb nationality. He left JNA in 1992 and helped to organize the first defense of Sarajevo (q.v.). His role in the Bosnian army has become mostly decorative in nature. Divjak is also founder of a charitable organization for orphans.

DIZDAR, MAK/MEHMEDALIJA (1917-1971). This well-known poet was born in Stolac (Herzegovina [q.v.]). In his native town he received his primary education and in Sarajevo (q.v.) his secondary education. After the Second World War, he was editor of the official Yugoslav news agency TANJUG and various papers, including the leading Sarajevo daily *Oslobođenje* (Liberation). From 1964 till his death he edited the Sarajevo literary journal *Život* (Life) (q.v.). It was under his editorial tenure that the journal attained prominence in cultural circles.

Dizdar's first book of poetry was published in 1936. However, during the war and the immediate post-war era he remained quiet. Only after the constraints of socialist realism began to crack, he began to publish again. Although his works from the mid-1950s and early 1960s were well accepted by the literary critics, his collection of poems entitled *Kameni spavač* (Lapidary sleeper) was acclaimed his most successful literary accomplishment. In this collection, Dizdar plunged to the depths of the suffering soul of his homeland and its tragic history as recorded in epigrams on medieval tombstones (stećci [q.v.]). In this collection he succeeded in harmonizing the universal impulses of human existence with the tragic destiny of his native land emanating through the sayings and epigrams on the giant tombstones that bore witness to an enigmatic past.

ĐOGO, RISTO (- 1994). A leading Serbian war propagandist. Editor of the Serb Radio-Television in the Serbian controlled part of Bosnia-Herzegovina. Before the war, he was an editor of Radio Sarajevo. As a result of an intra-Serb struggle, he was killed in 1994.

DOMOVINA/HOMELAND. A Croat monthly published in Sarajevo (q.v.) since 1994.

DONJI KRAJI/LOWER REGIONS. Medieval name for the region of Bosnia west of Vranica Mountain around the upper flows of the rivers Vrbas and Sana. The following counties (*župe*) were included in this district: Uskoplje (around present-day Gornji and Donji Vakuf), Luka (east of the town of Jajce on the east banks of the river Vrbas), Pliva (on the west bank of the river Vrbas around the river Pliva), Zemljanik (both sides of the river Vrbas around the town of Bočac), Vrbanja (around present-day Kotor Varoš), Banica (around the town of Ključ [q.v.]), and a small *župa* Lušci (west of *župa* Pliva).

The region of Donji Kraji was under the domain of the Croatian kings. But after the native dynasty died out, the district exchanged hands many times. The Bosnian *ban* Kulin (qq.v.) extended his rule over these districts at the end of the 12th century. The powerful Hrvatinić family had possessions in the region, and the best-known member of the family, Hrvoje Vukčić Hrvatinić (q.v.), became the most powerful nobleman in Bosnia and Croatia at the beginning of the 15th century.

ĐOZO, HUSEJIN (1912-1982). A Bosnian Muslim (q.v.) Islamic scholar. Studied at Al-Azhar University in Cairo. Returned to Bosnia in 1939 and became a *madrese* professor in Sarajevo (q.v.). Through his activities and because of pressures from a number of Muslim countries, the Theological Faculty in Sarajevo was opened in 1977. He was also the editor of the Muslim monthly *Preporod* (Rebirth). However, Đozo was removed from the editorial board by the regime in 1979. For his scholarly achievements, he became a member of the Egyptian Academy.

DRAŠKOVIĆ, VUK (1943-). A Serb nationalist writer and the head of a political party, Srpski Pokret Obnove (SPO) - Serbian Renewal Movement (q.v.). Born in Gacko, Bosnia and Herzegovina. His writings, including the novel *Nož* (The knife) were inspired mainly by his anti-Muslim and anti-Croat feelings. His works became the major source of the growing Serbian nationalism in the 1980s. After the collapse of the Communist regime, Drašković's newly formed political party (SPO) claimed to be a true successor of the Serbian *četnik* (q.v.) movement from the World War II era. The SPO formed its own paramilitary formation, the Serbian Guard (Srpska Garda), to fight in Croatia and Bosnia and Herzegovina. Although Drašković came into political conflict with President Slobodan Milošević (q.v.) and tried to portray his party as a democratic force opposed to the ruling Serbian Socialist Party, his contributions to the growth of Serbian nationalist euphoria and the involvement of his militia in ethnic cleansing (q.v.) were an important part of Serbian aggression from 1991 to 1995. By the end of 1993, he began to condemn the atrocities committed by the Serbs (q.v.), blaming other leaders or militias for such deeds, but he continued to advocate the creation of a Greater Serbia, a country that would include Serbia, Montenegro, Macedonia, all of Bosnia and Herzegovina, and parts of Croatia.

DURAKOVIĆ, NIJAZ (1949-). President of the Social Democratic Party (q.v.) and member of the Presidency of the Republic of Bosnia and Herzegovina. He was born in the town of Stolac and received his higher education at the University of Sarajevo, specializing in nationalism. After finishing his studies, he became a professor at the same university and has published a number of books, including his latest (1993) work *The Curse of the Muslims.*

From his young days, Duraković was an activist in the Yugoslav Communist Party and served at the top of its leadership. He was also a member of the collective Presidency in the former Yugoslavia (q.v.). From 1988 to 1991, he was president of the League of Communists of Bosnia and Herzegovina - Party for Democratic Change. The party, however, changed its name (1991) to Social Democratic Party of Bosnia and Herzegovina. Since then, Duraković has been elected twice as its president, and in October of 1993, he was named a member of the seven-member Presidency of the Republic of Bosnia and Herzegovina.

-E-

ECONOMY. Only about a third of Bosnia-Herzegovina is arable. Much of the cultivated land is scattered in mountainous or rocky terrain and is therefore not very productive. The Sava River valley (Posavina [q.v.]) is the only suitable region for a larger agricultural development.

Although the country has a strong industrial potential, and is rich in forestry and water resources and has relatively large mineral reserves, most of the population has traditionally made its living as small farmers. Industrial progress in the land has been stifled for centuries by various sociopolitical conditions.

A type of feudal economy and social relations remained in Bosnia and Herzegovina to the very end of the Ottoman rule, and in certain forms it lasted till the end of World War I. During the Ottoman centuries, especially during the imperial decline, most of the country's natural resources were not exploited. Even pre-Ottoman mining and smelting had mostly died out by the end of Ottoman rule. The overwhelming majority of people lived either as serfs or as landowners. Heavy assessments on peasants' annual yields, and other burdens, hindered all incentives to make agricultural improvements that would, in return, stimulate production and initiate processes of economic and social transformation. Only in the middle of the last century were there individual efforts toward economic modernization. But these did not have an impact on the Bosnian economy as a whole.

With the coming of Austro-Hungarian rule, Bosnia and Herzegovina entered a new era of economic development. The natural resources of the country and various government concessions attracted investments from other parts of the empire. The main industrial orientation was toward exploitation of the forests and mineral reserves. Only a few years after the occupation, there were more than 120 various industrial establishments with over 50,000 workers. The building of railroads, the opening of major banks, and an effort to increase agriculture, augmented by a more efficient bureaucracy and better educational system (q.v.), helped to bring about economic advancements.

These changes, however, did not have a major impact on most of the people in the country. The industrial and other economic developments, which in turn brought modernization and social changes, took place mainly in a few centers connected with a newly built railroad system. On the eve of World War I, almost 85 percent of the population still lived and worked in villages and was barely affected with the ongoing economic changes. A very high birth rate in the agricultural areas also contributed to slow economic improvement for these farmers and villages.

Moreover, even during the Austrian period, about half of the peasant population was still bound by remnants of feudalism. Despite its narrow confines and basically exploitative orientation, the economic changes brought about by the Austro-Hungarian administration did lay a foundation and set in motion the process of economic and social change in the country.

The collapse of the Austro-Hungarian Empire and Bosnia's entry (1918) into the new South Slavic state did not result in economic improvement. The size of the market for Bosnia's raw materials or half-finished products decreased greatly and an infusion of new capital from outside the land sharply diminished. The new country was not only smaller; its non-Habsburg components (Serbia, Montenegro, and Macedonia) were even less industrialized and could not be of any help to Bosnia and Herzegovina. Furthermore, because of the fears of foreign competition, Belgrade had an autarkic economic orientation that had a very negative effect on the former Habsburg regions: Slovenia, Croatia, and Bosnia-Herzegovina.

These factors, heightened by political and economic instability inside and outside the country in the 1920s and 1930s, caused economic stagnation. Moreover, only people loyal to the ruling regime, by various privileges, shady bank loans, and trade deals, accumulated a certain amount of wealth. But such "entrepreneurs" were not able to establish large and viable industries that could provide employment to the ever-increasing village population. During the entire interwar period, only about 130 new industrial enterprises were started in Bosnia and Herzegovina, mostly in timber industry, food processing, textile, and metal works. In 1931, only 6.7 percent of the total population worked in industry, mining, and various trade professions. Lack of industrial development, a high birth rate, and lack of education (q.v.) forced people to stay in increasingly poorer villages.

In post-World War II Yugoslavia (q.v.), as in all Communist-controlled countries, nationalization and socialization of the economy were implemented. A forced industrialization and limitations on land holdings were imposed. Policies of forced collectivization were enforced, but not on the same level in all parts of the country. During the first economic phase, which lasted till the early 1950s, the major emphasis was on developing heavy industrial bases, railroad buildings, irrigation systems, and the utilization of hydro energy. The central economic planners were very ambitious at the time and projected that they would make a quick transformation from an agricultural to an industrial economy. In this early post-war period, the economic role of Bosnia and Herzegovina was seen as vital for the development of the whole country. Bosnia with its coal and iron reserves was to be the most important metallurgical center. Herzegovina (q.v.) with its bauxite deposits was to be the center of the aluminum industry. But already in the 1950s it was clear that suc high goals could not be achieved and the planners had to look for a different theoretical road to the same socialist goals.

In the early 1950s, policies of decentralization were introduced and various economic reforms were promulgated in the decades that followed. The Yugoslav experimentation with self-management was hailed as a way of achieving an industrial and post-industrial socialist society that combined the best of socialism and capitalism. The economy, however, remained a tool in the hands of the Communist bureaucracy and its fate was always bound by the needs of the Communist Party.

Although Bosnia and Herzegovina did make major economic progress in the last 50 years, its economic position in the former Yugoslavia remained precarious. The economy always remained below the Yugoslav level. The GNP declined from 77 percent in 1952 to 66.4 percent in 1970, and in 1978 it went up to 67.4 percent in relation to the entire Yugoslav economy. Despite its natural potential, the republic continued to be an "underdeveloped" region and had to depend on federal funds for help in capital investments. The money flowed from the richer republics of Slovenia and Croatia to the federal center, then from there to the underdeveloped regions. However, it was not allotted according to economic needs or potential, but instead according to the sympathies of the federal bureaucrats. For example, from 1956 to 1968 Bosnia-Herzegovina received 13.72 percent and Serbia 43.48 percent of the Federal Investment Fund. From 1965 to 1970, Bosnia's share in the fund was 14.1 percent and that of Serbia was 46.6 percent. Bosnia's credit potential in 1969 was 7.8 percent and that of Serbia was 50.3 percent. Thus, despite socialist goals of industrialization and of transforming peasants into industrial workers, Bosnia and Herzegovina remained an agricultural land. In 1952, for example, out of every 100 residents 9.6 were industrial workers; in 1978 the ratio increased only to 18.5 per hundred.

In order to ease its economic and political tensions, the Yugoslav government began, in the mid-1960s, to export its workers to the West. Hundreds of thousands of workers found employment in Germany and other Western countries. Most of them became either permanent "guest workers" in Europe or moved to North America or Australia. A disproportionately large percentage of Croatians from Herzegovina (q.v.) and from other less productive regions of Bosnia became guest workers. While the cash brought into the country by such workers did help to raise the standard of living, it did not create a stable base for major economic progress. Because free enterprise was not permitted, most of the hard currency earned in the West was spent on better housing, cars, and equipment for family farms. None of this stimulated the process of solid economic growth in the country.

By the end of the Yugoslav period, a substantial industrial base had been achieved and in 1992 the economy was freed from Communist Party control, but the war in the country caused by Serbian separatists and Belgrade expansionists has destroyed not only most of the industrial infrastructure, but also most of the cities, towns, and villages. The material destruction and immense loss of human lives will have a critical impact on the economic development of the country. Its reconstruction will be of significant proportions and will require major international help. Bosnia and Herzegovina, however, is rich in natural resources and has skilled and hard-working people; there is hope that in peaceful times the economy will have a speedy recovery.

EDUCATION. During medieval times, the centers of learning were the monasteries. Literacy, however, was kept within the church circles and regal chanceries. Although the Christian church in Bosnia belonged to the Western tradition, the old Slavonic language and the Glagolitic script (q.v.) were kept in the liturgy, as was the case in neighboring southern Croatia. For inadequacies in the knowledge of Latin and lack of up-to-date books, learning in Bosnia was isolated from the main trends in the West. With the coming of the Franciscans (q.v.), however, the level of education increased, but the Latin language was pushing out the native cultural heritage.

The Muslim religious schools (*mekteb* or *mektep*) were introduced soon after the Ottoman intrusion into Bosnia. Their main purpose was to teach young children religious instructions in Arabic language. At the end of the Turkish rule there were 499 *mektebs* in Bosnia and Herzegovina.

In 1878, there were 110 primary schools in Bosnia and Herzegovina with 5,913 students. In 1910/1911 the number of schools rose to 487 and the number of students to 42,572. The illiteracy level, however, remained extremely high. Even in 1910, for example, 88 percent of those over seven years of age were illiterate. Only every seventh male and 15th female were literate. Among the Muslim population 5.3 percent were literate (99.7 percent of Muslim women were illiterate); among the Orthodox 9.9 percent, and among the Catholics 22.2 percent.

The first Orthodox schools in Bosnia and Herzegovina were founded toward the end of the Ottoman rule. There were 56 such schools on the eve of the Austrian occupation and their number increased to 107 by 1910. They were established and supported by the local Orthodox Church (q.v.). Textbooks and other educational assistance also came from Serbia and the Serbs (q.v.) from the Habsburg monarchy. The Orthodox schools in Bosnia were abolished at the beginning of World War I and were not revived after the war.

It was the Franciscan friars who sustained the seeds of learning among the Catholics in the country. There are indicators that their educational efforts were at least a little wider than the immediate church needs. The oldest monastic school from the Ottoman era dates from 1655. At the time of the Austrian occupation, there were 54 Catholic schools in the country. Women's religious orders also had their schools. The first such school was established in 1872. Soon the nuns had the best educational system in the country. Eventually, the nuns became the educators among the Croatian Catholics in primary schools, while the Franciscans focused on secondary and higher learning.

Although a law was passed to establish state schools toward the end of the Ottoman period, they did not appear till the Austro-Hungarian occupation. During the first three years of Austrian rule, 32 and, by 1886, 93 such schools were opened. Besides spreading literacy among the population, the new regime wished to limit the influence of the sectarian schools and their role in nationalistic revivals of the time. Thus there was a resistance to state schools, especially among the Muslim and Orthodox leaders. Although the number of primary schools increased, still less than 30 percent of children of school age were getting some kind of primary education on the eve of World War I.

There was also a small number of schools that were established by various ethnic communities in the country: Jewish (q.v.), German, Polish, Hungarian, and others.

During the interwar period, education declined in some parts of Bosnia and Herzegovina. Muslim and Catholic schools remained open. The state schools came under Serbian nationalistic control, thus the Serb leadership did not feel the need to have separate schools of their own.

The secondary and higher levels of education in Bosnia and Herzegovina evolved very slowly. Muslim middle-level schools for training religious leaders and *mekteb* teachers (*medrese*) were operating in Bosnia during the Ottoman times. The best-known such school was the Gazi Husref-beg *medrese* in Sarajevo (q.v.) established in 1537. At the time of the Austrian occupation, there were 43 such schools in the country. In the interwar period, the number of *medrese* declined. There were also *Šeriat* schools that taught Islamic jurisprudence and Oriental languages, and *ruždije,* schools that combined primary and secondary education, and offered religious and secular subjects.

Among the Orthodox, there was a "higher school" for girls and a school for priestly vocations. A number of secondary-level Catholic schools appeared toward the end of the last century: a teacher's college for women (Sarajevo), a Jesuit Gymnasium (high school) in Travnik, and two Franciscan Gymnasia (Visoko and Široki Brijeg). All four schools had a very high reputation and were attended also by non-Catholics. Three Catholic schools of theology, two in Sarajevo and one in Mostar (q.v.), were the first university-level institutions in the country.

State schools for training new teachers were also established under Austrian rule. Such schools opened in Sarajevo in 1886 and in Mostar in 1913, and a teacher's school for Muslim reformed *mektebs* in 1893. Various trade schools and a few state secondary schools were also founded.

At the beginning of this century, each of the three ethno/religious communities in Bosnia and Herzegovina formed a benevolent society to help young people to achieve higher education. Serbs had Prosvjeta (qq.v.), Croats Napredak (qq.v.), and the Muslims Gajret (qq.v.). These societies became very important in supporting education and encouraging cultural activities among the members of their respective communities. These associations, however, were banned after the Communist takeover.

After World War II, a new school system was introduced that conformed to socialist ideological needs. In 1948 about 45 percent of the population older than 10 years was still illiterate. Primary education became mandatory and it was extended from four to six, seven, and then eight years. But still many young people in remote villages did not attend school. Private schools were banned, except for a few that were limited to educating candidates for religious vocations. The Franciscans in Herzegovina (q.v.) were, however, forbidden to have a school even for their vocational needs. The number of state secondary schools greatly increased and new institutions of higher learning were established. The University of Sarajevo was formed in 1949. Three more universities were founded later, Banja Luka (1975), Tuzla (1976), and Mostar (1977) (qq.v.). The Academy of Sciences and Arts of Bosnia and Herzegovina (q.v.) was founded on June 22, 1966.

ELECTIONS - 1996. One of the stipulations of the Dayton peace accord (q.v.) required that elections for all elective offices on the state and local levels take place in Bosnia and Herzegovina within six to nine months after the signing of the peace treaty. Although the U.S. allies in Europe argued that the situation in Bosnia was not yet suitable for elections and they proposed that the vote be postponed, the elections did take place on September 14, 1996. The American side was determined to keep the Dayton peace process on track, hoping that the newly formed national institutions might serve as a unifying force in postwar Bosnia.

On election day, each of the three major national groups in Bosnia and Herzegovina, (Bosniacs, Croats, and Serbs [qq.v.]), cast ballots for their own candidate to the tripartite presidency of the country. Because Alija Izetbegović (q.v.), candidate of the Bosnian Muslim Party of Democratic Action (q.v.), won the highest number of votes, he became chairman of the newly elected presidency. The other two elected members of the presidency were Krešimir Zubak (Croat)(q.v.) and Momčilo Krajišnik (Serb)(q.v.).

Twenty-eight members were elected to the House of Representatives of Bosnia and Herzegovina from the Muslim-Croat Federation (q.v.) and 14 from the Serb Republic (q.v.). The Party of Democratic Action (SDA) gained 19, the Serbian Democratic Party (SDS) (q.v.) nine, the Croatian Democratic Union (HDZ) (q.v.) eight, the United List (ZLBiH) two, the Party for BiH (SBiH) two, and the Union for Peace and Progress (SMPSR) two seats in the House.

Representatives to the House of Peoples in the national government will be delegated from the House of Peoples in the Federation and from the National Assembly in the Serb Republic, respectively.

In the Muslim-Croat Federation, elections also took place for the House of Representatives of the Federation and for Cantonal Assemblies. In the House, the SDA won 78, the HDZ 36, the United List 11, the Party for BiH 10, the Democratic People's Union (DNZ) three, and the Croatian Party of Right (HSP)(q.v.) two seats.

In the Serb Republic, voters elected a president and the National Assembly of the Serb entity in Bosnia on the same day. The SDS candidate, Biljana Plavšić (q.v.), was elected president. The SDS gained 45, the SDA 14, the Union for Peace and Progress 10, the Serb Radical Party (SRS) six, the Democratic Patriotic Block two, the Party for BiH two, the United List two, the Serb Party of Krajina (SSK) one, and the Serb Patriotic Party (SPAS) one seat in the National Assembly.

Because of the loopholes in the Dayton agreement concerning voters' registration, the municipal elections were postponed by the Provisional Election Commission for mid-1997.

Although there were many irregularities and manipulations, including a 104 percent voter turnout, the elections were declared valid by the Organization for Security and Cooperation in Europe (OSCE), which organized and supervised the Bosnian vote. Robert Frowick, a U.S. diplomat, was the head of the OSCE's electoral operation in Sarajevo. For many, the success of the elections was not in numbers and percentages but in the fact that they did take place and in a relatively peaceful atmosphere.

The election results did not surprise anyone. The three leading nationalist parties (Muslim SDA, Serb SDS, and Croat HDZ) were clear victors. The hopes that the so-called non-nationalist parties or coalitions would have stronger showing were not fulfilled. The Union for Peace and Progress in the Serb Republic, led by an offshoot of Milošević's (q.v.) Serbian Socialist Party in Serbia, did receive more votes than expected, but it was not able to challenge the dominance of the SDS among the Bosnian Serbs. The next national elections are scheduled for 1998.

ETHNIC CLEANSING. A phrase used to describe mostly violent efforts to create ethnically pure regions during the 1991-1995 war in Croatia and Bosnia-Herzegovina. Although the expression and the practice are not new, their revival in the former Yugoslavia is credited to Vojislav Šešelj (q.v), leader of the Serbian Radical Party. In 1991, he began to advocate a struggle for an ethnically pure Greater Serbia. The following statements are taken from the U.S. Senate Foreign Relations Committee report published on August 15, 1992. "(1)The 'ethnic cleansing' campaign of the self-styled Serbian Republic of Bosnia-Herzegovina has substantially achieved its goals; an exclusively Serb-inhabited region has been created in territory contiguous to Serbia, occupying 70 per cent of the territory of Bosnia-Herzegovina, and with a territorial corridor connecting Serbia with Serb-inhabited territory in the Krajina region of Croatia. The new Serb territories were created by forcible expelling the Muslim populations that had been the overwhelming numerical majority in the regions of Bosnia-Herzegovina closest to Serbia. (2) Ethnic cleansing has been carried out with widespread atrocities. Random and selective killings are a routine part of the process of evacuating Muslim villages in Bosnia-Herzegovina. In some villages and towns, there were organized massacres of the Muslim population. We believe the death toll associated with forcible removal of the Muslim village population of Bosnia-Herzegovina far exceeds the death tolls from the bombardment of cities or from killings in prison camps. Unfortunately, this most lethal aspect of ethnic cleansing has received the least amount of public attention. (3) Detention camps were a routine way station for civilian population forcibly evacuated from villages and towns. Inadequate shelter, food and sanitation are the universal characteristics of these camps. Rape, beating, and killing occurred in some instances. (4) Bosnian Serb forces consider able-bodied Muslim and Croatian males older than 15 as potential fighters for the enemy and as potential assets in prison exchange. As a result, non-Serb boys and men have been and continue to be held in prison camps throughout the Serb-controlled areas of Bosnia-Herzegovina. As best we could determine, neither physical conditions nor the treatment of prisoners meets standards as laid out in relevant international protocols. The worst of these camps - Omarska, Luka, Prijedor and Manjača - are places where prisoners have been systematically beaten and starved. We found additional evidence of organized killings in some of these locations. (5) Killings in the camps often appear to be recreational and sadistic. There is evidence that paramilitary groups from Serbia and Montenegro have entered certain camps, often drunk and by night, for the purpose of torturing, killing, and raping. (6) Serb civilians in Bosnia-Herzegovina have been victims of violence by Muslim, Croatian and Bosnian Serb forces. Serb prisoners in Muslim and Croatian camps have not been treated in an internationally acceptable manner. In no sense, however, does the violence against the Serbs compare to the atrocities inflected on the Muslims, nor are conditions in Muslim or Croatian prison camps comparable to those in the Serbian death camps."

-F-

FEDERAL REPUBLIC OF YUGOSLAVIA/SAVEZNA REPUBLIKA JUGOSLAVIJA (SRJ). The new Yugoslav federation was officially proclaimed on April 27, 1992. It consists of the republics of Serbia and Montenegro. The federation is dominated by Serbia, which is by far the larger of the two, so Montenegrine ethnicity is being disregarded in favor of the Serbian identity. The largest minority in the country are the Kosovo Albanians that have been denied even basic ethnic and human rights. The region remains the most volatile trouble spot in the Balkans (q.v.).

For economic and political reason, the SRJ claims to be the only successor state of the Socialist Yugoslavia (q.v.), but that claim has been rejected by other republics of the former Yugoslavia and the international community.

FEDERATION OF BOSNIA AND HERZEGOVINA. A political entity composed of 51 percent of the country's territory which is shared by Bosniacs (Bosnian Muslims) and Croats (qq.v.). The Serb Republic (q.v.) makes the other 49 percent of the country. The two entities are united by a central government of the Republic of Bosnia and Herzegovina.

The first contours of a common Croat-Bosniac entity appeared at the beginning of 1994, after a year-long hostility between Muslims and Croats in central Bosnia and the Mostar (q.v.) region. The agreement was forged mostly under U.S. auspices in negotiations between the Bosniacs, Bosnian Croats, and the Republic of Croatia. It was signed in Washington, D.C., on March 18, 1994, in the presence of President Bill Clinton. The implementation of the Washington agreement, however, did not bring about the desired results. Thus another accord was signed in Dayton, Ohio, on November 10, 1995, in which the parties agreed to take "radical steps to achieve the political, economic and social integration of the Federation."

The Federation consists of ten "cantons," each with its own constitution, legislature, executive government, and courts.

The Federal Government includes a bicameral legislature, president and vice president, prime minister, and cabinet. The legislative body consists of a House of Representatives, elected Federation-wide, and a House of Peoples, with 30 Bosniacs and 30 Croats, and a proportionate number of "others." There is also a unified Federation Army above the corps level up to the Joint Command between the Croatian Defense Council (HVO) and the Army of Bosnia and Herzegovina (ABiH) (qq.v.). All disputes over the competence of cantons and the Federation are to be resolved by a Constitutional Court. The government of the Federation is structured in such a way that it should prevent either side from controlling the government.

The central government of the Republic of Bosnia and Herzegovina is responsible for foreign policy, foreign trade, customs, immigration, monetary policy, international law enforcement, communications, transportation, and air traffic control. The Federation is in charge of all other matters in this Croat-Bosniac entity.

FRANCIS JOSEPH I. Austrian emperor from 1848 to 1916. Bosnia-Herzegovina came under his domain in 1878. Because Austro-Hungarian rule brought to Bosnia modernization, economic development, and an improvement in education the old emperor was seen by many in Bosnia as a benevolent paternal figure.

FRANCISCANS. The followers of St. Francis of Assisi came to the present-day territory of Bosnia and Herzegovina in 1291. In 1339/40, a Franciscan Vicariate of Bosnia (an administrative division) was established. Its headquarters were at Mile, near the town of Visoko where the first Bosnian king was crowned in 1377. The territory of the vicariate stretched from the Adriatic to the Black Sea. Because of its huge size, the vicariate was eventually subdivided into seven custodies. By the end of the 14th century, Bosnian Franciscans had 35 monasteries. After the fall of the Bosnian medieval kingdom (1463), three vicariates (Dalmatia, Dubrovnik, and Croatian Bosnia), split from the original vicariate. In 1517, the Bosnian vicariate was raised to the level of a Franciscan province under the name of Bosna Argentina. The changes in its territorial jurisdiction were determined by the borders of the Ottoman Empire. The Franciscans in Herzegovina (q.v.) split from the Bosnian mother province and established their separate vicariate in 1852, which became a province in 1892.

Although after the fall of Bosnia in 1463, Sultan Mehment II the Conqueror issued a charter (*ahdnama*) stating the Catholics and their Franciscan clergy in Bosnia were free to practice their religion, the "freedom" of the Catholic Church (q.v.) was very restricted. It was often contingent on the Ottoman relationships with the Catholic powers in Central Europe and even more often on the whims of the local Muslim administrators and landlords. The fact that out of many Franciscan monasteries from the pre-Ottoman period only three existed at the beginning of the 18th century indicates the fate of the Franciscans and the Catholic population under Islamic rule.

The Franciscan community is the only guardian of the pre-Ottoman Bosnian heritage and the only institution in the country that spans the medieval, Ottoman, and modern history of Bosnia and Herzegovina.

-G-

GAČANOVIĆ, RASIM (1950-). Named minister of transportation and communications of the Federation of Bosnia and Herzegovina (q.v.) in January 1996. Bosniac by nationality. Born in Sarajevo (q.v.) and finished higher education in electrotechnology.

GAJRET/ZEAL from Arabic. A Muslim cultural and educational society in Bosnia and Herzegovina founded in Sarajevo (q.v.) in 1903. Initially, its main goal was the support of needy students in their pursuit of secondary and higher education (q.v.). Before World War I, the organization went through major turmoil because of the national question among the

Muslims (q.v.). Some of its leading members began to pull the society more and more to the Serbian national orientation. This led to a split in the society and a new organization, Narodna Uzdanica (People's Confidence) (q.v.), emerged out of it. Because of its pro-Serb orientation, Gajret's leadership came under Austro-Hungarian harassment after the Sarajevo assassination (q.v.) in 1914.

After the war, Gajret spread to other parts of the newly established Kingdom of Serbs, Croats, and Slovenes (q.v.). In the mid-1920s it had a number of student dormitories in Sarajevo and Mostar (q.v.). The society also engaged in various cultural activities among the Muslims. Gajret published (1907-1914 and 1921-1941) a cultural and literary journal under the same name. The association was banned by the Communist regime after World War II.

GANIĆ, EJUP (1946-). Member of Bosnia's state Presidency (Nov. of 1990), Vice-President of the Federation of Bosnia and Herzegovina (q.v.) (May of 1994), and a leading member of the (Bosnian Muslim) (q.v.) Party of Democratic Action. Ganić was born near Novi Pazar in the region of Sandžak (q.v.), present-day Serbia. He finished his higher education at Belgrade University and received a D. SC. in chemical engineering with a focus on thermal and fluid sciences at the Massachusetts Institute of Technology (1976). After teaching at the University of Illinois in Chicago for five years, he returned to Sarajevo (q.v.) in 1982 where he became a professor of chemical engineering at the University of Sarajevo and Executive Director of UNIS enterprise. He has been recognized and awarded by his national and international peers for his contributions in the field.

GLAGOLITIC SCRIPT /GLAGOLJICA. An old Croatian alphabet used also in the medieval Bosnian state. There are various theories about its origin. St. Cyril and Methodius used it in their work among the Moravian Slavs, but the script predates the holy brothers. The name *glagoljica* comes from the verb *to talk* (*glagoljati*). In Bosnia, *glagoljica* was slowly pushed out by a variant of the Cyrillic alphabet (q.v.), known, among other names, as *bosančica* (q.v.).

GLAS/VOICE. A Banja Luka (q.v.) regional paper that after the 1990 elections came under the control of the Serbian Democratic Party. In August of 1992, it became a very radical Serbian voice in Bosnia-Herzegovina. In August 1993, its name changed to *Glas zapadne Srbije*/Voice of Western Serbia.

GLAS MIRA/VOICE OF PEACE. The voice of the Marian shrine in Međugorje (q.v.). Its publication began in 1993 and it promotes devotion to the Virgin Mary.

GLASNIK ZEMALJSKOG MUZEJA U SARAJEVU/HERALD OF THE LAND MUSEUM IN SARAJEVO. This scholarly publication began in 1889 and with several interruptions it endured till the latest war in Bosnia-Herzegovina. The *Glasnik* has contributed greatly to the study and understanding of the Bosnian past.

GRABOVAC, NIKOLA (1943-). Appointed minister of commerce of the Federation of Bosnia and Herzegovina (q.v.) in January 1996. Croat nationality. Born in Bugojno and finished higher education in economics.

GREEN BERETS. Bosnian Muslim (q.v.) irregular armed forces formed in April 1992, believed to be the private militia of the Muslim political party, the Party of Democratic Action (SDA) (q.v.). They became a part of the Army of Bosnia and Herzegovina (q.v.).

-H-

HABENA/HERCEG-BOSNA NOVINSKA AGENCIJA/ HERCEG-BOSNA NEWS AGENCY. The agency was formed in August 1993 and is the official voice of the Croat Republic of Herceg-Bosna (q.v.). The headquarters of HABENA are in the village of Međugorje (q.v.). Its director is Božo Rajić, a leading member of the Croatian Democratic Union (HDZ) (q.v.), and initially the minister of defense of the coalition government of Bosnia-Herzegovina.

HADŽIĆ, NURI OSMAN (1869-1937). A writer and an important figure in the cultural life of Bosnian Muslims (q.v.) during the Austrian occupation. He was born in Mostar (q.v.), finished his secondary education in a Muslim law school (*Şeriat)* in Sarajevo (q.v.), and studied law in Vienna and Zagreb. After getting a law degree, he returned to Bosnia and worked in various government jobs till the end of World War I. After the war, he lived in Belgrade and worked in the state government.

Hadžić's earliest literary endeavors date from the days when he was a student. From 1894 to 1900, he and his friend, Ivan Milićević, published two novels and a number of short stories under the common pseudonym of Osman-Aziz. Besides writing novels, he contributed to many literary and cultural periodicals of his time. His writings are romantic reflections on the life and history of the Muslims in Bosnia and Herzegovina. Hadžić's works contributed to the cultural revival of his people at the time.

HAGADA. The Sarajevo (q.v.) *Hagada* is one of the most cherished Jewish religious and literary treasures around the world. This well-preserved and richly illuminated book of sacred texts was carried by the exiled Spanish Jews (q.v.) out of Spain in 1492. The book survived in Italy several hundred years and then it was brought through Dubrovnik to Sarajevo where it is scrupulously guarded. Miraculously, it survived

World War II and the destruction of Sarajevo in the last Bosnian war.

HDZ/HRVATSKA DEMOKRATSKA ZAJEDNICA. *See* CROATIAN DEMOCRATIC UNION.

HEBIB, AVDO (1936-). Became minister of interior of the Federation of Bosnia and Herzegovina (q.v.) in January 1966. Bosniac by nationality. Born in Gacko and finished higher education in psychology.

HERCEG-BOSNA. CROATIAN REPUBLIC HERCEG-BOSNA/HRVATSKA REPUBLIKA HERCEG-BOSNA. As the threat of war loomed and Serbian attacks on Croat villages in eastern parts of Herzegovina began at the end of September 1991, the counties in Bosnia-Herzegovina with the Croat majority organized themselves into the Croatian Community of Herceg-Bosna on November 18, 1991. Self-defense was initially the main purpose of this self-organizing Croat effort. This, and earlier moves to organize the Croat Defense Council, prevented the Serbs (q.v.) from grabbing more, or even the entire republic of Bosnia-Herzegovina, because the central government in Sarajevo was procrastinating with organizing its defense forces.

As the role and authority of the leadership of the Croat Union of Herceg-Bosna increased in the mainly Croat regions and as the intentions of the international, mainly European, community were becoming clearer that it wanted to divide Bosnia-Herzegovina according to ethnic lines, the Croat political power holders upgraded their status by proclaiming the Croat Republic of Herceg-Bosna on August 28, 1993. The Muslim-led Sarajevo government accused it of treason and of working for the breakup of the country. Although Sarajevo de jure never accepted the Republic's existence, de facto it had to acquiesce to the reality and to work with its leaders. The Croats (q.v.), on the other hand, emphasized that, in reality, they were the ones who had saved Bosnia-Herzegovina from total collapse by organizing themselves and fighting the Serbs from the very beginning of the aggression. The 1995 Dayton peace accord (q.v.) required the Croats to abandon their self-rule and merge into the common Muslim-Croat Federation of Bosnia-Herzegovina (q.v.).

HERCEGOVAČKI TJEDNIK. An independent popular Croat weekly in Herzegovina (q.v.) published from 1990 to 1992. It was a democratic voice that contributed to the opening of the society in the immediate post-Communist period.

HERZEG OR HERCEG STIPAN VUKČIĆ KOSAČA (ca 1404-1466). He was not only the most powerful nobleman in the Bosnian kingdom toward the end of its existence (1463), but practically an independent ruler of the lands today known as Herzegovina (q.v.) or Herzeg's lands.

Stipan's family roots go to Vuk Kosača, a nobleman who had possessions in the Podrinje (q.v.) (upper Drina) region. Vuk's descendants, who ruled the lands later known as Herzegovina till falling to the Turks in 1482, were known as the Kosačas. Vuk had two sons, Vlatko Vuković and Hran Vuković. While Vlatko did not have sons, his brother Hran had three: Sandalj, Vuk, and Vukac. They were known as Hranići-Kosača. Sandalj became the grand duke and, after the death of Hrvoje Vukčić Hrvatinić (1416) (q.v.), the most powerful feudal lord in the Bosnian kingdom. Although married twice, he did not have offspring of his own. Sandalj was, therefore, succeeded by his brother Vukac's son, Stipan Vukčić.

After succeeding his powerful uncle Sandalj Hranić (1435), the ruler in the region of present-day Herzegovina, Stipan proceeded to expand his possessions even further and to assert his feudal power. Relying on the Turks and even becoming their vassal, he acquired the lands of the neighboring feudal lords to the east and to the west of his inheritance, rebuffed the authority of the Bosnian king Stipan Tomaš (q.v.) who was also his son-in-law, repelled the attempts of the Hungarian-

Croat king to make him a vassal, and attempted to undermine the economic power of the republic of Dubrovnik.

Stipan's ambitions and impetuous lifestyle and rule earned him many enemies. A three-year war (1451-1454) erupted between him and the republic of Dubrovnik. The Bosnian king, his son-in-law, Stipan Tomaš, and even his oldest son, Vladislav, turned against him during this three-year war.

To emphasize his noble powers and political independence and ambitions, Stipan assumed (1448) the title of Herzeg (from German Herzog - grand duke). Some believe that he obtained the title from the Holy Roman emperor Frederick III, others that he assumed the title on his own. His domain became gradually identified with the title of Herzeg, and thus it became known as Herzegovina - Herzog's land.

After the fall of the Bosnian kingdom to the Ottomans in 1463, Herzeg Stipan and his sons regained the southern parts of the land. Because of dissensions between the Herzeg and his sons, Venetian interference, and overwhelming Ottoman power, the Turks took most of his land in 1465. After Herzeg Stipan's death in 1466, his son Vlatko continued to defend the remnants of his inheritance, but in 1482 Herzeg's last stronghold (Novi) fell to the Turks.

Herzeg Stipan's family life was as turbulent as his politics. He was married to Jelena from the neighboring Balšić family in Zeta (Montenegro). Three children were born from this marriage: Katarina (married Bosnian king Stipan Tomaš [q.v.] in 1446), Vladislav, and Vlatko. His wife left him, and the oldest son turned against him because the Herzeg openly took a young and beautiful Florentine woman as his mistress. The reconciliation of the family, however, took place in 1453, shortly before Jelena died. From his second marriage to Barbara, Herzeg had two children, Mara and Stipan. The second wife, however, died a day after giving birth to her son in 1459. With his third wife, Cecilija, whom he married in 1460, he did not have children.

The oldest brother, Vladislav, escaped (1469) to northern Croatia (Slavonia) where the Hungarian-Croatian king Mathias granted him two towns as feudal possessions. The second brother, Vlatko, accepted the Ottoman suzerainty (1469) in return for keeping four towns. In 1474, Vlatko tried again to solicit help from the West, but all his efforts proved to be futile. The fate of the Balkans (q.v.) was in the hands of the Ottomans. The last of Vlatko's strongholds (Novi) fell in 1482, and he found refuge on the Croatian island of Rab.

The Herzeg's youngest son, Stipan, born from the second marriage, was given as a hostage (1469) to the Ottomans by his brother Vlatko. He remained with the Turks for the rest of his life. After accepting Islam (q.v.), his name was changed to Ahmet. He rapidly climbed the ladder of success in imperial military bureaucracy. His wife was the daughter of Sultan Bayezit II. He was governor (*beylerbey*) of Anatolia and three times grand vezir before he died in 1516.

Herzeg Stipan was a follower and protector of the local Bosnian Church (q.v.). Many adherents of this church, believed to be a heretical sect, were persecuted in Bosnia yet found refuge in his domain. It seems that religious dogmas and religious differences were not too important to Herzeg Stipan, and perhaps not to most of the ruling elite in the country. There are strong indications, however, that the Herzeg did express "oral subordination" to the pope and that he embraced Catholicism in 1447.

HERZEGOVINA OR HERCEGOVINA. A geopolitical entity in the southeastern part of Bosnia-Herzegovina. It comprises close to 10,000 sq km (3,860 sq mi) of mostly rocky terrain and makes up about one-fifth of the entire country. In the east, it borders with Montenegro, and in the south-southwest, its neighbor is Croatia. In 1718, the republic of Dubrovnik gave to the Ottomans two exits to the Adriatic Sea: Neum-Klek at the north of its territory, and Sutorina at the south, at the entrance to the Bay of Kotor. By creating an Ottoman-controlled buffer zone, Dubrovnik wanted to protect its territories from Venetian aggression. For this reason, Herzegovina once had two exits to the Adriatic Sea. After the

Second World War, however, the southern exit was taken by the republic of Montenegro, while the exit at Neum-Klek was retained. The valley of the Neretva River is the main artery that connects Herzegovina with the rest of the country to the north and through Croatia to the Adriatic Sea in the south. Its main administrative, economic, and cultural city is Mostar (q.v.). Before the 1992 war, the region had about half a million inhabitants of mixed religious and ethnic background. Its western parts are populated mostly by Croats (q.v.), while the eastern areas are more ethnically mixed, but dominated by the Serbs and Muslims (qq.v.).

The traditional "dualistic" nature of Bosnia and Herzegovina, even in its name, is the result of geography and long historical processes. The mountain range in the middle of the country has been a natural divide between Bosnia, which is facing the north, and Herzegovina, oriented toward the southwest. Political developments also helped to sharpen the sense of separate Bosnian and Herzegovinian regions.

The roots of political Herzegovinian autonomy go back to the time of the first Bosnian king Tvrtko I (1353-1391) (q.v.). After his leading nobleman and military leader, Vlatko Vuković-Kosača, defeated the Turkish army near Bileća in 1388, Tvrtko sent him, as a commander of a large military contingent, to help Prince Lazar of Serbia in the battle of Kosovo (1389). As a reward for his military successes and efforts, the king granted Vuković the land of what is today the eastern part of Herzegovina (Zahumlje) (qq.v.), and neighboring parts of Montenegro and Serbia.

Vlatko's nephew and successor, Sandalj Hranić Kosača (1392-1435), expanded his inheritance by obliterating (1404) an old ruling family in the region (Sanković) and by stifling the power of other neighboring feudal lords. His possessions stretched from the river Lim in present-day Sandžak (q.v.) in the east to the Cetina River in Croatia to the west, and from the county of Rama in the north to the town of Kotor in the south. After the death of the grand duke Hrvoje Vukčić

Hrvatinić (1416) (q.v.), Sandalj became the most important feudal lord in the Bosnian kingdom.

Because Sandalj did not have male children, he was succeeded by his nephew Stipan Vukčić Kosača (1435-1466). He expanded his inheritance even further, asserted his independence from the Bosnia king, and, in 1448, he received from the Holy Roman emperor Frederick III (or some say assumed on his own) the title of Herzeg (q.v.). His territory became known as Herzegovina or the Herzeg's land. The earliest known written record that mentions Herzegovina as a geographic term comes form a Turkish military leader Isa-bey Ishaković who in his letter dating from 1454 or 1455 mentioned the "Herzeg's land."

The Herzeg's land resisted Turkish occupation for about 20 years after the fall of Bosnia. But Herzeg Stipan died in 1466 and his last stronghold (Novi or Herceg Novi) fell to the Turks in 1482.

The Ottoman administration reinforced the Herzegovinian regional name and singularity by creating a separate military district (*sandžak*) in Herzegovina (1470), and, in the first half of the 19th century (1833-1866), Herzegovina was a separate Ottoman province (*elayet*). Distinct political, religious, and other administrative structures during and after the Ottoman period have strengthened the geographic and historical divisions between Bosnia and Herzegovina so that even the name of the country reflects the existing dualistic dynamics between the two regions.

HOLBROOKE, RICHARD C. (1941-). Former assistant secretary of state for European and Canadian affairs from August 1994 to the end of February 1996. He served as a foreign service officer in the 1960s. During the 1970s, he became managing editor of *Foreign Policy* magazine and a contributing editor to *Newsweek*. He was appointed assistant secretary of state for East Asian and Pacific affairs by President Jimmy Carter. In the 1980s he went back to private life, but he joined the

Clinton administration and became U.S. ambassador to Germany before becoming assistant secretary.

Holbrooke played a major role in bringing about peace in Bosnia and Herzegovina. After the tragic death of Robert Frasure and two other American diplomats in August 1995 near Sarajevo (q.v.), he became the key U.S. peacemaking envoy to the former Yugoslavia (q.v.). Holbrooke became the prime mover of the peace process and the architect of the Dayton peace accord (q.v.) signed by the Bosniac, Croat, and Serb leaders on November 21, 1995.

HRUSTOVAČA. A cave two kilometers (1.2 mi) long, located 12 km (7.5 mi) from Sanski Most. Its ornaments and stone formations make it a beautiful natural phenomenon.

HRVATSKA RIJEČ/CROATIAN WORD. A Croat weekly in Sarajevo (q.v.). Its publication began in 1994.

HRVATSKI LIST. A Croatian weekly launched in Mostar (q.v.) in May 1993. It was a continuation of *Vrisak*, a local Široki Brijeg paper. *Hrvatski list* was owned by the Croat Republic of Herceg-Bosna (q.v.) and it served as the main hard-line propaganda tool. It ceased publication in 1995.

HRVATSKO VIJEĆE OBRANE (HVO). *See* CROAT DEFENSE COUNCIL.

HUM or ZAHUMLJE. A separate medieval geopolitical unit that probably emerged sometime in the eighth or ninth century in the region of present-day southeastern Herzegovina (q.v.). Its confines were approximately from the hills behind the city of Dubrovnik, including the Pelješac peninsula in the south to the Mount Vranica and land on both sides of the middle and upper flow of the river Neretva in the north; from a line somewhere between the towns of Trebinje and Popovo Polje in the east to the river Neretva in the west. Two towns were the main centers of the region: Blagaj, near the sources of the river Buna, and Hum, about 3.2 km (2 mi) southwest of present-day Mostar (q.v.). People in Dubrovnik called the region Zahumlje or the "land behind the hills." But the people living in the region called it Hum.

From the eighth century, when Hum and other neighboring territories belonged to the southern or "Red Croatia," to the beginning of the 14th century, this region exchanged hands often. The rulers of Croatia, Dioclea, Byzantium, Bulgaria, and Serbia one time or another extended their overlordship over Zahumlje. It was probably in 1322 when Bosnian *ban* Stipan II Kotromanić (qq.v.) incorporated most of Zahumlje into his realm. At the end of the 14th century, this territory came into the possession of the Kosača family and became the core of what later was known as Herzegovina.

HUMAČKA PLOČA/THE HUMAC TABLET. The oldest remnant of medieval writing in Bosnia-Herzegovina. It dates from the 10th or 11th century and is written in a mixture of Cyrillic and Glagolitic scripts (qq.v.). The Tablet was found in the village of Humac near the town of Ljubuški in Herzegovina (q.v.).

-I-

ILIDŽA. A suburb of Sarajevo (q.v.) known for its beauty and sulphurous healing waters. This biggest spa in Bosnia and Herzegovina is also the recreation center of the city of Sarajevo.

In Roman times, this was an administrative and resort center. Excavated Roman ruins testify that Ilidža was an important and prosperous colony. The natural healing powers of the Ilidža waters may also have been used by nearby settlements in the Middle Ages. It was under the Austro-Hungarian occupation, however, that Ilidža was reconstructed. Hotels, restaurants, and a park, including a beautiful three-kilometer-long alley connecting Ilidža with the source of the river Bosna (q.v.), were constructed at the time.

The spa, the spring of the river Bosna at the foot of Igman Mountain, old trees, and lush lawns make Ilidža a beautiful site.

ILLYRIAN MOVEMENT. Croatian national movement in the 19th century that stood for Slavic unity. The leaders of the movement advocated the adoption of the Illyrian name as a common identity of all South Slavs, including the Bulgarians. It began as a cultural program, but it turned into a political party. The Vienna regime saw it as a threat to the unity of the Habsburg Empire and banned the use of the Illyrian name in 1843. The movement was a prototype of Yugoslavism that emerged in the second half of the century. Illyrianism had a few fervent supporters among Croats (q.v.) in Bosnia and Herzegovina, mostly among the Franciscans (q.v.).

ILLYRIANS. Indo-European tribes found in the Balkan region from Greece to Slovenia. It is believed that "the formation of historical Illyrian peoples" took place around 1000 BC. Illyrian tribes formed their own political and territorial organizations and even a powerful Illyrian state emerged in the third century BC. However, after a long and fierce resistance (229 BC to AD 9), the Illyrians were conquered by the Romans who established the province of Illyricum on the eastern shores of the Adriatic Sea. Present-day Albanians are descendants of an ancient Illyrian tribe. In modern history, the Illyrian name was revived by Napoleon. After he gained Slovenia and the southern half of Croatia from Austria, he unified these lands into a single administrative unit (1809-1813) of the Illyrian Provinces.

IMPLEMENTATION FORCE (IFOR). An international NATO-led 60,000-member peace implementation force in Bosnia and Herzegovina. According to the Dayton peace accord (q.v.), initialed on November 21, 1995, by the presidents of Bosnia-Herzegovina, Croatia, and Serbia, large and heavily armed NATO-led troops were to be deployed in Bosnia and Herzegovina to supervise the implementation of the cease-fire agreement. This became the largest deployment of NATO forces, outside of its member states, in the history of the alliance.

The entire peacekeeping operation includes approximately 75,000 troops, out of which 60,000 are in Bosnia and 15,000 in neighboring countries. Although the bulk of the IFOR comes from NATO countries, over 30 countries, including Russia, have sent their military contingencies to this international operation. Those in Bosnia are authorized to take all necessary actions in order to maintain the cease-fire and protect themselves. The first contingent of NATO troops arrived in Bosnia on December 4, 1995, to make preparations for the deployment of the rest of the IFOR troops that were to arrive in January and February of 1996.

Bosnia and Herzegovina is divided into three sectors, each led by one of the main troop contributors. The United States, the largest contributor (20,000 troops) to the IFOR mission, is patrolling northeastern Bosnia, and its troops are based in the town of Tuzla (q.v.). The French forces (7,500 troops), that served as UN peacekeepers, remained in Bosnia and monitor the Sarajevo (q.v.) region and the southeastern part of the country. The British (13,000 troops), are policing the northwestern regions from their main base in Šipovo and command headquarters in Banja Luka (q.v.). The first commander of the IFOR was U.S. admiral Leighton Smith (q.v.), the former commander of NATO forces in southern Europe. Some of the countries that participate in the IFOR are:

In Bosnia and Herzegovina	
Austria	300
Belgium	400
Britain	13,000
Canada	1,000
Czech Rep.	1,000
Denmark	807
Egypt	635
Finland	450

France	7,500
Greece	300
Italy	3,200
Jordan	50
Luxembourg	20
Malaysia	1,533
Morocco	1,200
Netherlands	2,200
Norway	1,050
Pakistan	3,000
Poland	700
Portugal	911
Russia	1,700
Spain	1,750
Sweden	872
Turkey	1,600
Ukraine	500
United States	20,000
Outside Bosnia	
France	4,500
Germany	4,000
Greece	700
Hungary	419
Norway	50
Slovakia	200

In December 1996, the Implementation Force was converted into a 31,000-member "Stabilization Force" to prevent a renewal of fighting and offer limited civilian support in Bosnia and Herzegovina.

INDEPENDENT STATE OF CROATIA/NEZAVISNA DRŽAVA HRVATSKA (NDH). The NDH was proclaimed on April 10, 1941, after the collapse of royalist Yugoslavia (q.v.) under German and Italian assault. The new state, which also included Bosnia and Herzegovina, was established under the protection of the Axis powers. While the southern regions of the country were under Italian occupation, the rest of the country was under German "protection."

There were three main political factions among the Croats (q.v.) at the time: the nationalist forces, led by the *ustaša* (q.v.) revolutionary organization, which welcomed the opportunity to establish a Croat state and assume power; the Croatian Peasant Party (q.v.), supported by the majority of the Croatians before the war, which attempted to pursue a policy of noninvolvement; and the left-oriented groups, including segments of the Peasant Party, which joined the resistance movement led by the Communists.

While the *ustaša* rulers persecuted the Serbs, Jews (qq.v.), and the Croat Left, the Serbian *četniks* (q.v.) terrorized the Croatian and Muslim population in the regions they controlled, and also cooperated with the occupiers. The Communist-led partisans (Croats, Serbs, Muslims (qq.v.), and others) fought against the NDH and the *četniks*, and also engaged in terror of their own during and after the war. The NDH collapsed in May 1945.

INTERNATIONAL CONFERENCE ON FORMER YUGOSLAVIA (ICFY). Established in August of 1992 as a successor to the European Community Conference on Yugoslavia. After the UN secretary-general accused EC negotiators of making agreements on behalf of the UN without discussing them with him, the EC and UN established a common conference to deal with the urgent issues in the former Yugoslavia. The ICFY's initial meeting took place in London on August 26, 1992. Chairman of the European Community Conference, Lord Carrington (q.v.), resigned and Lord Owen (q.v.), a former British foreign secretary, became EC's special envoy and a co-chair of the ICFY. The UN secretary-general's special envoy and a co-Chair of the Conference was Cyrus Vance (q.v.), former U.S. secretary of state. The London meeting was hailed as a big success, mainly because the Serbian side agreed to notify the UN of all heavy weapons and their positions within 96 hours and place the weapons under UN supervision within seven days. The promises, however, turned out to be a farce like many others before and after that. The ICFY was also often called the Geneva Peace Conference because after its first session in London, its permanent place was in Geneva, Switzerland.

The ICFY had six Working Groups: Bosnia and Herzegovina; Humanitarian Issues; Ethnic and National Communities; Succession Issues; Economic Issues; and Confidence, Security-Building, and Verification Measures.

The most important efforts of the Conference were to find a suitable settlement in order to end the war in Bosnia and Herzegovina. A peace plan, known as the Vance-Owen plan, devised under the leadership of a Finnish diplomat, Marrti Ahtissari, proposed the division of Bosnia and Herzegovina into 10 semiautonomous regions. After Cyrus Vance resigned (April 1993) and a Norwegian diplomat, Thorvald Stoltenberg, became the UN envoy and a co-chair of the Conference, another similar peace plan was concocted by the ICFY. Both plans were tantamount to rewarding Serbian aggression and dividing Bosnia along ethnic lines.

INTERNATIONAL WAR CRIMES TRIBUNAL FOR THE FORMER YUGOSLAVIA. An international court established on February 22, 1993, by the United Nations Security Council (Resolution 808), under the 1949 Geneva Convention, to look into crimes against humanity and genocide committed in Bosnia-Herzegovina and Croatia since June 1991. This is the first war crimes tribunal since the Nüremberg and Tokyo trials after World War II. The Tribunal is located in The Hague, the Netherlands. Judge Richard J. Goldstone of South Africa was named by the UNSC as the chief prosecutor on July 8, 1994. By the end of June 1996, 76 people were indicted by the Tribunal.

The indictments and the indictees were: *November 4, 1994*, connected with the events in the Sušica camp in Bosnia-Herzegovina - Dragan Nikolić. *February 13, 1995*, Omarska camp: Željko Meakić, Miroslav Kvočka, Dragoljub Prcać,

Mladen Radić, Milojica Kos, Momčilo Gruban, Zdravko Govedarica, ? Gruban, Predrag Kostić, Nedeljko Pasaplj, Milan Pavlić, Milutin Popović, Željko Savić, Mirko Babić, Nikica Janjić, Dušan Knežević, Dragomir Šaponja, and Zoran Žigić. Duško Tadić and Goran Borovica were also indicted on the same day. *July 21, 1995*, linked with the Keraterm camp (q.v.): Duško Sikirica, Damir Došen, Dragan Fuštar, Dragan Kulundžija, Nenad Banović, Predrag Banović, Goran Lajić, Dragan Kondić, Nikica Janjić, Dušan Knežević, Dragomir Šaponja, Zoran Žigić, and Nedjeljko Timarac. On the same day, the following men were indicted for the crimes in the Bosanski Šamac camp: Slobodan Miljković, Blagoje Simić, Milan Simić, Miroslav Tadić, Stevan Todorović, and Simo Zarić, and also Goran Jelišić and Ranko Cesić for crimes in the Brčko (q.v.) camp. *July 25, 1995*, Milan Martić was indicted regarding the war crimes in Croatia. Radovan Karadžić and Ratko Mladić (qq.v.) were indicted on the same day because of their role in the war in Bosnia and Herzegovina. All of the above are of Serb nationality. *August 29, 1995*, Ivica Rajić, a Croat, was indicted concerning the events in central Bosnia. *November 7, 1995*, Mile Mrkšić, Miroslav Radić, and Veselin Sljivančanin, members of the Serb armed forces, were indicted for crimes in Vukovar, Croatia. *November 10, 1995*, Croat officials, Dario Kordić, Tihomil Blaškić, Mario Čerkez, Ivan Šantić, Pero Skopljak, and Zlatko Aleksovski were indicted dealing with the Lašva Valley events. Because of the massacres that followed the fall of Srebrenica (q.v.), Serbian leaders Radovan Karadžić and Ratko Mladić were indicted again on *November 16, 1995*. Đorđe Đukić, a Serb officer, was indicted on *February 29, 1996*. The case was discontinued because of the death of the accused. Dealing with the events in the Čelebići camp, three Bosnian Muslims, Zejnil Delalić, Hazim Delić, and Esad Landžo, and one Croat, Zdravko Mucić, were indicted on *March 3, 1996*. Dražen Erdemović was indicted on *May 29, 1996*. Dragan Gagović, Gojko Janković, Janko Janjić, Radomir Kovač, Zoran Vuković, Dragan Zelenović, Dragoljub

Kunarac, and Radovan Stanković were indicted on *June 26, 1996*, for Serb crimes in the Foča region.

Judge Goldstone's tenure expired on October 1, 1996, and he was replaced by Madam Justice Louise Arbour, a member of the Court of Appeals from Ontario, Canada.

ISLAM IN BOSNIA-HERZEGOVINA. The Muslims of Bosnia and Herzegovina, besides the Albanians, are the largest homogeneous Muslim community in Europe. The Sunni (traditional) variant of Islam came to this part of Europe with the Ottoman invasion of the Balkans (q.v.) in the 15th century. Although there are a number of controversies regarding the history of Bosnia and Bosnian Muslims (q.v.), most scholars agree that the appearance of Islam in the country predates the fall of the Bosnian kingdom (1463). The first foothold of Islam in Bosnia was in the region of present-day Sarajevo (q.v.), where the Ottomans established a frontier military post a few years before the fall of Bosnia. Furthermore, there is common consensus that the overwhelming majority of Bosnian Muslims are descendants of the local medieval population that converted to Islam.

A certain number of Muslims from present-day Bosnia-Herzegovina migrated into Croatia and Hungary during the Ottoman expansion into those areas. At the end of the 17th century, however, when the Ottoman Empire lost those lands to the Habsburgs and Venice, most of the Muslim population migrated back to the Ottoman-controlled Bosnia. Also, many Muslims found refuge in Bosnia-Herzegovina during the liberation of Serbia in the 19th century. On the other hand, major Muslim migrations from Bosnia-Herzegovina took place after the Austrian occupation (1878), after both world wars, and during the most recent war. According to the 1991 census, Muslims made up 43 percent of the total population in the country.

Bosnian Muslims did not have a separate religious hierarchy while under the Ottomans. In 1882, the first local *reis ul-ulema* (head of the religious community), and a four-man council of advisors (*medžlis*) were appointed by the Habsburg emperor. It was only in 1909, however, that Muslims in Bosnia-Herzegovina took full control over their own matters concerning religion and education (q.v.). Although the community directly or indirectly elected its leadership, the emperor in Vienna still had input in choosing the *reis ul-ulema*, who also had to receive the approval from the *Sheih-ul-Islam* in Istanbul to perform his duties.

In the first Yugoslavia (q.v.), there were two separate Muslim religious communities from 1918 to 1930. Muslims in Bosnia-Herzegovina, Croatia, and Slovenia made up one and Muslims in Serbia, Kosovo, Macedonia, and Montenegro belong to the other. In 1930, the two were unified and regional divisions (*muftistva*) were abolished. Till 1936, the seat of the *reis ul-ulema* was in Belgrade and then it was transferred to Sarajevo.

During Socialist Yugoslavia, there were four regional ruling assemblies (*sabors*): Sarajevo, Priština, Skolje, and Titograd. The Supreme Council was the highest organ that united the regional councils, and the *reis ul-ulema* was the head of the Muslim religious community for the entire country.

Today, however, the Muslims of Bosnia-Herzegovina have their separate religious administrative structures. The country is divided into seven regions (*muftistva*). The decision-making power is invested in the governing assembly *(sabor)*. The *Ri'aset* is the Executive Committee elected by the *sabor*. And the highest religious authority is invested in the *reis ul-ulema*, who resides in Sarajevo.

IZETBEGOVIĆ, ALIJA (1925-). First president of the Republic of Bosnia-Herzegovina. He was born in Bosanski Šamac. At the beginning of World War II, a young Izetbegović became an active member of a newly founded group named the Young Muslims (q.v.). Because he was among the leading members of the group who tried to revitalize the movement after the war, Izetbegović was accused of "activities against the people" and sentenced (1946) to three years of imprisonment by the

Communist regime. After serving the jail term, he finished his university studies in agronomy and law at Sarajevo University. He became a legal advisor to the PUT enterprise and a director of a building company in Sarajevo (q.v.).

Izetbegović's religious, intellectual, and political activities got him in trouble with the regime again in the early 1970s. In 1970, his treatise, known as the *Islamic Declaration*, became public. Although in it he called for a general Islamic renewal, without even mentioning Yugoslavia (q.v.) specifically, he and his supporters were accused of reviving the Young Muslims organization and of a "conspiracy" to set up an "ethnically pure" Islamic republic of Bosnia-Herzegovina. In 1983, Izetbegović was tried again, with 11 other Bosnian Muslims (q.v.), and sentenced to 14 years of prison. Out of that, he served five years.

In the post-Communist era, Izetbegović with his ethno/religious-oriented friends formed the Party of Democratic Action (SDA) (q.v.) and he became the leader of the Bosnian Muslims. After his party won the majority of votes in the first multiparty elections (Nov. 1990), he became a member of the presidency of Bosnia and Herzegovina, and in December 1990 was elected the president of the seven-member multiethnic state presidency. Besides the *Islamic Declaration*, he has written several texts dealing with Islam. In 1993, he received the King Faisal's Award for service to Islam.

In the September 1996 elections, Izetbegović received an overwhelming vote of confidence from the Bosniac (q.v) electorate for the presidency of the Republic of Bosnia and Herzegovina, but he narrowly defeated the Serbian presidential candidate for the two-year chairmanship of the presidency.

IZRAZ/EXPRESSION. A Sarajevo (q.v.) monthly journal for literary and art criticism. Its publication began in 1957 and ceased in 1991.

-J-

JABLANICA LAKE/JABLANIČKO JEZERO. This lake was created in 1955 to power hydroelectric generators located on the Neretva River near the town of Jablanica, on the road between Sarajevo and Mostar (qq.v.). The lake is about 30 km (18.5 mi) long, 2.5 km (1.6 mi) wide, and 70 m (230 ft) deep. It has become an attractive excursion spot and tourist attraction. South of it begins the awe-inspiring Neretva canyon.

JAVNOST/POPULACE. Newspaper published by Bosnian Serbs (q.v.) since 1990. It became a major propaganda tool in preparations for the war against the non-Serbs in the country. After the start of the war (April 1992), its publication was moved to Pale (q.v.), the Bosnian Serb stronghold near Sarajevo (q.v.).

JEWS IN BOSNIA-HERZEGOVINA. Although probably a small number of Jews lived in present-day Bosnia-Herzegovina from Roman times, their number increased significantly as a result of two immigration waves, first from Spain at the end of the 15th century and, second, from various parts of the Habsburg monarchy after Bosnia and Herzegovina came under Austro-Hungarian rule in 1878.

Many of the Jews expelled from Spain found refuge in the Ottoman Empire and some of those established themselves in Sarajevo (q.v.). The small number of Jews that already lived there were easily absorbed by the better-educated and highly cultured Sephardic Jews arriving from Spain. The first Sarajevo Jewish community was established in 1565 and it remained a closely knit religious and ethnic group throughout the century. Although they adapted to the new homeland and became a viable segment of the population at large, they retained their Spanish language (Ladino) and other customs they brought with them.

The second Jewish community emerged in Sarajevo after a new wave of immigrants came to Bosnia from various parts of

Austria-Hungary, especially from the Slavic speaking regions. Many Jews came to this former Ottoman province looking for an economic opportunity or as Austro-Hungarian state employees. The new immigrants were better educated and more progressive Ashkenazic Jews. They established a separate community of their own in Sarajevo in 1879 and, a few years later, in Tuzla and Banja Luka (qq.v.). Because of the political, economic, and social changes in Bosnia, and also because of the newly arrived, more vibrant Jews from Central Europe, the old Sephardic Bosnian community was awakened from its conservatism and Orientalism, and the differences between the two groups began slowly to blur. After the creation of the Kingdom of the Serbs, Croats, and Slovenes in 1918 (known as Yugoslavia after 1929) (q.v.), a number of Jews from Serbia also moved to Sarajevo and other Bosnian towns.

Statistics indicate that on the eve of World War II, there were 11,800 Jews in Bosnia-Herzegovina and after the war only about 1,300. While some escaped the persecutions, most members of the Jewish community became victims of the Nazis and their local collaborators. Although the number of Jews began to increase after the war, many migrated to the newly established Israeli state in 1948. Before the 1992 war, there were approximately 3,000 Jews in Bosnia and Herzegovina. Most of them, however, have left the country as a result of the war. Those few that are still in Bosnia are organized in a single commune that numbers less than 500 members in Sarajevo, and a small number reside in other towns in Bosnia and Herzegovina.

JNA/JUGOSLAVENSKA NARODNA ARMIJA. *See* YUGOSLAV PEOPLE'S ARMY.

JOVIĆ, MIRKO. Leader of the Serbian People Renewal Party (Srpska Narodna Obnova-SNO), one of the most radical Serbian nationalist organizations in the post-Communist era. His paramilitary force, White Eagles (Beli orlovi), was one of the most brutal instruments of ethnic cleansing (q.v.) during the war in Croatia and Bosnia.

-K-

KÁLLAY, BENJÁMIN (1839-1903). A Hungarian nobleman and a common minister of finance in the Austro-Hungarian Empire, and ex officio responsible for imperial policies in Bosnia-Herzegovina from 1882 to 1903. Before becoming minister of finance, he served in Belgrade for seven years in the Austrian foreign service. He learned the Serbian language, wrote a history of the Serbs (q.v.), and was considered a specialist on the Balkans (q.v.).

Although Kállay was instrumental in bringing about a number of progressive changes in the country, he became best known for trying to protect Bosnia-Herzegovina from Serb and Croat nationalism and for promoting a separate Bosniac nationhood among the three main religious (Muslim, Orthodox, and Catholic) groups in the province. His efforts, however, did not bring about the desired results.

KAPETANOVIĆ, IZUDIN (1953-). Named prime minister of the Federation of Bosnia and Herzegovina (q.v.) at the end of January 1996. Bosniac by nationality. Born in Tuzla (q.v.) and finished higher education in electrotechnology. Because the powers of the Republic of Bosnia and Herzegovina have not been transferred to the Federation, as agreed in the Dayton peace accord (q.v.) at the end of 1995, the office of prime minister of the Federation remains fictional.

KARAĐORĐEVIĆ, ALEKSANDAR (1888-1934). A member of the Karađorđević dynasty in Serbia and the ruler of the Kingdom of Serbs, Croats, and Slovenes (q.v.) (1918-1934). After a period of quasi-parliamentary politics, King Aleksandar abolished the Constitution, banned political parties, divided the country into new administrative districts, changed the name of the country to Yugoslavia (q.v.), and declared a personal dictatorship on January 6, 1929.

The new administrative borders greatly hindered the unity of Bosnia and Herzegovina. Turbulent nationalist tensions marked the political life in the country during his reign. The assassination of Croatian deputies in Belgrade's parliament by a Serb deputy in June 1928 led to radicalization of the political life in the country. As a result, Aleksandar was assassinated by Croatian and Macedonian nationalists in Marseilles, France, in 1934.

KARADŽIĆ, RADOVAN (1945-). Political leader of the Bosnian Serbs (q.v.) from 1992 to 1996. By implementing the will and nationalist program of Slobodan Milošević (q.v.), president of Serbia, he emerged from obscurity and stepped to the forefront of the nationalist Serbian movement in Bosnia-Herzegovina in post-Communist Yugoslavia (q.v.).

Karadžić was born in the village of Petnjica, county of Šavnik in Montenegro. He came to Sarajevo (q.v.) to study medicine (psychiatry), specializing in neurosis and depression. He also spent a year (1974-75) at Columbia University, New York City, as a graduate student. After finishing his studies, he, his wife Ljiljana (also a psychiatrist), son, and daughter remained in Bosnia. He worked in the state hospital system, with Unis Corporation, and was also a psychiatrist to the Sarajevo soccer team. He served a prison term in the former Yugoslavia for embezzlement. Karadžić is also a published poet. In 1993, he received the highest awards for poetry in his native Montenegro. However, the honors did not reflect his literary achievements but rather the regime's appreciation of what he had done for the "Serbian cause" in Bosnia-Herzegovina.

Karadžić was a cofounder of the country's Serbian Democratic Party (SDS) (q.v.) in 1990 and he became the leader of the self-proclaimed Serb Republic of Bosnia-Herzegovina (q.v.). In 1992, he led the Bosnian Serb rebellion against the legitimate government in Sarajevo in order to break up the country and to unite the Serb Republic with Serbia and Montenegro. Because of his leading role in implementing the policy of ethnic cleansing (q.v.) and genocide of the non-Serbs in Bosnia, he was indicted by the UN-sponsored International War Crimes Tribunal (q.v.) in The Hague on July 25, 1995, and again on November 16, 1995.

Through significant American pressure on Serbia and its leader Slobodan Milošević, Karadžić was forced to resign the office of president of the Serb Republic in August 1996 and to remove himself from the political scene in the country. His influences among Bosnian Serbs, however, remain strong.

KERATERM. A concentration camp near the town of Prijedor. It remained open from May 1992 till November 1995. It is estimated that about 40,000 people passed through it. From May 30 to June 4, 1992, about 1,000 civilians were killed in the camp, and on July 27, 1992, in Pavilion III, 1,200 non-Serbs, mostly Muslims (q.v.), were killed. The camp was especially reactivated after the Serb, began to lose territory in Croatia and Bosnia-Herzegovina in the summer of 1995. The commander of the camp in 1995 was Slobodan Vlačina, and his two brothers, Ninoslav and Ranko, were his assistants.

KIKANOVIĆ, MIRSAD (1954-). Appointed minister of finance of the Republic of Bosnia and Herzegovina in January 1996. Served in the administration of the regional government of the Tuzla (q.v.) canton. Bosniac nationality. He has finished higher education in economics.

KINGDOM OF SERBS, CROATS, AND SLOVENES. *See* YUGOSLAVIA.

KISELJAK. A Croat town 34 km (21 mil) from Sarajevo (q.v.) on the road to Jajce. It has been known for its mineral waters since the 15th century. Its bitter-salty water is being used as a remedy for numerous health problems (diabetes, gout, urinary diathesis, etc.). The Kiseljak natural mineral water is being sold in many places as a health remedy. The area is inhabited by the Croats (q.v.). During the last war it became major profiteering center.

KLJUČ. A town 220 m (720 ft) above sea level in western Bosnia. It had over 40,000 inhabitants before the last war. Its old fortress was one of the strongest medieval Bosnian bastions. The region around the town was known as Donji Kraji (q.v.) before the Ottoman invasion. The last Bosnian king, Stipan Tomašević (q.v.), was captured by the Turks there and killed in Jajce in 1463. At the time of Austrian occupation (1878) a strong resistance to the Habsburg armies was put up by Bosnian Muslims (q.v.) in the region of Ključ.

KLJUIĆ, STJEPAN (1939-). Former member of the seven-member state presidency of Bosnia-Herzegovina. Born in Sarajevo (q.v.) and a journalist by profession. In 1971, he was dismissed from his job at the leading Sarajevo daily *Oslobođenje* because the regime suspected him of antistate activities. From that time till 1990 he was a Sarajevo correspondent to the Zagreb (Croatia) daily *Vjesnik*. In 1990, Kljuić became the leader of the most popular Croatian party in Bosnia-Herzegovina, the Croatian Democratic Union (q.v.) and a member of the presidency. However, because of his disagreement with the policies of Croatia's president Franjo Tudjman toward Bosnia-Herzegovina, Kljuić was removed in November 1992 from his party position and also from the presidency. But while his split from the party was permanent, he was reinstated to the presidency a year later. Kljuić's support for the preservation of the state of Bosnia-Herzegovina was unwavering and he was an advocate of Muslim-Croat cooperation. In June 1994, Kljuić founded a Republican party (q.v.) which was not based on ethnic or confessional support but sought to attract membership from various segments of society in Bosnia. It remains, however, a minor political formation. During the September 1996 elections, the Republicans were part of a five-party United List BiH coalition.

KOČIĆ, PETAR (1877-1916). A leading Serbian writer in Bosnia during the Austrian period. He was born in the village of Stričići near Banja Luka (q.v.). Already during the years of his secondary education in Sarajevo (q.v.), he was in trouble with the Austrian regime because of his Serbian nationalism. After being expelled from school, he went to Belgrade where he finished high school. However, he returned to the Habsburg Empire and studied at the University of Vienna. He was a political activist all of his life and editor of several newspapers. In 1910, Kočić was elected to the Bosnian parliament and became the leader of the nationalist opposition.

Storytelling and drama were Kočić's main literary forms. In them, he describes the life of his native region and the life of the Serb peasantry in Bosnia under Austrian rule. All of his works reflect his political and social beliefs and nationalist emotions, many times in satirical form.

KOLJEVIĆ, NIKOLA (1936-1997). Former chair at the English department at Sarajevo University and vice president of the Serb Republic (q.v.) of Bosnia and Herzegovina from 1992 to 1997. Koljević was born in Banja Luka (q.v.). Finished higher education at the University of Belgrade. From 1960 to 1962 he worked at *Glas* (q.v.) enterprise in Banja Luka, then moved to Sarajevo where he worked at the Svjetlost publishing house. From 1965 to 1990, he taught philology at the University of Sarajevo.

Koljević emerged as a leading figure in the Serbian Democratic Party (SDS) (q.v.) in Bosnia after the first multiparty elections at the end of 1990 and became a member of the Bosnian multiethnic presidency. However, he resigned the post in April 1992 and became vice president of the self-declared independent Serb Republic. He was thought to be a moderate nationalist but he remained "Karadžić's (q.v.) intellectual shadow" and supportive of the most radical policies till the end of the war. Moreover, it was Koljević who originally called upon the Yugoslav People's Army (JNA) (q.v.)

to "protect Serbs" (q.v.) in Bosnia in April of 1992. After shooting himself in the head, he died in January 1997.

KOMŠIĆ, IVO (1948 -). A Croat member of the presidency of Bosnia-Herzegovina till the 1996 elections. Born in the town of Kiseljak (q.v.) and finished law school in Sarajevo (q.v.). Once an official in the Socialist Republic of Bosnia and Herzegovina, professor at Sarajevo University, became a vice president of the Party of Democratic Reform, former Communist Party, in March 1991. He split with the reformists and cofounded the Croatian Peasant Party (q.v.) of Bosnia-Herzegovina (1993) and was its president till October 1995. He stood for the integrity of the Bosnian state and cooperation between the Muslims and Croats (qq.v.) in their defense against Serbian aggression.

In the September 1996 elections, Komšić ran among the Croats as a candidate of the United List BiH coalition for the presidency of Bosnia and Herzegovina. He received only about 10 percent of the Croat vote.

KOS/KONTRA OBAVJEŠTAJNA SLUŽBA/COUNTER-INTELLIGENCE SERVICE. KOS was the main intelligence service of the Yugoslav People's Army (JNA)(q.v.) and the most powerful guardian of Socialist Yugoslavia and its communist regime. Its significance came to prominence in the mid-1960s when KOS discovered that the country's main internal security agency, UDBA (Uprava Državne Bezbjednosti/Directorate of State Security) and its head, vice president Aleksandar Ranković, had been spying on Tito (q.v.) himself. KOS was the main instrument in Tito's handling of all nationalist and liberal forces in the country, especially in the brutal crash of the Croatian Spring in December of 1971. After Tito's death, KOS's loyalty was shifting more and more toward the advocates of Serbian centralism and, by the end of the 1980s, KOS's leadership was closely tied to Serbian president Slobodan Milošević and his aggressive Serbian nationalism. It was no accident that Col. Gen. Marko

Negovanović, the head of KOS before the 1991 war, was made Serbia's defense minister.

The network of the KOS members was a major problem for the Croats and Muslims (qq.v.) in their struggle against the Serbs (q.v.) and the JNA, especially at the beginning of the last war.

KOSAČA, KATARINA (1424-1478). Daughter of Stipan Vukčić Kosača, better known as Herzeg Stipan (q.v.), and Jelena Balšić, whose noble family ruled in neighboring Zeta (Montenegro). Because her father adhered to the Bosnian Church (q.v.), she was probably raised as a Bosnian *kr'stjan.* But sometime before her marriage to Bosnian king Stipan Tomaš (q.v.) (1446) at the age of 22 she became not only legally but genuinely a Catholic. Her support of the Catholic Church (q.v.), especially of the Franciscan order, in Bosnia, was well known. She even became a member of the order herself.

Katarina and King Stipan Tomaš had two children, Sigismund and Katarina. After the death of King Tomaš (1461), the new king, her stepson Stipan Tomašević (q.v.), treated her and her children well. Even her rebellious father, who had been in a constant struggle with her husband, made peace with the new king.

Because of the swift Turkish invasion of Bosnia (1463) and the confusion that followed, she had to flee the country. After an arduous trip from Bosnia, she found refuge in the city of Dubrovnik, but her two children were not so fortunate. They were captured by the Turks.

She was received politely by Dubrovnik's commercial aristocracy, but her presence was a liability to the city that was trying to live in peace with the Turks. For that reason and hoping to solicit help for the liberation of her country, she moved to Rome. The queen and members of her court were well received by the church authority. Her hopes, however, that the pope might help liberate Bosnia soon dissipated. She was treated royally and supported monetarily, but nothing more tangible was undertaken on behalf of her country.

The queen's captive children were another painful concern. All her efforts to ransom them from the Turks failed. Moreover, both of them converted to Islam (q.v.), so her son Sigismund and also her younger half-brother Stipan were lost to the Bosnian cause. They entered the Ottoman service and became high officials in the empire. Sigismund, renamed Ishak, became a *sandžak* bey, but the fate of her daughter was unknown.

Before Queen Katarina died on October 25, 1478, she bequeathed the kingdom of Bosnia to the Holy See. She was buried in the church of the Franciscan *Aracoeli* monastery in Rome. In popular stories among the Bosnian Croatians Queen Katarina remains in high esteem as a saintly woman and a patron of the common folk.

KOTROMANIĆI. A ruling dynasty in medieval Bosnia. The beginnings of the family ascendance are not clear. They are mentioned for the first time in documents of the city of Dubrovnik at the beginning of the 14th century, but it is likely the family was already well established in the country. It is believed that Stipan Prijezda the Great (1254-1287) was the first Kotromanić. His mother was the daughter of the Croatian nobleman Kotroman, and Stipan probably assumed the nickname *Kotroman* after his mother's ancestry. His successors were known as the Kotromanići, or sons of Kotroman.

KRAJINA/FRONTIER or BORDER LAND. When the Croatian noble family Nelipići separated the Zahumlje (q.v.) region from Croatia at the end of the 12th century, the region between the river Cetina and the river Neretva became known as Krajina or Frontier. The territory, except for the town of Omiš, came under the rule of Bosnian *ban* Stipan II Kotromanić (qq.v.) in 1324. A few years later, however, *ban* Tvrtko (q.v.) had to relinquish Krajina (and Zahumlje) back to the ruler of Croatia (1357). In 1390, however, Tvrtko gained Krajina again. The region came into the possession of the powerful feudal family

Kosača and became a part of the autonomous domain of Herzeg Stipan Vukčić Kosača (q.v.). This region fell to the Ottomans in (1498). Parts of present-day western Herzegovina (q.v.) belonged to the medieval Krajina district.

KRAJIŠNIK, MOMČILO (1944-). A leading member of the Serbian Democratic Party (q.v.) and former president of the Assembly of Bosnia and Herzegovina. After the creation of the self-proclaimed independent Serb Republic (q.v.) in Bosnia, he was elected president of its assembly and became one of the principal figures among the separatist Serbs (q.v.) in Bosnia. He rejected the Dayton peace accord (q.v.) and urged the Serbs to leave Sarajevo (q.v.) rather than to live under the Muslim-led government.

After Radovan Karadžić (q.v.), as an indicted war criminal, was forced from the office of the president of the Serb Republic by international pressure in August 1996 and banned from political life in Bosnia and Herzegovina, Krajišnik was selected by the Serb Democratic Party (q.v.) leadership to be its candidate for the three-man presidency of Bosnia and Herzegovina. Although he was unexpectedly challenged by Milošević's (q.v.) Socialist Party candidate, Krajišnik achieved an easy victory and became one of the three members of Bosnia's presidency.

KRANJČEVIĆ, SILVIJE STRAHIMIR (1865-1908). A leading Croat writer in Bosnia at the end of the last century. Born in Senj (Croatia), where he finished his primary and secondary education. He began theological studies in Rome, but soon he returned to Zagreb where he finished the teachers' college. From 1886 till his death, Kranjčević taught elementary education in various towns in Bosnia and Herzegovina, Mostar (q.v.), Livno, Bijeljina, and Sarajevo (q.v.). Throughout his adult life, he was in constant struggle with various economic, political, and health predicaments.

Kranjčević is perhaps the most significant poet of the last century, not only in Bosnia and Herzegovina but also in

Croatian literature (q.v.). His literary debut began during his high school days. Although many of his poems are inspired by the Croatian patriotism of the day, he successfully lifts himself to a level of universal themes of life struggles, doubts, alienation, and human idealism versus social conventions and injustices. His poems and reflections cut, like a blade, into the question of the meaning of human existence. Among Kranjčević's best-known poems are "Narodu," "Hrvatskoj majci," "Moj dom," "Radniku," "Iza spuštenih trepavica," "In tyrannos," "Povijesti sud," "Mojsije," and "Zadnji Adam."

Kranjčević was also the editor of the literary journal *Nada* (1895-1903), probably the best literary publication in Bosnia and Herzegovina at the time. It reflected the contemporary European literary movement of modernism. Kranjčević died in Sarajevo, leaving an enormous literary treasure.

KRESO, ENVER (1946-). Became minister of energy, mining, and industry of the Federation of Bosnia and Herzegovina (q.v.) in January 1996. Bosniac by nationality. Born in Mostar (q.v.) and finished higher education in electrotechnology.

KULENOVIĆ, DŽAFER-BEG (1891-1956). A leading Bosnian Muslim (q.v.) politician between the two world wars and during World War II. He was born near Kulen-Vakuf. He received his secondary education in Sarajevo, Tuzla, and Mostar (qq.v.). He finished his law studies in Vienna and Zagreb. Kulenović was of Croatian national orientation from his youth till his death. In 1919, he became a member and in 1939 president of the Yugoslav Muslim Organization. Kulenović was also a representative in the Belgrade parliament and a leading voice against Serbian unitarism. After the collapse of the First Yugoslavia in April 1941, he became Deputy Prime Minister in the Independent State of Croatia (q.v.). In 1945, he emigrated to the West and ended up in Syria, where he lived till the end of his life. His son Nahid was murdered for political reasons by Yugoslav secret agents in Germany in 1969.

KULIN. *Ban* (viceroy) (q.v.) of Bosnia (ca. 1164-ca. 1204). Kulin probably became *ban* of Bosnia in 1164, after *ban* Borić (qq.v.) was removed from power by the Hungarian-Croatian king. Soon, however, Bosnia and *ban* Kulin came under Byzantine suzerainty. In 1180, Kulin freed his land from the Byzantine lordship and with the Hungarian-Croatian king Béla III invaded Byzantium as far as the city of Sofia in Bulgaria. Kulin successfully used the conflict between the two competing regional powers, Byzantium and Hungary, and advanced his autonomy, expanded the original Bosnian territory to the north (Usora, Soli, and Lower Regions [qq.v.]) and to the south (region around Neretva River). Although he nominally recognized the sovereignty of Hungarian kings over Bosnia, he laid the foundations for the future Bosnian statehood. Attributes and titles used by the pope and others to praise him suggest that he was a powerful nobleman and a generous ruler. Legends glorifying him and his "good times" remain in the memory of Bosnian people today.

The first allegation that an unorthodox Christian teaching was present in Bosnia appeared during Kulin's rule. Dioclean (approximately the present-day Montenegro) ruler Vukan in his letter (1199) to Pope Innocent III accused Kulin himself and his family of adhering to a Manichean-like heresy. In all likelihood, Vukan had an ulterior (political) reason for such accusations because there is no reason to believe that Kulin was anything but faithful to Rome. To ease the pope's concerns and to prevent a possible crusade against Bosnia by Hungarian rulers eager to control Bosnia, Kulin sent a delegation to Rome and invited the pope to send a legate to Bosnia to investigate the matter. Kulin's embassy to the pope cleared the issues in Rome. Also, the political and religious leaders met with the pope's legate in 1203 at Bilino Polje, near Zenica (q.v.). All heterodox practices were renounced and the orthodox Catholic teaching was reaffirmed by the assembly. These wise moves by *ban* Kulin averted a major political crisis and a direct clash with the pope and the Hungarian king, who was not pleased with Bosnia's assertion of autonomy.

KURTOVIĆ, TODO (1919-). One of the leading political personalities in post-World War II Bosnia-Herzegovina and Yugoslavia (q.v.). Born in Trebinje. A member of the Communist Party from 1941 and a participant in the partisan movement during World War II. Kurtović finished the "Higher Political School" in Belgrade and held various high positions in the Party, the republic of Bosnia-Herzegovina, and in Yugoslavia after 1945. He lives in Sarajevo.

KUSTURICA, EMIR (1955-). A world-renowned filmmaker. Born in Sarajevo (q.v.). After finishing higher education in his native city, he graduated from the famed film academy in Prague (Filmová a televizní fakulteta Akademie múzickỳch uměni/FAMU), where he absorbed the Czech humanistic film tradition along with various Western influences. The first part of his career includes two locally produced feature films and various television productions. Kusturica's real debut was the release of *Do You Remember Dolly Bell?* in 1981, which he directed. This love story won him the Golden Lion Award in the first film category at the Venice Festival. His next film, *When Father Was Away on Business* (1985), a political scene in 1950s Yugoslavia (q.v.) from the perspective of a young boy, brought to Kusturica the Golden Palm, the International Critics Prize at Cannes, and a nomination for an Academy Award as Best Foreign Language Film. His third feature, *Time of the Gypsies* (1989), exploring the exploitation of gypsy children smuggled from Yugoslavia to the West to beg and steal for their masters, earned Kusturica the Best Director Prize at Cannes and the Roberto Rossellini Career Achievement Award in Rome. In 1992, he released *American Dreaming*. His latest production, *Underground*, has brought Kusturica a major controversy. Half of the film was shot in Serbia from June 1994 to January 1995, with the help of Serbian movie studios and money, which was against the international embargo imposed on Serbia by the UN. More important, however, the film reflects Serbian nationalist propaganda against its neighbors and the West. The artistic side of the film reflects its cheap propagandistic character. From the beginning of the 1992-1995 war in Bosnia, Kusturica did not hide his pro-Serb sympathies, and for that reason he is not well thought of in his native city at the present time.

-L-

LANGUAGE. In the former multinational Yugoslavia (q.v.) language was much more than a means of communication. It touched the core of intranational relations. The country had three official languages: Macedonian, Slovene, and "Croato-Serbian" or "Serbo-Croatian." The Serbian and Croatian languages were "united" for political and ideological reasons in 1954. Because the Croats (q.v.) considered the unification to be a form of Serbian imperialism, they persisted in keeping Croatian as a separate language. In Bosnia and Herzegovina, where Muslims, Serbs (qq.v.), and Croats lived, Serbian language influences were significant and the use of both alphabets, Latin and Serbian Cyrillic (q.v.), was enforced in schools and official media.

At the present, there is no single official language in Bosnia-Herzegovina. The Serbs use Serbian, the Croats Croatian, and the Muslims, in their desire to assert their newly discovered Bosniac nationality, have inaugurated the Bosniac language; there are clear signs that they would like to impose their idiom as the official language in the country.

LITERATURE. The oldest remnant of medieval writing in Bosnia and Herzegovina dates from the 10th or 11th century (Humačka ploča/The Humac Tablet) (q.v.) and the earliest known codices go back to the 12th century. These treasures are linked to an earlier Latin and even Greek literary heritage that is found in the region. Initially, the manuscripts were written in Glagolitic (q.v.) and later in Bosnian Cyrillic script (*bosančica*) (qq.v.), and most of them were in the *ikavian* dialect of the Croatian language. Besides religious texts and regal documents, a few writings of a secular nature were also written in medieval Bosnia, like genealogies, chronicles, and even a variant of a story about Alexander the Great (*Aleksandrida*). The epigraphic writing, however, has a special place in the cultural heritage of Bosnia and Herzegovina. Most such inscriptions are found on numerous stećci (q.v.), unique tombstones found in Bosnia-Herzegovina, the neighboring southern regions of Croatia, and parts of Montenegro and Serbia that used to be under Bosnian rulers. Many of these writings express much more than the usual data about the deceased and have a literary value of their own.

The medieval writing in Bosnia, as in other European lands, is closely linked to the needs of the church and most of the texts are religious in nature. Among the best-known codices are Miroslav's gospel (12^{th}c.), Batal's gospel (14th c.) Srećković's gospel (15^{th}c.), Hval's collection (1404), and, the most beautiful codex, the Missal of Duke Hrvoje Vukčić Hrvatinić (1404) (q.v.). *How Satan Created the World* and *Apocalypse of the Bosnian Christians* are among the best-known works of the medieval dualist Christian sect in Bosnia.

With the fall of the Bosnian kingdom and the coming of the Ottomans, major cultural and religious shifts took place. The Islamic civilization that the Ottomans brought to the region took root and thrived. The importance of the Bosnian dualist church declined and it slowly faded away. The Catholic Church (q.v.), revitalized by the Franciscans (q.v.) toward the end of Bosnian independence, spun into major decline under the Islamic dominion. Furthermore, Orthodox Christianity began to spread in the country. During the Ottoman period (1463-1878), literary activities in Bosnia split in three main directions, corresponding to the three major religious communities: Muslim, Catholic, and Orthodox.

A number of educated Muslims (q.v.) from Bosnia and Herzegovina wrote in Oriental languages (Persian, Arabic, and Turkish) and made a major contribution to the literature and general growth of knowledge in the Ottoman Empire. The Persian language was used mostly for poetic expression, Arabic for religious texts, law, and scholarly commentaries, and

Turkish for a variety of other needs. Numerous native sons gave their literary contribution in Oriental languages. Some of them became well-known copiers and commentators of old texts.

The second type of literary expression that evolved among the Bosnian Muslims (q.v.) was the so-called *aljamiado* literature. The expression comes from the Spanish *alhamia* (from Arabic *al-'agamiya*) meaning non-Arabic, foreign. In literature, it denotes texts in non-Arabic languages written in Arabic script.

This type of literary writing, especially poetry, was very common among the literate Muslims of Bosnia and Herzegovina. Many religious, didactic, satiric, and love songs, as well as prayers, sayings, and even a dictionary in poetic style were written in the native language and in Arabic letters. This literary form provided the writers with a useful combination through which they could verbalize the riches of their indigenous culture but still remain a part of a wider Islamic civilization. The oldest known aljamiado text in Bosnia dates from 1588 (*Hirvat türkisi* — Croatian song by a man named Mehmed). Aljamiado literature increased in the later Ottoman centuries as the writings of the Bosnian Muslims in Persian, Arabic, and Turkish diminished. This form of artistic expression was most popular in the 19th and into the 20th century. Among the best-known names of aljamiado literature in Bosnia and Herzegovina are Muhamed Hevaji Uskufi and Hasan Kaimi (17th c.), Mula Mustafa Bašeskija, Kadija Hasan, Mehmed Razija, Šefkija, Illhamia (18th c.), poetess Umihana Čuvidina, Arif Sarajlija, Jusufbeg Čengić, Rizabeg Kapetanović, Ahmed Karahodža, Omer Humo (19th c.), and Alija Sadiković at the beginning of twentieth century.

In the middle of the nineteenth century, however, as a result of the Ottoman reforms, a new cultural life began to emerge among the Muslims of Bosnia and Herzegovina. It was during the rule of the progressive governorship of Topal Šerif Osman-pasha (1860-1869) that a first printing press began to operate in Sarajevo (q.v.) which in turn stimulated literary activities among the Muslims and members of the other two religious communities. Western influences in education (q.v.) and literature began to penetrate a very traditional Bosnian society. During the Ottoman rule in Bosnia, the Serbian Orthodox monasteries were not significant literary centers. The low level of the monks' education prevented them from making a serious cultural contribution. Besides some copying of church books, they wrote a few chronologies and hagiographic works. These works were written in Russo-Serbian-church language and Cyrillic alphabet (q.v.).

As a result of their national awakening, however, in the first half of the 19th century, Bosnian Serbs (q.v.) came in closer touch with the Serbian cultural activities in the Habsburg Empire and in Serbia. Under such influences, the local Serbs began to collect and publish folk literature. But under the influence of the Serbian language reformer and national ideologist, Vuk Karadžić, all such works were declared Serbian regardless of their ethnic origin. In 1849, he published an article ("Serbs All and Everywhere") in which he claimed that all people of Bosnia-Herzegovina and most of Croatia were Serbs. Besides some journalistic and polemical writing, most of the Serbian literary activities of the last century, therefore, centered around the collection of folk wisdom.

While the early Bosnian Muslim literature evolved under the umbrella of Islamic civilization, Serbian under Byzantine-Russian influence, Croatian literature was tied to the Western intellectual and spiritual tradition. The beginnings of Croatian literary activities under the Turkish rule are closely tied to the Franciscans and their book publishing for religious needs: theological and liturgical manuals, catechisms and simple religious texts for the common people, and translations of some Catholic authors in the West. Besides the religious texts, chronologies, school textbooks, and books with simple medical advice were written. Furthermore, the first attempts to synthesize Bosnian history were made by the Franciscans.

Among the more significant contributors to the Croatian literacy in Bosnia from the Turkish period were Matija

Divković and Stipan Matijević (16th - 17th centuries); Stjepan Margitić, Lovro Šitović, Nikola Lašvanin, Filip Laštrić, Beno Benić (18th c.); Ivan F. Jukić, Petar Bakula, and Grga Martić (q.v.) in the nineteenth century.

The Franciscans were writing in the Croatian language and in a style understandable to the simple folk. As such, they had an important influence on the linguistic development and popular literature among the Croatians in the later centuries. Their early works were printed in the Bosnian Cyrillic (*bosančica*), while by the first half of the 18th century the Latin script prevailed among the Croats (q.v.) in Bosnia.

Besides literary expressions in the native language, there were a number of Catholic Croatian writers from Bosnia who wrote in Latin. One such author was Juraj Dragišić (ca 1450-1520). He was a well-known Franciscan humanist and university professor. The Latinist tradition among the Bosnian Franciscans continued into the 19th century. They published works on subjects such as theology, philosophy, linguistics, poetry, and medicine.

Because the Franciscans considered education essential to the national revival of the last century, a number of them became very active in organizing schools and in publishing. One such enthusiast was Fr. Ivan F. Jukić who published in 1850 the first modern journal in Bosnia and Herzegovina *(Bosnian Friend)*. Toward the end of the nineteenth century, as a result of previous educational efforts, lay people began to join the literary circles.

Besides the three major ethno/religious literatures, the Jewish community (q.v.), although small in number, had a literary input in Bosnia and Herzegovina. It started with the coming of the Sephardic Jews to Bosnia at the beginning of the 16th century. Their writings before the Austrian occupation of the country (1878) deal mainly with religious education, chronicles, epigraphic inscriptions, and, later on, lyric poetry. But while Jewish life in Bosnia and Herzegovina remained relatively quiet during those centuries, one of their members, Nehemija Hija Hajon, stands out. He was the passionate missionary of a cabalistic heresy and published several religious works in the West at the end of the 17th and beginning of the 18th century. Furthermore, one of the most important Jewish cultural, religious, and literary treasures is preserved in Bosnia. That is the Sarajevo *Hagada* (q.v.), a religious manuscript with rich illustrations that originated in Spain.

Only after a rabbinical school was established in Sarajevo at the end of the 18th century did Jewish literary activities lift to higher artistic levels. Besides the Hebrew language, Jewish literature was also orally transmitted and written in Ladino (Sephardic Jews) idiom.

The Austrian period (1878-1918), besides the political changes, saw major shifts in cultural activities in Bosnia and Herzegovina among all of the ethno/religious groups. Although the new cultural processes were not of the same intensity among the Muslims, Orthodox, or Catholics, these changes did push literary activities out of the religious realm and into the secular domain in all three communities. Serb opposition to Vienna and closer ties with Serbia increased. Croats strove for closer links to cultural activities in Croatia. Both Serb and Croat literatures became a vehicle for reaffirmation of nationalist feelings and political activism. Among the Muslims, although their literary activities increased, there was confusion regarding their cultural and national affiliation. The old Ottoman pride and tradition were fading away, and the new sense of identity had not yet been formed.

Benevolent and cultural societies among the three communities were established at the beginning of this century. They helped to nurture young literary talents. At the same time, the proliferation of newspapers and literary journals took place in the country. As a result, the literary activities in Bosnia-Herzegovina began to catch up with modern trends. Among the Bosnian Serb writers of the time, the best-known names were Aleksa Šantić (q.v.), Jovan Dučić, Petar Kočić (q.v.), Sima Milutinović-Sarajlija, and Svetozar Ćorović. They were gathered around the publications of *Bosanska Vila* in

Sarajevo and *Zora* in Mostar (q.v). Among the Muslims, Mehmend-beg Kapetanović-Ljubušak was the first to write in Bosnian language and Latin script. He was an advocate of the Bosniac identity. Others were Safvet-beg Bašagić, Musa Ćazim Ćatić, Osman Nuri Hadžić, Edhem Mulabdić (qq.v.)(these considered themselves as Croatians), and Osman Đikić (he identified with the Serbs). Leading publications among the Muslims were *Behar*, *Biser*, and *Muslimanska biblioteka*. Among the Croatian Catholic writers were Grga Martić, Ivan A. Milićević, Tugomir Alaupović, Mirko Jurkić, Petar Bakula, Ivan Zovko, and the best-known Silvije S. Kranjčević (q.v.). Their publications were *Hercegovački bosiljak*, *Glas Hercegovaca*, *Novi prijatelj Bosne*, *Osvit*, and, the most important literary publication, Kranjčević's *Nada*.

The best-known names among the modern Muslim writers are Ahmed Muradbegović, Enver Čolaković, Hasan Kikić, Alija Nametak (q.v.), Hamza Humo, Skender Kulenović, Midhat Begić, Derviš Sušić, Nedžad Ibrišimović, Alija Isaković, Izet Sarajlić, Abdulah Sidran, Feđa Šehović, and Alan Horić, who lives in Canada. Meša Selimović and Mak Dizdar (qq.v.) stand out among the best writers in the literature of Bosnia and Herzegovina. Čolaković, Kikić, and Nametak were the pioneers of modern literary expression in Bosnia and Herzegovina. Begić's critical comparisons of Bosnia-Herzegovina poets are specially valuable and, as a leading literary critic and theorist, he became well respected in European circles. Selimović became especially known for incorporating Bosnian Islamic tradition and the Koran in his writings. His works deal with the relationship between the rulers and the ruled in which the individual is always the victim. Dizdar, through his works, entered the world of medieval Bosnia by utilizing the inspiring literary and philosophical inscriptions from the ancient tombstones in the country. On the other hand, Sarajlić in his poems (many dedicated to the "heroes of socialist labor") glorified the former Communist regime and Leninist totalitarianism. Although being of Muslim religion or of Islamic cultural background,

Alija Nametak and Mak Dizdar considered themselves Croats, and Meša Selimović declared himself to be of Serb nationality.

Among the Serbs, Branko Ćopić, Mladen Oljača, Marko Marković, Vojislav Lumbarda, Mirko Kovač, Vuk Krnjević, Petar Zubac, Duško Trifunović, Dara Sekulić, Rajko Nogo, and Nenad Radanović are the best-known literary names. The works of Ćopić and Oljača are known for their servitude to the ideals of "socialist realism." Both writers remained faithful to the Communist regime. Kovač, on the other hand, in his works resisted the ideas of socialist revolution as well as Serbian nationalism. Reacting to the Serb aggression in Croatia (1991) and Bosnia-Herzegovina (1992), he went so far as to declare himself a Croat writer.

Among the Croats, Antun. B. Šimić (q.v.), Stanislav Šimić, Jaksa Kušan, Novak Simić (q.v.), Nikola Šop, Janko Bubalo, Lucijan Kordić, Vitomir Lukić, Andjelko Vuletić, Veselko Koroman, Ivan Loverenović, Vlado Pavlović, Gojko Sušac, Ićan Ramljak, Mirko Marijanović, Ivan Kordić, Krešimir Šego, Stojan Vučićević, Marijo Suško, and Nikola Martić stand out. The best-known Bosnian writer is Ivo Andrić (q.v), the 1961 Nobel Prize winner for literature, who is by birth a Croat, but did not consider himself, except in his younger years, a part of Croat literary circles. The poetry of A. B. Šimić represents a defiance of the traditional literary forms. Already as a young student he founded various publications in which he promoted contemporary European literary movements. In the post-World War II period, Bubalo destroyed all of his early works out of fear of the Communist regime. But after 1970, he became a leading poet of Catholic persuasion. Kordić spent five decades in the West, and became a leading Croat poet in exile. Stojan Vučićević, as a high school student, was condemned to three years in jail for his political views, and his works reflect his political stands. Ramnjak is a well-known author of children's books in which he incorporated Croatian village life and traditions.

The best-known modern Jewish writer in Bosnia is Isak Samokovlija (q.v.). His works reflect the life of the Sephardic

Jews, their efforts to preserve their cultural identity, and the challenges that people face in the universal struggle between good and evil.

LJILJAN. A leading Bosnian Muslim (Bosniac) (q.v.) nationalist weekly with a forceful Islamic orientation. With the support of Saudi Arabia, it began publication in Zagreb, Croatia, in 1992. Its attacks on Croatia and its leadership led to the ban of the paper in Croatia (1993). Since then it has been operating from Ljubljana, Slovenia. The Bosnian edition is printed in the town of Visoko. Although it claims to be independent, it is close to the Sarajevo government and the ruling (Muslim) Party of Democratic Action (SDA) (q.v.). Its editor, Džemaludin Latić, is also one of the leading ideologues of the SDA.

LJUBIĆ, BOŽO (1949-). Named minister of health of the Federation of Bosnia and Herzegovina (q.v.) in January 1996. Croat nationality. Born in Široki Brijeg and finished higher education in medicine.

LJUBIJA. A small mining town in northwestern Bosnia, near Prijedor. Although its mines were known from the times of the Romans, and the Saxon miners worked there in the Middle Ages, the first major explorations were made by the Austro-Hungarian mining experts before World War I. They found that the region abounded in a very rich iron ore. During the era of socialist Yugoslavia (q.v.), Ljubija became the largest mine of iron ore in the country.

Recently, the town came into prominence because its mine pits were used as mass graves for thousands of Muslims and Croats (qq.v.) who became victims of the Serbian ethnic cleansing (q.v.) campaign. During 1992, the mine pits were places of executions and burials, but as the Serbs (q.v.) began to lose territory in 1995, remains from other mass graves in western Bosnia were transferred to the Ljubija mines as hiding places, and attempts were made to erase the crime by destroying the remains. It is estimated that about 8,000 people have been disposed of in the Ljubija mines.

LJUBIJANKIĆ, IRFAN (1952-1995). Foreign minister of the Republic of Bosnia-Herzegovina. He was born in the town of Bihać (q.v.). After finishing medical studies in Belgrade in 1977, he worked in Africa and Zagreb, Croatia, and his native Bihać. In the first post-Communist elections, Ljubijankić was elected to the Sarajevo Parliament, became a leading member of the ruling Muslim political party (SDA [q.v.]), and was appointed president of the Bihać district (1991). In October 1993, he was named foreign minister, and on May 28, 1995, Ljubijankić was assassinated. The helicopter carrying him and his assistants was downed by the Serbs (q.v.).

LJUJIĆ MIJATOVIĆ, TATJANA (1941-). A Serb member of the seven-member state presidency of Bosnia-Herzegovina from 1992 to 1996. She was born in Sarajevo (q.v.). Mijatović finished her education in Sarajevo and Belgrade in natural environment and preservation. Besides her professional activities, she was a political activist during the Communist and post-Communist period in the country. Among other functions, she was delegate to the Assembly of the Republic of Bosnia-Herzegovina and president of the Association of Women during the Yugoslav period. She became a member of the state presidency of Bosnia-Herzegovina at the end of 1992. After the 1992 war began, she remained in the besieged Sarajevo, rejected the policies of the Serbian nationalist leadership, and supported the preservation of the state of Bosnia-Herzegovina. She is a member of the Serbian Civic Council in Sarajevo (qq.v.).

LOWER REGIONS. *See* DONJI KRAJI.

-M-

MACKENZIE, LEWIS (1940-). Canadian general and commanding officer of UN forces in Bosnia-Herzegovina (Sarajevo Sector) between June and September 1992. In June 1992, he opened the Sarajevo (q.v.) airport to relief flights and became an instant hero. The fame, however, lasted a short time because of his zealous insistence that all three sides in the Bosnian war were equally to blame.

After his removal from the Sarajevo post, he became an open advocate of pro-Serbian positions in Bosnia-Herzegovina. Some of his speaking engagements were sponsored by SerbNet, a Serb-American lobby group. His stand, in essence, was to let the "three serial killers" settle their own scores. But his military "realism" actually supported the Serbs (q.v.) because they had an overwhelming power superiority. He was accused by the Bosnian government of serious misconduct for participating in the alleged abuses of women while he was in Bosnia.

MacKenzie was born in Truro, Nova Scotia. He graduated from Xavier Junior College in 1960 and has a B.A. (1989) from the University of Manitoba. He served in the Queen's Own Rifles of Canada and as intelligence officer in Calgary and Germany. He served under the UN flag in several places around the world: Gaza Strip, Cyprus, Egypt, and Central America. MacKenzie attended Staff College in Kingston, NATO Defense College in Rome, and U.S. Army War College in Carlisle, PA, as an International Fellow.

MANDIĆ, DOMINIK (1889-1973). Franciscan priest and historian from Herzegovina (q.v.). He was born in the village of Lise (Široki Brijeg) near Mostar (q.v.). He received his higher education in Mostar and Fribourg, Switzerland, where he received a doctorate in theology. Mandić served in various important positions in his Franciscan order in Herzegovina and in Rome. In 1952, he came to the United States where he dedicated himself to studying the history of Bosnia and

Herzegovina. Mandić published numerous works on the subject, especially on the period of medieval Bosnia.

MARKOVIĆ, ANTE (1924-). Last prime minister of socialist Yugoslavia (q.v.) (1989-1991). Born in the town of Konjic in Herzegovina (q.v.) to a Croat family. Received higher education in Zagreb in electrical engineering. He served as an industrial manager and a member of the Economic Councils in the government of the Republic of Croatia and of Yugoslavia. He served as prime minister and president of the presidency of Croatia. When Marković took office as prime minister of Yugoslavia (March 1989) the country was in major economic, political, social, and ethnic turmoil. His radical reform proposals, well acclaimed and supported by the West, were the last attempt to prevent and correct instability in the country. He strove to steer the country to a free-market economy believing that a sound economy would keep the various peoples together. Although Yugoslavia had reached the point of no return by the beginning of 1990, Marković attempted to preserve the unity of the country by forming his own all-Yugoslav Reform Party, "an alliance of reformist forces to build a new and prosperous Yugoslavia," in the summer of 1990. But, instead of preserving the unity of the country, he presided over the first phase of the war of disintegration. It was on his watch that the Yugoslav People's Army (q.v.) began the attack on Slovenia in June of 1991.

MARTIĆ, GRGA (1822-1905). A distinguished Franciscan, poet, and cultural and political activist. Born in Rastovača near the town of Posušje, he received his education in Kreševo, Požega, Zagreb and Stolni Biograd (Székesfehérvár). Martić served as a parish priest, a lecturer at the Franciscan school in Kreševo, and as missionary in Bulgaria and Romania. In 1856 he became the representative of the Franciscan province for relations with the Turkish government and consular representatives in Sarajevo (q.v.). It was in this position that he became a spokesman, not only for the Catholics in Bosnia and

Herzegovina, but quite often for the Orthodox and local Muslim causes.

Martić not only promoted education (q.v.) and cultural activities, but also wrote a number of literary works himself in epic and lyric folk tradition. In his writings, he promoted freedom and liberation of the people of Bosnia and Herzegovina, whom he saw as part of a wider Slavic family. Initially, he was a supporter of Austrian rule, but soon after the occupation (1878) he became disappointed with the new regime and withdrew from political activities. At the end of his life, he dictated his memoirs, which were published after his death, and which give insight into his life, as well as the history of Bosnia and Herzegovina in the second half of the last century.

MEĐUGORJE. A village in Herzegovina (q.v.) that has become a famous Marian shrine since 1981. Six children (Vicka, Mirjana, Marija, Ivanka, Ivan, and Jakov) claimed that the Virgin Mary appeared to them on June 24, 1981. Daily visions continued in which Mary urged all humanity to conversion, prayer, love, and peace. As people began to flock to the hill of apparitions, the Communist regime at the time began to harass the visionaries, local Franciscan priests, and pilgrims. While the local bishop openly declared that nothing supernatural was taking place in Međugorje, the Vatican neither approved nor prohibited the pilgrimages to this place, which many believe to be holy. Millions of people from around the world have visited Međugorje since 1981 and are still gathering there in prayer. Many books have been written, and even a motion picture (*Gospa*) has been made about this extraordinary phenomenon in a small Herzegovinian village.

MEMIJA, MUFID. Named director-general of Radio-Television of Bosnia and Herzegovina (RTVBH) (q.v.) at the end of 1992. During the Communist era, Memija was a leading Sarajevo (q.v.) journalist and "a highly agile exponent of self-management socialism and the politics of non-alignment." But in the post-Communist period, he became a loyal champion of the official policy of the ruling Muslim party (SDA [q.v.]). Because of the political and pro-Muslim shifts at the RTVBH, about 60 staff members, mostly Croats and Serbs (qq.v.), left the organization at the beginning of 1993. The non-Muslims who remained at their posts became insignificant and their loyalty to multiethnic Bosnia was abused.

MERHAMET/MERCY. A Bosnian Muslim (q.v.) charitable organization. Although an independent society, it closely cooperates with other Muslim organizations in the country and in the world. Its role came to prominence especially during the 1992-1995 war. It helped to alleviate the suffering of thousands of Muslims (q.v.) caught up in the war tragedy.

MIJATOVIĆ, CVIJETIN (1913-). A leading political figure in Bosnia-Herzegovina and Yugoslavia (q.v.) after World War II. Born in Lopare, near Tuzla (q.v.), Mijatović was a Left activist in his youth and became a member of the Communist Party in 1933. In the 1930s, he was sent to Bosnia to spread Marxist propaganda and establish Communist cells. During World War II, Mijatović was an active organizer of the partisan movement and a political Commissar in his native region. After the war, he served in various high positions in Sarajevo (q.v.) and Belgrade. From 1958 to 1961, he was also the editor of *Komunist*, the official organ of the Communist Party of Yugoslavia and from 1961 to 1965 served as ambassador to the Soviet Union. After his return from Moscow, Mijatović held the highest political positions in Bosnia-Herzegovina.

MIKULIĆ, BRANKO (1928-1995). A Bosnian Croat politician born in Podgrađe near Gornji Vakuf. One of the leading Communist Party and republican functionaries in Bosnia and Herzegovina during the Titoist era. After serving in various local party positions in central Bosnia, he became a member of the Central Committee and also the secretary of the Executive Committee of the Communist Party of Bosnia-Herzegovina in the 1960s. Mikulić also served as president of the Executive Committee of the Assembly of the republic. In 1986, he became prime minster of Yugoslavia (q.v.). At that time, the country was going through rapidly growing economic hardships, including a galloping inflation and workers' unrest. His economic reforms, which included major austerity measures, were unsuccessful and unpopular. Inflation rose to 120 percent in 1987 and 250 percent in 1988, and the Yugoslav debt reached $33 billion. After a vote of nonconfidence in the Federal Assembly, on December 30, 1988, Mikulić was forced to resign.

MILOŠEVIĆ, SLOBODAN (1941-). President of Serbia and the leader of the Serbian nationalist forces. He was born in Požarevac, Serbia. His father was an Orthodox priest from Montenegro. His mother was a primary school teacher and a Communist activist. His parents divorced in his childhood, and, later both committed suicide. Milošević studied law at the University of Belgrade. He became a member of the Communist Party (League of Communists of Yugoslavia) and a political activist in 1959. As a party functionary and protégé of Serbia's Communist leader Ivan Stambolić, he successfully moved up through the party ranks. Milošević worked as an advisor on economic effairs to the mayor of Belgrade; deputy director and then director of Tehnogas; head of the Belgrade Information Service; president of Beogradska Udružena Banka (1978-83); and leader of the Belgrade League of Communists (1984-86). A clever manipulator who turned against his former patrons, he succeeded to become the president of the League of Communists of Serbia in 1986 and, at the time, he was considered to be a reliable party conservative. His wife, Mirjana Marković, a daughter of a well-known hard-line Communist official, is a professor of Marxist philosophy at the University of Belgrade and a strong political activist.

In 1987, Milošević began to emerge as a leading nationalist voice in Serbia. Harvesting the rise of Serbian nationalism and also stimulating it by promising to achieve the Serbian dream of a Greater Serbia, he solidified the control of the republic's Communist Party and of Serbia itself. In 1989, the Serbian parliament elected Milošević president of the republic. In May 1990, he renamed the League of Communists of Serbia the Socialist Party of Serbia (SPS) and won the elections in December of the same year. Although most Serbs (q.v.) generally supported the idea of a Greater Serbia, Milošević became the most important factor in bringing about Serbian aggression on the neighboring republics and, consequently, the collapse of Yugoslavia (q.v.). As the man most responsible not only for the war in Slovenia, Croatia, and Bosnia-Herzegovina, but also for crimes against humanity committed by the Serb forces during the war, he was nicknamed the "Butcher of the Balkans" by Western media, and former U.S. secretary of state Lawrence S. Eagleburger listed him among the war criminals in December of 1992. Realizing that the Serb warmachine was losing steam, and trying to salvage at least some of the gains, Milošević turned to negotiations that led to the Dayton peace accord (q.v.) in November 1995.

MIRKO. An IFOR (q.v.) publication designed for the youth of Bosnia and Herzegovina. The name is a derivative of the word *mir*, which means peace. This monthly magazine is published in Latin and Cyrillic scripts. It contains articles on movies, music, fashion, and other themes of interest to young people. It began publication in the Spring of 1996.

MLADA BOSNA/YOUNG BOSNIA. A loosely organized revolutionary nationalist movement among school boys before World War I in Bosnia-Herzegovina. Most of its members were of Serbian ethnic origin and the organization was connected to two nationalist organizations in Serbia, Narodna obrana (People's Defense) and Ujedinjenje ili smrt (Unification or Death) — better known as the Black Hand. These two societies were the moving forces behind the Serbian agitation to unite all the Serbs (q.v.), especially those in Bosnia-Herzegovina, with Serbia. Thus, the Young Bosnia movement became an instrument, and also a loose cannon, of Serbian anti-Austrian and pro-Serbian activities, especially after the Austrian annexation of Bosnia in 1909. Its members were involved in several assassination attempts of Austrian officials, and some served as volunteers in the Serbian armed forces during the two Balkan wars (1912-1913) (q.v). But they are best known for the Sarajevo assassination (q.v.) of the archduke Franz Ferdinand, the heir apparent to the Habsburg throne on June 28, 1914. The event touched off World War I.

MLADIĆ, RATIMIR (RATKO) (1943-). Commander of the Serb secessionist armed forces in Bosnia-Herzegovina. Mladić was born in the village of Božinovići, near Kalinovik, 25 miles south of Sarajevo (q.v.). It was claimed that his father was killed by the Croat *ustaša* (q.v.) forces during the Second World War and, therefore, Mladić was avenging the loss of his father during the 1991-1995 war. In recent months, however, he has admitted that his father, as Tito's (q.v.) partisan, was killed by the Serbian *četniks* (q.v.) and not by the Croats (q.v.).

Mladić graduated from the Yugoslav military academy in Belgrade in 1965. In the same year Mladić became a member of the Communist Party. In 1991, after serving in Macedonia, he became a deputy commander of the Yugoslav military forces in the troubled region of Kosovo. In June of the same year, Mladić was transferred to Croatia, where the secessionist local Serbs (q.v.), the Yugoslav People's Army (q.v.), and paramilitary forces from Serbia began to clash with the Croatian people and government. While in Croatia, he proved himself to be loyal to the Serbian nationalist cause and thus rose to the rank of colonel. As a proven hard-liner, he was transferred to Bosnia-Herzegovina (May 1992) to take command of Bosnian Serb military operations and also was named a brigadier general. His regular armed forces were augmented by various Serbian regular and paramilitary groups from Serbia.

Mladić was close to Serbia's president Slobodan Milošević (q.v.) who paid his and his officers' salaries and provided him with military supplies. His relationship with his immediate political superiors, however, especially Radovan Karadžić (q.v.), became stormy in 1994. Mladić implemented the most brutal military tactics against non-Serbs during the 1992-1995 war. He became known for his tactics of encircling Bosnian cities and mercilessly shelling civilian objects and population. His command to "stretch the brains" of his enemies became well-known. Mladić's son is also pursuing a military career, while his daughter, who was a medical student in Belgrade, committed suicide during the Serb offensive against the Goražde "safe area" in March 1994. He was indicted by the International War Crimes Tribunal (q.v.) in The Hague on July 25, 1995, and again on November 16, 1995, for crimes against humanity, breaches of the Geneva convention, and genocide. As a result of the Dayton peace accord (q.v.) he was marginalized, but he would not give up his powers. On November 9, 1996, he and his entire general staff were officially fired by the new President of the Serb Republic in Bosnia, Biljana Plavšić (q.v.). She named an obscure officer, Gen. Pero Colić, as his successor. Finally, on November 27, 1996, Mladić announced he was stepping down, but by naming Gen. Manojlo Milovanović as his successor he provoked another confrontation with the political leadership in the Serb Republic.

MORANKIĆ, IBRAHIM (1948-). Named minister of environment development and ecology of the Federation of Bosnia and Herzegovina (q.v.) in January 1996. He is of Bosniac (q.v.) nationality, born in Tuzla (q.v.), and finished higher education in architecture.

MORILLON, PHILIPPE (1935-). French lieutenant general who served as the United Nations Protection Force (UNPROFOR) (q.v.) commander in Bosnia from December 1992 to July 1993.

Morillon came into prominence in March 1993 when he visited the besieged Muslim towns of Cerska, Konjević Polje, and Srebrenica (q.v.) in eastern Bosnia. After his visit to

Srebrenica, thousands of Muslim refugees prevented him from leaving the town. In solidarity with the besieged people, he declared that he would stay with them till UN help arrived.

By his efforts several hundred civilians, including about 100 wounded, were evacuated from the town, and he became an instant celebrity around the world. His celebrity status, however, did not last long. He, too, became a symbol of UN and Western indecisiveness in the Bosnian tragedy.

MOST/BRIDGE. A journal published in Mostar (q.v.) from 1976 to 1991 dealing with philosophical, social, and cultural issues. It also published literary contributions of various writers in the former Yugoslavia (q.v.) and translations of foreign authors.

MOSTAR. This attractive city is the main political, cultural, and economic center of Herzegovina (q.v.). It is located only 59 meters (193 ft) above sea level, surrounded by rocky mountains in the valley of the Neretva River, which flows through the town into the Adriatic Sea. In 1991, the population of the city was close to 76,000 and that of the Mostar county was over 126,000. Muslims made up 34.6 percent, Croats 34 percent, and Serbs 18.8 percent (qq.v.) of the population.

While most other towns in Herzegovina date from ancient times, the first indication that there was a settlement at the site of present-day Mostar comes from the mid-15th century. There are, however, strong indications that in Roman times, an early Christian diocese (Savsenterum) was located somewhere near the city. This suggests that this part of the Neretva valley was attractive to various settlers in the early times.

A document from 1452 says that two towers and a bridge hanging over the Neretva River existed where the Old Bridge (q.v.) was later built. Another source from two decades later (1474) tells us that the settlement around the hanging bridge was called Mostar. The name comes from the word *mostari*, meaning the "men who guard the bridge and collect the crossing toll."

The town, therefore, grew around a wooden bridge hanging on massive chains across the river with a watch tower on each of its sides. Being at an important trade and military location, the settlement slowly overshadowed the nearby town of Blagaj, which used to be the medieval capital of the Herzegovina region. One of the early sacral monuments of the town was a Franciscan monastery built in 1450 and demolished by the Ottomans in 1563.

At the beginning of the Turkish occupation, because the old wooden bridge was unstable and risky to cross, the town grew mostly on the eastern side of the river. A stone bridge built in 1566 (later known as the Old Bridge) permanently connected eastern and western Herzegovina, and the town of Mostar began to evolve into an important strategic base in the Ottoman Empire. Besides its military relevance, the city became the heart of commercial, political, and cultural life in Herzegovina.

Besides the famous Old Bridge, Mostar was enriched by superb Islamic architectural achievements. Among them are the Karađoz-Bey's Mosque, the Roznamejiya Mosque, the minaret of the Ćejvan-ćehaja's Mosque, the Koski Mehmet Pasha's Mosque, and a number of other religious or secular objects dating from the 16th and 17th centuries. During the Ottoman centuries, many scholars and writers (who were highly esteemed in the Islamic world) came from this town. Among them were Mustafa Ejubović - Shejh Jujo (1650-1707), Dervish Pasha Bajezidagić (1566-1603), Husami Husejn Čatrnja (middle of 17th century), Ahmed Mostarac (first half of the 18th century), and others.

In modern times, Mostar also gave rise to many poets, writers, singers, and artists. At the end of the last and the beginning of this century, Mostar was a very active cultural center in Bosnia and Herzegovina. It was also a hotbed of Muslim, Serbian, and Croatian national activism.

The beauty of Mostar is expressed in the synthesis of various civilizations and cultures. Its old nucleus (Kujundžiluk — the Coppersmith's Bazaar) and many mosques reflect a rich

Ottoman and Islamic past. A short distance away, one finds examples of Austrian and typical Western architecture left from the Habsburg and interwar era. Socialist-style structures, industrial plants in the vicinity, and newly grown neighborhoods witness to the recent past. Its mosques and Christian churches were clear manifestations of the religious mix of its population. It seemed that the single span of the Old Bridge joined the Oriental, Mediterranean, and Central European heritage into a single monument to all those who left a mark in this historic and charming city.

Unfortunately, however, the war that began in the spring of 1992 has brought tremendous destruction and a great loss of human life. At first, Serbian forces occupied the city. Then the Croat Defense Council liberated it in May 1992. By the end of the year, however, the two victims of the war, Bosnian Muslims and Croats (qq.v.), began to fight each other and some of the most brutal fighting of the conflict took place in Mostar. The city itself became divided into zones: the eastern part was controlled by the Muslims and the western by the Croats. Even the ancient link between the two parts of the town, the Old Bridge, became a casualty of the war. The Croat forces destroyed it on November 9, 1993. Only after the Washington Agreement (March 1994) between the Croats and the Bosnian Muslims did a slow reconciliation of the two sides begin. To mediate between the two communities and help rebuild of the city infrastructure, the European Union took the responsibility of administrating the city. Its efforts, however, were not very successful. Even after the election of a common city administration in June of 1996, the city practically remains divided into two ethnic communities.

MOSTARIENSIA. A scholarly journal in humanistic sciences published by the University of Mostar (q.v.) since 1994. Its contributors are mostly professors at that university.

MUJAHEDEENS/HOLY WAR WARRIORS. A number of Mujahedeens came to Bosnia from the Middle East (Afghans,

Turks, Syrians, and others) to fight the *jihad* (holy war) against the Orthodox Serbs and the Catholic Croats (qq.v.). A number of local Muslim men joined the Mujahedeen units that were operating under the umbrella of the Army of Bosnia-Herzegovina (q.v.). Besides helping the Bosnian Muslims (q.v.) fight the war, their second mission was to teach the local Muslims "true" Islamic practices and bring about an Islamic society in Bosnia. According to the stipulations of the Dayton peace accord (q.v.), all foreign fighters had to leave Bosnia-Herzegovina. Many of these foreigners, however, have taken Bosnian passports. Fears are that these holy warriors are exponents of Islamic fundamentalism from the Middle East.

MULABDIĆ, EDHEM (1864-1954). A leading Bosnian Muslim (q.v.) writer and cultural activist. He was probably born in Maglaj to a family that was in state service. He benefited from the contemporary Ottoman reforms and as a young man he received education in a lower-secondary type of school, known as *ruždije*. After the Austrian occupation, with a great personal effort to adjust to the new political and cultural situation, he entered the teachers' college in Sarajevo (q.v.) and became one of its best students. In 1890, he became a teacher in the town of Brčko (q.v.). Two years later, however, he became the head of a Muslim school for teachers in Sarajevo and, at the same time, his literary activities began.

Mulavidić, most of all, was a cultural activist. In 1900, he and his friends, Safvet-beg Bašagić and Osman Nuri Hadžić (qq.v.), began to publish the literary and informative bi-monthly *Behar*, which, under his leadership, was a major voice of Bosnian Muslim literary talents till 1906. After a long break, the paper appeared again in 1927 as *Novi behar*/New Behar. He was editor and contributor of several almanacs and papers, and cofounder of various cultural societies, Gajret/Zeal, Narodna Uzdanica/People's Confidence (qq.v.), and Društvo muslimanske omladine/Society of Muslim youth, among them.

Mulavidić wrote numerous stories and novels from the life of the Muslim community in Bosnia at a time of major social and cultural changes, many of them for the purpose of uplifting the cultural level of that community. In his national orientation he considered himself a Croat of Muslim religion.

MURATOVIĆ, HASAN (1940-). Named prime minister of the Republic of Bosnia and Herzegovina on January 21, 1996. Bosniac nationality. Born in Olovo. Finished higher education in Ljubljana, Slovenia, in mechanical engineering and was professor at the University of Sarajevo. Before the appointment, he was a minister without portfolio and president of the State Committee for relations with the United Nations.

MUSLIM ARMED FORCES/MUSLIMANSKE ORUŽANE SNAGE (MOS). A Bosnian Muslim (q.v.) military formation that stands for a Muslim-controlled Bosnia with a strong religious orientation, some would say even fanaticism. They came under the influence of Mujahedeens (q.v.), volunteers from the Middle East that came to Bosnia to fight for the Muslim cause.

MUSLIM BOSNIAC ORGANIZATION/MUSLIMANSKA BOŠNJAČKA ORGANIZACIJA (MBO). A small political party among Bosnian Muslims (q.v.). It was founded (October 1990) by a few leading personalities who were expelled from the principal Muslim formation, the Party of Democratic Action (SDA) (q.v.). The former vice president of the SDA and a long-time political emigrant in the West, Adil Zulfikarpašić (q.v.) became the president of the newly formed MBO. Its other leading figures are Muhamed Filipović and Hamza Mujagić. The party claimed to have a liberal-democratic political orientation in contrast to the ethno/religious program of the SDA. Because Zulfikarpašić was negotiating with the Serbs (q.v.) on his own and even proposed a Muslim-Serb alliance declaring that Yugoslavia (q.v.) should be preserved as a single state with Bosnia-Herzegovina as a single entity in it, he was accused by the Bosnian Muslims and Croats (q.v.) of betrayal.

MUSLIM DEMOCRATIC PARTY/MUSLIMANSKA DEMOKRATSKA STRANKA (MDS). This party was formed in 1992 by its president Armin Pohara and his confidants. Pohara blamed President Alija Izetbegović (q.v.) and his ruling party for misjudging the Serbian intentions and failing to organize the Muslim population to defend themselves against the Serb onslaught, and also for not cooperating with the Croats (q.v.) in a common cause. The MDS advocated a Muslim-Croat alliance and even a confederation between Bosnia-Herzegovina and Croatia. The party lost most of its appeal after the Muslim-Croat conflict erupted in the spring of 1993.

MUSLIMS or BOSNIAN MUSLIMS. *See* BOSNIACS.

-N-

NAMETAK, ALIJA (1906-1987). One of the pioneers of modern literary expression in Bosnia and Herzegovina. Born in Mostar (q.v.). Educated in his native city and in Zagreb, where he studied Slavic literature and history. After his graduation from Zagreb University, he worked for a while in Podgorica (Montenegro). However, he spent most of his life in Sarajevo (q.v.), where he worked in various cultural institutions and was editor of a literary journal *Novi Behar*. His literary works deal with life in his native Herzegovina (q.v.), especially the life of the Muslim community after World War I. He keenly observed how the new historical events undermined the old social and moral structures, especially social stability, traditions, and virtues of the old Muslim nobility. The painful adjustments to the new way of life is Nametak's main literary theme. Besides his own writing, Nametak edited and published several collections of Bosnian folk stories and songs.

NAPREDAK/PROGRESS. The Croatian Cultural Association Napredak is the oldest existing Croatian cultural and benevolent society in Bosnia-Herzegovina. Napredak was formed in 1907 from two existing organizations with similar goals established in Mostar and Sarajevo (qq.v.), respectively, in 1902. Napredak soon became a very vibrant society and had a major impact on the cultural and educational life of the Croats (qq.v.) in the country. It provided scholarships for students, published books, founded libraries, organized choirs and other cultural activities, sponsored economic endeavors, and proved to be the backbone of Croat cultural life in Bosnia-Herzegovina. In 1935 it had over 20,000 members and was one of the most successful societies in the entire country.

After the Second World War, Napredak was banned and its property confiscated. After the collapse of the Communist regime in 1990, the society was revived and has become again a dynamic cultural force. Its presence is especially felt among the citizens of the besieged Sarajevo where Napredak engages in humanitarian and cultural activities despite the dreadful conditions of the city since 1992.

NARODNA UZDANICA/PEOPLE'S CONFIDENCE. A Muslim cultural and educational society. It was formed in 1923 by leading members of the Muslim educated elite that since 1908 opposed a pro-Serb nationalist orientation in the Gajret (q.v.), a Muslim cultural society founded in 1903. The Uzdanica was banned instantly by the Belgrade regime, but a year later the ban was lifted. The organization prospered, especially in the 1930s. Local chapters throughout Bosnia and Herzegovina organized various cultural activities among Muslim youth. It had four boarding houses for its high school students (Sarajevo, Mostar, Tuzla, and Banja Luka [qq.v.]) and one in Zagreb for university students. In contrast to Gajret which enjoyed the sympathies of the regime, Uzdanica was seen as an antistate organization. After World War II, the Communist regime banned both Gajret and Uzdanica and out of them created Preporod (Rebirth) for the Muslims (q.v.) in Bosnia. But it, too, was banned in 1949, just as all other similar ethnic or religious organizations in Titoist Yugoslavia (q.v.). However, Preporod was revived in 1991, after the collapse of the Communist regime.

NAŠA OGNJIŠTA/ OUR HEARTHS. A Croat religious monthly paper published by the Herzegovinian Franciscans (q.v.) in Tomislavgrad for the last 25 years. The paper and its editors were harassed and persecuted during the Communist period. It even had to change its name for a number of years in order to survive the repression.

NAŠI DANI/OUR DAYS. Journal of the Sarajevo University students from 1953 to 1990. The publication remained faithful to the official Marxist ideology during the period. However, under the influence of wider student movements in 1968, its "political correctness" was jeopardized and the editorial board of the time was dismissed. In 1990, the publication moved from a Marxist to a liberal ideology without attaching itself to any political party and changed its name to *Valter*. It stopped publication in 1994.

NATIONAL PARKS. The mountains of Bosnia and Herzegovina are very rich in flora, fauna, and virgin forests. Many regions have been set aside as natural preserves. Two of the most important places are the national parks of Sutjeska, in the southeastern, and Kozara in the northwestern part of the country.

The core of the Sutjeska Park is the Sutjeska River and a massive gorge around it. The high mountains of Zelengora and Maglić, and especially the Perućica primeval forest preserve area, are of extraordinary beauty and of enormous importance for the preservation of nature. The virgin forests of Perućica are among the most special beauties in all of Europe. These ancient woods stretch along the stream by the same name. At a short distance from its flow into the Sutjeska River is the famous Skakavac waterfall that plunges 70 meters (230 ft) from a large rock into a deep gap. This beautiful park is accessible to tourists, mountaineers, and sports enthusiasts.

The Sutjeska region is also known for a major battle that took place in May-June 1943 between Tito's (q.v.) partisans and German forces.

The Kozara National Park is about 20 kilometers (12.5 mi) from Kozarac, near the town of Prijedor. Its main attractions are the mountain Kozara and beautiful landscapes and virgin nature. A major World War II battle took place between Tito's partisans and the Germans on the Kozara mountain.

NERETVA BATTLE. A major battle between Tito's (q.v.) partisans and the German forces in the Rama-Konjic region in the Neretva valley which took place in March 1943. The bridges over the Neretva River were blown up, and, under great pressure from the German troops, pontoon bridges were used by the partisans to transfer their corps to the eastern side of the river. The battle became a myth in socialist Yugoslav historiography and resulted in a motion picture entitled the "Battle of Neretva."

NEW LAYOUT. A newspaper published by the Liberal Party of Banja Luka (q.v.). Its publication began at the end of 1992. After seven issues, it was shut down by the ruling Serbian Democratic Party (q.v.).

NEWS MEDIA. The main broadcasting service, Radio-Television of Bosnia and Herzegovina (RTVBH) (q.v.), was almost choked to death soon after the war broke out in April 1992. Most of the 11 main transmitters and 186 relay stations were lost by the legitimate government and most of the country's territory was inaccessible to Sarajevo radio and television. There are, however, around 15 local television and many radio stations in the government controlled areas. From the fall of Communism till the occupation of most of Bosnia and Herzegovina in the summer of 1992, Sarajevo television pretended neither to see nor to speak evil. It remained in a world of its own, believing that the Yugoslav People's Army (q.v.) could not turn against

Bosnia, a true "Yugoslav" republic. In the summer of 1992, however, the RTVBH came under the wing of the Sarajevo government, or better to say, the ruling Muslim party (SDA [q.v.]).

Among the papers that are either close to or controlled by the Muslim-led government, are the following: In Sarajevo (q.v.), *Oslobođenje* (q.v.)(also in Zenica), *Svijet*, *Večernje novine* (q.v.)(also in Tuzla [q.v.]), *Dani* (q.v.), *Dnevni avaz*, *Oglasi*, *Narodne novine*, *Sarp*, *Bosna*, *Sarajevo Times*, and *Behar*. In Zenica (q.v.), *Islamski glas*, *Štit*, and *Slobodna Bosna* (q.v.) (moved from Sarajevo). *Bosnoljubljen* and *Čelić* in northeastern Bosnia, *Trn* in Tešanj, and *Zmaj od Bosne* in Tuzla. While *Oslobođenje* was close to the former prime minister Haris Silajdžić (q.v.), *Večernje novine* was the main daily voice of President Izetbegović's (q.v.) faction in the SDA. The *Zapadna Bosna* was a mouthpiece of Fikret Abdić (q.v.), a renegade to the Muslim cause, and his Autonomous Province of Western Bosnia. The main Muslim/Bosniac nationalist voice outside the country is the weekly *Ljiljan* (q.v.), printed in Slovenia. Although it claims to be independent, it is under the control of the Sarajevo government, and is considered to be the voice of Islamic religious forces.

-O-

O'GRADY, SCOTT (1965-). Captain in the U.S. Air Force who was blasted from the cockpit when his F-16 was hit by a Serb SA-6 surface-to-air missile above Serb-controlled territory in Bosnia, near Bihać (q.v.), on June 2, 1995. His mission was to enforce the UN-mandated no-fly-zone over Bosnia when his plane was hit. Captain O'Grady survived six days in enemy territory eating insects, drinking rainwater, and enduring the cold Bosnian weather. On several occasions he was only feet away from Serbian patrols. Six days later, he was rescued by the 24th Marine Expeditionary Unit from the *Kearsarge* helicopter carrier, which was sailing in the Adriatic off the coast of Croatia in a bold raid behind enemy lines. O'Grady, who was born in Brooklyn, New York, and had lived in Spokane, Washington, before joining the Air Force, became an instant hero after his survival and rescue.

ODIJEK/ECHO. Sarajevo (q.v.) weekly publication dealing with matters of culture, art, literature (q.v.), and various social issues. It promoted artistic activities among the younger generations. Its publication began in 1947 and lasted till the 1992 war.

OLD BRIDGE. *See* STARI MOST.

ORTHODOX CHURCH. The demarcation line established in AD 395 between the Eastern and Western parts of the Roman Empire, stretching along the river Drina (between Bosnia and Serbia), evolved into a permanent faultline between Western and Byzantine civilizations. Even the final split between the Eastern (Orthodox) and the Western (Catholic) churches (1054) was along the same border. The perimeters between the two spheres, however, began to be affected by the rise of the medieval Serbian state and its autonomous Orthodox Church.

The medieval Serbian state resulted from the collapse of the Byzantine Empire. The so-called Latin Empire was established in Constantinople (1204-1262) and the republic of Venice began to assert its dominance in the Mediterranean. The Byzantine tragedy proved to be an excellent opportunity for the neighboring small principality of Raška (later known as Serbia) to advance its interests in the region. With the help of the West, Raška became a kingdom in 1217. By shifting its allegiance to the East again, the Serbian church gained its independence from the Byzantine political and church authority in 1219. Both state and church powers were in the hands of the Nemanjić family.

As the political power of the Serbian rulers expanded to the southwest into traditional Catholic lands at the end of the 12th century, so did the institutions and influence of the Orthodox Church. The founder of the Serbian church, Sava Nemanjić, out of eight newly established episcopates placed one at Dabar (1219), on the very border with Bosnia, and two in the newly acquired Catholic territories of Zeta (later Montenegro) and Hum (later Herzegovina) (qq.v.). Clearly, Sava had an ambitious vision of expanding his church and Serbian state borders to the west. The Serbian excursion into Hum, however, did not last very long. Their political and religious authority was rolled back by the rise of the Bosnian state and the republic of Dubrovnik. Although the Orthodox episcopate in Hum lasted only till the 1250s, the Serbian church did establish its presence in the southeastern parts of present-day Herzegovina.

A visible increase of Serbian Orthodox population in the Bosnian medieval kingdom occurred during the reign of Tvrtko I (1353-1391) (q.v.) when he occupied parts of southwestern Serbia (1376). Even the monastery of Miloševo, the burial place of Sava Nemanjić, came under Bosnian rule. A relatively small number of Orthodox adherents in present-day Bosnia-Herzegovina were found in some locations of northeastern Bosnia and eastern Herzegovina, but Serbian church institutions did not establish permanent footing in the territory of present-day Bosnia and Herzegovina till after the Ottoman conquest (1463).

Under the Ottomans, major religious and even ethnic shifts began to take place in Bosnia and Herzegovina. The local Bosnian Church (q.v.), already weak, practically vanished soon after the Turkish conquest. The Catholic Church (q.v.) which flourished toward the end of the Bosnian kingdom, began to lose its strong position and eventually became the church of a minority. Islam (q.v.), as a state religion, became dominant in the country and many natives converted to the religion of the new state. Furthermore, because of Turkish invasions, Orthodox Christianity established itself in Bosnia. It grew from a small minority in pre-Ottoman times to the largest of the three religious groups in Bosnia-Herzegovina at the end of the Turkish rule. The main reasons for this growth were migrations and conversions.

With the Ottoman invasion of Bosnia (1463), a significant migration of the Christian Orthodox population began from the eastern and southern Balkans (q.v.) to the northwest. These migrants served as guardsmen, pass-watchers, frontier raiders, herdsmen, and transporters of military supplies. In return, they colonized devastated frontier regions, organized their settlements, preserved their tribal autonomy, and received various privileges. Most of those who migrated to Bosnia (and Croatia), along with the Ottoman armies, were of the Orthodox religion, but not necessarily of Serbian ethnicity. Most of them were partly slavicized Balkan Vlachs that lived in the region from Roman times. Those who migrated and the converts to Orthodoxy came under the pastoral care of the Serbian Orthodox Church and eventually all melted into the Serbian national body. Thus, the Islamic empire became the most important catalyst in the spread of Orthodoxy and Serbianism across its traditional boundaries in the Balkans (q.v.).

Once the Ottomans solidified their rule over the Balkan Orthodox regions, they modified their policy toward the Serbian Orthodox Church. Although from the middle of the 15th century the church was subordinated to the Greek-controlled archbishopric in Ohrid and despite hardships it had to go through, it was a part of the Ottoman-recognized Orthodox religious community *(millet).* In comparison to the Catholic Church under the Ottomans, it had a privileged status. Furthermore, because the Ottomans needed Serbian support in their struggle against the Catholic Habsburg lands and because of sympathies of the grand vezir at the time, who was from Bosnia himself, the Serbian patriarchate of Peć was restored in 1557. By regaining church independence, the Serbian religious and national body became an autonomous entity in the Ottoman Empire that promoted its interests under the Islamic rule. Moreover, the borders of the Serbian church greatly increased to the west (Bosnia and parts of Croatia) and numerous churches and monasteries were built in the new regions, mostly on the foundations of former Catholic churches. The close cooperation between the Serbian patriarchate and the Ottomans lasted till 1690, when patriarch Arsenije III Crnojević, as the Habsburg ally, was forced to flee, together with many Serbs (q.v.), from Serbia to Srijem in the Habsburg Empire.

With the growth of the Orthodox population during the Ottoman centuries, the church's institutional structures also evolved in Bosnia and Herzegovina. The jurisdiction of the episcopate of Dabar, established by Sava Nemanjić on the border between Serbia and Bosnia (1219), stretched into Bosnia. In 1557, after the revival of the patriarchate of Peć, this church seat was moved to Bosnia itself, and became known as the Dabro-Bosnian episcopate. In 1575, the same episcopate was transferred to a former Catholic monastery in Rmanj in western Bosnia and in 1713 to Sarajevo (q.v.).

The Serbian medieval rulers and the church leaders gave special attention to the Hum region (eastern Herzegovina). This was the first region to feel the penetration of growing Serbian political and religious power. After it came under the Nemanjić domain, the Hum episcopate was established (1219). Because of the lack of Orthodox believers in Hum and the pressures from the republic of Dubrovnik, the residence of the episcopate was moved to the Lim region in Serbia in the early 1250s. Moreover, by the unification of Hum to Bosnia (1322) the Orthodox Church lost the firm ground in Herzegovina till the arrival of the Ottomans.

In the early 17th century (1611), the revived Orthodox episcopate of Hum was divided into two church regions. In the next century, however, the two parts were reunited again into the Zahumlje-Herzegovina episcopate. The local bishops resided mostly in monasteries around the town of Trebinje till 1777, when the seat of the episcopate was moved to the city of Mostar (q.v.).

In northeastern Bosnia, an Orthodox episcopate was established in Zvornik in the early 16th century (ca. 1532). This church center was transferred to Tuzla (q.v.) in 1852 and since then has been known as the Zvornik-Tuzla episcopate.

Besides the three older metropolitan episcopates, a new one was formed in the town of Banja Luka (q.v.) in northwestern

Bosnia in 1900. Because the Sarajevo church district was too big, this episcopate was separated from it and is known as the Banja Luka-Bihać episcopate.

In addition to the parochial structures of the church, Orthodox monasteries were also established in Bosnia and Herzegovina. They too came into existence after the Ottoman conquest. During the 16th and 17th centuries, three such monasteries were established in Herzegovina and eight in Bosnia. These religious houses became the most important centers of Serbian Orthodoxy and Serbian national life in the country.

Because the patriarchate of Peć was abolished in 1766, the jurisdiction over the Orthodox Church in Bosnia and Herzegovina came under the patriarch of Constantinople. From that time till 1880, a few years after Bosnia-Herzegovina was occupied by the Habsburgs, the church leadership in the country was in the hands of the Greek bishops (Phanariotes), who were foreigners and cared little for the local needs of the church or the people. Because money was the most important factor for the ordination of priests, the quality of Orthodox clergy in Bosnia-Herzegovina was below the necessary level for religious leadership and vitality.

After the Habsburg occupation of the country in 1878, the new rulers were not sure how to gain the cooperation of the Orthodox Church in Bosnia-Herzegovina while limiting Serbia's influences over that church and the Orthodox people in the country. A solution was worked out with the patriarch in Constantinople (1880) by which the Patriarch had jurisdiction over the "Greek-Eastern Church" in Bosnia-Herzegovina, and Vienna was allowed to nominate its bishops. In turn, the patriarch in Constantinople was paid an annual fee by Vienna, and the local bishops were put on the state payroll. By 1891, all three episcopates were transferred from the Greek bishops into the hands of the native sons, the Serbian hierarchy. As a result of the collapse of the Habsburg Empire and of the creation of the Kingdom of Serbs, Croats, and Slovenes (Yugoslavia after 1929) (q.v.), the four episcopates in Bosnia-Herzegovina united with the metropolitan episcopate of Serbia in 1918. In 1920, the Serbian Orthodox Patriarchate was established in Belgrade and since then the Orthodox Church of Bosnia and Herzegovina has been under its jurisdiction.

OSLOBOĐENJE/LIBERATION. Sarajevo's (q.v.) main daily paper. It began (1943) as a partisan propaganda news-sheet for the National Liberation Struggle and the Communist movement in Bosnia-Herzegovina during the Second World War. From the very beginning to the collapse of the Communist regime in Yugoslavia (q.v.), *Oslobođenje* was an orthodox paper, never wavering in its support of the regime and its ideology. Even in the post-Communist era, at the time when Slovenia was attacked and the war in Croatia raged, *Oslobođenje* zealously supported the Yugoslav People's Army (JNA) (q.v.) and remained faithful to the dogma of Yugoslavism. The paper, and Sarajevo's news media in general, were not able to name the war aggressor for a long time.

After the siege of Sarajevo began, the paper continued to be published under war conditions and attempted to keep a multi-ethnic image. Although it claims to be an independent paper and above ethnic affiliations, its critics consider it too close to the official line of the Sarajevo Muslim-dominated government, especially to the former prime minister Haris Silajdžić (q.v.).

Oslobođenje has received numerous international honors and awards in the last five years for defying the atrocious war conditions and keeping the voice of freedom alive. It was honored by the Sakharov Prize for Human Rights, the Oscar Romero Award, and the Freedom Award, among others.

Serbian authorities in Pale (q.v.) near Sarajevo also publish their own *Oslobođenje*, that claims to be the true successor to the original paper.

OSTOJIĆ, VELIBOR. A leading member of the Serbian Democratic Party (SDS) (q.v.) and minister of information in the coalition government of Bosnia-Herzegovina before April

1992. But once the war began, he became involved in the first stages of ethnic cleansing (q.v.) in eastern Bosnia.

OWEN, DAVID A. LORD (1938-). Former EC mediator and co-chairman of the Peace Conference on Former Yugoslavia (1992-1995). He, together with Cyrus Vance (q.v.), and then with Thorvald Stoltenberg (q.v.), proposed two peace plans that would divide Bosnia-Herzegovina into semiautonomous cantons or three ethnic ministates. Both proposals fell through. He was replaced as EC negotiator by Carl Bildt in June 1995. He was accused of being ready to reward Serbian aggression in Bosnia and Herzegovina.

Owen was born in Plympton, South Devon. He finished medical school and served in various positions, including foreign secretary, in the British national government.

-P-

PAGANIA/THE PAGAN LAND. Medieval name for the region west of Hum or Zahumlje (q.v.). It stretched from the Neretva River to the Cetina River in the present-day Republic of Croatia. The southwestern parts of western Herzegovina (q.v.) also belonged to the region of Pagania.

PALE. A village near Sarajevo (q.v) that became headquarters of the Bosnian Serb hard-line leadership during the 1992-1995 war in Bosnia and Herzegovina.

PARTY OF DEMOCRATIC ACTION/STRANKA DEMOKRATSKE AKCIJE (SDA). The ruling party in Bosnia and Herzegovina and the leading political formation among the Bosnian Muslims (q.v.). At the time of its founding (May 1990), it was perceived as a political organization that would rally not only the Muslims of Bosnia-Herzegovina but also the Muslims throughout the former Yugoslavia (q.v.). As the war erupted and Yugoslavia dissolved, its activities in Serbia, Montenegro, and Macedonia were greatly contained and even suppressed. The SDA has, however, active membership in Croatia and some other foreign countries in the West.

Initially, the SDA portrayed itself, and the Bosnian Muslim community, as a convenient bridge between Serbs and Croats (qq.v.), and the East and West. Thus it tried hard and for too long to be "neutral" during the 1991 war in Croatia. Despite visible signs that the war would spread to Bosnia, the SDA failed to make any preparations for the coming onslaught. Once the war in Bosnia began, it developed reluctant relations with Croatia and the Croats in Bosnia-Herzegovina. The "alliance" even broke down at the beginning of 1993 and turned into an open conflict over the 30 percent of the country that was not occupied by the Serbs.

Because the SDA received 37.8 percent of the electoral votes in the first multiparty election (1990), it won 86 of the 240 seats in the national Assembly. The president of the SDA, Alija Izetbegović (q.v.), who was elected to the collective nine-member rotating presidency, was chosen as the first president of the presidency and he formed the first coalition government made up of Muslims, Serbs, and Croats.

Although the party program emphasizes freedom and equality of all citizens, regardless of nationality, religion, race, gender, or political affiliation, there are signs that the SDA would like to achieve a dominant Muslim role in the country. The arguments are that they make up the majority of the population and, as the Croats and Serbs have their respective national states, so should the Bosniacs (Bosnian Muslims).

President Izetbegović plays a dominant role in the party, and his support is especially strong among more conservative Muslim forces and the Muslim religious leaders, while the more cosmopolitan wing of the party is rallied around Prime Minister Haris Silajdžić (q.v.). A small but influential group of SDA members split from the party ranks and formed the Muslim Bosniac Organization (MBO) (q.v.) in October 1990. After Prime Minister Silajdžić split from President Izetbegović at the beginning of 1995, he organized a political formation of his own. He was not able, however, to diminish the SDA's hold on power in the September 1996 elections. Izetbegović and his party successfully retained control of the Bosniac electorate.

PAŠIĆ, HILMO (1934-). Became minister of justice and general administration of the Republic of Bosnia and Herzegovina. Served in the Sarajevo (q.v.) district administration and, before the war, in various positions in the Socialist Republic of Bosnia and Herzegovina. Of Bosniac nationality. Finished law studies.

PAVELIĆ, ANTE (1889-1959). Leader of the *ustaša* (q.v.) movement and head of the Independent State of Croatia (NDH) (q.v.) during World War II. He was born in the town of Bradina (Herzegovina [q.v.]). Pavelić finished his primary education in Bosnia, secondary in Croatia, and, in 1915, he finished law studies at the University of Zagreb, Croatia. From his youth, Pavelić was a member of the Croatian Party of Right (q.v.), which emphasized Croatia's historical state rights and independence. He was also the founder of the Croatian Workers Federation. In 1922 and 1927, Pavelić was elected to represent the city of Zagreb in the provincial and national assembly.

After the assassination of leading Croat politicians in Belgrade's Parliament (1928) and the imposition of King Aleksandar's dictatorship (1929), Pavelić turned to revolutionary methods to fight Serbian domination of the country and established the *ustaša* — Croatian Revolutionary Organization. Its main objective was the breakup of Yugoslavia (q.v.) and liberation of Croatia. In the same year, Pavelić left the country and a few months later he was sentenced to death in absentia by the state court in Belgrade (July 17, 1929) for "antistate activities."

In 1941, Pavelić returned with the help of the Axis powers to become the head of the Independent State of Croatia (NDH), which also included Bosnia and Herzegovina. During his regime there were persecutions of Jews, Serbs, and Croats (qq.v.) who were considered disloyal to the state. When the Croat state collapsed at the end of World War II, he left the country and lived in Argentina where he survived an assassination attempt by Yugoslav agents in 1957. Finally, he and his family moved to Spain, where he died.

PEJANOVIĆ, MIRKO (1946-). A member of the seven-member state presidency of Bosnia-Herzegovina from 1992 to 1996. He was born near Tuzla (q.v.). Of Serb nationality. After working as a teacher for a few years, he pursued higher education at the University of Sarajevo, specializing in sociology. Besides serving in various local government functions in the city of Sarajevo (q.v.), Pejanović also served as a sociopolitical analyst for the governments of the republic of Bosnia-Herzegovina and of the former Yugoslavia (q.v.). During the first multiparty elections in the country (1990), he was president of the Democratic Party of Socialists. After the 1992 war began, he remained in Sarajevo and opposed the Serbian nationalist leaders. In 1992, he became a member of the Bosnian state presidency and a member of the state delegation to the peace talks in Geneva from 1992 to 1994. Pejanović is a cofounder and president of the Serb Civic Council (SCC) (q.v.), an organization formed in March 1994 by leading Serb intellectuals in Sarajevo who accept the independence of Bosnia-Herzegovina and its multiethnic life.

PITANJA KNJIŽEVNOSTI I JEZIKA/QUESTIONS ON LITERATURE AND LANGUAGE. A journal dealing with issues of literature and language (qq.v.) published at the University of Sarajevo from 1954 to 1958.

PLAVŠIĆ, BILJANA (1930-). President of the Serb Republic of Bosnia-Herzegovina (q.v.) and a former professor at the University of Sarajevo. She was born near Tuzla (q.v.) and finished higher education in natural sciences and mathematics at the University of Zagreb, Croatia. First, she worked at the Faculty of Philosophy at the University of Sarajevo (1956-1960), then at the Faculty of Natural Sciences and Mathematics at the same University (1961-1977). After a two-year break, she returned to the same university and taught there till 1990.

Plavšić became a member of the Bosnian multiethnic presidency after the first multiparty elections at the beginning of 1991. However, she resigned from the presidency in April 1992, joined the Serb warring faction, and became vice president of the Serb Republic in Bosnia and Herzegovina. Plavšić proved herself to be one of the most ardent advocates of Serbian separatism, and remained an outspoken proponent of the Serb nationalist cause throughout the war.

After Radovan Karadžić (q.v.), as an indicted war criminal, was forced out by international pressure from the office of the president of the Serb Republic in August 1996 and banned from political life in Bosnia and Herzegovina, Plavšić became his replacement. In the September 1996 elections, she was elected president of the Serb Republic.

PODGORJE. Medieval territory in present-day northeastern Herzegovina (q.v.) created at the end of the 10th century out of the northern parts of Travunja and Zahumlje (qq.v.).

PODRINJE. Literally it means "regions below the river Drina." In pre-Ottoman times, the name designated a territory east of the upper flow of the Drina River; between the rivers Drina and Lim. It included the towns of Sokol, Pljevlje, Prijepolje, and the Serbian monastery Miloševo. *Ban* Tvrtko (qq.v.) was the first Bosnian ruler to gain this area (1366). Podrinje remained under the Bosnian rulers till the Turkish occupation.

POLITICAL PARTIES. A parliamentary system did not exist in Bosnia and Herzegovina during the first decades of the Austrian rule, or earlier under the Ottomans. The first semblance of parliamentary life that emerged from 1910 to 1916, although with a limited franchise and lacking direct legislative powers, resulted from three factors. First, there was a belief on the part of the imperial Austro-Hungarian bureaucrats that Bosnia and Herzegovina was secure enough to allow more local political participation. Second, it became clear by the end of the last century that the supraethno/religious Bosnian (Bošnjak or Bosniac) identity, championed by Minister Benjámin Kállay (q.v.) (the Joint Finance Minister responsible for Bosnia and Herzegovina from 1882 to 1903) was rejected even by the Bosnian Muslims (q.v.). Third, during the first decade of this century, the Orthodox and Muslim communities in the country gained religious-educational autonomies and were beginning to transform the gathering of cultural power into a political force.

The first political party in Bosnia and Herzegovina, the Muslim People's Organization, was established in 1906. It advocated Bosnian autonomy under the sultan's sovereignty. Socially, it advocated freedom of the customary tenants (*kmets*) in order to make them free agricultural laborers. Its leader was Alibeg Firdus and later Šerif Arnautović. A second Muslim political party, the Croatian Muslim Progressive Party, was founded in 1908 under the leadership of Ademaga Mešić. It sympathized with the pro-Croatian policies and ethnic orientation while preserving Islamic religious heritage. It attracted many leading Muslim intellectuals with the publication *Muslimanska Sviest* (Muslim consciousness). Because the Muslim People's Organization shifted its program closer to the Croatian side, some pro-Serb Muslims split from the party. However, they were not strong enough to form a party. Their only candidate, Osman Đikić, in the first parliamentary elections of 1910 failed to be elected.

Toward the end of 1907, three Serbian activist groups, business, intellectuals, and pro-peasant, formed the Serbian People's Organization. In the same year, another Serbian political party was formed, the Serbian People's Independent Party in Sarajevo (q.v.), but because of its weak following it soon faded away.

Among the Croatians in Bosnia and Herzegovina there were two major parties before World War I. The Croatian People's Organization was founded in 1908 and the Croatian Catholic Union in 1910. The first emphasized its secular and supra-confessional orientation while the second had a strong Catholic-centered program. The first political orientation was supported by the Franciscans (q.v.), and the main champion of the second was the archbishop of Sarajevo, Josip Stadler.

In the first parliament, elected in 1910, the Serbs had 31 mandates, the Muslims 24, and the Croats 16 (qq.v.). The working of the parliament was not, however, predetermined by the ethno/religious affiliation of its members. Various political shifts were taking place on different issues. The local government always attempted to have a "working majority" from all three ethno/religious communities.

After the creation of the Kingdom of Serbs, Croats, and Slovenes in 1918 (Yugoslavia after 1929) (q.v.), the unitarist ideology prevailed and the various nations in the country were declared to be simply "tribes" of a "single Yugoslav nation." Regardless of this ideological axiom, however, the political parties in the country continued to be based on ethnic and religious affiliation.

In 1919, the Democratic Party was organized out of three Serbian political circles and a small pro-Serb Muslim group. Its main ideological orientation was a Serb-dominated version of "Yugoslavism." Although its leaders advocated "national unity," at least they were willing to discuss the concerns of non-Serbs. They rejected, however, all forms of federalism in the country. In the 1920 elections, the Democrats received only 5.59 percent of votes in Bosnia-Herzegovina.

But most of the Orthodox (Serbian) population supported the Serbian Radical Party and the Alliance of Agrarian Workers or Serbian Agrarians. The Radicals and their political allies considered the Serbs to be a nation while the others (Croats and Slovenes) were tribes. According to them, the new state was resting upon the Serbian historical state tradition and the Serbs were not equal but superior to the others in the country. It was theirs to "melt" the others into Serbs, and not, as some Yugoslavist idealists believed, that all of the nationalities should transform themselves into a common Yugoslav ethnicity. The Radicals, reflecting a strain of social Darwinism, claimed that the Serbs had a stronger national will and higher moral aspirations and, therefore, history was on their side.

The left wing parties, Social Democrats and Communists, were marginal forces in Bosnia-Herzegovina. Most of the Social Democratic membership shifted to the Communist side. The Social Democrats in the 1920 elections, for example, received only 0.84 percent and the Communists, who were soon outlawed, 5.46 percent of votes in Bosnia.

The Yugoslav Muslim Organization (JMO) was established in 1919, from some smaller groupings among the Muslims. It attracted most of the Muslim political forces in Bosnia and Herzegovina. Besides its efforts to keep the administrative unity of Bosnia and Herzegovina and to protect the interests of its constituency, the JMO's main aim was to keep the Muslim population from political factionalism according to class divisions or from being caught between Serbian and Croatian nationalist rivalry. While there were small and insignificant pro-Serb Muslim political groupings (Muslim Husbandmen's Party, Muslim People's Party, and Muslim List of Šerif Arnautović), the JMO had overwhelming Muslim support in Bosnia and Herzegovina. The JMO, unlike the Serbian and Croatian political parties, was defined only in religious and not in ethnic terms. The ethnic identity of the Muslims was left unclarified at the time. For example, after the 1920 elections, out of 24 JMO delegates 15 declared themselves to be Croats, two Serbs, five undeclared, and one Bosnian. And after the 1923 elections, out of 18 JMO deputies and their alternates, all, except its leader Mehmed Spaho (q.v.), declared themselves as Croats. Spaho decided to be a Yugoslav. Although the JMO made compromises with the ruling Serbian centralist forces, it was, with Slovenes and Croats, in a federalist political camp in the country.

The Croatian People's Organization was revived and from it two parties later evolved: the Croat Husbandmen's Party and the Croat People's Party. The first one had a much larger support among the Croat electorate, especially among the liberal minded Croats, while the second was a clerical party. Soon, however, a third Croatian political formation appeared in Bosnia-Herzegovina. In 1921, the Croatian Peasant Party (HSS) (q.v.) (from 1918-1925, known as Croatian Republican

Peasant Party -HRSS), the main political force in neighboring Croatia, began to spread its organizations there, and, already in the 1923 elections, gained overwhelming support among the Croat electorate. It also attracted some following among the Muslims. The two other parties were practically wiped out after 1923. The core of the political program of the Croat parties was federalism. They advocated national equality and decentralized government.

After the assassination of the Croatian political leadership in Belgrade's parliament in 1928 and the imposition of the royal dictatorship on January 6, 1929, King Aleksandar banned all political parties. An all "Yugoslav" political organization, however, was formed according to royal wishes. After the assassination of the king in 1934, a quasiparliamentary life was revived and in the 1935 elections, even under tremendous political pressure, the opposition led by the Croatian Peasant Party, had an impressive showing. But the advent of the war and the Communist takeover in 1945 eliminated all party politics in the country till 1992.

After the Communist Party gave up monopoly of power in the former Yugoslavia, ethno/religious political formations in Bosnia and Herzegovina were rapidly constituted in the first half of 1990. The Party of Democratic Action (SDA) (q.v.) was formed in May 1990. Under the leadership of Alija Izetbegović (q.v.), it became the party that gathered most of the Bosnian Muslim electorate. Although Bosnian-centered, its goal at the time was to be a major political voice of all those who adhered to Islamic cultural and religious tradition in the former Yugoslavia. Therefore, chapters of the SDA were formed in other republics of the former country. The party program stood for the integrity of Bosnia-Herzegovina and preservation of its multiethnic, multireligious character within a decentralized Yugoslavia. Although its symbols were religious, the party leadership maintained that it stood for a civil society and a secular state. A group of SDA dissidents, led by an influential émigré returnee, Adil Zulfikarpašić (q.v.), formed a splinter party, the Muslim Bosniac Organization (MBO) (q.v.). The MBO emphasized the nonreligious nature of its program and was considered closer to the Serbs than the SDA was. There was also a Bosnian Republican Party that was secular and closer to the Croats in its program. But it did not find a meaningful response among the Muslim population.

Most of the Bosnian Serbs gathered around the Serbian Democratic Party (SDS) (q.v.) and its leader, Montenegrine-born psychiatrist Radovan Karadžić (q.v.). During the election campaign in the summer of 1990, the party's main emphasis was on protection of the Serbian rights in Bosnia and Herzegovina and not on a scheme to create a Greater Serbia. The Serbian Renewal Movement (SPO)(q.v.) was also in the Bosnian first-election arena, but it had marginal support among the Bosnian Serbs. Karadžić and his party were the favorites of the Serbian president Slobodan Milošević (q.v.).

The main Croatian political party in Bosnia-Herzegovina was the Croatian Democratic Union (HDZ) (q.v.), also the strongest party in Croatia. Its program emphasized that it stood for the integrity of Bosnia and Herzegovina but as a country of three equal peoples: Muslims, Serbs, and Croats. Its main concerns were Serbian expansionism and a possible Muslim domination in the country. The HDZ lacked strong leadership in Bosnia and Herzegovina, mainly because it was subservient to the ruling sister party bosses in Croatia. Two other Croatian parties were formed in the country, Croatian Democratic Party (HDS) and Croatian Party of Right (HSP) (q.v.), but the HDZ had overwhelming Croat support.

Among 41 registered parties that emerged at the end of the Communist era, the following also managed to win a representation in the National Assembly in the first post-Communist elections: Democratic Party of Socialists (DSS); League of Communists — Party of Democratic Change; Alliance of Reform Forces of Yugoslavia for Bosnia and Herzegovina (SRSJ BiH); Democratic League of Greens (DSZ); and Liberal Party (LS).

The November-December 1990 elections were clearly won by the three major ethno/religious parties. The SDA won 35.81 percent of the votes, SDS 29.11 percent, and HDZ 18.75 percent of the vote. In the Chamber of Municipalities, out of

110 seats, SDA won 43, SDS BiH 38, HDZ BiH 23, Party of Democratic Change 4, DSS 1, and SPO 1. In the Chamber of Citizens, out of 130 seats, SDA won 43, SDS BiH 34, HDZ BiH 21, Party of Democratic Change 15, SRSJ BiH 12, MBO 2, DSS 1, DSZ 1, and LS 1. According to ethnic background, the 1990 National Assembly was composed of 99 Muslims, 85 Serbs, 49 Croats and 7 "Yugoslavs". Many in the country believed at the time that there was a chance to resolve the longtime simmering but ignored ethnic problems in a peaceful way, but only a few months later, it became clear that an armed insurrection and aggression against Bosnia and Herzegovina was imminent.

Out of 49 registered political parties in 1996, 24 ran in the first post-war national elections on September 14, 1996 (q.v.). The Party for Bosnia and Herzegovina (SBiH), formed and led by former Bosnia's Foreign Minister Haris Silajdžić (q.v.), became the second-strongest political formation among the Bosnian Muslims. The Socialist Party (SPRS), an offshoot of the ruling Slobodan Milošević's party in Serbia, received an unexpectedly high number of votes in the September elections. The three nationalist parties (SDA, SDS, and HDZ), however, were clear winners and they retained their hold on power among their respective constituencies.

POSAVINA. A fertile region in northern Bosnia along the Sava river. The main towns in the region are: Bosanski Brod, Bosanski Šamac, Brčko (q.v.), Derventa, Doboj, Gradačac, Modriča, Odžak, and Orašje. The Posavina "corridor" is the only link between the eastern and western parts of the Serbian held territory of Bosnia-Herzegovina. Thus, it is not only economically but also strategically an important part of the country. The region was inhabited mostly by the Croats (q.v.). While, in some parts of the country, conflict between the Croats and Muslims (q.v.) escalated during 1993, in Posavina the two communities were not only able to prevent mutual quarrels but also to fight together against the Serbs (q.v.) from 1992 till the end of the war. Although the Serbs were a minority in the region, the Dayton peace accord (q.v.) allotted most of Posavina to the Serbian controlled Bosnia.

POZDERAC, HAKIJA (1919-). Born in Cazin. Became a member of the Communist Party in 1942. Finished technical school in Belgrade. In the post-World War II period, he was a public prosecutor in Bihać and Banja Luka (qq.v.) and a faithful instrument of the Communist Party. He held various positions in the hierarchy of the party and in Yugoslav state bureaucracy till his retirement. Presently he lives in Belgrade.

POZDERAC, HAMDIJA (1923-1988). Born in Cazin, town in northwestern Bosnia. Became a Communist Party member in 1942 and an active member of the partisan movement during World War II. His education included the Higher Party School in Moscow. He taught for a while at the University of Sarajevo. Pozderac became a higher functionary in the Communist Party and political structure in Bosnia-Herzegovina and Yugoslavia (q.v.), including membership in the Central Committee of the Party in the republic. Among other high offices, he became a member of the federal presidency and was in line to become the president of the presidency on May 15, 1988. A few months earlier, however, a financial scandal erupted in one of the largest economic enterprises in the country (Agrokomerc) that involved him, other members of his family, and his younger protégé, Fikret Abdić (q.v), among many others. Because of this affair Pozderac was removed from the Central Committee of the League of Communists of Yugoslavia in October of 1987 and from the presidency in September of 1988.

PREGLED/SURVEY. A well-known Sarajevo (q.v.) scholarly journal. Its publication began in 1910. Between the two World Wars, the journal was a voice of the Left-oriented intellectuals concerned about social and philosophical issues. In the post-World War II period, it was affiliated with the University of Sarajevo and had a strong Titoist orientation. Its publication ceased in 1991. Its English edition was entitled *Survey.*

PREPOROD/REBIRTH. Official bi-weekly religious organ of the Muslim community in Bosnia-Herzegovina. Its publication began 25 years ago. The paper came under the Communist regime's attack in 1979 and its entire editorial board was dismissed, including a well-known theology professor, Husejin Đozo (q.v.), and was replaced with a more "government friendly" staff.

PRLIĆ, JADRANKO (1959-). Named minister of foreign affairs of the Republic of Bosnia and Herzegovina in January 1996. Before that, he served as deputy premier and deputy defense minister in the Republic and Federation of Bosnia and Herzegovina (q.v.). He also served as the president of the Executive Committee of the Municipal Assembly of the city of Mostar (q.v.), director of Apro-Korporacija enterprise, and vice president of the Executive Committee of the Socialist Republic of Bosnia and Herzegovina. Born in Đakovo (Croatia). Of Croat nationality. Finished higher education in economics.

PROSVJETA/EDUCATION. Serbian cultural and educational society in Bosnia and Herzegovina founded in 1902. Its main goal at the beginning was the material support of Serbian students in their efforts to finish secondary and higher education. With time, however, it became a leading Serbian cultural association that published textbooks, almanacs, and other literature (q.v.). It also established various libraries, helped to organize and enlighten Serbian peasants, and promoted various cultural activities. These activities also promoted national consciousness and were a part of the mainstream of the Serbian nationalist movement in Bosnia-Herzegovina.

In 1914, the Prosvjeta was banned and its leadership imprisoned by the Austro-Hungarian regime for "antistate" activities. In the post-World War I era, Prosvjeta tried to expand its activities besides Bosnia-Herzegovina into other regions of the newly established Kingdom of Serbs, Croats, and Slovenes (q.v.), but without much success, except in some parts of southern Croatia and Sandžak (q.v.).

Its official organ was also named *Prosvjeta*. From 1908 to 1914 it was a monthly and, after 1919 till World War II, a bimonthly publication. The association was banned when the Communists took over power after World War II.

PUCAR, ĐURO-STARI (1899-1979). A leading Communist politician in Bosnia immediately after World War II. He was born in Kosići, near Bosansko Grahovo. By profession he was a blacksmith. While learning his trade in Vojvodina, he also accepted Marxism-Leninism and became a member of the Communist Party in 1922 and an activist in the city of Subotica. After getting out of jail in 1939, he returned to Bosnia. During World War II, Pucar was an organizer of the partisan movement in western Bosnia and became a member of the leading political structures among Tito's (q.v.) partisans. After the war, he held the highest post in Bosnia-Herzegovina, was among the leading figures in Yugoslavia (q.v.), and has received the highest party and state honors. Party loyalty was his best distinction.

PULJIĆ, VINKO (1945-). Cardinal of the Catholic Church (q.v.) and the archbishop of Vrhbosna (Sarajevo [q.v.]), the largest Roman Catholic diocese in Bosnia-Herzegovina. Born near the city of Banja Luka (q.v.). Ordained to the priesthood in 1970. Consecrated archbishop in January 1991 and invested into the College of Cardinals in November 1994. He was the youngest cardinal at the time and the first from Bosnia-Herzegovina.

Throughout the 1992-1995 war period, the archbishop remained in besieged Sarajevo. He was tireless in helping the needy and in his calls for a peaceful resolution of the conflict in the region. Besides advocating the preservation of a multiethnic Bosnia-Herzegovina, he emphasized that all citizens in the country have three principal rights: the right to life, the sanctity of home, and the right to personal identity.

PUTEVI/PATHS. A bi-monthly journal for literary and other cultural issues. It was published in Banja Luka (q.v.) from 1960 till the beginning of the 1992 war. From 1955 to 1960 it was published under the name *Korijeni* (Roots).

-R-

RADIO 99/INDEPENDENT STUDENT RADIO. A private radio station in Sarajevo (q.v.) formed by young intellectuals and journalists. The station operates from the former Communist Party headquarters in the city and its "patron" is the Social Democratic Party (SDP) (q.v.), the former League of Communists. It carries summaries of news from a variety of foreign sources and diverse interviews relevant to the situation in the country. Its editor in chief is Adil Kulenović, a former information officer with the Social Democratic Party.

RADIO CD. A private radio station in the town of Zenica (q.v.), owned and operated by Zoran Mišetić, a Croat advocating a multinational Bosnia. It began its operation at the end of 1991, and the station was critical of all political parties, including the ruling Muslim party (SDA [q.v.]). In April 1993, armed Mujahedeens (q.v.) came to the station to kidnap Mišetić. Because of his absence, the studio was sacked, two journalists were taken as hostages, and the voice of the Radio CD was silenced. Mišetić escaped to Croatia and received international awards for "opposing intellectual cleansing."

RADIO-TELEVISION OF BOSNIA AND HERZEGOVINA/RADIO-TELEVIZIJA BOSNE I HERCEGOVINE (RTVBH). Formerly Sarajevo Radio-Television (RTVSA). The same company is split into TVBH (Television of Bosnia-Herzegovina) and RBH (Radio of Bosnia-Herzegovina).

RAGUŽ, MARTIN (1959-). Appointed minister without portfolio in the government of the Federation of Bosnia and Herzegovina (q.v.) in January 1996. Of Croat nationality.

Born in Stolac and finished higher education in political science.

RAPID REACTION FORCE (RRF). A 10,000-strong international military unit established in June 1995 in order to strengthen the UN mission and protect its personnel in Bosnia-Herzegovina. It went into action for the first time on July 23, 1995, on the road to Sarajevo (q.v.) over Igman Mountain after Serb artillery had killed two French peacekeepers. With the signing of the Dayton peace accord (q.v.), members of the RRF were merged into the newly established larger Implementation Force (IFOR) (q.v.) in December 1995.

RAVNO. A Croat village in southeastern Bosnia-Herzegovina attacked by Serbian forces on September 29, 1991. The village was destroyed; a number of civilians were killed, and others had to flee. Unofficially, this marked the beginning of Serbian aggression in Bosnia-Herzegovina.

REČICA, NUDŽEIM (1960-). Became minister of social policies, displaced persons and refugees of the Republic of Bosnia and Herzegovina in January 1966. Worked as deputy minister for refugees and as director of Office for Repatriation, and, before the war, in Energoinvest enterprise. Bosniac nationality. He finished higher education in economics.

REPUBLICAN PARTY/REPUBLIKANSKA STRANKA (RS). A small political party in Bosnia founded (1994) by Stjepan Kljuić (q.v.), former member of the state presidency and the former head of the Croatian Democratic Union (HDZ) (q.v.). The party seeks to attract membership from various segments of Bosnian society regardless of religion or ethnicity.

RIZVANBEGOVIĆ, FAHRUDIN (1945-). Named minister of education, culture, and sports in January 1996. Bosniac nationality. Born in Stolac and finished higher education in South Slavic languages and literatures.

ROSE, SIR MICHAEL (1940-). A British lieutenant general who served as a commander of the United Nations Protection Force (UNPROFOR) (q.v.) in Bosnia for a year from January 21, 1994, till January 24, 1995. After an initial "triumph," when the Serbs (q.v.) pulled back their heavy weapons a short distance from Sarajevo (q.v.), Sir Michael Rose was despised by the Bosnian government and many others for his seeming reluctance to offend the Serbs in order to deter their attacks, such as those on Goražde in April 1994 and their push into the Bihać (q.v.) pocket in November of the same year. He was very disinclined to call for NATO air strikes against the Serbs. After he was relieved from his duty in Bosnia-Herzegovina, he tried to dissuade the U.S. Congress from supporting Senator Robert Dole's resolution that would require the U.S. government to lift the arms embargo (q.v.) against Bosnia-Herzegovina by May 1, 1995. His acceptance of an elaborate painting of himself surrounded with Serbian national emblems, at the time of his departure from Sarajevo, is seen by some as a symbol of his partiality toward the Serbs while commanding UN troops.

Rose was born in Quetta and educated at Cheltenham, Oxford, and the Sorbonne. He was commissioned into the Coldstream Guards in 1964 and served in Aden, Germany, and Northern Ireland. Before his appointment to Bosnia, he was commander of the United Kingdom's Field Army and Inspector-General of the Territorial Army.

-S-

SACIRBEY (ŠAĆIRBEGOVIĆ), MUHAMED (1956-). Ambassador to the United Nations and Foreign Minister of Bosnia and Herzegovina. He was born in Sarajevo (q.v.). His family left the country in 1963, lived in Western Europe and in Northern Africa, and came to the United States in 1967. Sacirbey finished his higher education at Tulane University in Louisiana, where he received a doctorate of jurisprudence in 1980. Two years later he earned an MBA at Columbia

University (New York), School of Business. From that time till 1992, he held high positions in various large American firms, including Standard and Poor's Corporation, Security Pacific Merchant Bank, Mortgage-Structured Real Estate Finance Group, and Princeton Commercial Corporation.

In May 1992, Sacirbey was appointed Bosnian ambassador and permanent representative to the United Nations. In the beginning of June 1995, he was appointed minister of foreign affairs. In January 1996, however, he returned to his previous post as Bosnian ambassador to the United Nations. Sacirbey is one of the best-known and most articulate Bosnian state officials.

SAMOKOVLIJA, ISAK (1889-1955). The best-known Jewish (q.v.) writer in Bosnia and Herzegovina in modern times. Born in Goražde. Finished secondary education in Sarajevo (q.v.) and medical studies in Vienna. From his literary debut in 1927 till his death, he published numerous short stories, dramas, and poems. Most of his stories reflect the history of Sephardic Jews through which the author sees his own vision of the past. His writings, however, ponder not only the Jewish struggle for existence but also a wider universal quest to overcome the complexities of human life.

Samokovlija was also the editor of the literary journal *Brazda* (1948-51) and of the publishing house Svjetlost.

SANDŽAK or SANJAK/DISTRICT. Area: 8,686 sq km (2,250 sq mi). Population: 500,000. Capital: Novi Pazar. A border region between present-day Serbia and Montenegro that was a part of the Bosnian medieval state and also of the Bosnian *pashaluk* (Ottoman province). This narrow strip of land, known as the Sandžak of Novi Pazar (new bazaar), wedged between Serbia and Montenegro, was permanently severed from the Bosnian *pashaluk* in 1877. Although it remained under Ottoman jurisdiction, Austria-Hungary was granted permission by the Congress of Berlin (1878) (q.v.) to station troops in the region. In 1908, however, Vienna pulled its troops from this strategically important junction. After the 1912-1913 Balkan wars (q.v.) and the defeat of the Ottomans, the Sandžak of Novi Pazar was divided between Montenegro and Serbia. Before World War I, 75 percent of Sandžak's population was Muslim; after the war, 51 percent; and 33 percent in 1969. Many Sandžak Muslims, who identify with the Bosnian Muslims (q.v.), emigrated to Turkey and to Bosnia, where some of them reached high political positions. The political situation and relations between Serbs and Muslims (qq.v.) in Sandžak remained tense.

ŠANTIĆ, ALEKSA (1868-1924). A well-known poet from the so-called Mostar (q.v.) literary circle, consisting of a group of writers that promoted Serb literary and cultural activities in Herzegovina (q.v.) at the end of the last century. Šantić was born in Mostar. After studying in Ljubljana and Triest, he returned to Mostar in 1883 and, together with a few other patriots, he began to cultivate nationalist and cultural activities among the Serbs (q.v.) in Herzegovina. Among other endeavors, they published the literary journal *Zora* (1896-1901).

Šantić began to write poetry in his youth. However, his early literary expression is self-taught and modeled on the poetry of older Serbian writers. Only at the beginning of this century did he evolve into an original and reputable lyric poet. Patriotism, intimate love, and nature are his main themes. His style and language are light and close to folk lyric expression.

SARAJEVO. The capital of Bosnia and Herzegovina. The population in the 10 city counties in 1991 was over 527,000 of which 49.2 percent were Muslims, 29.8 percent Serbs, and 6.6 percent Croats (qq.v.). The city stretches on the slopes of the magnificent mountains of Trebević and Igman along the narrow valley of the river Miljacka at around 600 m (close to 2,000 ft) above sea level. Also in its vicinity is the source of the river Bosna (q.v.), after which the country was named.

Archeological findings have confirmed that not only a Neolithic settlement, but also an entire Neolithic culture prospered in the area. In the first century AD, the Romans, most probably attracted by the sulphurous springs of present-day Ilidža (q.v.), built a settlement there. The nucleus of the Bosnian medieval state began to evolve in that part of the country during the 10th century. At the core of the principality was the town of Vrhbosna, the main political, economic, and religious center. An independent Catholic diocese was established for Bosnia in the middle of the 11th century, and the cathedral of St. Peter was built in Vrhbosna at that time. In the 15th century Vrhbosna was taken by the Ottomans, who were already controlling the eastern Balkans (q.v.). In 1435, the military fort of Hodidjed was captured by the Turks. A few decades later a military commander in the region, Isa-bey Ishaković, built for himself the villa Saray in the area. He also established (1462) a religious endowment for the upkeep of the newly built *tekija* (*tekke*) for the Mevlevi dervish order and free room and board for needy people. These buildings and devout institutions were the beginnings of the present-day city of Sarajevo.

The oldest known record of the name of the city comes from 1507. The name Vrhbosna faded away and it was preserved only in the use of the Catholic Church (q.v.). The city passed through its "Golden Age" in the 16th century, during the governorship of Gazi Husref-Bey (1521-1541), who enriched it with major monuments, which formed the old *Čaršija* (the Old Market) of Sarajevo. Those monuments are Husref-Bey Mosque, the Kuršumli-Maderse, the Imaret, the Clock-Tower, the Bursa-Bezistan, and the Hammam. These buildings became not only the architectural pride of Sarajevo, but also the main educational and cultural centers of the Bosnian Muslims (q.v.).

Other Islamic architectural monuments in Sarajevo are the Ali-Paša mosque (1560-61), the Baščaršija mosque (early 16th c.), the Sultan's mosque (1566), the Čekrkčija mosque (1526), and the Ferhat-Paša mosque (1561-62). Among the non-Islamic monuments stand the Old Synagogue (1580), the City Hall (1896), the Orthodox Church (1720), and the Catholic Cathedral (1889).

Being located on the main route between the Ottoman capital and Central Europe, various trades with well-organized craft guilds (*esnafs*) prospered in Sarajevo for a long time. Present-day *Čaršija* and its core (*Baščaršija*) were the centers of Sarajevo's rich and colorful business life for centuries. Foreign commerce was also exuberant during the prosperous Ottoman centuries, especially with the city of Dubrovnik. Special living quarters for Dubrovnik merchants were located on the west bank of the Miljacka River, known as *Latinluk*, or the Latin quarters. The prosperity of Sarajevo was ensured while the empire was expanding further into Central Europe. The city was a major economic, cultural, and religious hub of an expanding superpower. The fortunes turned against the Ottomans in the 17th century, however, and the city began to stagnate. Bosnia and Herzegovina was no longer a springboard for expansion but a bulwark against the Habsburg onslaught. It became clear that the city was vulnerable when Prince Eugene of Savoy, a famed Habsburg military leader, burned the city to the ground in 1697. Various other misfortunes (fires, earthquakes, and epidemics) contributed to the decline of the city till its slow recovery in the second half of the 19th century and its growth into a modern city in the last few decades.

Besides the concentration of political and economic power in the city, Sarajevo is the most important cultural center in the country. It has a National Theater, a Puppet and Children's Theater, a Philharmonic orchestra, a Chamber Theater, a university, Catholic theological schools, the Academy of Sciences and Arts (q.v.), National Library, Gallery of art, various museums, and many other cultural, educational, and religious institutions.

The city also hosted the Winter Olympics in 1984. Many sport facilities were built at that time, and the Olympics have put Sarajevo on the map as a major tourist attraction. The city, unfortunately, has also become a symbol of human suffering and merciless destruction. Hundreds of innocent people have been killed and most of the city, including priceless historic monuments, have been destroyed by Serbian artillery that kept Sarajevo under siege from May 1992 till February 1996.

SARAJEVO ASSASSINATION. The assassination of the archduke Franz Ferdinand, the Habsburg heir apparent to the Austro-Hungarian throne, and his wife Sophie took place in Sarajevo (q.v.) on June 28, 1914. The seven-member assassination team (Gavrilo Princip, Trifko Grabež, Nedjeljko Čabrinović, Danilo Ilić, Vaso Čubrilović, Cvijetko Popović, and Muhamed Mehmedbašić) belonged to a revolutionary organization called Mlada Bosna (Young Bosnia) (q.v.). All of them, except for one, were young men of Serbian ethnic background who wanted to liberate Bosnia from the Habsburgs and unite it with Serbia.

Although there is some disagreement as to how much official Serbia was involved in the assassination, there is no doubt that the assassins were in direct connection with the revolutionary nationalist organization the Black Hand, whose leadership was directly linked with the military command of Serbia. Furthermore, three of the assassins (Princip, Grabež, and Čabrinović) were trained, armed, and sent from Serbia, where they were living, to Sarajevo to join the other members of the team in an attempt to slay the archduke who was visiting the city.

After an initial failure of the assassins and following some fatal mistakes on the part of the royal visitors, Princip succeeded in killing the archduke and his wife on the streets of Sarajevo. Princip and his companions became instant Serbian heroes, and the event sparked World War I.

SELIMOVIĆ, MEHMED-MEŠA (1910-1982). One of the best-known Bosnian writers. Born in the town of Tuzla (q.v.), he finished his primary and secondary education in his native town and graduated from the University of Belgrade with a degree in literature. During World War II, Selimović joined the Communist-led partisan movement, became a political commissar, and a member of the propaganda bureau toward the end of the war. In the post-war era, he was a member of theCommunist cultural elite in Belgrade, then a professor and art director of "Bosna-film" in Sarajevo (q.v.). Finally, he turned to full-time writing and became a leading figure in various literary and cultural organizations in Bosnia and Herzegovina.

Selimović as a writer was acclaimed by the critics only after the appearance of his novel *Derviš i smrt* (Dervish and Death) in 1966. In the novel, he successfully incorporated the traditions of Bosnian Muslims (q.v.) and the teachings of the Koran with the questions of an individual's fate caught in the universal struggle of good and evil. Selimović died in Belgrade.

SERB CIVIC COUNCIL (SCC)/SRPSKO GRAĐANSKO VIJEĆE (SGV). A political organization of the Serbs (q.v.) in Bosnia-Herzegovina that stands for safeguarding the country's borders without internal ethnic divisions. The Council was formed at the beginning of 1994 in Sarajevo (q.v.). It grew out of a Citizens' Forum, organized by Sarajevo Serbs in 1992. Some 34 Serb intellectuals belong to the Council. It is a grassroots organization that opposed Radovan Karadžić (q.v.) and the Pale (q.v.) Serb regime. The leader of the Serb Civic Council is Mirko Pejanović (q.v.) who was also a member of the presidency of Bosnia-Herzegovina.

SERB RADIO-TELEVISION/SRPSKA RADIO-TELEVIZIJA (SRT). The broadcasting network of the self-proclaimed Serb republic of Bosnia-Herzegovina (q.v.) and the main propaganda tool of the Serb nationalist forces in Bosnia-Herzegovina.

SERB REPUBLIC NEWS AGENCY/SRPSKA REPUBLIKA NOVINSKA AGENCIJA (SRNA). Established in April of 1992 in the Serb Republic of Bosnia-Herzegovina (q.v.), a day after the independence of the "republic" was proclaimed. It was the mouthpiece of the Serbian extremists and known for its unreliable reporting.

SERB REPUBLIC OF BOSNIA-HERZEGOVINA. A political entity in Bosnia and Herzegovina under Serbian control proclaimed in Sarajevo (q.v.) on March 27, 1992, by the Bosnian Serb leader Radovan Karadžić (q.v.) and an Assembly of 70 deputies. Although it was announced that the town of Banja Luka (q.v.) was to be its temporary capital, Pale (q.v.), a Sarajevo suburb, became its stronghold. The proclamation of the Republic came after Serb nationalists created several autonomous *krajinas* (regions) in Bosnia and Herzegovina in the fall of 1991.

Furthermore, in November 1992, Karadžić announced that the "Serb Republic of Bosnia-Herzegovina," and the "Serb Republic of Krajina" in Croatia had established a confederation. The loyalty of these Serb entities was to the "all-Serb state of Yugoslavia" (q.v.) and not to the legitimate states in which they were formed. Both entities were an instrument of Slobodan Milošević's (q.v.) policy of creating a Greater Serbia.

After the Serbs (q.v.) took control of about 70 percent of Bosnia, Milošević began to shift his policy from confrontation to negotiation in order to consolidate the Serb gains. The Bosnian Serb leadership, however, was not ready for any compromise. It demanded peace on its terms. This led to an alienation of the Bosnian Serb leadership from the power holders in Belgrade, and in August 1994, Milošević announced that Yugoslavia was severing its economic and political ties with the Bosnian Serb Republic. Although this was more a political move than a real severance, disagreements over the tactics were real. Because of external pressures and internal political and economic needs, Milošević finally disregarded the Bosnian Serb leadership and in the name of the Bosnian Serb Republic negotiated the Dayton peace accord (q.v.) in November 1995. The agreement legitimized the existence of the Serb Republic, which controls 49 percent of Bosnia and Herzegovina. Since then, both Radovan Karadžić, the president of the Serb Republic, and General Ratko Mladić (q.v.), commander of the Republic's military forces, have been indicted by the International War Crimes Tribunal (q.v.) in The Hague.

SERBIAN DEMOCRATIC PARTY/SRPSKA DEMOKRATSKA STRANKA (SDS). A political party in Bosnia-Herzegovina that united two main Serb political forces, socialists and neo-fascists. The SDS was formed in Bosnia in July 1990 by Radovan Karadžić (q.v.) and other leading Serb nationalists in the country with the blessing of Serbian president Slobodan Milošvić (q.v.) and his Serbian Socialist Party in Serbia. The Bosnian SDS was a sister party of the SDS in Croatia, which had been formed earlier and led the Serb rebellion in Croatia.

The most important point of the SDS program was its insistence on the national unification of Serbs (q.v.) living in Bosnia-Herzegovina and Croatia with Serbia. Although a few other Serb parties were formed in Bosnia-Herzegovina, the SDS quickly gained the largest following among the local Serbs, mainly because it had Milošvić's support. In the 1990 elections, it gained 72 seats out of the 240-seat bicameral legislature. The SDS opposed Bosnian independence and, after proclaiming Serbian regional autonomies, its armed Territorial Defense and paramilitary forces, with the assistance of the regular units of the former Yugoslav People's Army (JNA) (q.v.), occupied 70 percent of the country that was to be united with Serbia. After the formation of the Serb Republic of Bosnia and Herzegovina (q.v.) in April of 1992, the SDS retained the majority in the Serb self-proclaimed government assembly. Even after it seemed that Milošvić, had begun to abandon the idea of a Greater Serbia, at least for the time being, the SDS retained its hard-line stand. The party, however, was forced by Milošvić to accept the Dayton peace accord (q.v.) terms and its leader, Radovan Karadžić, was indicted by the International War Crimes Tribunal (q.v.) as a war criminal. The SDS leaders, however, have retained the support of the more extreme nationalist elements and of the Serbian Orthodox Church (q.v.) leaders.

SERBIAN ORTHODOX CHURCH. *See* ORTHODOX CHURCH.

SERBIAN RENEWAL MOVEMENT/SRPSKI POKRET OBNOVE (SPO). A Serbian ultranationalist political party led by Vuk

Drašković (q.v.). It claims to be an extension of the *četnik* (q.v.) movement from World War II. Because the Serbian Democratic Party had the support of the regime in Belgrade, the SPO gained only a minor following in Bosnia and Herzegovina. Although the nationalist goals of the SPO and Drašković were the same as those of Slobodan Milošvić (q.v.), the party remained in opposition to the socialist government in Belgrade.

SERBS. One of the Slavic peoples in the Balkans (q.v.). There is not yet a full agreement among scholars regarding their origin and national name. According to Byzantine emperor Constantine Porphyrogenitus, Serbs moved from north-central Europe to the Balkans (q.v.) in the early seventh century.

The initial phase of the Serbian political autonomy began around the year 800, under the name Raška in present-day southern Serbia. But the Serb self-rule was constantly challenged by stronger neighbors, Bulgaria or Byzantium. Only after Byzantine and Bulgarian power was greatly diminished, did the Serbs assert their political independence under the leadership of Stevan Nemanja (1168-1196).

Raška became a kingdom in 1217 and the independent Serbian Orthodox Church (q.v.) was established in 1219. Serbia reached the peak of its medieval power during the reign of Stevan Dušan (1331-1355), who, after a quick expansionist success, assumed the title of emperor (tsar) of the Serbs and Greeks. His rush to appropriate the title of the Byzantine emperors is indicative of his ambitions more than of the real power of the Serbs. Shortly after his death in 1355, the "imperial" power began rapidly to decline. Besides internal weaknesses, Serbia became a victim of Ottoman expansionism.

Although Serbia retained a semblance of autonomy under the Ottomans till 1459 by shifting the remnants of its power to the Danube regions in the north, the 1389 battle of Kosovo symbolizes the real end of the Serbian medieval state. This relatively minor battle became not only the symbol of national tragedy but the source and dream of a new future when vengeance over old enemies will occur and a new glorious Serbia will arise.

Regardless of the harsh life under Muslim rule, the Serb religious and ethnic identity was preserved mainly by the efforts of the church. In accordance with Islamic law, the Orthodox Christians were treated as an autonomous community in the state. Moreover, the Serbian independent patriarchate of Peć was restored in 1557 and the Serbian Orthodox Church was the guardian not only of religion but of national dreams.

After long centuries under the Ottomans, the Serbs struggle for independence began at the beginning of the last century. From the time of the first uprising (1804) till the time of the Congress of Berlin (1878) (q.v.) Serbia moved from securing autonomy to a fully recognized independent state. It was proclaimed a kingdom in 1882.

In alliance with Bulgaria, Greece, and Montenegro it declared war on Turkey in 1912, after which Serbia doubled the size of its territory by acquiring northern Macedonia. The Sarajevo assassination (q.v.) of the Austrian archduke Francis Ferdinand on June 28, 1914, by a Serb nationalist led to Serbia's conflict with Austria, and World War I. In 1918 Serbia became part of the Kingdom of Serbs, Croats, and Slovenes, renamed Yugoslavia in 1929 (q.v.) and ruled by the Serbian Karađorđević dynasty.

During the Ottoman invasions and domination of the Balkans (q.v.), a major population movement took place in the region. Many Orthodox Vlachs and Serbs from the eastern and southern Balkans (q.v.) migrated westward to Bosnia-Herzegovina, Croatia, and Hungary.

This population movement from the past created a cultural and religious mix that became a major predicament in the process of forming modern national consciousness and nation-states in this century. For the Serbs, the lands the Serbs migrated to are also Serbia. Consequently, the idea of gathering "Serbian lands" has been a major cause of friction among the Serbs and their neighbors throughout this century.

ŠEŠELJ, VOJISLAV (1945-). President of the Serb Radical Party (SRS). Born and educated in Sarajevo (q.v.), Šešelj received a Ph.D. in the Marxist doctrine of military defense. He was a member of the Communist Party and a reserve officer. In 1984, however, he was sentenced to eight years in prison for political reasons. Released after serving 21 months of the jail term, Šešelj became a leading Serbian nationalist voice. In 1991, he revived the Serbian Radical Party and the ultranationalist paramilitary *četnik* (q.v.) organization. He even received the title of "duke" from a well-known World War II *četnik* war criminal living in the United States. His militia implemented the most brutal tactics of warfare in Croatia and Bosnia-Herzegovina during the 1991-1995 war. Former U. S. secretary of state Lawrence S. Eagleburger listed him, among others, as a war criminal.

In the December 1992 elections in Serbia, the Radical Party won 73 out of 250 seats in the Belgrade parliament. Šešelj became a junior partner to Serbia's president Slobodan Milošević (q.v.) till the latter consolidated his power. Although Šešelj has become a marginal figure in Serbian politics since 1993, he has the support of the Serbian Orthodox Church (q.v.) and other right-wing forces, and his political career is not over yet, unless he gets indicted by the International War Crimes Tribunal (q.v.) in The Hague for war crimes.

SILAJDŽIĆ, HARIS (1945-). Former prime minister of Bosnia-Herzegovina. Born in Sarajevo (q.v.), where he also received his primary and secondary education. His father was an imam at one of the oldest mosques (*Begova džamija*) in the city. He graduated (1971) in Islamic studies at Benghazi University in Libya and taught Arabic language at the University of Priština, Kosovo. In 1980, he received a Ph.D. in history at the same university. His dissertation dealt with U.S. policies toward Albania in 1912-1913.

Silajdžić's political career began in 1990, when together with Alija Izetbegović (q.v.), later president of Bosnia-Herzegovina, he became one of the founders of the Bosnian

Muslim Party of Democratic Action (SDA) (qq.v.). Soon after his party won the December 1990 elections, he became minister of foreign affairs. He spent most of the time outside the country at the beginning of the war campaigning for support of Bosnia. In October of 1993, he became prime minister, returned to Sarajevo, and became the most popular politician in the city. He was also elected prime minister of the Muslim-Croat Federation (q.v.) in 1994.

Silajdžić became a well-liked personality among the Western diplomats and one of the few Bosnian politicians able to articulate the Bosnian tragedy and its cause to the world. He portrays himself as a moderate in contrast to a more conservative faction in the SDA led by President Izetbegović. Because of political disagreements and personality clashes, Silajdžić submitted a letter of resignation in August of 1995, but for the sake of unity in a war-torn country, he continued to serve as prime minister till he definitely resigned in January 1996. Since then, he has formed a new political party (Party for Bosnia and Herzegovina-SBiH). He ran against President Alija Izetbegović for Bosnia's new collective presidency in the September 1996 elections and won only about 14 percent of the vote. Silajdžić was appointed co-chair to the prime minister of Bosnia-Herzegovina at the beginning of 1997.

ŠIMIĆ, ANTUN BRANKO (1898-1925). A poet and literary critic. Born in Drinovci, Herzegovina (q.v.). He studied in his native village, Široki Brijeg, Mostar (q.v.), Vinkovci, and in Zagreb, where he lived from 1915 till his death. Despite poverty, sickness, and a short life, his exceptionally creative talents and powerful insights have had a major impact in Croatian literature (q.v.).

Being well informed about the contemporary European literary movements, Šimić became very critical of the traditional literary expressions of his older colleagues. His criticism became at once controversial and stimulating, and his expressionist poetry represents a defiance of the traditional literary forms. As a young student, he founded various publications in which he promoted contemporary European literary movements. The importance of Šimić's writings, however, was (re)discovered a few decades after his death.

SIMIĆ, NOVAK (1906-1981). A well-known writer from Bosnia. Born in the town of Vareš in 1906 to a Serb family. Finished higher education in Zagreb, Croatia, where he lived till his death. This poet and superb storyteller successfully depicted and scrutinized individual and social conflicts of modern day city life; personal struggles, rejections, failed love relations, and the general fate of human existence in a modernizing world. His best work is a novel *Braća i kumiri* (Brothers and Idols). In the post-World War II period, he was also the editor of the literary journal *Republika* in Zagreb. Although of Serb nationality, he considered his works to belong to Croatian literary expression.

SLOBODNA BOSNA/FREE BOSNIA. A weekly sensationalist newspaper that began publication at the end of 1991 in Sarajevo (q.v.). Its editor in chief was Senad Avdić. When the war began in Bosnia, the journalists working for the paper drifted to their respective ethnic camps. The paper became more and more a Bosnian Muslim (q.v.) voice. It escaped the Sarajevo siege and was moved to Zenica (q.v.) at the end of 1992.

SMAJIĆ, AHMET (1958-). Became minister of agriculture, aquiculture and forestry of the Federation of Bosnia and Herzegovina (q.v.) in January 1996. Bosniac nationality. Born in Rogatica and finished higher education in agronomy.

SMITH, LEIGHTON W., JR. (1939-). Admiral in U.S. Navy and commander of an international NATO-led 60,000-member peace Implementation Force (IFOR) (q.v.) in Bosnia and Herzegovina since December of 1995. Smith was born in Mobile, Alabama, and graduated from the Naval Academy in 1962. He served in various U.S. Navy deployments, including three combat cruises in waters off North Vietnam where he flew numerous missions. He was involved in direct support of

Desert Shield/Desert Storm operations during the war with Iraq. In 1994, he received his fourth star and became commander of U.S. Naval Forces in Europe and commander in chief of Allied Forces in Southern Europe. Admiral Smith has been awarded several medals for his distinguished service.

SMITH, RUPERT (1943-). A British lieutenant general who commanded the UN Protection Force (UNPROFOR) (q.v.) in Bosnia and Herzegovina from January to the end of 1995. It was on his watch that the UN policy makers began to shift from a rigorous "impartiality" and "proportionate response" in Bosnia toward a more assertive role of NATO air power, in response to the lack of Serb cooperation and their shelling of the UN "safe areas." His suggestion to create a Rapid Reaction Force (q.v.) to protect UNPROFOR from any, but mainly Serb, attacks and hostage taking, was also accepted. Although his calls for NATO air strikes in May were answered, it was in July, after the Serbs (q.v.) captured Srebrenica (q.v.) and killed thousands of Muslim men in the aftermath, that General Smith's strategy began to bear fruit. The power of decision over the air strikes was taken from the UN civilians and given to military commanders, which cleared the way for a forceful response to the Serb attacks on the civilian population in Sarajevo (q.v.) at the end of August. Thus, effective bombings along with a U.S. diplomatic initiative brought about a cease-fire and then the signing of the Dayton peace accord (q.v.) in November 1995.

Smith was educated at Haileybury and the Royal Military Academy, Sandhurst. He was commissioned in 1964 into the Parachute Regiment. He served in Kenya, British Guyana, Australia, Malta, Libya, Cyprus, Saudi Arabia, Malaysia, Belize, Zimbabwe, Northern Ireland, and the Persian Gulf. In September 1992, he became assistant chief of the Defense Staff in the Ministry of Defense.

SOCIAL DEMOCRATIC PARTY (SDP) OF BOSNIA AND HERZEGOVINA. The leading opposition party in the country. It evolved from the former League of Communists of

Yugoslavia (Yugoslav Communist Party). As the center of the Communist party and of the Yugoslav state was collapsing at the end of the 1980s, the Communist leadership in the former Yugoslav republics began to transform their parties into more open political organizations. Thus the League of Communists of Bosnia and Herzegovina — Party for Democratic Change was born in 1988. In March of 1991, however, the name of the party was changed to Social Democratic Party of Bosnia and Herzegovina.

The leadership of the Social Democratic Party claims that their party has discarded all the vestiges of the Communist past and has become a modern European-style social democratic party. The program of the Social Democratic Party of Bosnia and Herzegovina advocates preservation of the external borders of the country and rejects its internal division according to ethnic lines. Two journals (*Opredjeljenja* and *Sveske*) and a bi-weekly newspaper *(Styl)* were published by the Social Democratic Party. The publications, however, ceased during the war.

SOKOL/SOKOL GRAD. A medieval town located on the Pliva river near Jajce. In 1363, the Hungarian-Croatian king Louis Hungary (1342-1382) invaded Bosnia from the north and came to the fortified town of Sokol, at the center of the county (*župa*) of Pliva. His intentions were to subordinate Bosnia and its *ban* Tvrtko I (qq.v.). But King Louis could not take the city and his campaign was unsuccessful. The main defender of Sokolgrad was Vukac Hrvatinić, father of the famous Herceg Hrvoje Vukčić Hrvatinić (q.v.). As a reward for Hrvatinić's friendship and help, Tvrtko granted Vukac the county of Pliva. Sokolgrad lost its significance with the rise of the nearby town of Jajce and it was taken by the Ottomans in 1496. There were other medieval Bosnian fortifications with the same name (Sokol).

ŠOLA, ATANASIJE (1878-1960). A Bosnian Serb political leader at the beginning of this century. He was born in Triest where he finished lower education. He began his higher studies in

Paris, but did not finish them. Šola lived in Mostar (q.v.) where, by his strong opposition to the Austro-Hungarian annexation of Bosnia and Herzegovina (1908), he came to prominence. In 1911, he was elected to the Bosnian *Sabor* (Diet). After the Sarajevo assassination (q.v.) of Franz Ferdinand, Šola was arrested for antistate activities and sentenced to 12 years of imprisonment in 1916. At the end of the war, however, the National Council of the Serbs, Croats (qq.v.), and Slovenes for Bosnia and Herzegovina elected him president of the National government in Sarajevo (q.v.) in 1919.

SOLI. Territory in northeastern Bosnia between the rivers Sava, Drina, Drinjača, and Brka. The name derived from the salty springs and salt mines found in the region. The main regional town is Tuzla (q.v.). Its name comes from the Turkish word *tuz* (salt). The region came under the rule of the Bosnian *bans* (q.v.) in the middle of the 12th century.

ŠOLJIĆ, VLADIMIR. Named minister of defense of the Federation of Bosnia and Herzegovina (q.v.) in January 1996. Of Croat nationality. Born near Široki Brijeg in 1943 and finished higher education in mechanical engineering in Rijeka, Croatia, and Mostar (q.v.). He became a victim of the U.S. demand that his Iranian-allied Muslim deputy and also an Islamic religious functionary, Hasan Čengić, resign in return for the delivery of $100 million worth of U.S. arms to Bosnia's Muslim-Croat Federation. Šoljić resigned his office in mid-November 1996. He was named president of the Muslim-Croat Federation at the beginning of 1997.

SPAHO, MEHMED (1883-1939). A leading political figure among the Bosnian Muslims (q.v.) during the 1920s and 1930s. He was born in Sarajevo (q.v.), finished primary and secondary education in his native town, and law school in Vienna. Immediately before and during the First World War he worked at the Sarajevo Board of Trade. Spaho was a part of the National Council of the Serbs, Croats (qq.v.), and Slovenes, which took power in Bosnia from the Austrian authorities in 1918. From the beginning (1918) of the Kingdom of Serbs, Croats, and Slovenes (Yugoslavia after 1929) (q.v.) till his death, Spaho spent most of his time serving in various ministerial positions in Belgrade governments.

Besides his government positions, Spaho became the leading figure among the Bosnian Muslims and the most influential Muslim politician in Yugoslavia in the interwar period. He joined the Yugoslav Muslim Organization (JMO) in 1919 and was its president from 1921 till his death in 1939. Spaho's main goals were to preserve the administrative borders of Bosnia and Herzegovina, to keep the unity among the Bosnian Muslims, and, by political maneuvering between the Serbs and Croats, to advance the Bosnian Muslim cause. Spaho died in 1939 in Belgrade under suspicious circumstances.

SREBRENICA. A town located 400 meters (1312 ft) above sea level in the eastern part of Bosnia. It had an important silver mine already in Roman times. The name Srebrenica is derived from the word *srebro*, meaning silver. In the Middle Ages, Saxonian experts were brought to the town to improve the mining. Because of its silver, the town was a constant target of various invaders during pre-Ottoman centuries, especially of the Serbs (q.v.). During the Ottoman period, however, the exploitation of Srebrenica's mines was neglected. Mining in the region began to flourish again under Austro-Hungarian rule.

In recent times, Srebrenica became known to the world for being the first out of six United Nations "safe areas" declared in Bosnia in 1993. This small town became a haven for about 40,000 Bosnian Muslim (q.v.) refugees fleeing the Serbian forces that were in the process of ethnic cleansing (q.v.) in eastern parts of the country. Lieut. Gen. Philippe Morillon (q.v.), commander of the United Nations troops in Bosnia at the time, came to Srebrenica and prevented the town from being overrun by the Serbs. On March 16, 1993, he declared: "I will stay here among these people until the day that their survival is assured." But on July 11, 1995, the Serbian forces entered Srebrenica, masses of refugees were forced to run, and many people were massacred while the United Nations officials did nothing meaningful to stop the Serbian onslaught. It is estimated that several thousand Muslim men were executed after the fall of Srebrenica.

SRPSKI POKRET OBNOVE (SPO). *See* SERBIAN RENEWAL MOVEMENT.

STARI MOST/THE OLD BRIDGE. A magnificent stone bridge that spanned the east and west banks of the Neretva River in the city of Mostar (q.v.) was known as the Stari Most — the Old Bridge. The building of this masterpiece was commissioned by Sultan Suleiman the Magnificent. Its architect was Master Hajrudin — a pupil of the great Ottoman builder Sinan. This single-span stone bridge, 30 meters (98 ft) wide and 24 meters (79 ft) high, was one of the most beautiful architectural monuments and tourist attractions, not only in the country, but in all of Europe.

Before the Turkish occupation of this part of the country, there was a medieval wooden bridge hanging on massive iron chains at approximately the same location where the Old Bridge was built. A stone tower was also located on each end of the original bridge. Though modified, these medieval stone structures have survived till today. The tower on the right bank of the river is known as Halebija Tower, and the other as Herzeguša.

As the Old Bridge stood splendidly above the rapid stream of the Neretva River, it seemed as if it stood above the ages and mortal predicaments. The bridge also seemed to fuse various cultural elements into a single harmony. But after being "wounded" many times, the Old Bridge became a casualty of the war on November 9, 1993.

STEĆAK. A monthly magazine published in Sarajevo (q.v.) by the Croatian cultural society, Napredak (q.v.). The publication began in January 1994. In May 1995, the magazine received the prestigious International Union of Catholic Journalists

"Pierre Chevallier" Award in Geneva, Switzerland, for its contribution to freedom of expression and promotion of literary expression in war-torn Bosnia. In the same year *Stećak* received the International Catholic Union of the Press Award for its exemplary defense of freedom of information, as well as the Italian "Paolo Borsellino" Award in January 1996.

STEĆCI. (sing. STEĆAK). The name comes from the Croatian verb *stajati* (to stand). Unique medieval tombstones found in present-day Herzegovina (q.v.), interior Bosnia, parts of southern Croatia, and southwestern parts of Serbia. Estimates are that there are close to 60,000 stećci in the region. A debate continues among scholars about their origin and significance. It was believed at first that the stećci only marked the final resting places of the followers of the medieval Bosnian Church (Bosnian Christians) (q.v.), but it has become clear that the stećci were raised by the members of Catholic and Orthodox Churches (qq.v.) too, and that these massive tombstones even predate the appearance of the autonomous Bosnian Church.

Some scholars suggest that their origins are found in the pre-Christian Croatian burial practices. At first, according to this plausible hypothesis, there were ceremonial stone heaps (*gomile*) above and around the place where the dead were buried. Those that could afford it began placing a large stone, *stećak*, over their graves. For that reason, stećci are usually found near the old stone heaps and on the hill tops.

Stećci come in three basic shapes in various sizes: slabs, boxes, and sarcophagi. Many of them are rich in ornaments and in various symbols (the sun wheel, the crescent moon, the cross, the swastika, rosettes, braids, clover leaves, hunting scenes, and others). A small number of them have inscriptions, usually in the Bosnian Cyrillic (*bosančica*)(q.v.). Despite many uncertainties about the stećci, clearly they are artistic and literary treasures that witness to a medieval culture which transcends present religious differences and problems in this part of Europe.

Some other names for *stećak* are *biljeg* or *bilig* (marker), *kalup*, *slamenija* (figure), and *mašeta* (from Italian maseto-big stone).

STIPAN II, KOTROMANIĆ (q.v.). *Ban* (q.v.) of Bosnia (1312-1353). He was the son of Stipan I Kotromanić (1287-1302) and Elizabeth, daughter of Dragutin, the king of Serbia (1276-1282), who had to give up his throne and became a vassal of his brother-in-law, Hungarian King Ladislas IV (1272-1290), who gave him the region of Mačva as his feudal possession.

Stipan II was also a blood relative to the powerful Croatian Šubić family that overthrew his father, *ban* Stipan I in 1302. From that time till 1318, the Šubić family had the overlordship in Bosnia. Their growing feudal power, however, became a concern to the Hungarian-Croatian king, neighboring Venice, other feudal families in the area, and the free cities along the Croatian coastline.

Ban Mladen II (Šubić), believing that young Stipan Kotromanić was his faithful relative and a junior partner, installed him as *ban* of Bosnia (1312). But young Stipan turned his back on his Šubić cousins. By supporting the power of the king, he consolidated his domain and advanced his expansionist aims at the expense of the neighboring Croat nobility. The Hum region (later known as Herzegovina) (qq.v.), Krajina (coastal region between the rivers Neretva and Cetina) (q.v.), and Završje or Tropolje (region around the town Livno) recognized, at this time, the Bosnian *ban* as their overlord. Toward the end of his rule (1350), Stipan had to face the expansionist attack on Bosnia by the Serbian ruler Stevan Dušan, but the *ban* succeeded to free his lands from a short Serbian incursion.

This able *ban*, signed treaties with Dubrovnik (1334) and Venice (1335), invited Franciscans (q.v.) to Bosnia in 1340, coined the first Bosnian money, extended the borders of his realm from the Sava River to the sea, and from the Cetina River in the west to the Drina in the east. It was Stipan II who set the stage for the rise of the Bosnian kingdom.

Stipan II was married three times. His second wife, Elizabeth, was from a noble Polish family. His daughter Jelisava (Elizabeth) married (1353) the Hungarian-Croatian king Louis I (1342-1382) and became the mother of the famous Polish-Lithuanian Queen Jadviga (Hedwiga). All of his sons died before he did, and for that reason he was succeeded (1353) by his nephew Stipan Tvrtko (q.v.), who became the first Bosnian king.

STIPAN TOMAŠ. Bosnian king (1444-1461). He was an illegitimate son of the late king Ostoja. While his older brother Radivoj was a leading political adversary of the king Tvrtko II and, with the help of the Turks, declared himself king of Bosnia (c.1432), Tomaš, on the other hand, lived a secluded and humble life before he was elected to the throne. He was brought up in the schismatic Bosnian Church (q.v.). In his adult life, however, he became a full-fledged Catholic and, after his first marriage to a woman of humble background was annulled by Pope Eugene IV (1445), he married Katarina, daughter of Stipan Vukčić Kosača (Herzeg Stipan) (qq.v.), a powerful and rebellious lord from Herzegovina (q.v.).

Although the activities of Catholic religious orders were encouraged and generously supported, at first the king resisted the persecution of the Bosnian *kr'stjan*s who had support among the feudal lords. He promoted a religious coexistence to keep peace and unity in the country. At the beginning of his rule, Stipan Tomaš even declined to accept the crown from the pope in order to preserve a factional equilibrium among various internal and external forces. But he was under constant pressure from the popes and Hungarian kings to make good on his promise to eradicate the "heresy" in the country. Thus, after securing his position as a king, he did turn to persecutions (after 1450) of the adherents to the Bosnian Church who, by this time, were a small minority in the country. They found protection with Herzeg Stipan in his domain of Herzegovina.

Throughout the reign of Stipan Tomaš, the country was entangled in various strifes with neighboring rulers and in internal discontent. More important, the Turkish onslaught in the Balkans (q.v.) shadowed his entire reign. To strengthen his position, Tomaš decided to seek the protection of the West and its powerful Catholic Church. He turned to the neighboring Hungarian-Croatian king Vladislav (1440-1444) and his energetic military commander John Hunyadi. They did affirm him as the king of Bosnia and promised him assistance, but, in return, Tomaš gave Hunyadi all the privileges in Bosnia and even promised to pay him an annual tribute. King Tomaš, on the other hand, had turbulent relations with the Serbian ruler, Despot (title of Serbian rulers under Turkish suzerainty) George Branković and his successors, Turkish vassals themselves, and Stipan Vukčić Kosača, a defiant grand duke of the Hum (q.v.) region and the king's father-in-law. Branković wanted to grab parts of northeastern Bosnia, namely the rich mining town of Srebrenica (q.v.), and Vukčić constantly opposed the king's power.

Continuous conflicts and shifting alliances were taking place in the region. Major factors that prevented a much-needed unity in order to prevent Turkish expansion into Central Europe were the republic of Venice, the Croatian nobility, the free cities along Croatia's coast, the Hungarian king and various pretenders to the throne after Vladislav's death at the fatal battle of Varna (1444), the republic of Dubrovnik, the Serbian despots, Herzeg Stipan, the Bosnian king, and various feudal families. Even King Tomaš, although in a grave predicament himself, wanted to reassert his rule over territories that Bosnia lost after the death of Tvrtko I (q.v.). The Turks, however, were not only the main beneficiaries but were also the instigators of such feuds so they could soften the resistance to their expansionist designs.

After the fall of Constantinople (1453), the Balkans (q.v.) were ready for the final Turkish assault. Stipan Tomaš, although realizing the significance of the event, had to congratulate the sultan on his success, express his allegiance, and plead for the sultan's grace. Moreover, on the invitation of Herzeg Stipan, Sultan Mehmet II (1432-1481) sent his troops to southeastern Bosnia, and in 1456 the sultan demanded the surrender of four strongholds and an annual tribute in kind. At the same time, the Bosnian king, through his envoys, portrayed the gravity of the events in the Balkans (q.v.) to Rome and other Western capitals and pleaded for help. He emphasized that it was in the interest of Western neighbors to help him fight the Ottomans, but little help came from anywhere.

After a brilliant victory of John Hunyadi over the Turks in Serbia (1456) and the successful struggle against the Turks of the famous George Castrioti (Scanderbeg) in Albania, Stipan Tomaš decided to undertake a campaign against the Turks himself. But despite the pope's efforts on his behalf, the response to this Bosnian crusade was meager. More important, the sudden death of Hungarian king Ladislas Postumus (1444-1457) and problems of the Hungarian succession caused a political and military paralysis in the country that was Bosnia's main patron. Although Tomaš had some local successes at the beginning of the campaign, he quickly realized that the project was doomed to fail. Thus, in April of 1458, he concluded a peace with Mehmet II that brought Bosnia a step closer to the Ottoman occupation.

Following continuous attempts by Serbia to gain and hold the Srebrenica region in Bosnia, king Tomaš and despot Lazarus, son of George Branković, became friends. They even arranged a marriage between Tomaš's son Stipan Tomašević (q.v.) and Lazarus's daughter Jelena Margareta-Mara. But Lazarus died before the marriage took place. Since there were other claims to the despot's inheritance, the marriage was postponed. Finally, with the approval of the new Hungarian-Croatian king Mathias Corvinus (1458-1490), the marriage between Tomašević and Mara did take place in 1459 and Tomaš's son became despot of Serbia. King Tomaš believed that this would strengthen his weak position against the Turks, but his involvement in what little was left of Serbia became an additional burden.

As a Catholic and an outsider, the new despot Stipan was perceived as an agent of Hungary. The Serb residents of Smederevo, a famous medieval fort at the confluence of the Morava and Danube Rivers, were especially angry. Since

Stipan resided at Smederevo, the local Serbs (q.v.) helped the Turks to take this most important fortification in the region, rather than to see the Bosnian prince as their ruler. Moreover, the Bosnian king, his son Stipan, and his brother Radoje were falsely accused of treason in the West for the fall of Smederevo. This intrigue became a major problem for Tomaš and instead of getting help against the Turks he had to clear his name and his reputation to the potential allies.

Toward the end of Tomaš's reign, the situation in Bosnia was increasingly grave. The Ottomans required (1460) from the king a free passage through Bosnia and he had to acquiesce to their demands. He even asked Venice to either help him defend Bosnia or take it as their possession, but Venice did not want to escalate its confrontation with the Turks over Bosnia. Instead, the Venetian Senate promised small help, urged Tomaš to reconcile with Herzeg Stipan, and, in case the king had to flee the country, gave him permission to come to Venice.

As if Tomaš did not have enough problems with the Turks and his internal opponents, he became an ally of Venice against the *ban* (q.v.) of Croatia who attempted to regain possessions taken earlier by the republic. It was during this miniwar in 1461 that Stipan Tomaš died, leaving the country, which was in a perilous situation, to his son Stipan Tomašević.

STIPAN TOMAŠEVIĆ. King of Bosnia (1461-1463), the son of king Stipan Tomaš (q.v.) from his first marriage to a woman of humble background. His succession to the throne came on the eve of Bosnia's capitulation to the powerful Ottoman Empire. Sultan Mehmet II (1432-1481) was already making preparations for the final assault on Bosnia, and Tomašević did not have a trusted ally who could help him and his country. Stipan's father Tomaš had been an ally of Venice and even lost his life in a battle against Croatian nobility fighting on the side of Venice. Thus, the *ban* (q.v.) of Croatia was not eager to help Bosnia. Neither was the Hungarian-Croatian king Mathias Corvinus (1458-1490) who still suspected, although falsely, Stipan Tomašević of treason in losing the famous Smederevo fort to the Turks. Namely, Stipan Tomašević married Jelena Margareta-Mara, daughter of Serbian despot Lazarus in 1459 and became despot of Serbia himself. The new sovereign, however, as a Bosnian and a Catholic, was resented by the Serbs (q.v.). His enemies in Smederevo helped the Turks to take the city, but the young despot Stipan, his father Bosnian king Tomaš, and the king's brother Radoje were falsely accused of treason in the West for the fall of Smederevo. Even Herzeg Stipan (q.v.), the ruler of Hum (q.v.), was an opponent of king Stipan Tomašević.

To make preparations for the defense of the country, Stipan Tomašević began to make peace with his opponents, including his stepmother Katarina Kosača (q.v.) and her father Herzeg Stipan, and he sought help from outside the country. In order to boost his prestige among his noblemen and neighboring rulers, he sent a delegation to Rome to request a royal crown from the Holy See. Pope Pius II saw that such a move would strengthen Stipan's position and, therefore, the defense of Bosnia and the Christian West. The crown was sent and Stipan was solemnly crowned in the presence of the pope's legate in Jajce 1461. On Stipan's request, the pope also established new dioceses in Bosnia to boost the vitality of the church. These very symbolic events and the king's success in achieving peace and unity in the country, however, proved to be inadequate to save Bosnia.

The first significant problem Stipan had to face was the displeasure of Mathias Corvinus. Mathias considered Bosnia a vassal-state and the coronation implied full sovereignty of Bosnia; it made King Stipan an equal to Mathias. This was unacceptable to him. All papal attempts to calm Mathias had little effect. Finally, to placate him, Stipan Tomašević paid a large sum of money to the Hungarian king. Furthermore, the Bosnian king had to cede four fortifications to Mathias, enter a common defense alliance against the Turks, and cease paying annual tribute to the sultan. After the sultan heard of the Hungarian-Bosnian treaty and that the tribute to him would cease, Mehmet II hastened his plans concerning Bosnia.

Stipan Tomašević began his preparation for the defense of the country. He pleaded for help from abroad but got only empty promises. Realizing his predicament, Stipan sent two envoys to Istanbul in the spring of 1463. They begged the sultan's pardon, promised to pay the tribute, and asked for a 15-year truce. While giving a positive answer to the Bosnians and lulling them into a false sense of security, the sultan, with his massive army, marched toward Bosnia only days after the envoys returned.

In the early spring of 1643, the Turkish forces entered upper Bosnia from Serbia and through the Drina valley. King Stipan and his family were at the royal residence in the town of Jajce. The news that the royal town of Bobovac, believed to be an impregnable fort, fell through treason created panic and confusion. Resistance collapsed throughout Bosnia, and King Stipan tried to escape to Croatia, but a detachment of the Ottoman army caught up with him in the fortified town of Ključ (q.v.). Instead of laying a siege, the Ottoman commander negotiated the surrender of the king and the fort. A charter was issued guaranteeing the king's life, safety, and freedom. Trusting the Ottoman promises, Stipan Tomašević surrendered with the Ključ garrison in mid-May 1463. The king's life, however, was not spared. He was brought to the sultan in Jajce and beheaded there along with his uncle Radivoj. The rest of Bosnia fell rapidly and the region of the original medieval Bosnia became a Turkish *sandžak* (military district).

Queen Mara, Stipan Tomašević's wife, while trying to escape from Bosnia was captured by the Croatian *ban*. She escaped and in October 1463 came to Dubrovnik. From there she moved to the city of Split, which was under Venice at the time, where she lived in a Benedictine monastery until Venetians forced her to leave Split. She went to Istria and then to Hungary where her mother lived. The last known news about the queen came from 1498. At that time, she was in Jerusalem.

STOJANOV, DRAGOLJUB. Named minister without portfolio in the Republic of Bosnia and Herzegovina in January 1996. Serb nationality. Served as minister of foreign trade in the Republic of Bosnia and Herzegovina and professor of economics at the University of Sarajevo.

STOLTENBERG, THORVALD (1931-). Former Norwegian minister of foreign affairs who replaced Cyrus Vance (q.v.) in May 1993 as UN peace negotiator in the former Yugoslavia (q.v.). In September 1993, he and the EC negotiator Lord Owen (q.v.) proposed a peace plan that would divide Bosnia and Herzegovina into three ethnic semiindependent states. However, their plan failed.

Stoltenberg became a special envoy of the UN secretary general in Bosnia, after the Sarajevo government refused to deal with Yasushi Akashi (q.v.), a special UN envoy to the former Yugoslavia, and the head of the entire UN mission in the Balkan region. He became infamous for his explanation of the war in Bosnia. According to him, the Bosnian Muslims and Bosnian Croats (qq.v.) were in fact "ethnic Serbs" (q.v.) and the war was a product of "socio-economic forces; the poor Serb peasants were fighting with the richer Muslims."

Stoltenberg was born and educated in Oslo. He served in various positions in Norway's Ministry of Foreign Affairs, including as secretary of its Embassy in Belgrade (1961-1964). He is board member of the Oslo Labor Party and has served in the city government. He studied international law and international relations in Austria, Switzerland, the United States, and Finland. From October 1989 to January 1990, he served as the United Nations high commissioner for refugees.

-T-

TADIĆ, MATO (1952-). Appointed minister of justice of the Federation of Bosnia and Herzegovina (q.v.) in January 1996. Of Croat nationality. Born in Brčko (q.v.) and finished law school.

TITO. Josip Broz, better known as Tito (1892-1980). President of the former Yugoslavia (q.v.). He was born in the village of Kumrovac, in northwestern Croatia, a part of the Austro-Hungarian Empire at the time. As a young locksmith apprentice and a Social Democratic Party member, he served in the Austrian army during World War I. After being captured by the Russians, he joined the Red Army in 1917. In 1920, he returned to the newly formed South Slavic state where he became an ardent Communist activist. Because he was persecuted and served a jail sentence for his political and terrorist activities, Broz became noticed by the local Communist leaders and by the Comintern. In 1939, after the purge of the exiled Yugoslav Communists in Moscow, Tito, as Stalin's faithful follower, was picked (1939) to be the general secretary of the Communist Party of Yugoslavia. From that time till his death he dominated the party, and after 1945, Yugoslav politics.

After Germany attacked the Soviet Union (June 22, 1941), Tito began to organize attacks against the Axis powers and their collaborators on the territories of the collapsed Yugoslav state, and became the commander of the Communist-led partisan forces. Because of his guerrilla activities, he was recognized by the Western Allies as the leader of the Yugoslav resistance in 1943. With Soviet and Allied help Tito became the winner of the war in the region, and took over power in the reunified and Communist-controlled Yugoslavia in 1945. Under his leadership, a vast number of people were executed, jailed, and terrorized as "enemies of the people" during and after the war, and many escaped to the West.

Tito faced a major crisis when Yugoslavia was expelled from the Soviet bloc in 1948. The West, however, hoping that this was only the first crack in the Communist camp, helped Tito to maintain his personal power and preserve the country's independence. After a short period of disorientation, he embarked on ideological experimentation that included national communism, workers' councils, self-management, and market socialism. Furthermore, Tito successfully used the Cold War conditions and exploited both East and West for his benefit. He also promoted the idea of the Non-Allied movement among the newly independent countries in the so-called Third World, and became one of its main leaders.

Tito believed that decentralization of some decision-making processes in Yugoslavia was possible as long as the Communist Party held the monopoly of power, especially control of the military. Because of such assumptions, a "controlled federalism" was implemented in Yugoslavia, after the conservative forces were subdued in the mid-1960s. But by the early 1970s, the true nature of Tito's "liberal socialism" became obvious. The economy stagnated, a massive emigration to the West was taking place, a liberal movement in Croatia was brutally crushed, and all voices of freedom were subdued. Tito in his lavish lifestyle, however, remained a popular figure. In the international community, many believed that he had successfully resolved the national question in Yugoslavia and that he was a strong barrier against possible Soviet expansionism in the Balkans. His sympathizers in the country, on the other hand, praised him for being clever in using the East and the West in procuring Western aid, mainly cheap loans that secured a higher standard of living for the bureaucrats who, in turn, watched over the country.

Although various observers argue that the "Yugoslav experiment" did work, it became clear soon after Tito's death in May 1980 that Tito's "bigger than life" figure, an exalted image of Yugoslav "brotherhood and unity," and a praised Yugoslav socialist model were little more than a myth of the time.

TOMIĆ, NEVEN (1958-). Appointed minister of foreign trade of the Republic of Bosnia and Herzegovina in January 1966. Previously served as minister of finances of the Republic and the Federation of Bosnia and Herzegovina (q.v.). Before the war, he served in various administrative positions at the city of Mostar (q.v.). Croat nationality. Born in Mostar (q.v.) and finished higher studies in economics.

TRAVUNJA. A separate district dating from the eighth or ninth century that is partially in the present-day southeastern end of Herzegovina (q.v.). Medieval Travunja included the town of Kotor in the southeast to Dubrovnik in the northwest, and from the Adriatic Sea toward the northeast along the present border between Bosnia-Herzegovina and Montenegro. The town of Trebinje was its main center. The region was ruled by members of the Serbian Nemanjić family from the end of the 12th century till 1377, when it was annexed to the Bosnian state by the first Bosnian king, Tvrtko I (q.v.).

TREATY OF KARLOWITZ/KARLOVCI (1699). By signing this peace treaty, the Ottomans lost Hungary, northern Croatia, and Transylvania to the Habsburgs; Dalmatia, the Morea, and Agean Islands to Venice; Podolya and southern Ukraine to Poland, and Azov and lands north to the Dniester to Russia. The treaty marks the beginning of the Ottoman withdrawal from Europe and the switch from its offensive to a defensive position in relation to European powers. As a result, Bosnia-Herzegovina became an Ottoman line of defense toward the West, its borders began to resemble today's contours, and a large number of Muslim landlords and populations migrated to Bosnia from Hungary and Croatia.

TUĐMAN, FRANJO (1922-). President of the Republic of Croatia since 1990. He was born in 1922 in Veliko Trgovišće near Zagreb. As a young man, he joined the Communist movement and the partisan resistance during World War II, and became an army general. After the war, he was a carrier officer working in the Ministry of National Defense in Belgrade. He also received a Ph.D. in history. In 1960, Tuđman left the military and became the director of the Institute for the History of the Labor Movement of Croatia, associate professor of history at Zagreb University, and a member of the parliament of the Socialist Republic of Croatia. In the late 1960s, however, he came in conflict with the regime. He was dismissed from the Institute in 1967 and was given a two-year jail term in 1972, and three more years in 1981.

On the eve of the demise of Communism in Yugoslavia (q.v.), and then of the state itself, he stepped to the forefront of the opposition forces and became president of the Croatian Democratic Union (HDZ) (q.v.). The HDZ won the first multiparty elections and Tuđman was elected president of Croatia in 1990, and again in 1992.

One of the more controversial issues regarding Tuđman's presidency has been his policy toward Bosnia and Herzegovina. During the entire 1991-1995 war, there was a constant mutual mistrust between him and the Muslim leadership in Sarajevo. He was suspected of making a deal with Slobodan Milošević (q.v.) of Serbia to divide Bosnia and Herzegovina between the Serbs and Croats (qq.v.). In practice, however, he went along with the dictates of the West.

TUZLA. A town in northeastern Bosnia located 232 meters (761 ft) above sea level. The Tuzla Basin is one of the most industrialized parts of Bosnia and Herzegovina.

It is not known for certain when the settlement was established, but it must have originated in ancient times because of large deposits of salt in the region. In medieval times, the region was known as Soli (Salts) and the present name of the town comes from the Turkish word for salt (*tuz*). Besides salt, the Tuzla region is rich in coal deposits and other minerals. Because of its strategic location and salt production, the Ottomans made Tuzla an important administrative and military center. In the first half of the last century, the Tuzla region was known for its fierce resistance to Ottoman reforms of the time.

According to the 1991 census, Tuzla municipality had 131,000 inhabitants. Out of that 47.6 percent were Muslims, 15.6 percent Croats, 15.5. Serbs (qq.v.), 16.5 percent Yugoslavs, and 4.7 percent others. Among larger cities in Bosnia and Herzegovina, only in Tuzla did former Communists ("the Reformists") win the 1990 elections. The town remained under the Sarajevo Muslim-dominated government and was relatively free of interethnic violence during the 1992-1995 war. The most significant war tragedy in the city occurred on May 25, 1995, when an artillery shell fired by the Serb forces landed in a crowded cafe killing 71 and injuring 150 young people. Since the end of the war, the city leadership has been under pressure to let the Muslim party (SDA [q.v.]) take control of the town and the region.

TVRTKO I (1353-1391) - *Ban* (q.v.) and first king of Bosnia. Stipan Tvrtko was the oldest son of Bosnian *ban* Stipan II's (q.v.) brother, Vladislav Kotromanić (q.v.), and Jelena Šubić. Because Vladislav was in poor health, he transferred his right of succession to his youthful son Tvrtko.

The first major problem the young and ambitious *ban* encountered was pressure from the Hungarian-Croatian king Louis I (1342-1382) to assert his kingly powers over the nobility, especially in Bosnia. Furthermore, Louis I was the son-in-law of Tvrtko's predecessor Stipan II and considered himself the rightful heir to the Bosnian banship. Moreover, the threat of Serbia's expansionism into Bosnia dissipated after the early death of its ambitious ruler Steven Dušan (1355), and Louis wanted to prevent Bosnia's possible assertion of autonomy. Thus, under a dictated agreement (1357) Louis I acquired lordship over the southwestern regions of the country under the pretext of obtaining his wife's rightful dowry. However, even after undertaking a major military campaign against Bosnia in 1362, the king could not subdue the resistance of the local feudal lords. Their support of Tvrtko was strong enough to repel the king's pressures at this time.

By 1365, the relations between the king and Tvrtko were normalized; the *ban* reaffirmed his loyalty to the king as his suzerain and the king recognized him as the *ban* of Bosnia. The antebellum status in the country was reestablished. But the agreements with the king obligated Tvrtko to expel the followers of the Bosnian Church (q.v.) from the country because the king considered them heretics. This was, however, a political move against the Bosnian feudal lords who supported the local church traditions and resisted the royal powers. This provision brought Tvrtko in conflict with the local gentry and the leaders of the Bosnian Church. An open rebellion erupted in 1365. Tvrtko was dethroned and, with his mother, had to flee the country to the court of King Louis I. However, with a small army that the king furnished and with the help of the nobility that remained faithful to him, Tvrtko crushed the rebellion (1367) and regained power.

By 1370, Tvrtko not only consolidated his power but began to expand his realm. First he turned to Serbia, the neighboring kingdom that was falling apart. The youthful Uroš IV (1356-1367), successor to his powerful father Dušan, was unable to prevent local lords from grabbing total power in their realms. Uroš was even assassinated by an ambitious member of the aristocratic oligarchy. Besides the internal predicaments, the rise of the Ottoman Turks was overshadowing the events in Serbia. After the defeat of Serbian forces in 1371 on the banks of the Maritza River (Chernomen), Serbia had to declare allegiance to the sultan and pay tribute.

Prince Lazar (1371-1389) of Serbia, therefore, became a Turkish vassal and, simultaneously, became embroiled with other Serbian feudal lords. A situation like this was a tempting opportunity for Tvrtko to expand his domain. He became involved in the Serbian power struggle by supporting Lazarus to defeat his enemies and, as a result, Tvrtko gained Travunja (q.v.) (southern Herzegovina [q.v.] and parts of Montenegro) with the sea coast to the port of Kotor and parts of Serbia (Podrinje [q.v.]). Disintegrating processes in Serbia on one hand, King Louis' preoccupations with his Polish-Lithuanian affairs on the other, then his death in 1382, followed by a civil war in Hungary, made it possible for Tvrtko to achieve his ambitions. He expanded Bosnian borders and made it the most powerful contemporary Christian country in the Balkans (q.v.).

In a quiet move (1377), without informing either King Louis I or Prince Lazarus of Serbia, Tvrtko had himself crowned king of Bosnia, and, probably in a second ceremony at the Serbian Monastery at Miloševo, as king of Serbia.

Realizing that there was a strong resistance among the Croatian nobility to the crowning of 12-year-old Maria (1382) as the legitimate successor to her father Louis I, he stirred their defiance in order to prepare the way for the expansion of his domain further into Croatia. But when an open rebellion erupted, led by Ivan Paliža in Vrana near Zadar, Bosnian help did not come and the rebellion was easily crushed. Tvrtko also made peace with Maria's advisors and acquired from them (1385) the port of Kotor (in present-day Montenegro).

Using the succession strife in Hungary and Croatia that continued till 1387 and the help of Croatian noblemen that found refugee in his kingdom, Tvrtko forced his sovereignty upon southern Croatia. In 1390, he even took the tile of "King of Croatia and Dalmatia." His early death in March 1391, however, prevented him from consolidating his possessions and further expanding the Bosnian kingdom.

The instant rise of Tvrtko's personal and state power was doomed to collapse from the very start because of Bosnia's internal and external weaknesses. The problem of succession became a consistent impediment for stability in the country. A strong royal power became a prey to an ever-ambitious feudal oligarchy. Furthermore, the advancing Turkish armies were already at the gate of Bosnia.

In 1391 the Turks invaded southeastern Bosnia, devastated the countryside, and established a foothold in the land for further incursions. Moreover, the rise of Bosnia, in the first place, was possible only because of the neighboring countries' weaknesses. Any recovery on their part was an imminent threat to Bosnia. Thus the newly acquired regions of Croatia were slipping away from Bosnian control right after Tvrtko's death. His successor, Dabiša, in return for being recognized the king of Bosnia, had to accept the suzerainty (1393) of the Hungarian king Sigismund, including the provision that after his death the Bosnian royal crown would pass to Sigismund as a legitimate monarch of the country.

Tvrtko was married (1374) to Doroteja, one of the two daughters of Bulgarian ruler Ivan Stracimir who was captured in 1365 and kept as a prisoner till 1369 by the Hungarian king Louis I. After Ivan's return to Bulgaria, his two daughters were kept at Louis' court for ransom. Thus, Doroteja came to

Bosnia from Hungary. Tvrtko II was the only child born of this marriage. After Doroteja's death, Tvrtko I was arranging his second marriage (1390) to a daughter of Duke Albert III from the Habsburg family. But his sudden death on February 14 or 15, 1391, ended all his plans and ambitions.

-U-

UNITED NATIONS PROTECTION FORCE (UNPROFOR). On February 21,1992, the UN Security Council adopted Resolution 743 to establish a United Nations Protection Force (UNPROFOR) to be sent to Croatia in order to guarantee the implementation of the Vance (q.v.) peace plan that had gone into effect a month earlier. UNPROFOR was fully deployed in early June 1992. Its main assignments were to supervise the withdrawal of the former Yugoslav People's Army (JNA) (q.v.) from Croatia, take control of the Serb occupied regions that did not recognize the Zagreb government, disarm the local Serb rebels, stabilize the region so that the Croats (q.v.) expelled from the Serb-controlled territories could safely return and live in their homes, and assure that an ethnically balanced local authority could be established in regions that were under the control of the rebels. UNPROFOR accomplished only the first assignment successfully. The Serb forces not only did not disarm, they and the Serb civilian authorities in the so-called protected areas received a semiofficial status under the protection of the UN forces.

At the beginning, the headquarters of the UN mission in Croatia were in Sarajevo (q.v.). But after the shelling began in April 1992, the UN withdrew from the city. On June 11th, however, an advanced party of about 150 UN Canadian troops, led by Brigadier Lewis McKenzie (q.v.), and a few French military monitors came to Sarajevo from Croatia. Their assignment was to open the Sarajevo airport for relief flights. On June 29, the UN Security Council authorized (Resolution 761) redeployment of 1,000 more Canadian UNPROFOR troops form Croatia to Sarajevo. Again, on September 14, 1992, the Security Council authorized (Resolution 776) the enlargement of UNPROFOR's mandate and strength in Bosnia-Herzegovina to provide for the protection of humanitarian convoys. The UN peacekeeping contingent in Bosnia was also known as UNPROFOR-2, to distinguish it from UNPROFOR in Croatia. The number of UN troops in the region was on the steady increase and by the end of November 1994 there were close to 39,000 UN peacekeepers from 37 countries in the Balkans (q.v.); out of that, close to 23,000 were in Bosnia-Herzegovina. As a part of the Dayton peace accord (q.v.), the UNPROFOR was replaced by the Implementation Force (IFOR) (q.v.) under NATO command in December 1995. The following officers were the UNPROFOR commanders: Lt. Gen. Satish Nambiar (India) from March 3, 1992, to March 3, 1993; Lt. Gen. Lars-Eric Wahlgren (Sweden) from March 3, 1993, to July 1, 1993; Gen. Jean Cot (France) from July 1, 1993, to March 10, 1994; Lt. Gen. Bertrand Guillaume de Sauville de Lapresle (France) from March 10, 1994, to February 28, 1995; and Lt. Gen. Bernard Janvier (France) till the end of the UNPROFOR mandate.

USORA. Territory around the lower flow of the Bosna River (q.v.); from the Brka River in the east to the Ukrina River in the west and from the Sava River in the north to the mountains Konjuh and Borje in the south. The region was named after the Usora River. The central town in the region is Doboj. The region became a part of Bosnian domain in the 13th century.

USTAŠA/REBEL. The Ustaša Croatian Revolutionary Organization was founded in 1929 by Ante Pavelić (q.v.), a Zagreb lawyer and Croatian representative in the parliament of the Kingdom of Serbs, Croats, and Slovenes (q.v.) in Belgrade, and by his political confidants. After the assassination of Stjepan Radić, the leading Croatian politician after World War I, and his associates in the Belgrade parliament (1928) and after the imposition of a dictatorship by King Aleksandar (1929), Pavelić and his comrades turned to revolutionary means in order to shatter the Yugoslav state and bring about Croatia's independence. Accordingly, all means were to be used in order to bring about these goals. Furthermore, as the Yugoslav state was a product of the post-World War I Versailles order, they believed the existing European state system had to be modified and the principle of self-determination of peoples be respected. For that reason the movement associated itself with the other revisionists of the time, especially those that were against the Yugoslav state, like the Internal Macedonian Revolutionary Organization (IMRO) and Hungary.

In 1934, members of *ustaša* and IMRO assassinated King Aleksandar in Marseilles during his visit to France. After the collapse of Yugoslavia in April of 1941, Pavelić and his followers formed the Independent State of Croatia (NDH) (q.v.) with the help and under the protection of the Axis powers. Bosnia-Herzegovina was part of the NDH, and a sizable number of Croats (q.v.) (Catholics and Muslims [q.v.]) from Bosnia-Herzegovina were members of the *ustaša* movement or joined their armed units during the war. The movement is blamed for its nationalist extremism and collaborationism, but to the Croatian nationalists it symbolized most of all uncompromising anti-Yugoslavism.

-V-

VANCE, CYRUS (1917-). Former U.S. secretary of state who served as personal envoy of the UN secretary general in the search for peace in the former Yugoslavia (q.v.) from October 1991 to April 1993. He put together a UN-sponsored "permanent cease-fire" agreement between Croatia and Serbia that took effect in January 1992 and lasted, with some major breaks, till the summer of 1995. Representing the UN, he co-chaired with former British foreign secretary David Owen (q.v.) as the EC representative of the Geneva Conference on peace in Bosnia-Herzegovina. They proposed a peace plan that would divide Bosnia-Herzegovina into 10 semiautonomous cantons. But the proposal fell through. After Vance resigned, he was succeeded by Thorvald Stoltenberg (q.v.), former Norwegian minister of foreign affairs.

VEČERNJE NOVINE/EVENING PAPER. An afternoon Sarajevo (q.v.) newspaper published by the same company as the daily *Oslobođenje* (q.v.), whose profile and political tenets it shared. Although under difficult circumstances, it was also published during the war. The paper is an unofficial voice of the Muslim-led Sarajevo government.

VIŠEGRAD. A town located 344 meters (1,128 ft) above sea level on the border with Serbia in eastern Bosnia. The county of Višegrad in 1991 had a little over 21,000 inhabitants, out of which 63 percent were Muslim, 33 percent Serbs (qq.v.), and four percent others.

During the Ottoman centuries, the town was an important link on the road from Bosnia to Istanbul. Višegrad is best known for its famous stone bridge over the Drina River. It was built as an endowment of Mehmet Paša Sokolivić (Sokullu Mehmet Paşa), a native son taken as a boy-tribute by the Turks to Istanbul. Because of his talents, he advanced rapidly to the top of Ottoman bureaucracy and became a famous grand vizier (1565-1579) the second only to the sultan. The bridge was built by a superb Ottoman architect, Mimar Sinan, between 1571 and 1577. It has 11 arches and is 175.5 meters (576 ft) long. The fame of the bridge was immortalized in modern times by the world-renowned Bosnian writer Ivo Andrić (q.v.), who received the Nobel Prize for literature (1962) for his novel entitled *The Bridge on the Drina.*

VJESNIK MIRA also *GLASNIK MIRA*/HERALD OF PEACE. A weekly paper published by IFOR (q.v.) in Bosnia and Herzegovina since December 1995. Its purpose is to provide information on mine awareness, separation of forces, elections, and world and local news. It is published in both Latin and Cyrillic scripts.

VJETRENICA. A cave that is one of the most beautiful phenomena in the country. It is located near the village of Zavala, above the river Trebišnjica in southeastern Herzegovina (q.v.). Its main chamber, halls, and corridors stretch 7.5 km (4.7 mi) and are famous for their beauty. The stone curtains, stalactites, and stalagmites of various shapes, small lakes, brooks, the wind, and the acoustics adorn this natural beauty. The Golden Hall near the main entrance is its most famous section.

VOJSKA REPUBLIKE SRPSKE (VRS). *See* ARMY OF THE SERB REPUBLIC.

VUKČIĆ HRVATINIĆ, HRVOJE (¿-1416). A leading nobleman in Bosnia and Croatia. Parts of medieval Bosnia known as the Lower Regions (q.v.) (around the upper flow of the river Vrbas) were in the possession of the nobleman Hrvatin at the end of the 13th century. His descendants, called Hrvatinići or sons of Hrvatin, became the leading aristocratic family in Bosnia and southern Croatia. At the time of the struggle between Stipan II Kotromanić (qq.v.) of Bosnia (1312-1353) with Mladen II Šubić of Croatia, two of Hrvatin's sons (Pavao and Vukac) sided with Mladen, and the third (Vukoslav) with Stipan II. The victorious Kotromanić at first punished the two Hrvatinić brothers who did not support him by taking their inheritance, but in time they all reconciled.

Hrvoje Vukčić Hrvatinić was the son of Vukac Hrvatinić and became the best-known aristocrat of Bosnia and southern Croatia at the end of the 14th century. In 1380, he was named grand duke of the Bosnian kingdom by the first Bosnian king Tvrtko I (q.v.). After Tvrtko's death he expanded his power and possessions, and even became regent for the Bosnian king Stipan Ostoja (1398-1404).

Because the fate of the Hungarian-Croatian king Sigismund was unknown for a few months after his defeat by the Ottomans at Nicopolis (Sept. 25, 1396), a leading Croatian nobility elected Ladislas of Naples as the new king. But, after Sigismund returned alive and well, he, by deceit, executed

Ladislas's main supporters (1397). Rebellion against Sigismund resulted among Croatian and Bosnian aristocracy. Hrvoje Vukčić defeated Sigismund's forces in 1398 and expanded his territory westward to the river Una and northward to the river Sava. This made him the leading personality in the pro-Ladislas party. The king of Naples came to Zadar in 1403 and as a pretender to the throne was crowned there as the king of Hungary and Croatia. Instead of proceeding to Hungary, however, to seize the throne, he appointed Hrvoje Vukčić Hrvatinić as governor of Croatia and Hungary and returned to Naples. Ladislas also gave Hrvoje the islands of Brač, Hvar, Vis, and Korčula and made him duke (Herzeg — from *Herzog* in German) of the city of Split. His main residences were at the town of Jajce in Bosnia and in Split on the Adriatic coast. He was married to Helen, daughter of Ivan Nelipić, of a well-known Croatian princely family, and had a son Balša. Hrvoje became the most influential nobleman at the time, not only in Bosnia, but also in Croatia.

To establish his lordship over Bosnia and southern Croatia, Sigismund unsuccessfully waged several campaigns against Hrvoje, as the leader of the opposition. After King Ostoja joined Sigismund's party, Hrvoje with other leading Bosnian aristocracy, removed him and elected young Stipan Tvrtko II (1404-1409) to the throne. Realizing that he could not accomplish his goal alone, Sigismund summoned a large army from other European countries under the pretext of a crusade against the heretics in Bosnia, Dalmatia, and Croatia. This time (1408) he achieved a victory over Bosnia, captured the Bosnian king Stipan Tvrtko II, and executed about 170 leading men in the country. Hrvoje made peace with Sigismund and retained his possessions.

Sigismund's vengeance, however, turned against Hrvoje in 1413, when Hrvoje invaded the lands of another well-known nobleman, Sandalj Hranić of Hum (later Herzegovina) (qq.v.), while Hranić fought the Turks in Serbia as an ally of Sigismund. The Herzeg Hrvoje was declared a rebel and a heretic, and his possessions were to be taken from him. But Hrvoje made an alliance with the Turks and with their help routed Sigismund's army (1415) near Doboj, thereby maintaining his power. Following this victory, Turkish troops raided Croatia and penetrated as far as Celje in Slovenia, and asserted their influence in Bosnian affairs. Hrvoje's triumph, however, was short-lived. He died a year later at the town of Kotor on the banks of the river Vrbas.

Two well-known codices were written for this famous nobleman, Hval's *Collection* (1404) and the *Missal* of Duke Hrvoje Vukčić Hrvatinić (1404).

-W-

WAR CASUALTIES. The United States officials estimate 250,000 dead or missing in Bosnia as a result of the war from 1992 to 1995. The Muslim-led Bosnian government believes that more than 150,000 died or are missing on its side alone, including 17,000 children, and more than 175,000 were wounded. This count includes more than 10,600 dead (including more than 1,600 children) in Sarajevo (q.v.) alone. Neither Bosnian Croats nor Serbs (qq.v.) have officially given estimated numbers of their casualties.

-Y-

YOUNG MUSLIMS/MLADI MUSLIMANI. An organization among the Bosnian Muslims (q.v.) that could be categorized as a movement that attempted to gather young Muslims, especially more educated ones, in order to promote religious ideals. Because in the eyes of its followers Islam is all encompassing, this organization was not only religious in nature but also dealt with all aspects of individual and communal life in the Bosnian Muslim community. It also had a pan-Islamic dimension in its program. An official document (Our Movement) from the time of its founding states that the "Young Muslims are not some new sect or *mesheb*. It is an educational, fighting Islamic organization."

Although the organization was formed in March of 1941, its followers claim that its real beginnings were in 1939. There are indications that the founding of the Young Muslims in Bosnia was directly connected to a similar organization (Esubani muslimini — Young Muslims) in Egypt, where some of the leading members of the Bosnian organizations studied theology. The Croat-Serb agreement (Sporazum) of 1939, a generally negative view of Islam in Europe, and a lack of leadership on the part of the religious officials in Bosnia, prompted a group of educated Bosnian Muslims to start the movement. Initially, its followers and sympathizers were recruited in Sarajevo (q.v.) from the First Gymnasium (High School) for boys, a Muslim organization Trezvenost, and Muslim students studying at the University of Belgrade. The *ustaša* (q.v.) regime during the war did not look favorably on the followers of the Young Muslims and therefore the organization was officially dormant during World War II, but its members were in touch with each other and involved in religious and charitable activities.

After the war, the Young Muslims organization was reactivated under a new and younger leadership, but already in March 1946 a number of its leading members, including Alija Izetbegović (q.v.), were arrested. Soon after, the Young Muslims became a secret underground organization with branches in about 30 locations in Bosnia and Herzegovina and in Zagreb, Croatia. The branches in Mostar (q.v.) and Zagreb became the most active. The group even published in *samizdat* (self-published) form a few issues of *Mudzahid* and *Kolo*.

The new wave of arrests began in 1948 and culminated in 1949. The trials of August 1949 gave the last blow to the organization. In 1970, however, the Yugoslav regime accused Alija Izetbegović and his supporters, after his treatise (*Islamic Declaration*) became public, of conspiracy to revive the Young Muslims organization. Although the organization was never animated, its former followers have become very influential in today's ruling Muslim party in Bosnia and Herzegovina.

YUGOSLAV PEOPLE'S ARMY/JUGOSLAVENSKA NARODNA ARMIJA (JNA). The armed forces of the socialist Yugoslavia (q.v.), the successor of the World War II partisan movement. Besides the Communist Party, the JNA was the most important pillar of Yugoslavism and the socialist revolution. Because its officer core was overwhelmingly Serb-dominated, it was seen by the country's non-Serbs as an instrument of Serbian interests under the cover of Yugoslavism. The JNA quickly transformed itself into a Serb military force during the breakup of Yugoslavia (1991-1992). Officially it ceased to exist at the end of April 1992.

YUGOSLAVIA. As a result of the peace settlement of 1918, the Kingdom of Serbs, Croats, and Slovenes (q.v.) was formed of various parts of the former Austro-Hungarian Dual Monarchy, namely Slovenia, Croatia, Bosnia-Herzegovina, and Vojvodina, and the kingdoms of Serbia and Montenegro. The creation of the new state was a result of romantic Slavism and resistance to the Habsburg, Hungarian, and Italian domination, but most of all it was a by-product of the post-World War I European power balance. In the eyes of the peacemakers in Paris, the newly created country was to serve as an important link in a chain of independent states from the Baltic Sea in the north to the Adriatic in the south in protecting the West from the spread of the Bolshevik Revolution and a possible German revival. After King Aleksandar Karađorđević imposed his dictatorship in 1929, the country was renamed Yugoslavia.

The "national question" remained the state's Achilles' heel and the main cause of its dismemberment in 1941 and again in 1991. From the outset, the country came under Serbian military and bureaucratic domination, which the others, mostly Croats (q.v.), resisted. Nationalist antagonisms and social problems resulted in persecutions, assassinations, and, finally, the breakup of the country in 1941. Yugoslavia was revived in 1945 under the name of Socialist Federative Republic of Yugoslavia (SFRY) as a part of the post-World War II European settlement, and came under the rule of a

Communist regime within the Soviet bloc. The state was made up of six republics: Bosnia-Herzegovina, Croatia, Macedonia, Montenegro, Serbia, and Slovenia. The republic of Serbia had two autonomous provinces: Kosovo and Vojvodina.

After its expulsion from the Soviet bloc (1948), Yugoslavia embarked on its own brand of socialism, also known as Titoism, named after the country's leader, Josip Broz Tito (q.v.). Many thought that Tito successfully bridged nationalist problems and that the Yugoslav social and economic institutions were models for the eventual convergence of socialism and capitalism. But the collapse of the Communist regimes in Europe proved that the whole Yugoslav experiment was of temporary success and never had solid foundations. The country itself collapsed in 1991. Its former republics, Slovenia, Croatia, Bosnia-Herzegovina, and Macedonia, became independent states, while Serbia and Montenegro formed the Federal Republic of Yugoslavia (q.v.) in April of 1992.

-Z-

ZAHUMLJE. *See* HUM.

ZAPADNE STRANE/WESTERN PARTS, also known as TROPOLJE/THREE-FIELD REGION or ZAVRŠJE/THE EDGE LANDS. Names used in pre-Turkish Bosnia for the region of Glamoč, Livno, and Tomislavgrad (Duvno). This area belonged to the Croatian kingdom till the middle of the 14th century. The Bosnian *ban* Stipan II Kotromanić (qq.v.) extended his authority over the region sometime around the year 1330.

At times the three counties (Glamoč, Livno, and Duvno) were ruled as a single administrative unit, with Livno as the main center. At other times, all three became separate counties.

ZAVNOBiH (THE TERRITORIAL ANTI-FASCIST COUNCIL OF THE NATIONAL LIBERATION OF BOSNIA AND HERZEGOVINA/ ZEMALJSKO ANTIFAŠISTIČKO VIJEĆE NARODNOG OSLOBOĐENJA BOSNE I HERCEGOVINE).

The ZAVNOBiH was the branch of the Anti-Fascist Council of the National Liberation of Yugoslavia (AVNOJ) (q.v.). Its constitutive meeting took place in Mrkonjić Grad (Varcar Vakuf) on November 25/26, 1943. The Council elected its presidency and delegates to the AVNOJ (q.v.) meeting that took place a few days later. Officially, this body became the highest political authority in Bosnia and Herzegovina till the end of the war.

ZENICA. An industrial city located 309 m (1,013 ft) above sea level, 84 km (52 mi) northwest of Sarajevo (q.v.). Indications are that in Roman times the town of Bistua with a separate church diocese existed in the vicinity. Its modern growth and industrial development began when the Austro-Hungarian administration built in Zenica metal smelting and refining furnaces and rolling mills in the last century. In the post-1945 era, Zenica became one of the most important industrial complexes in Yugoslavia (q.v.).

During the present war, Zenica became the command center for the Second Corps of the Army of Bosnia-Herzegovina (q.v.) and, because of the siege of Sarajevo, an important center for various operations of the Bosnian government. In 1991, the county of Zenica had 145,577 people, out of which 55.2 percent were Muslims, 15.6 percent Croats, and 15.5 percent Serbs (qq.v.). By the end of the war, however, the city had come under complete Muslim control.

ŽEPA. A town in eastern Bosnia that was declared by the UN a "safe area" (May 1993) for the Bosnian Muslims (q.v.) who were under the Serbian onslaught. The enclave, however, fell to the Bosnian Serbs (q.v.) on July 25, 1995.

ZID (ZDRAVKO I DRUŠTVO/ZDRAVKO AND COMPANY). An FM music station in Sarajevo (q.v.) owned by Zdravko Grebo, a Muslim who operated outside nationalist camps. It began broadcasting in March 1993. Besides music, it broadcasts news bulletins and it is a favorite station of the younger generation in the city.

ZIMMERMANN, WARREN (1934-). Last U.S. ambassador to the former Yugoslavia (q.v.) (1989-92) and also a political officer in the American embassy in Belgrade from 1965 to 1968. In implementing (and helping to shape) the U.S. policy toward Yugoslavia, he remained a staunch supporter of Yugoslav unity even when its collapse was imminent. Misreading the events and counting on Serbian forces to keep the ailing country together by force, he even declared (March 25, 1992) that the United States "will be side by side with Serbia in war and peace" despite "sporadic misunderstanding." After the Serb onslaught in Bosnia, however, Zimmermann advocated a strong American political and military involvement in the region and a firm posture against the Serb aggression.

ŽIVOT/LIFE. A Sarajevo (q.v.) monthly journal dedicated to literary and other cultural issues. It published works from literature (q.v.), theater, language, music, art, and various discussions and controversies on cultural issues. The journal began publication in 1952 and reached its best years in the 1960s, when its editor was the well-known writer Mak Dizdar (q.v.). It ceased publication in 1991.

ZUBAK, KREŠIMIR (1947-). He became president of the Muslim-Croat Federation of Bosnia and Herzegovina (q.v.) in May of 1994. In September 1996, Zubak was elected a member of the three-man presidency of the Republic of Bosnia and Herzegovina. He also served as president of the Presidency Council of the Croat Republic of Herceg-Bosna (q.v.) from February 1994 till the dissolution of the Republic at the beginning of 1996.

Zubak was born in Doboj to a Croat family. He finished law school in Sarajevo (q.v.) and served in various judiciary positions before the war. From 1980 to 1984 he was undersecretary in the Ministry of Justice of the Socialist Republic of Bosnia and Herzegovina.

ZULFIKARPAŠIĆ, ADIL (1923-). An ambitious and influential Bosnian Muslim (q.v.) political activist and businessman. Born in the town of Foča. As Tito's (q.v.) partisan during World War II and a Communist, he became a major general and a minister in the post-war Yugoslav government. After becoming a political immigrant in the West, he became a well-to-do businessman and founder of the Institute of Bosnian Studies in Zurich that promoted a Bosniac national identity, claiming that Catholics, Orthodox, and Muslims in Bosnia-Herzegovina were of Bosniac ethnicity.

In 1990, Zulfikarpašić returned to his native land and became a political ally of President Alija Izetbegović (q.v.) in founding the Party of Democratic Action (SDA) (q.v.). However, he on his own drafted an agreement with the Serb leadership stating Muslims and Serbs (q.v.) would be allies in preserving Yugoslavia (q.v.) but Bosnia-Herzegovina would be maintained as a political entity. Because of this and other disagreements with Izetbegović, he was expelled from the SDA. Then, Zulfikarpašić and his confidants formed a separate political party, the Muslim Bosniac Organization (MBO) (q.v.).

Although he envisioned that the Bosnian Muslims (Bosniacs) would play an intermediary role between the Croats (q.v.) and Serbs, his political position while in exile and after his return to Bosnia was always closer to the Serbs than to the Croats. Presently he lives in Switzerland.

BIBLIOGRAPHY

INTRODUCTION

Bosnia and Herzegovina is indisputably one of the most complex newly independent countries in Europe. It is a region where major empires once clashed, and, today, three religions, cultures, and ethnic groups converge and interact. The encounter of these peoples has been both peaceful and violent, and their views on Bosnia's past, present, and future are often diametrically opposed. These factors are reflected in most of the writings on Bosnia and Herzegovina.

For a country this small, there is a surprisingly vast bibliography, in several languages. To grasp the complexities of Bosnia's past, one has to study the history of its immediate neighbors and the former imperial powers in the region, mainly the Ottomans and Habsburgs. For that reason, I have given readers some basic bibliography on the histories of these two imperial powers, as well as on the Balkans and East Central Europe as a whole. Although most of the cited works are in English, especially those published in the last few decades, many entries are in several other languages. I hope this inclusion will be helpful to those who have a deeper interest in the country's past and present. For the same reason, I have listed various articles dealing with Bosnia.

The 1992-1995 war in Bosnia and Herzegovina has spawned a significant amount of writing concerned with the Bosnian tragedy. This dictionary includes many but not all of the recent works on Bosnia and Herzegovina. As the future of the country and its very existence are still being debated, it is expected that many more works on Bosnia and Herzegovina will be published in the near future.

Unfortunately, there are no solid and comprehensive works on the history of Bosnia and Herzegovina in English. However, before anyone starts an extensive study of the country, I recommend they first read Ivo Banac's *The National Question in Yugoslavia: Origins, History, Politics* (Ithaca: Cornell University Press, 1984), to have a better grasp of the history of national tensions in the area, and Noel Malcolm's *Bosnia: A Short History* (London: Macmillan, 1994), which is the only survey of the history of Bosnia and Herzegovina in English.

The organization of the Bibliography is as follows:

1. ENCYCLOPEDIAS AND HANDBOOKS

Bosnia-Hercegovina, Croatia, Slovenia. Country Report. The Economist Intelligence Unit. London: The Unit, 1996.

Bosnia and Herzegovina. Peace Handbooks No. 12. London: Foreign Office, Historical Section, 1920.

Enciklopedija Jugoslavije. Zagreb: Leksikografski zavod, 1955-1971; 2nd ed. 1980- .

Enciklopedija leksikografskog zavoda. Zagreb: Leksikografski zavod, 1955-1964; 2nd ed. 1966-1969; 3rd ed. 1977-1982.

Hrvatska enciklopedija. Zagreb: Konzorcij Hrvatske enciklopedije, 1941-1945.

Narodna enciklopedija srpsko-hrvatsko-slovenačka. Zagreb: Bibliografski zavod, 1925-1929.

2. BIBLIOGRAPHIES

Academic Writer's Guide to Periodicals, vol. 2, *Eastern Europe and Slavic Studies.* Kent, OH: Kent State University Press, 1971.

Alilović, Ivan. *Bibliografija hrvatskih pisaca Bosne i Hercegovine između dvaju ratova.* Zagreb: HKD sv. Ćirila i Metoda, 1989.

American Bibliography of Slavic and East European Studies. Columbus, OH: American Association for the Advancement of Slavic Studies, 1956- .

Arheološki leksikon Bosne i Hercegovine. Sarajevo: Zemaljski muzej Bosne i Hercegovine, 1988.

Bamborschke, Urlich and Werner Waltrud. *Bibliographie slavistischer Arbeiten aus den wichtigsten englischsprachigen Fachzeitschriften sowie Fest- und Sammelschriften 1922-1976.* Bibliographische Mitteilungen des Osteuropa-Instituts an der Freien Universität Berlin, Bd. 19. Berlin: Osteuropa-Institut on der Freien Universität Berlin; Wiesbaden: In Kommission bei O. Harrassowitz, 1981.

Birkos, Alexander S. *East European and Soviet Economic Affairs: A Bibliography (1965-1973).* Littleton, CO: Libraries Unlimited, 1975.

Bosansko-hercegovačka bibliografija knjiga i brošura 1945-51. Sarajevo: Svjetlost, 1953.

Ćeman, Mustafa. *Bibliografija bošnjačke književnosti.* Zagreb: Sebit, 1994.

Communist Eastern Europe: Analytical Survey of Literature. Washington, DC: Department of the Army, 1971.

Friedman, Francine. *Yugoslavia: A Comprehensive English-Language Bibliography.* Wilmington, DE: Scholarly Resources, 1993.

Gazić, L. "Les collections des manuscrits orientaux à Sarajevo." *Prilozi za orijentalnu filologiju* 30 (1980) 153-57.

Halpern, Joel. *Bibliography of English Language Sources on Yugoslavia.* 2nd ed. Amherst, MA: Department of Anthropology, University of Massachusetts, 1969.

Hink, T. *European Bibliography of Soviet, East European and Slavonic Studies.* (English, French, and German). Birmingham: University of Birmingham, 1975- .

Horak, Stephan M. *Russia, the USSR, and Eastern Europe: A Bibliographic Guide to English Language Publications, 1964-1974.* Littleton, CO: Libraries Unlimited, 1978.

—. *Russia, the USSR, and Eastern Europe: A Bibliographic Guide to English Language Publications, 1975-1980.* Littleton, CO: Libraries Unlimited, 1982.

—. *Russia, the USSR, and Eastern Europe: A Bibliographic Guide to English Language Publications, 1981-1985.* Littleton, CO: Libraries Unlimited, 1987.

Horecky, Paul L., ed. *Southeastern Europe: A Guide to Basic Publications.* Chicago: University of Chicago Press, 1969.

Horton, John Joseph. *Yugoslavia.* World Bibliographical Series. Revised and expanded edition. Oxford: Clio Press, 1990.

Jelenić, Julian. *Bio-bibliografija franjevaca Bosne Srebreničke.* Vol. 1. Zagreb, 1925.

Kerner, Robert J. *Slavic Europe: A Selected Bibliography in the Western European Languages Comprising History, Language and Literatures.* Cambridge: Harvard University Press, 1918. [New York: Russell & Russell, 1969].

Leskovsek, Valentin. *Yugoslavia: A Bibliography.* Vols. 9, 12-14. New York: Studia Slovenica, 1974-1982.

Matulić, Rusko. *Bibliography of Sources on Yugoslavia.* Palo Alto, CA: Ragusan Press, 1981.

Mihailovich, Vasa D. *A Comprehensive Bibliography of Yugoslav Literature in English, 1593-1980.* Columbus, OH: Slavica Publishers, 1984.

Nurudinović, Bisera. *Bibliografija jugoslovenske orientalistike: 1918-1945.* Sarajevo: Orijentalni institut, 1986.

Pearson, Raymond. *Russia and Eastern Europe, 1789-1985: A Bibliographical Guide.* Manchester: Manchester University Press, 1989.

Petrovich, Michael B. *Yugoslavia: A Bibliographic Guide.* Washington, DC: Slavic and Central European Division, Library of Congress, 1974.

Prpić, George J. *Croatia and the Croatians: A Selected and Annotated Bibliography in English.* Scottsdale, AZ: Associated Book Publishers, 1982.

Remington, Robin Alison. *The International Relations of Eastern Europe: A Guide to Information Sources.* International Relations Information Guide Series, vol. 8. Detroit: Gale Research Co., 1978.

Roth, Klaus and Gabriele Wolf, eds. *South Slavic Folk Culture: A Bibliography of Literature in English, German, and French on Bosnian-Hercegovinian, Bulgarian, Macedonian, Montenegrin and Serbian Folk Culture.* Columbus, OH: Slavica, 1993.

Russia and Eastern Europe, 1789-1985: A Bibliographical Guide. History and Related Disciplines, Selected Bibliographies. Manchester: Manchester University Press, 1989.

Šabanović, Hazim. *Književnost Muslimana BiH na orijentalnim jezicima.* (Bibliografija). Sarajevo: Svjetlost, 1973.

Savadjian, Léon. *Bibliographie balkanique.* 8 vols. Paris: Société Générale d'Imprimerie et d'Edition, 1920-1939.

Slavic Studies: A Guide to Bibliographies, Encyclopedias, and Handbooks. Wilmington, DE: Scholarly Resources, 1993.

Štitić, Lina. *Bibliografija knjiga i periodičnih izdanja štampanih u Hercegovini, 1873-1941.* Mostar: Izdanje Savjeta za kulturu Narodnog odbora sreza Mostar, 1958.

Stokes, Gale. *Nationalism in the Balkans: An Annoted Bibliography.* New York: Garland, 1984.

Terry, Garth M. *Yugoslav History: A Bibliographic Index to English-Language Articles.* Bibliography of Southeast Europe History, vol. 1. Nottingham: Astra Press, 1985.

Trisić, N. D. et al. *Sarajevski atentat u svijetlu bibliografskih podataka: Dopune, 1954-1964.* 2nd ed. Sarajevo: Muzej grada, 1964.

Živković, Pavo. *Bibliografija objavljenih izvora i literature o srednjovjekovnoj Bosni.* Sarajevo: Zavičajni muzej Travnik, 1982.

3. GEOGRAPHY

Bosnia and Herzegovina: Macmillan Atlas of War and Peace. New York: Macmillan, 1996.

Burdett, Anita L. P., ed. *The Historical Boundaries between Bosnia, Croatia, Serbia: Documents and Maps, 1815-1945.* 2 vols. [England]: Archive editions, 1995.

Carter, Francis W. *An Historical Geography of the Balkans.* London: Academic Press, 1977.

Cornish, Vaughn. "Bosnia, the Borderland of Serb and Croat." *Geography* 20:4 (1935) 260-70.

Djaja, Mato et al. *A Review of the Old and the New in Bosnia and Hercegovina.* Sarajevo: Narodna prosvjeta, 1959.

Englefield, Greg. "Yugoslavia, Croatia, Slovenia: Re-emerging Boundaries." *Boundry and Territory Briefing* 3. Durham, England: International Boundaries Research Unit, 1992.

Gašparević, R. *Bosna i Hercegovina na geografskim kartama od prvih početaka do kraja XIX vijeka.* Sarajevo: ANUBiH, 1970.

Great Britain, Naval Staff Intelligence Dept. *Bosnia: Geography.* London: H.M.S.O., 1918.

Helfert von, Josef A. Freiherr. *Bosnische: Geschichte, Kulturgeschichte, Land und Leute.* Vienna: Manz, 1887.

Jukić, I. F. (Slavoljub Bošnjak). *Zemljopis i poviestnica Bosne.* Zagreb, 1851.

Klemenčić, Mladen, ed. *A Concise Atlas of the Republic of Croatia and of the Republic of Bosnia and Hercegovina.* Zagreb: Lexicographical Institute, 1993.

—. "Territorial Proposals for the Settlement of the War in Bosnia-Hercegovina." *Boundary and Territory Briefing* 1:3. Durham, England: International Boundaries Research Unit, 1994.

Kovačević, Ešref. *Granice Bosanskog pašaluka prema Austriji i mletackoj republici po odredbama Karlovačkog mira.* Sarajevo: Svjetlost, 1973.

Kreševljaković, H. and H. Kapidžić. *Vojno-geografski opis Bosne pred Dubički rat 1785.* Sarajevo: Naučno društvo BiH, 1957.

Magocsi, Paul Robert. *Historical Atlas of East Central Europe.* Seattle and London: University of Washington Press, 1993.

Sainte-Marie, E. de. *L'Herzégovine. Étude géographique, historique et statistique.* Paris: Baer, 1875.

Sterneck, H. *Geografische Verhältnisse, Communicationen und das Reisen in Bosnien, der Herzegovina und Nord-Montenegro. Aus eigener Anschauung geschildert.* Vienna: Braumüller, 1877.

Strausz, Adolf. *Bosnien, Land und Leute: Historisch-ethnographisch-geographische Schilderung.* 2 vols. Vienna: Gerold's Sohn, 1882.

United States. Central Intelligence Agency. *Bosnia and Herzegovina, summary map.* [Washington, DC], Central Intelligence Agency, [1993].

—. *Sarajevo and Vicinity.* Computer generated block diagram of Sarajevo region. Aerial view. Washington, DC: Central Intelligence Agency, 1992.

4. TRAVEL AND DESCRIPTION

"Adventures among the Austrians in Bosnia." *Blackwood's Magazine* 133 (1883) 197-207.

Asbóth, János. *An Official Tour through Bosnia and Herzegovina.* London: Swan Sonnenschein, 1890.

—. *Bosnien und die Herzegowina: Reisebilder und Studien von Johann von Asbóth.* Vienna: A. Hölder, 1888.

—. *Bosznia és a Herczegovina: uti rajzok és tanulmányok.* Budapest: Pallas, 1887.

Baedeker, Karl. *Austria, Including Hungary, Transylvania, Dalmatia, and Bosnia: Handbook for Travelers.* Leipzig: Baedeker, 1896.

Baernreither, J. M. *Bosnische Eindrücke.* Vienna, 1908.

Barry, John Patrick. *At the Gates of the East: A Book of Travel among Historic Wonderlands.* London: Longmans, Green, 1906.

Blau, Ernst Otto. *Reisen in Bosnien und der Herzegowina: Topographische und pflanzengeographische Aufzeichnungen.* Berlin, 1877.

Blowitz, H.G.S.A.O. "A Trip to Bosnia-Herzegovina." *Nineteenth Century* 36 (1894) 621-44.

Capus, Guillaume. *A travers la Bosnie et l'Herzégovine: Études et impressions de voyage.* Paris: Librairie Hachette, 1896.

Ćelebi, Evliya. *Putopis:odlomci o jugoslovenskim zemljama.* H. Šabanović, ed. and tr. Sarajevo: Svjetlost, 1973.

Ćelebija, E. *Iz Sejahatname.* Sarajevo: G ZM, 1908.

Chaumette des Fossés, J. B. A. *Voyage en Bosnie dans les années 1807 et 1808.* Paris: É. Didot, 1816.

Coffin, Marian Cruger. "Where East Meets West." *National Geographic Magazine* 19:5 (1908) 309-44.

Creagh, James. *Over the Border of Christendom and Eslamiah, a Journey through Hungary, Slavonia, Servia, Bosnia, Herzegovina, Dalmatia, and Montenegro, to the North of Albania, in the Summer of 1875.* 2 vols. London: Tinsley, 1876.

Curtis, William E. "The Great Turk and His Lost Provinces." *National Geographic Magazine* 14:2 (1903) 46-61.

—. *The Turk and His Lost Provinces.* New York: Revell, 1903.

Cypriena and Despreza. *Südslavische Wanderung im Sommer 1850.* Leipzig, 1851.

Davis, W. M. "An Excursion in Bosnia, Hercegovina, and Dalmatia." *Bulletin of the Geographical Society of Philadelphia* 3 (1901) 21-50.

Dawkins, W. Boyd. "Bosnia-Herzegovina and Dalmatia." *Nature* 54 (1896) 78-80.

Dell, Anthony. "A Holiday in Bosnia." *Contemporary Review* 126 (1924) 613-21.

[Dunkin, Robert.] *In the Land of the Bora: Or Camp Life and Sport in Dalmatia and the Herzegovina, 1894-1895-1896.* London: Paul, Trench, Trubner, 1897.

Evans, Arthur J. *Illyrian Letters: A Revised Selection of Correspondence from the Illyrian Provinces of Bosnia, Herzegovina, Montenegro, Albania, Dalmatia, Croatia, and Slavonia, Addressed to the* Manchester Guardian *during the Year 1877.* London: Longmans, Green and Co., 1878.

—. *Through Bosnia and Herzegovina on Foot during the Insurrection, August and September 1875: With an Historical Review of Bosnia.* London: Longmans, Green, 1876.

Gibbons, John. *London to Sarajevo.* London: G. Newnes, 1930.

Giljferding, Alexander F. *Putovanje po Hercegovini, Bosni, i Staroj Srbiji.* Trans. from Russian and ed. Branko Čulić. Sarajevo: Veselin Masleša, 1972.

Goedorp, Victor. "With a Camera in Bosnia." *Wide World Magazine* (Feb. 1902) 494-500.

Gordon, Jan and Cora J. Gordon. *Two Vagabonds in the Balkans.* New York: McBride, 1925.

Hadžiselimović, Omer, ed. *Na vratima Istoka: Engleski putnici o Bosni i Hercegovini od 16. do 20. vijeka.* [Summary in English]. Sarajevo: Veselin Masleša, 1989.

Holbach, Maude M. *Bosnia and Herzegovina: Some Wayside Wanderings.* London: Lane, 1910.

Jokić, Gojko. *Bosnia-Hercegovina: A Tourist Guide.* Belgrade: Turistička štampa, 1969.

Kuripešić, Benedikt. *Itinerarium oder der Botschaftsreise des Josef von Lamberg und Niclas Jurischitz durch Bosnien, Serbien, Bulgarien nach Konstantinople 1530.* Ed. E. Lamberg-Schwarzenberg. Innsbruck, 1910.

—. *Putopis kroz Bosnu, Srbiju, Bugarsku u Rumuniju 1530. godine.* Sarajevo: Svjetlost, 1950.

"A Lady's Visit to Herzegovinian Insurgents." *Cornhill Magazine* 34 (1876) 60-73.

Mackenzie, Georgina Mary Muir and Adelina P. Irby. *Travels in the Slavonic Provinces of Turkey-in-Europe.* 2 vols. New York: Strahan, 1866.

Maurer, Franz. *Eine Reise durch Bosnien, die Saveländer und Ungarn.* Berlin: C. Heymann's Verlag, 1870.

—. "Mitteilungen über Bosnien: Die Bosniaken." *Das Ausland* 42 (1869) 1022-27.

Mažuranić, Matija. *Pogled u Bosnu ili Kratak put u onu krajinu učinjen 1839-40.* 2nd ed. Zagreb: Narodne novine, 1938.

McKenzie, Kenneth. "East of the Adriatic: Notes on Dalmatia, Montenegro, Bosnia, and Herzegovina." *National Geographic Magazine* 23 (Dec. 1912) 1159-87.

Michel, Robert. *Fahrten in den Reichslanden: Bilder und Skizzen aus Bosnien und der Hercegovina.* Vienna, Leipzig: Deutsch-österreichischer Verlag, 1912.

Mihić, Ljubo. *Turistički motivi i objekti u Hercegovini.* Belgrade: Turistička štampa, 1968.

Munro, Robert. *Rambles and Studies in Bosnia-Herzegovina and Dalmatia.* London: Blackwood, 1895.

Nickles, S. "Where East Meets West: The Republic of Bosnia-Hercegovina." *Country Life* 17:10 (1974) 1142-43.

Paton, A. A. *Highlands and Islands of the Adriatic, Including Dalmatia, Croatia, and the Southern Provinces of the Austrian Empire.* 2 vols. London: Chapman and Hall, 1849.

"A Peep at Bosnia." *Sharpe's London Magazine* 3 (1853) 334-40.

Pelletier, René. *Chez les Yougoslaves, de la Save à l'Adriatique: Sarajevo et sa région.* Paris: Belles-lettres, 1934.

Perrot, Georges. *Souvenirs d'un voyage chez les Slaves du Sud (1868).* Tour du Monde, 1870.

Pertusier, C. *La Bosnie considérée dans ses rapports avec l'Empire Ottoman.* Paris, 1822.

Renner, H. *Durch Bosnien und die Hercegowina kreuz und quer.* Berlin: Geographische Verlagshandlung D. Reimer, 1896.

Rhodes, Anthony Richard Ewart. *Where the Turk Trod: A Journey to Sarajevo with a Slavic Mussulman.* London: Weidenfeld & Nicolson, 1956.

Šamić, Midhat. *Les Voyageurs français en Bosnie à la fin du XVIIIe siècle et au début du XIXe et le pays tel qu'ils l'ont vu.* Paris: Didier, 1960.

Sandwith, Humphry. "A Trip into Bosnia." *Fraser's Magazine* (Dec. 1873) 698-713.

"Servia, Bosnia and Bulgaria." *Geographical Magazine* 3 (1876) 257-59.

"A Short Trip into Bosnia." *Household Words* 3 (1851) 182-87.

Spencer, Edmund. *Travels in European Turkey, in 1859, through Bosnia, Servia, Bulgaria, Macedonia, Thrace, Albania, and Epirus; with a Visit to Greece and the Ionian Isles: And a Homeward Tour through Hungary and the Slavonian Provinces of Austria on the Lower Danube.* 2 vols. London: Colburn, 1851.

Stojanović, Mihailo M. *Kroz Bosnu i Hercegovinu: Utisci s puta srpskih učitelja 1901 g.* Belgrade: S. Horovic, 1902.

Thompson, Ellinor F. B. "Ride through Bosnia and the Herzegovina." *Nineteenth Century* 61 (1907) 685-700.

Thompson, Harry C. *The Outgoing Turk: Impressions of a Journey through the Western Balkans.* London: Heinemann, 1897.

Trevor, Roy. *My Balkan Tour: An Account of Some Journeyings and Adventures in the Near East Together with a Descriptive and Historical Account of Bosnia and Herzegovina, Dalmatia, Croatia and the Kingdom of Montenegro.* London: Lane, 1911.

Usborne, J. "Idylic valley in Yugoslavia [Neretva valley]." *Country Life* 21:1 (1960) 126-29.

Wilkinson, John Gardner. *Dalmatia and Montenegro: With a Journey to Mostar in Herzegovina, and Remarks on the Slavic Nations; The History of Dalmatia and Ragusa; the Uscocs; &c &c.* 2 vols. London: Murray, 1848.

5. DEMOGRAPHY

Bogićević, V. "Emigracije muslimana Bosne i Hercegovine u Tursku u doba Austro-Ugarske vladavine 1878-1918." *Historijski zbornik* 3 (1950) 175-88.

Breznik, D., ed. *The Population of Yugoslavia.* Belgrade: Demographic Research Center, Institute of Social Sciences, 1974.

Eterovich, Francis H. "Geographic and Demographic Statistics of Croatia and Bosnia-Herzegovina." In F. H. Eterovich and C. Spalatin, eds. *Croatia: Land, People, Culture,* vol. 1, 3-19. Toronto: University of Toronto Press, 1964.

Gelo, Jakov, Marinko Grizelj, and Anđelko Akrap. *Stanovništvo Bosne i Hercegovine: Narodnosni sastav po naseljima.* Zagreb: Državni zavod za statistiku, 1995.

Handžić, Adem. *Population of Bosnia in the Ottoman Period: A Historical Overview.* Istanbul: Research Center of Islamic History, Art, and Culture, 1994.

Heinz Fassmann. "European East-West Migration, 1945-1992." *International Migration Review* 28 (1994) 520-38.

Kapidžić, Hamdija. "Pokret za iseljavanje srpskog seljaštva iz Hercegovine u Srbiju 1902 godine." *Godišnjak društva istoričara Bosne i Hercegovine* 11 (1960) 23-54.

Kashuba, M. S. *Novaia etnopoliticheskaia karta Balkan*. Moscow: In-t etnologii i antropologii, 1995.

Markotić, Ante F. *Demografski razvitak Hercegovine*. Mostar: IKRO Prva književna komuna, 1983.

Pejanović, Đorđe. *Stanovništvo Bosne i Hercegovine*. Belgrade: Naučna knjiga, 1955.

Prpić, George. *Tragedies and Migrations in Croatian History*. Toronto: Hrvatski put, 1973.

Republički zavod za statistiku Bosne i Hercegovine. *Popis stanovnistva i stanova 1971*. Sarajevo: Republički zavod za statistiku, 1976.

Schweninger, F. "Die Bevölkerung in Bosnien und der Herzegowina nach der Konfession." In *Petermann's Mitteilungen* 59, vol. 2 (1913) 196-97.

Stanovništvo Bosne i Hercegovine: Narodnosni sastav po naseljima. Zagreb: Republika Hrvatska. Državni zavod za statistiku, 1995.

6. SURVEY OF REGIONAL HISTORIES

THE BALKANS

Anderson, Matthew Smith. *The Eastern Question, 1774-1923*. New York: St. Martin's Press, 1966.

Arato, Endre. "The Effect of International Politics and External Forces on the National Liberation Movement of the Balkan Peoples in the 19th Century." *Acts du Premier Congrès International des Études Balkaniques et Sud-est Européennes* 4 (1969) 739-48.

The Balkan Wars, 1912-1913: The War Correspondence of Leon Trotsky. Trans. Brian Pearce; ed. George Weissman and Ducan Williams. New York: Monad Press, 1980.

Bercovici, Konrad. *The Incredible Balkans*. New York: Putnam's, 1932.

Brown, James F. *Nationalism, Democracy, and Security in the Balkans.* Brookfield, VT: Dartmouth, 1992.

Castellan, Georges. *History of the Balkans: From Mohammed the Conqueror to Stalin.* Trans. Nicholas Bradley. Boulder, CO: East European Monographs; Distributed by Columbia University Press, New York, 1992.

Cviic, Christopher. *Remaking the Balkans.* New York: Council on Foreign Relations Press, 1991.

"Europe and the Balkans." *Current History* (Nov. 1993). The entire issue is devoted to the region.

Fine, John Van Antwerp, Jr. *The Early Medieval Balkans: A Critical Survey from the Sixth to the Late Twelfth Century.* Ann Arbor: University of Michigan Press, 1983.

—. *The Late Medieval Balkans: A Critical Survey from the Late Twelfth Century to the Ottoman Conquest.* Ann Arbor: University of Michigan Press, [1987].

Fox, Frank. *The Balkan Peninsula.* London: A.& C. Black, 1915.

Gautier, Xavier. *L'Europe à l'épreuve des Balkans.* Paris: J. Bertoin, 1992.

Gewehr, W. M. *The Rise of Nationalism in the Balkans, 1800-1930.* New York: Holt, 1931.

Heuven van, Marten. *The United States and the Balkans.* Santa Monica, CA: RAND, 1994.

Jankovic, Branimir M. *The Balkans in International Relations.* New York: St. Martin's Press, 1988.

Jelavich, Barbara. *History of the Balkans.* 2 vols. Cambridge: Cambridge University Press, 1983.

Jelavich, Barbara and C. Jelavich, eds. *The Balkans in Transition: Essays on the Development of Balkan Life and Politics since the Eighteenth Century.* Berkeley: University of California Press, 1963.

Jelavich, Charles and Barbara Jelavich. *The Balkans: The Modern Nations in Historical Perspectives.* A Spectrum Book. Englewood Cliffs, NJ: Prentice-Hall, 1965.

—. *The Establishment of the Balkan National States, 1804-1920.* Seattle: University of Washington Press, 1977.

Johnsen, William T. *Deciphering the Balkan Enigma: Using History to Inform Policy.* Carlisle Barracks, PA: U.S. Army War College — Strategic Studies Institute, 1995.

Kaplan, Robert D. *Balkan Ghosts: A Journey through History.* New York: St. Martin's Press, 1993.

Kennan, George F. "The Balkan Crisis: 1913 and 1993." *The New York Review of Books* (Jul. 15, 1993) 3-7.

Lampe, John R. and Marvin R. Jackson. *Balkan Economic History, 1550-1950.* Bloomington: Indiana University Press, 1982.

Larrabee, Stephen F. *The Volatile Powder Keg: Balkan Security after the Cold War.* Lanham, MD: University Press of America, 1994.

MacKenzie, David. *Ilija Garašanin, Balkan Bismarck.* Boulder, CO: East European Monographs; Distributed by Columbia University Press, New York, 1985.

The Other Balkan Wars: A 1914 Carnegie Endowment Inquiry in Retrospect, with a New Introduction and Reflection on the Present Conflict by George F. Kennan. Washington, DC: Carnegie Endowment, 1993.

Pamir, P. *The Balkans: Nationalism, NATO and the Warsaw Pact.* London: Institute for the Study of Conflict, 1985.

Roggeman, Herwig. *Krieg und Frieden auf dem Balkan: Historische Kriegsursachen, wirtschaftliche und soziale Kriegsfolgen, politische und rechtliche Friedens-voraussetzungen.* Berlin: Berlin Verlag A. Spitz, 1993.

Rossos, Andrew. *Russia and the Balkans: Inter-Balkan Rivalries and Russian Foreign Policy, 1908-1914.* Toronto: University of Toronto Press, 1981.

Schevill, Ferdinand and Wesley March Gewehr. *The History of the Balkan Peninsula from the Earliest Times to the Present Day.* New York: Harcourt, Brace [1933].

Shoup, Paul S., ed. *Problems of Balkan Security: Southeastern Europe in the 1990s.* Washington, DC: Wilson Center Press, 1990.

Slav and Turks: The Border Lands of Islam in Europe. London: "Leisure Hour" Office, 1876.

Stavrianos, L. S. *The Balkans Since 1453.* New York: Rinehart, 1959.

Stoianovich, Traian. *Balkan Worlds: The First and Last Europe.* Armonk, NJ: M.E. Sharpe, 1994.

Weithmann, Michael. *Balkan-Chronik: 2000 Jahre zwischen Orient und Okzident.* Graz: Verlag Styria, 1995.

Wolff, Robert L. *The Balkans in Our Times.* New York: W. W. Norton, 1967.

Wyon, R. *The Balkans from Within.* London: Finck, 1904.

OTTOMAN EMPIRE

Kunt, I. M. *The Sultan's Servants: The Transformation of Ottoman Provincial Government, 1550-1650.* New York, Columbia University Press, 1983.

Lachmann, Renate, ed. and tr. *Memoiren eines Janitscharen oder Türkische Chronik.* Graz, Vienna, Cologne: Styria, 1975.

Miller, William. *The Ottoman Empire and Its Successors, 1801-1922.* Cambridge: The University Press, 1936.

Rycaut, P. *The Present State of the Ottoman Empire.* London: J. Starkey and H. Brome, 1668.

Shaw, Stanford J. and Ezel Kural Shaw. *History of the Ottoman Empire and Modern Turkey.* 2 vols. Cambridge: Cambridge University Press, 1976-1977.

Suger, Peter F. *Southeastern Europe under Ottoman Rule, 1354-1804.* Seattle: University of Washington Press, 1977.

HABSBURG EMPIRE

Jaszi, Oscar. *The Dissolution of the Habsburg Monarchy.* Studies in the Making of Citizens. Chicago: University of Chicago Press, 1929.

Kann, Robert A. *A History of the Habsburg Empire, 1526-1918.* Berkeley: University of California Press, 1977.

—. *The Multinational Empire: Nationalism and National Reform in the Habsburg Monarchy 1848-1918.* New York: Columbia University Press, 1950.

May, Arthur J. *The Passing of the Hapsburg Monarchy, 1914-1918.* Philadelphia: University of Pennsylvania Press, 1966.

Zbynek, Zeman. *The Break-up of the Habsburg Empire, 1914-1918: A Study in National and Social Revolution.* London and New York: Oxford University Press, 1961.

EAST CENTRAL EUROPE

Banac, Ivo, ed. *Eastern Europe in Revolution.* Ithaca: Cornell University Press, 1992.

Bannan, Alfred J. and Achilles Edelenyi, eds. *Documentary History of Eastern Europe.* New York: Twayne, 1970.

Dvornik, Francis. *The Making of Central and Eastern Europe.* Gulf Breeze, FL: Academic International Press, 1974.

—. *The Slavs: Their Early History and Civilization.* Boston: American Academy of Arts and Sciences, 1956.

Fejtö, Francois. *A History of the People's Democracies: Eastern Europe since Stalin.* New York: Praeger, 1971.

Ference, Gregory C., ed. *Chronology of 20th Century East European History.* Washington, DC: Gale Research, 1994.

—. *The East European Revolutions.* London: Methuen, 1952.

Gimbutas, M. *The Slavs.* London: Thames and Hudson, 1971.

Glenny, Misha. *The Rebirth of History : Eastern Europe in the Age of Democracy.* 2nd ed. London: Penguin Books, 1993.

Held, Joseph, ed. *The Columbia History of Eastern Europe in the Twentieth Century.* New York: Columbia University Press, 1992.

—. *Dictionary of East European History since 1945.* Westport, CT: Greenwood Press, 1994.

Marriott, J. A. R. *The Eastern Question: An Historical Study in European Diplomacy.* Oxford: Clarendon, 1925.

Nicolle, David. *Hungary and the Fall of Eastern Europe, 1000-1568.* London: Osprey, 1988.

Obolensky, Dimitri. *The Byzantine Commonwealth: Eastern Europe, 500-1453.* New York: Praeger, 1971.

Polonsk, Antony. *The Little Dictators: The History of Eastern Europe since 1918.* London and Boston: Routledge and Kegan Paul, 1975.

Rothschild, Joseph. *East Central Europe between the Two World Wars.* Seattle and London: University of Washington Press, 1974.

—. *Return to Diversity: A Political History of East Central Europe since World War II.* New York and Oxford: Oxford University Press, 1989.

Schöpflin, George. *Politics in Eastern Europe.* Oxford: Blackwell, 1993.

Sedlar, Jean W. *East Central Europe in the Middle Ages, 1000-1500.* Seattle and London: University of Washington Press, 1994.

Seton-Watson, Hugh. *Eastern Europe between the Wars 1918-1941.* Cambridge: Cambridge University Press, 1946.

Seymore, Bruce II., ed. *The Access Guide to Ethnic Conflicts in Europe and the Former Soviet Union.* Washington, DC: ACCESS: A Security Information Service, 1994.

Stadtmüller, G. *Geschichte Südosteuropas.* Munich: Verlag für Geschichte und Politik, 1950.

Stone, N. *Europe Transformed: 1878-1919.* Glasgow: Fontana, 1983.

Sugar, Peter F., ed. *Eastern European Nationalisms in the Twentieth Century.* Lanham, MD: University Press of America, 1995.

—. *Ethnic Diversity and Conflict in Eastern Europe.* Santa Barbara: ABC-Clio, 1980.

Walicki, Andrezej. *The Slavophile Controversy: History of a Conservative Utopia in Nineteenth-Century Russian Thought.* Oxford: Clarendon, 1975.

FORMER YUGOSLAVIA

Akhavan, Payam and Robert Howse, eds. *Yugoslavia, the Former and Future: Reflections by Scholars from the Region.* Washington, DC: The Brookings Institution, 1995.

Banac, Ivo. "The Dissolution of Yugoslav Historiography." In Sabrina P. Ramet and Ljubiša S. Adamovich, eds. *Beyond Yugoslavia: Politics, Economics, and Culture in a Shattered Community,* 39-65. Boulder: Westview Press, 1995.

—. "Historiography of the Countries of Eastern Europe: Yugoslavia." *American Historical Review* 97:4 (Oct. 1992) 1084-1104.

—. "The Origins and Development of the Concept of Yugoslavia." In Martin Van den Heuvel and J. G. Siccama, eds. *The Disintegration of Yugoslavia,* 1-22. Amsterdam: Rodopi, 1992.

—. "Serbia's Deadly Fears." *The New Combat* (Autumn 1994) 36-43.

Clissold, Stephen. *A Short History of Yugoslavia: From Early Times to 1968.* Cambridge: Cambridge University Press, 1968.

—, ed. *Yugoslavia and the Soviet Union 1939-1973: A Documentary Survey.* New York: Oxford University Press, 1975.

Cohen, Philip. *Serbia's Secret War.* College Station, TX: Texas A&M University Press, 1996.

Čuvalo, Ante. "The Yugoslav Experiment: Time for a Scholarly Reassessment." *American Croatian Review* 2:1 (1995) 1-3.

Danopoulos, Constantine P. and Daniel Zirker, eds. *Civil-Military Relations in the Soviet and Yugoslav Successor States.* Boulder: Westview Press, 1996.

Djilas, Aleksa. *The Contested Country: Yugoslav Unity and Communist Revolution 1919-1953.* Cambridge: Harvard University Press, 1991.

Djilas, Milovan. *Land without Justice.* New York: Harcourt, Brace, 1958.

Dragnich, Alex. N. "The Rise and Fall of Yugoslavia: The Omen of the Upsurge of Serbian Nationalism." *East European Quarterly* 23 (1989) 183-198.

Duncan, W. Raymond and G. Paul Holman, Jr., eds. *Ethnic Nationalism and Regional Conflict: The Former Soviet Union and Yugoslavia.* Boulder: Westview Press, 1994.

Garde, Paul. *Vie et mort de la Yougoslavie.* Paris: Fayard, 1992.

Hondius, Frits W. *The Yugoslav Community of Nations.* The Hague and Paris: Mouton, 1968.

Kerner, Robert J. et al. *Yugoslavia.* Berkeley: University of California Press, 1949.

Kostelski, Z. *The Yugoslavs: The History of the Yugoslavs and Their States to the Creation of Yugoslavia.* New York: Philosophical Library, 1952.

Lampe, John R. *Yugoslavia As History: Twice There Was a Country.* Cambridge: Cambridge University Press, 1996.

Lauer, Reinhard and Werner Lehfeldt. *Das jugoslawische Desaster: Historische, sprachliche und ideologische Hintergründe.* Wiesbaden: Harrassowitz, 1995.

Memorandum on the Establishment of a Special Status for Sanjak. Novi Pazar: Muslim National Council of Sanjak, 1993.

Nyrop, Richard F., ed. *Yugoslavia: A Country Study.* Washington, DC: American University Press, 1982.

Palairet, M. R., ed. *Yugoslav Statistics 1834-1919: Croatia, Serbia and Bosnia.* (Microfilm with printed guide). Cambridge: Chadwyck-Healy, 1991.

Pavlowitch, Stevan K. *The Improbable Survivor: Yugoslavia and Its Problems, 1918-1988.* Columbus: Ohio State University Press, 1988.

Peril, Lila. *Yugoslavia, Romania, Bulgaria.* Camden, NJ: Thomas Nelson, 1970.

Singleton, Fred. *A Short History of the Yugoslav Peoples.* Cambridge: Cambridge University Press, 1985.

Stumbo, Bella. "Slobo and Mira." *Vanity Fair* (Jun. 1994) 126-31, 166-67, 170-71.

Sundhaussen, Holm. *Experiment Jugoslavien: Von der Staatsgründung bis zum Staatszerfall.* Mannheim: B.I. Taschenbuchverlag, 1993.

Trifunovska, Snezana, ed. *Yugoslavia through Documents: From Its Creation to Its Dissolution.* Dordercht, Boston: Martinus Nijhoff, 1994.

West, Rebecca. *Black Lamb and Grey Falcon: A Journey through Yugoslavia.* New York: Penguin, 1982 [1940].

West, Richard. *Tito and the Rise and Fall of Yugoslavia.* New York: Carroll and Graf, 1995.

7. BOSNIA AND HERZEGOVINA

GENERAL

Avdić, Kamil Y. *Bosna u historijskoj perspektivi.* Vienna, 1973.

Balić, Smail. *Bosnien und der deutschsprachige Kulturraum: Eine historische-zeitgenössische Skizze.* Cologne: Böhlau, 1992.

Bašagić-Redžepašić, Safvet beg. *Kratka uputa u prošlost Bosne i Hercegovine.* Sarajevo, 1900.

Basovic, L. "Brief Survey of Libraries and Librarianship in Bosnia and Hercegovina." *Journal of Library History* 13:1 (1978) 1-10.

Benac, Alojz et al. *Bosnia and Herzegovina.* Sarajevo: Svjetlost, 1980.

Bogdan, Ivo. *Bosnia y Herzegovina.* Buenos Aires: Studia Croatica, 1965.

Borsody, Stephen. "Bosnia and Herzegovina." In *Encyclopedia of Islam.* Vol. 1, 1261-77. Leiden, Netherlands: E. J. Brill, 1960.

Bosnia and the Bosnian Muslims. Four issues. Sarajevo: n.p. [1991].

"Bosnien und die Bosnier." *Die Grenzboten* 35:3 (1876) 57-69 , 96-106.

Capus, A. *Bosnie et l'Herzégovine.* Paris, 1898.

Clark, Arthur L. *Bosnia: What Every American Should Know.* New York: Berkeley Books, 1996.

Coquelle, P. *Histoire du Monténégro et de la Bosnie depuis les origines.* Paris: E. Leroux, 1895.

Ćorović, V. *Istorija Bosne.* Belgrade: Srpska kraljevska akademija, 1940.

Darby, H. C. "Bosnia and Hercegovina." In A.S. Clissold, ed. *A Short History of Yugoslavia,* 58-72. Cambridge: C.U.P., 1966.

Dedijer, Jefto. *Hercegovina.* Belgrade: Srpska kraljevska akademija, 1909.

Dell, Anthony. "Other Branches of the Slav Family." In James Alexander Hammerton, ed. *Peoples of All Nations.* Vol. 6, 4576-4601. London: Fleetway House, 1924.

Djurdjev, B. "Bosna." In *The Encyclopedia of Islam.* Vol. 1, 1261-75. Leiden: Brill, 1960.

Đordić, Marjan. *Bosanska Posavina.* Zagreb: Polin, 1996.

Draganović, Krunoslav and Dominik Mandić. *Herceg-Bosna i Hrvatska.* Split: Laus, 1991.

Draganović, Krunoslav et al. *Poviest hrvatskih zemalja Bosne i Hercegovine od najstarijih vremena do godine 1463.* Sarajevo: Napredak, 1942.

Eterovich, Francis H. and Christopher Spalatin, eds. *Croatia: Land, People, Culture.* 3 vols. Toronto: University of Toronto Press, 1964.

Fermendžin, Euzebije, ed. *Acta Bosnae potissimum ecclesiastica cum insertis editorum documentorum regestis ab anno 925 usque ad annum 1752.* Zagreb: JAZU, 1892.

Filipović, Nedim, ed. *Savjetovanje o istoriografiji Bosne i Hercegovine, 1945-1982.* Sarajevo: ANUBiH, 1983.

Ganić, Ejup N. *Bosanska otrovana jabuka.* Sarajevo: Bosanska knjiga, 1995.

Gazi, Stjepan. *A History of Croatia.* New York: Philosophical Library, 1973.

Hadžić, A. *Bosna.* Novi Sad: Matica Srpska, 1959.

Herzegovina. Zagreb: NIRO and MOK-Mostar, 1981.

Imamović, M. and I. Lovrenović. *Bosnia and Its People: Bosnia and Herzegovina — A Millennium of Continuity.* Sarajevo, Oslobođenje, 1992.

Klaić, Vjekoslav. *Geschichte Bosniens von den ältesten Zeiten bis zum Verfalle des Königreiches.* Tr. I. von Bojničić. Leipzig: W. Friedrich, 1885.

—. *Poviest Bosne.* Zagreb: Matica Hrvatska, 1882.

Krcsmarik, J. "Bosnia and Herzegovina." In Martijn Theodoor Houtsma et al. *The Encyclopedia of Islam: A Dictionary of the Geography, Ethnography and Biography of the Muhammedan Peoples,* 754-65. Leyden: Brill, 1913.

Malcolm, Noel. *Bosnia: A Short History.* London: Macmillan, 1994.

Mandić, Dominik. *Bosnien und Herzegowina: Geschichtlich-kritische Forschungen.* Rome; Chicago: ZIRAL, 1978.

—. "The Croatian character of Bosnia and Hercegovina." In A. F. Bonifačić and C. S. Mihanovich, eds. *The Croatian Nation in Its Struggle for Freedom and Independence: A Symposium,* 101-39. Chicago: "Croatia" Cultural Publishing Center, 1955.

—. *Crvena Hrvatska u svijetlu povijesnih izvora.* Rome: ZIRAL, 1972.

—. *Etnička povijest Bosne i Hercegovine.* 2nd ed. Rome; Chicago: ZIRAL, 1982.

—. *Hrvatske zemlje.* Rome: ZIRAL, 1972.

—. *Kroaten und Serben: Zwei alte verschiedene Völker.* Bad Kissingen: Heiligenhof, 1989. [*Hrvati i Srbi dva stara različita naroda.* Munich; Barcelona: Hrvatska Revija, 1971.]

Maners, Lynn. *The Bosnians: An Introduction to Their History and Culture.* CAL Refugee Fact Sheet No. 8. Washington, DC: Service Center — Center for Applied Linguistics, 1993.

Milobar, F. *Bosnien und das kroatische Staatsrecht.* Zagreb: Anton Schols, 1898.

—. *Das geschichtliche Verhältnis Bosniens zu Kroatien und Ungarn.* Zagreb, 1989.

Olivier, Louis. *La Bosnie et l'Herzégovine.* Paris: Armand Colin, 1902.

Peroche, Gregory. *Histoire de la Croatie et des nations slaves du sud, 395-1992.* Paris: F.X. de Guibert, 1992.

Preveden, Francis Ralph. *A History of the Croatian People.* 2 vols. New York: Philosophical Library [1956, 1962].

Radić, Stjepan. *Živo hrvatsko pravo na Bosnu i Hercegovinu.* Zagreb, 1908.

Redžić, Enver, ed. *Prilozi za istoriju Bosne i Hercegovine.* Sarajevo: ANUBiH, 1987.

Rośkiewicz, J. *Studien über Bosnien und die Herzegowina.* Leipzig, Brockhaus, 1868.

Schimek, Maximilian. *Geschichte des Königreiches Bosnien und Rama vom Jahre 867. bis 1741.* Vienna: Chr. Friedr. Wappler, 1787.

Spalajković, M. *La Bosnie et l'Herzégovine.* Paris: Arthur Rousseau, 1899.

Stojanović, Stanoje. *Istorija Bosne i Hercegovine.* Belgrade: Državna štamparija, 1909.

Stoyanovich, Nikola. *Bosnie-Herzégovine.* Geneva, 1917.

Suger, P. F. "Bosnia-Hercegovina National Archive in Sarajevo." *Journal of Central European Affairs* 18 (1958) 179-82.

Tomić, Ivan M. *Whose Is Bosnia-Hercegovina?* London: Zbornik, 1992.

Tvrtković, Paul. *Bosnia Hercegovina: Back to the Future.* London: Paul Tvrtković, 1993.

PREHISTORY AND ANCIENT

Basler, Đuro. *Spätantike und frühchristliche Architektur in Bosnien und der Herzegowina.* Vienna: Verlag der österreichische Akademie der Wissenschaften, 1993.

Benac, A. "Recently Excavated Bronze Age Tumuli in the Kupresko-Polje, Bosnia, Yugoslavia." *Antiquity* 64 (1990) 327-34.

Gimbutas, Marija. "The Neolithic Cultures of the Balkan Peninsula." In Henrik Birnbaum and Speros Vryonis Jr., eds. *Aspects of the Balkans: Continuity and Change.* The Hague: Mouton, 1972.

—. "Obre, Yugoslavia: Two Neolithic Sites." *Archaeology* 23 (1970) 287-97.

Imamović, Enver. *Antički kultni i votivni spomenici na području Bosne i Hercegovine.* Sarajevo: Veselin Masleša, 1977.

Markotić, Vladimir. "Archaeology." In F. H. Eterovich and C. Spalatin, eds. *Croatia: Land, People, Culture,* vol. 1, 20-75. Toronto: University of Toronto, 1964.

Pašalić, Esad. *Antička naselja i komunikacije u BiH.* Sarajevo: Zemaljski muzej, 1960.

—. *Sabrano Djelo.* Priredio Alojz Benac. Sarajevo: Svjetlost, 1975.

Patsch, C. *Bosnien und Hercegovina in römischer Zeit.* Sarajevo: Zavod za istraživanje Balkana, 1911.

Stipičević, A. *The Illyrians.* Tran. by S. Čulić-Burton. Park Ridge, NJ: 1977.

Wilkes, John J. *Dalmatia: History of the Roman Provinces.* Cambridge: Harvard University Press, 1969.

—. *The Illyrians.* Oxford: Blackwell, 1992.

MEDIEVAL PERIOD

Anđelić, Pavao. *Bobovac i kraljevska Sutjeska: Stolna mjesta bosanskih vladara u XIV i XV stoljeću.* Sarajevo: Veselin Masleša, 1973.

Babić, Anto. *Iz istorije srednjovjekovne Bosne.* Sarajevo: Svjetlost, 1972.

Ćirković, Sima M. *Herceg Stefan Vukčić-Kosača i njegovo doba.* Belgrade: SANU, Naučno delo, 1964.

—. *Istorija srednjovekovne bosanske države.* Belgrade: Srpska Književna Zadruga, 1964.

—. "Jedan prilog o Banu Kulinu." *Istorijski časopis* 9-10 (1959) 71-77.

Draganović, Krunoslav. *Katarina Kosača bosanska kraljica: Prigodom 500-godišnjice njezine smrti.* Sarajevo: Vrelo života, 1978.

Fermendžin, E., ed. *Acta Bosnae potissimum ecclesiastica cum insertis editorum documentorum registi ab anno 925 usque ad annum 1752.* Monumenta spectantia historiam slavorum meridionalium, vol. 23. Zagreb, 1892.

Fine, John Van Antwerp, Jr. "Was the Bosnian Banate Subject to Hungary in the Second Half of the Thirteenth Century?" *East European Quarterly* 3 (1969) 167-77.

Guldescu, Stanko. *History of Medieval Croatia.* The Hague: Mouton, 1964.

Klaić, Nada. *Srednjovjekovna Bosna: Politički položaj bosanskih vladara do Tvrtkove krunidbe (1377 g.).* Zagreb: Grafički zavod Hrvatske, 1989.

Miller, William. "Bosnia before the Turkish Conquest." *English History Review* 13 (1898) 643-66.

Poparić, Bare. *Tužna povijest Hercegove zemlje.* Zagreb: Matica Hrvatska, 1942.

Šišić, Ferdo. *Vojvoda Hrvoje Vukšić Hrvatinić i njegovo doba (1350-1416).* Zagreb: Matica Hrvatska, 1902.

Thálloczy von, Ludwig. *Studien zur Geschichte Bosniens und Serbiens im Mittelalter.* Munich and Leipzig: Duncker and Humbolt, 1914.

Truhelka, Ćiro. "Das mittelalterliche Staats-und Gerichtswesen in Bosnien." *Wissenschaftliche Mitteilungen aus Bosnien und der Herzegowina* 10 (1907) 71-155.

Turčinović, J. ed. *Povijesno-teološki simpozij u povodu 500. obljetnice smrti bosanske kraljice Katarine.* Sarajevo: Kršćanska sadašnjost, 1979.

Vego, Marko. *Iz historije srednjovjekovne Bosne i Hercegovine.* Sarajevo: Svjetlost, 1980.

—. *Postanak srednjovjekovne bosanske države.* Sarajevo: Svjetlost, 1982.

—. *Povijest Humske zemlje (Hercegovine).* Samobor, 1937.

—. "Prikazi i kritike." *Glasnik zemaljskog muzeja Bosne i Hercegovine* 9 (1954) 183-85.

Vidov, Božidar. *Herceg Stjepan Vukčić-Kosača i naziv Hercegovina: Stjepan II. Tomašević i Mara - posljedni hrvatski kralj i kraljica Druge narodne dinastije.* Toronto: n.p. 1980.

OTTOMAN ERA (1463-1878)

Akarslan, Mediha. *Bosna-Hersek ve Türkiye Çemberlitas.* Istanbul: Agaç Yayincilik, 1993.

Arbuthnot, George. *Herzegovina, or, Omer Pacha and the Christian Rebels.* London: Longman, 1862.

Atanasovski, Veljan. *Pad Hercegovine.* Belgrade: Narodna knjiga, Istoriski institut, 1979.

Austro-Turcica 1541-1552: Diplomatische Akten des habsburgischen Gesandtschaftsverkehrs mit der Hohen Pforte im Zeitalter Suleymans des Prachtigen. Bearbeitet von Srećko M. Džaja unter Mitarbeit von Gunter Weiss; in Verbindung mit Mathias Bernath, herausgegeben von Karl Nehring. Munich: R. Oldenbourg, 1995.

Babinger, Franz. *Das Archiv des bosniaken Osman Pascha.* Berlin: Reichsdruckerei, 1931.

—. "Fünf bosnisch-osmanische Geschichtsschreiber." *Glasnik zemaljskog muzeja* 40 (1930) 169-72.

—. *Die Geschichtsschreiber der Osmanen und ihre Werkes.* Leipzig: O. Harrassowitz, 1927.

Bašagić, Safvetbeg. *Znameniti Hrvati Bošnjaci i Hercegovci u turskoj carevini.* Zagreb: Matica Hrvatska, 1931.

Bašeskija, Mula Mustafa Sevki. *Ljetopis (1746-1804).* Trans. Mehmed Mujezinović. 2nd ed. Sarajevo: Veselin Masleša, 1987.

Bosna-Hersek ile ilgili arsiv belgeleri, 1516-1919. Ankara: T.C. Basbakanlik Devlet Arsivleri Genel Müdürlügü, 1992.

Bralić, P. St. *Monografia storica sulle crudeltà musulmane in Bosnia-Erzegovina*. Estratta del periodico romano *La Palestra del Clero*. Rome: Tipografia sociale, 1898.

Buconjić, Nikola. *Povijest ustanka u Hercegovini i boj kod Stoca*. Mostar, 1911.

Čubrilović, V. *Bosanski ustanak 1875-1878*. Belgrade: Srpska kraljevska akademija, 1936.

Ćurić, Hajrudin. *Arhivska zbirka Vladimira Desnice: Prilozi radu Obrovačkog odreda i ustanak u Bosni 1875-1878*. Sarajevo: Akademija nauka i umjetnosti Bosne i Hercegovine, 1971.

Đurđev, Branislav and Milan Vasić, eds. *Jugoslavenske zemlje pod turskom vlašću (do kraja XVIII stoljeća): Izabrani izvori*. Zagreb: Školska knjiga, 1962.

Effendi, Omer. *History of the War in Bosnia during the Years 1731/8 and 9*. Trans. from Turkish by C. Fraser. Oriental Translation Fund. London: Murray, 1830.

Ekmečić, Milorad. *Ustanak u Bosni 1875-1878*. Sarajevo: Veselin Masleša, 1960.

Fawcett, Millicent Garrett. *The Martyrs of Turkish Misrule*. London: Cassell Petter & Galpin, 1877.

Freeman, Edward Augustus. "Bosnia and Bulgaria." *Edinburgh Review* 144 (1876) 535-72.

Gaj, Velimir. *Balkan divan: Viesti, misli i prouke o zemlji i narodu, navlast u Bosni i Hercegovni*. Zagreb: Vlastita naklada, 1878.

Gavranović, Berislav, ed. *Bosna i Hercegovina od 1853-1870 godine*. Sarajevo: Naučno društvo NR Bosne i Hercegovine, 1956.

Hadžijahić, Muhamed. "Bune i ustanak u Bosni sredinom 18. stoljeća." *Historijski Zbornik* 33-34 (1980-81) 99-137.

Irby, Adelina Paulina. "Bosnia in 1875." *Living Age* 12 (1875) 643-51.

—. "Work among the Bosnian Fugitives." In Donald Macleod, ed. *Good Works for 1876*, 638-42. London: Daldy, Isbister, 1876.

Jakšić, Grgur. *Bosna i Hercegovina na Berlinskom kongresu; Rasprava iz diplomatske istorije*. Belgrade: SANU-Naučna knjiga, 1955.

Jelavich, Barbara. "The British Traveler in the Balkans: The Abuses of Ottoman Administration in the Slavic Provinces." *Slavonic and East European Review* 33 (1955) 396-413.

Kanuni i Kanun-name. Monumenta turcica vol. 1. Sarajevo, 1957.

King, Edward. "A Day with the Voivoda." *Lippincott's Magazine* 18 (1876) 477-87.

Koetschet, J. *Aus Bosniens letzter Türkenzeit.* Ed. G. Grassl. Vienna: A. Hartleben, 1905.

Koetschet, J. *Osman Pascha, der letzte grosse Wesier Bosniens, und seine Nachfolger.* Ed. G. Grassl. Sarajevo, 1909.

Kreševljaković, Hamdija. *Kapetanije u Bosni i Hercegovni.* Sarajevo: Naučno društvo NR Bosne i Hercegovine, 1954.

Miller, William. "The Turks in Bosnia." *Gentleman's Magazine* 61 (1897) 585-602.

Muradbegović, Ahmed. *Omer-paša Latas u Bosni 1850-1852.* Zagreb: Matica Hrvatska, 1944.

Nagata, Yuzo. *Materials on the Bosnian Notables.* Tokyo: Institute for the Study of Languages and Cultures of Asia and Africa, 1979.

Pavičevič, Branko, ed. *Rusija i bosansko-hercegovački ustanak 1875-1878.* Titograd: Crnogorska akademija nauka i umjetnosti, 1986.

Peledija, Enes. *Bosanski ejalet od karlovačkog do požarevačkog mira 1699-1718.* Sarajevo: Veselin Masleša, 1989.

Pertusier, C. *La Bosnie considérée dans ses rapports avec l'Empire Ottoman.* Paris, 1822.

Petrović, Rade, ed. *Medjunarodni naučni skup povodom 100-godišnjice ustanka u Bosni i Hercegovini, drugim balkanskim zemljama i istočnoj krizi 1875-1878. godine.* Sarajevo-Ilidža, 1-3. oktobra 1975. Sarajevo: ANUBiH, 1977.

Pisarev, Iurii A. and M. Ekmechich, eds. *Osvoboditel'naia bor'ba narodov Bosnii i Gertsegoviny i Russiia, 1850-1864: Dokumenty.* Moscow: Izd-vo. Nauka, 1985-8.

Prelog, Milan. *Povijest Bosne u doba osmanlijske vlade.* 2 vols. Sarajevo: J. Studnička i drug, [1912].

Ranke von, Leopold. *Die Letzten Unruhen in Bosnien.* Vienna, 1832.

Šabanović, Hazim. *Bosanski Pašaluk: Postanak i upravna podjela.* Sarajevo, Svjetlost, 1982.

—. "Bosansko krajište." *Godišnjak društva istoričara Bosne i Hercegovine* 9 (1957) 177-219.

—. "Pitanje turske vlasti u Bosni do pohoda Mehmeda II 1463 godine." *Godišnjak društva istoričara Bosne i Hercegovine* 7 (1955) 37-51.

—. "Vojno uredjenje Bosne od 1463. g. do kraja XVI stoljeća." *Godišnjak društva istoričara Bosne i Hercegovine* 11 (1960) 173-223.

Samardžić, Radovan. *Mehmed Sokolović.* Belgrade: Srpska književna zadruga, 1971.

Shaw, S. J. "The Ottoman View of the Balkans." In C. Jelavich and B. Jelavich, eds. *The Balkans in Transition: Essays on the Development of Balkan Life and Politics since the Eighteenth Century,* 56-80. Berkeley: University of California Press, 1963.

Šišić, Ferdo. *Bosna i Hercegovina za vezirovanja Omer-paše Latasa (1850-1852).* Subotica: Srpska kraljevska akademija, 1938.

Skarić, Vladislav. "Popis bosanskih spahija iz 1123 (1711) godine." *Glasnik zemaljskog muzeja* 42 (1930) 1-99.

Šljivo, Galib. *Omer-Paša Latas u Bosni i Hercegovini: 1850-1852.* Sarajevo, Svjetlost, 1977.

Stillman, William James. *Herzegovina and the Late Uprising: The Causes of the Latter and the Remedies.* London: Longmans, Green, 1877.

Sućeska, Avdo. "Bedeutung und Entwicklung des Begriffes A'yân im Osmanischen Reich." *Südostforschungen* 25 (1966) 2-26.

—. "Neke specifičnosti Bosne pod Turcima," *Prilozi* 4 (1968) 43-57.

—. "The Position of Bosnian Muslims in the Ottoman State." In *Ottoman Rule in Middle Europe and Balkan in the 16th and 17th Centuries,* 142-175. Papers presented at the 9th Joint Conference of the Czechoslovak-Yugoslav Historical Committee. Ed. Oriental Institute, Czechoslovak Academy of Sciences. Prague: Academia, 1978.

—. "The Position of the Bosnian Moslems in the Ottoman State." *International Journal of Turkish Studies* 1 (1980) 1-24.

Tepić, Ibrahim. *Bosna i Hercegovina u ruskim izvorima, 1856-1878.* Sarajevo: Veselin Masleša, 1988.

Terzuolo, Eric Robert. "The Garibaldini in the Balkans, 1875-1876." *International History Review* 4 (1982) 111-26.

Thoemmel, G. *Geschichtliche, politische und topographisch-statistische Beschreibung des Vilayet Bosnien das ist das eigentliche Bosnien, nebst türkisch Croatien, der Hercegovina und Rascien.* Vienna: Wenedikt, 1867.

Umar Busnavi. *History of the War in Bosnia during the Years 1737-8 and 9.* London: Oriental Translation Fund; Sold by Murray, 1830.

Zah, František. *Bosna u tajnim politickim izvještajima Františeka Zacha iz Beograda:1843-1848.* Uvod i izbor Vaclav Zacek. Ed. Milorad Ekmečić. Sarajevo: ANUBiH, 1976.

HABSBURG PERIOD TILL WORLD WAR I (1878-1914)

Der Aufstand in der Hercegovina, Süd-Bosnien und Süd-Dalmatien 1881-1882. Vienna: Abteilung für Kriegsgeschichte des k.k. Kriegs-Archivs, 1883.

"The Austro-Hungarian Monarchy Absorbs Bosnia and Herzegovina." In Alfred J. Bannan and Achilles Edelenyi, eds. *Documentary History of Eastern Europe,* 235-58. New York: Twayne, 1970.

"Baron de Kallay's Achievement." *Spectator* 75 (1895) 428-29.

Barre, André. *La Bosnie-Herzégovine: Administration autrichienne de 1878 à 1903.* Paris: Michaud, 1904.

Bauer, Ernest. *Zwischen Halbmond und Doppeladler — 40 Jahre österreichische Verwaltung in Bosnien und Herzegowina.* Vienna: Herold, 1972.

Bericht über die Verwaltung von Bosnien und der Herzegovina. Vienna, 1906.

Bogićević, Vojislav, ed. *Građa o počecima radničkog pokreta u Bosni i Hercegovini od 1878-1905: Dokumenta iz austrougarskih arhiva.* Sarajevo: Državni arhiv NR BiH, 1956.

"Bosnia, Herzegovina, and Austria." *British Quarterly Review* 67 (1878) 206-17.

Colonna, M. *Contes de la Bosnie.* Paris, 1897.

Čuprić-Amerein, Martha M. *Die Opposition gegen die österreichisch-ungarische Herrschaft in Bosnien-Hercegovina (1878-1914)*. Bern and New York: P. Long, 1987.

Ćurić, Hajrudin. *Prilozi bosansko-hercegovačkoj istoriji XIX vijeka*. Sarajevo: Naučno društvo NR Bosne i Hercegovine, 1960.

Cvijić, Jovan. *Aneksija Bosne i Hercegovine i srpski problem*. Belgrade: Državna štamparija Kraljevine Srbije, 1908.

Dillon, E. J. "Annexation of Bosnia and Herzegovina." *Contemporary Review* 94 (1908) 526-31.

—. "Bosnia and Herzegovina." *Contemporary Review* 65 (1894) 735-60.

—. "Foreign Affairs." *Contemporary Review* 94 (1908) 748-64.

—. "Germany and Austria and the Occupation of Bosnia and Herzegovina." *Contemporary Review* 94 (1908) 758-64.

—. "The Near Eastern Crisis." *Contemporary Review* 94 (1908) 513-32.

Donia, Robert J. "The Battle for Bosnia: Habsburg Military Strategy in 1878." *Posebna izdanja*, vol. 43, 109-20. Sarajevo: ANUBiH, 1979.

—. "The Habsburg Imperial Army in the Occupation of Bosnia and Hercegovina." In Bela K. Kiraly and Gale Stokes, eds. *Insurrections, Wars, and the Eastern Crisis in the 1870s*, 375-91. Boulder, CO: Social Science Monographs, 1985.

—. *Islam under the Double Eagle: The Muslims of Bosnia and Hercegovina, 1878-1914*. Boulder, CO: East European Monographs; Distributed by Columbia University Press, New York, 1981.

—. "The Politics of Factionalism: The Bosnian Moslems in Transition, 1878-1906." Ph.D. dissertation, University of Michigan, 1976.

Duce, Alessandro. *La crisi bosniaca del 1908*. Milano: A. Giuffrè, 1977.

Đurkovečki, Mirko. *Politička historija Bosne iza okupacije*. Zagreb, 1920.

Ehli-Islam. *Bezakonja okupacione uprave u Bosni i Hercegovni*. Novi Sad, 1901.

Eichler, Eduard. *Das Justizwesen Bosniens und der Hercegovina*. Vienna: K.u.K. Hof. und Staatsdruckerei, 1889.

Ekmecic, Milorad. "Impact of the Balkan Wars on Society in Bosnia and Hercegovina." In Bela K. Kiraly and Dimitrije Djordjevic, eds. *East Central European Society and the Balkan Wars*, 260-85. Boulder, CO: Social Science Monographs, 1987.

—, ed. *Otpor austrougarskoj okupaciji 1878. godine u Bosni i Hercegovini*. Naučni skup. Sarajevo, 23. i 24. oktobra 1978. Sarajevo: ANUBiH, 1979.

Evans, Arthur J. "The Austrian Counter-Revolution in the Balkans." *Fortnightly Review* 33 (1880) 491-524.

—. "The Austrians in Bosnia." *Macmillan's Magazine* 38 (1878) 495-504.

Fournier, August. *Wie wir zu Bosnien kommen*. Vienna: Reisser, 1909.

Gavranović, Berislav, ed. *Bosna i Hercegovina u doba austrougarske okupacije 1878. godine*. Sarajevo: Akademija nauka i umjetnosti Bosne i Hercegovine, 1973.

Gemeinhardt von, Heinz Alfred. *Deutsche und österreichische Pressepolitik während der bosnischen Krise 1908/09*. Husum: Matthiesen, 1980.

Grđić, Vasilj. *Der Banjaluka-Prozess*. Berlin: Arbeitsausschuss deutsher Verbände, 1933.

Gross, Mirjana. "Hrvatska politika u Bosni i Hercegovini od 1878. do 1914." *Historijski zbornik* 19-20 (1966-1967) 9-68.

Harris, David. *A Diplomatic History of the Balkan Crisis of 1875-1878*. London: H. Milford, 1936.

Holeček, Josef. *Bosniia i Gertsegovina za vremia okkupatsii*. Moscow, 1902.

Hulme-Beaman, Ardern G. "Notes of a Fortnight in Bosnia." *Fortnight Review* 52 (1889) 395-409.

Hurst, Ben. "The Fate of Bosnia: Some Impressions of an Immediate Observer." *Catholic World* 88 (1909) 513-22.

Imamović, Mustafa. *Pravni Položaj i unutrašnji politički razvitak Bosne i Hercegovine od 1878. do 1914*. Sarajevo: Svjetlost, 1976.

Ivanovitch, Mil. R. "Europe and the Annexation of Bosnia and Herzegovina." *Fortnightly Review* 91 (1909) 1-18.

Jelavich, Charles. "The Revolt in Bosnia and Hercegovina, 1881-2." *Slavonic and East European Review* 31 (1953) 420-436.

Jerábek, Rudolf. *Potiorek: General im Schatten von Sarajevo.* Graz: Verlag Styria, 1991.

Kadić, Ante. "The Occupation of Bosnia (1878) as Depicted in Literature." *East European Quarterly* 28:3 (1994) 281-96.

Kapidžić, Hamdija. "Austro-ugarska politika u Bosni i Hercegovini i jugoslovensko pitanje za vrijeme prvog svjetskog rata." *Godišnjak istoriskog društva Bosne i Hercegovine* 9 (1957) 7-53.

—. *Bosna i Hercegovina pod austrougarskom upravom: Članci i rasprave.* Sarajevo: Svjetlost, 1968.

—. *Hercegovački ustanak 1882 godine.* Sarajevo: Veselin Masleša, 1958.

—. "Položaj Bosne i Hercegovine za vrijeme austrougarske uprave (državnopravni odnosi)." *Prilozi* 4:4 (1968) 59-80.

Kharuzin, Aleksei Nikolaevich. *Bosniia-Gertzegovina: Ocherki okkupatsionnoi provintsii Avstro-Vengrii.* St. Petersburg: Gos. Tip., 1901.

Kotsebu, P. A. *Politicheskoe, ekonomicheskoe i voennoe znachenie prisoedinenniia Bosnii i Gertsegoviny k Avstro-Vengrii.* Ekaterinburg, 1911.

Kraljačić, Tomislav. *Kalajev režim u Bosni i Hercegovini (1882-1903).* Sarajevo: Veselin Masleša, 1987.

Kuba, Ludvik. *Ctení o Bosne a Hercegovine: Cesty a studie z roku 1893-1896.* [V Praze] Druzstevní práce, 1937.

Lang, Robert Hamilton. "The Austrians in Bosnia." *Fortnightly Review* 32 (1879) 650-71.

Langer, William L. "The 1908 Prelude to the World War." *Foreign Affairs* 7 (1929) 633-49.

Lanin, E. B. "Bosnia and Herzegovina." *Contemporary Review* 65 (1894) 735-60.

Lavrov, Petr A. *Anneksiia Bosnii i Gertsegoviny i otnoshenie k nei slavianstva.* St. Petersburg, 1909.

Legh, T. W. "A Ramble in Bosnia and the Herzegovina." *New Review* (Nov. 1891) 470-80.

Macartney, Carlile Aylmer. "Bosnia-Herzegovina, 1875-1903." In *The Habsburg Empire: 1790-1918,* 740-48. New York: Macmillan, 1969.

Mandić, Mihovil. *Povijest okupacije Bosne i Hercegovine (1878).* Zagreb: Matica Hrvatska, 1910.

Masaryk, T. G. *Der Agramer Hochverratsprozess und die Annexion von Bosnien und Herzegovina.* Vienna, 1910.

Masleša, V. *Mlada Bosna.* Belgrade, 1945.

Medlicott, William Norton. *The Congress of Berlin and After: A Diplomatic History of the Near Eastern Settlement, 1878-1880.* London: Methuen, 1938.

Miller, William. "Bosnia under the Austrians." *Gentleman's Magazine* 61 (1898) 340-52.

Muelder, Milton E.G. "The Austro-Hungarian Administration of Bosnia and Hercegovina 1878-1910." Ph.D. dissertation, University of Michigan, 1939.

Nintchitch, Momtchilo. *La Crise bosniaque (1900-1908) et les puissances européennes.* Paris: Alfred Costes, 1937.

Die Occupation Bosniens und der Hercegovina durch k.k. Truppen im Jahre 1878. Vienna: Abteilung für Kriegsgeschichte des k.k. Kriegs-Archivs, 1879.

Okey, Robin F.C. "Cultural and Political Problems of the Austro-Hungarian Administration of Bosnia and Herzegovina." Ph. D. dissertation, Oxford University, 1972.

Die österreichisch-ungarische Monarchie in Wort und Bild. Band 23 *(Bosnien-Herzegovina*). Vienna, 1901.

Roebke-Berns, R. D. "Austrian Social Democratic Foreign Policy and the Bosnian Crisis of 1908." *Austrian History Yearbook* 17-18 (1981-82) 104-23.

Šarac, Nadim. *Položaj radničke klase u Bosni i Hercegovini pod Austro-Ugarskom okupacijom 1878-1914.* Belgrade, 1951.

Schmid, F. *Bosnien und die Herzegovina unter der Verwaltung Österreich-Ungarns.* Leipzig: Veit, 1914.

Schmitt, Bernadotte Everly. *The Annexation of Bosnia 1908-1909.* Cambridge: University Press, 1937; New York: H. Fertig, 1970.

—. "The Bosnian Annexation Crisis." *Slavonic Review* 9 (Dec. 1930) 312-34; 9 (Mar. 1931) 650-61; 10 (Dec. 1931) 408-19; 10 (Apr. 1932) 641-57.

Seton-Watson, Robert William. [Scotus Viator]. "The Hungarian Crisis and the Southern Slavs." *Spectator* 103 (9 Oct. 1909) 547-49.

—. *The Role of Bosnia in International Politics (1875-1914).* London: Oxfod University Press, [1932].
—. "Russian Commitments in the Bosnian Question and an Early Project of Annexation." *Slavic Review* 8 (1930) 578-88.
—. *The Southern Slav Question and the Habsburg Monarchy.* New York: H. Fertig, 1969.
—. [Viator]. "The Truth about Bosnia and Herzegovina." *Fortnight Review* 90 (1908) 1007-16.
Skarić, Vladislav, Nuri-Hadžić, Osman and Nikola Stojnović. *Bosna i Hercegovina pod austrijskom upravom.* Belgrade: G. Kon, [1938].
Slijepčević, Đ. *Pitanje Bosne i Hercegovine u XIX veku.* Cologne: n.p., 1981.
Snyder, Philip Stephen. "Bosnia and Herzegovina in Cisleithanian Politics 1878-1879." Ph.D. dissertation, Rice University, 1974.
Stojanović, Nikola. *Hercegovačko-bokeljski ustanak 1882.* Belgrade: Vojno delo, 1963.
Sugar, Peter Frigyes. "Austria-Hungary and the Balkan Crisis: An Ingenious Improvisation." In Bela K. Kiraly and Gale Stokes, eds. *Insurrections, Wars, and the Eastern Crisis in the 1870s,* 66-85. Boulder, CO: Social Science Monographs, 1985.
Sweet, D. A. "The Bosnian Crisis." In Francis Henry Hinsley, ed. *British Foreign Policy under Sir Edward Grey,* 178-92. Cambridge: University Press, 1977.
Tolstoy, Leo. *The Crisis of Civilization.* Translation of the essay "On the Annexation of Bosnia and Herzegovina by Austria." Bristol: R. V. Sampson, 1965.
Tuttle, Herbert. "The Occupation of Bosnia." *Nation* 27 (Sept. 12, 1878) 161-62.
Wank, Solomon. "Aehrenthal and the Sanjak of Novibazar Railway Project: A Reappraisal." *Slavonic and East European Review* 42 (1964) 353-69.
Wittrock, Georg John Veit. *Österrike-Ungern i bosniska krisen, 1908-1909.* Uppsala: Almqvist & Wiksells boktryckeri-a; Leipzig: O. Harrassowitz, 1939.
Wurmbrand, Norbert. *Die richtliche Stellung Bosniens und Herzegowina.* Vienna: F. Deuticke, 1915.

WORLD WAR I AND FIRST YUGOSLAVIA (1914-1941)

Almira, José. *Le déclic de Sarajevo.* Paris: Édition Radot, 1928.

Banac, Ivo. *The National Question in Yugoslavia: Origins, History, Politics.* Ithaca: Cornell University Press, 1984.

Beard, Charles and George Radin *The Balkan Pivot: Yugoslavia: A Study in Government and Administration.* New York: Macmillan, 1929.

Boban, Ljubo. *Sporazum Cvetković-Maček.* Belgrade: Institut društvenih nauka, 1965.

Brehm, Bruno. *They Call It Patriotism.* Boston: Little, Brown, and Company, 1932.

Chopin, Jules. *Le complot de Sarajevo (28 juin 1914): Études sur les origines de la guerre (une carte).* Paris: Editions Bossard, 1918.

Cornish, Vaughan. "Bosnia, the Borderland of Serb and Croat." *Geography* 20:4 (1935) 260-70.

Ćorović, Vladimir. *Političke prilike u Bosni i Hercegovini.* Belgrade: Politika, 1939.

Dedijer, Vladimir. *The Road to Sarajevo.* New York: Simon and Schuster, 1966.

Dor, Milo. *Der Letzte Sonntag: Bericht über Attentat von Sarajewo.* Munich: Amalthea, 1982.

Dragnich, Alex N. *The First Yugoslavia: The Search for a Viable Political System.* Stanford: Hoover Institute Press, 1983.

Durham, Edith M. *The Sarajevo Crime.* London: George Allen and Unwin, 1925.

Fay, Sidney Bradshaw. *The Origins of the World War.* New York: Macmillan, 1966.

Fischer-Baling, Eugen. *Die kritischen 39 Tage von Sarajewo bis zum Weltbrand.* Berlin: Ullstein, 1928.

Gilfond, Henry. *Black Hand at Sarajevo.* Indianapolis, IN: Bobbs-Merrill, 1975.

Graham, Stephen. *Alexander of Yugoslavia: Strong Man of the Balkans.* London: Cassell, 1938.

Hoptner, J. B. *Yugoslavia in Crisis, 1934-1941.* New York: Columbia University Press, 1962.

Išek, Tomislav. *Djelatnost Hrvatske seljacke stranke u Bosni i Hercegovini do zavodjenja diktature.* Sarajevo: Svjetlost, 1981.

Lafore, Laurence D. *The Long Fuse: An Interpretation of the Origins of World War I.* Philadelphia and New York: Lippincott, 1956.

Lederer, Ivo J. *Yugoslavia at the Paris Peace Conference.* New Haven: Yale University Press, 1963.

Ljubibratić, Dragoslav. *Mlada Bosna i sarajevski atentat.* Sarajevo: Muzej grada Sarajeva, 1964.

Maček, Vladko. *In the Struggle for Freedom.* New York: Robert Speller & Sons, 1957.

MacKenzie, David. *Apis: The Congenial Conspirator: The Life of Colonel Dragutin T. Dimitrijevic.* Boulder, CO: East European Monographs; Distributed by Columbia University Press, New York, 1989.

—. "Serbia As Piedmont and the Yugoslav Idea, 1804-1914." *East European Quarterly* 28:2 (1994) 153-82.

Mićanović, Slavko. *Sarajevski atentat.* Zagreb: Stvarnost, 1965.

Nickels, Sylvie. *Assassination at Sarajevo.* New York: Grossman, 1969.

Owings, W. A. " 'Young Bosnia' in the Light of a Generation-Conflict Interpretation of Student Movements." *Balkanistica* 2 (1975) 99-116.

Pauli, Hertha. *The Secrets of Sarajevo.* New York: Appleton-Century, 1965.

Pfefer, L. *Istraga u sarajevskom atentatu.* Zagreb: Nova Evropa, 1938.

Pozzi, Henri. *Black Hand over Europe.* London: F. Mott, 1935; Zagreb: Croatian Information Center, 1994.

Pribitchévitch, Svetozar. *La Dictature du roi Alexandre.* Paris: Bossuet, 1933.

Purivatra, Atif. "Formiranje Jugoslavesne Muslimanske Organizacije i njen razvoj do prevazilaženja krize početkom 1922. godine." In *Istorija XX veka: Zbornik radova.* Vol. 9, 387-445. Belgrade: Institut društevnih nauka, 1968.

—. *Jugoslavenska muslimanska organizacija u političkom životu Kraljevine Srba, Hrvata i Slovenaca.* Sarajevo: Svjetlost, 1974.

—. "Nacionale koncepcije Jugoslavenske muslimanske organizacije," *Jugoslovenski istorijski časopis* 4 (1969) 141-48.
Remak, Joachim. *Sarajevo: The Story of Political Murder.* New York: Criterion Books, 1959.
Šarac, Nedim. "Šestojanuarska diktatura 1929. godine na području Bosne i Hercegovine." *Pregled* 4 (1974) 365-88.
Šehić, Nusret. *Četništvo u Bosni i Hercegovini, 1918-1941.* Sarajevo: ANUBiH, 1971.
Seton-Watson, R. W. *Sarajevo: A Study in the Origins of the Great War.* London: Hutchinson, 1926.
Spaho, Mehmed. "Jugoslavenska Muslimanska Organizacija." *Nova Evropa* 7:17 (1923) 505-06.
Stojadinović, Milan. *Ni rat ni pakt: Jugoslavija izmedju dva rata.* Buenos Aires: El Economista, 1963.
Stoyanovich, Nikola. "The Problem of Bosnia-Herzegovina." *World Court* 4 (1918) 245-49.
Strauss Feuerlicht, Roberta. *The Desperate Act.* New York: McGraw-Hill, 1968.
Südland, L. V. [Ivo Pilar]. *Južnoslavensko pitanje.* Zagreb: Matica Hrvatska, 1943. Translation of *Die südslawische Frage und der Weltkrieg.* Vienna, 1918.
Vane, J. M. *The Yugoslav Crisis, 1918-1945.* New York: New Book, 1945.
Vasiljevic, Dusan. "The South Slav Problem from the Bosnian Point of View." *New Europe* 9 (1918) 79-84.
Vrbanic, George Franz. *The Failure to Save the First Yugoslavia: The Serbo-Croatian Sporazum of 1939.* Chicago: ZIRAL, 1991.

WORLD WAR II AND SOCIALIST YUGOSLAVIA (1941-1991)

Allcock, John B. "In Praise of Chauvinism: Rhetorics of Nationalism in Yugoslav Politics." *Third World Quarterly* 11 (1989) 208-22.
Anonymous. *Hercegovina u NOB-u.* Sarajevo: Berdon, 1986.
Antonić, Zdravko. *Ustanak u istočnoj i centralnoj Bosni 1941.* Tuzla: Univerzal, 1983.
Auty, Phyllis. *Tito.* New York: McGraw-Hill, 1970.

Babić, Nikola. *ZAVNOBiH i izgradnja Bosansko-Hercegovačke državnosti.* Sarajevo: Muzej revolucije Bosne i Hercegovine, 1970.

Bailey, Ronald H., ed. *Partisans and Guerrillas.* Alexandria, VA: Time-Life Books, 1978.

Banac, Ivo. *With Stalin against Tito: Cominformist Splits in Yugoslav Communism.* Ithaca and London: Cornell University Press, 1988.

Beloff, Nora. *Tito's Flawed Legacy: Yugoslavia and the West Since 1939.* Boulder, CO: Westview, 1985.

Bilandžić, Dušan. *Jugoslavija poslije Tita (1980-1985).* Zagreb: Globus, 1986.

Campbell, John C. *Tito's Separate Road.* New York: Harper and Row, 1967.

Deakin, F. W. D. *The Embattled Mountain.* New York: Oxford University Press, 1971.

Dedijer, Vladimir and Antun Miletić. *Genocid nad Muslimanima 1941-1945: Zbornik dokumenata i svjedočenja.* Sarajevo, Svjetlost, 1990.

Dimitrijević, Vojin. "The International Community and the Yugoslav Crisis." *Balkan Forum* 4:2 (1996) 45-79.

Djilas, Milovan. *The New Class.* New York: East World, 1957.

—. *Rise and Fall.* San Diego: Harcourt, Brace, Jovanovich, 1985.

—. *Wartime.* New York: Harcourt, Brace, Jovanovich, 1977.

Heuser, Beatrice. *Western Containment Policy in the Cold War: The Yugoslav Case, 1948-53.* London, New York: Routledge, 1989.

Humo, Avdo. *Moja generacija.* Sarajevo: Svjetlost, 1984.

Jelić-Butić, Fikreta. "Bosna i Hercegovina u koncepciji stvaranja Nezavisne Države Hrvatske." *Pregled* 12 (1971) 663-70.

Kočović, Bogoljub. *Žrtve drugog svetskog rata u Jugoslaviji.* London: Naše delo, 1985.

Lendvai, Paul. *Eagles in Cobwebs.* London: Macdonald, 1970.

Ludall, Harold. *Yugoslavia in Crisis.* Oxford: Clarendon, 1989.

Massacre of Croatians in Bosnia and Hercegovina and Sandzak. [Toronto: Croatian Islamic Center], [1978.]

McFarlane, Bruce. *Yugoslavia: Politics, Economics and Society.* London: Pinter, 1988.

Meir, Viktor. "Yugoslavia's National Question." *Problems of Communism* (Mar.-Apr. 1983) 47-60.

Milazzo, Matteo J. *The Chetnik Movement and The Yugoslav Resistance.* Baltimore: Johns Hopkins University Press, 1975.

Milivojević, M. *Descent into Chaos: Yugoslavia's Worsening Crisis.* London: Alliance for the Institute for European Defence and Strategic Studies, 1989.

Mladenović, O., ed. *The Yugoslav Concept of General People's Defense.* Belgrade: Međ. Politika, 1970.

National Republican Institute for International Affairs. *The 1990 Elections in the Republics of Yugoslavia.* Washington, DC: 1991.

Omrčanin, Ivo. *Tito.* Washington, DC: Samizdat, 1986.

Pavlowitch, Stevan K. *Tito, Yugoslavia's Great Dictator: A Reassessment.* Columbus: Ohio State University Press, 1992.

Pešelj, Branko M. "Constitutional Characteristics of the Socialist Republic of Bosnia and Hercegovina." *Review of the Study Centre of Jugoslav Affairs* 1:5 (1965) 328-38.

Prcela, John and Stanko Guldescu, eds. *Operation Slaughterhouse.* Philadelphia: Dorrance, 1970.

Ramet, Pedro. *Nationalism and Federalism in Yugoslavia 1962-1991.* 2nd ed. Bloomington: Indiana University Press, 1992.

—. "Yugoslavia and the Threat of Internal and External Discontent. *Orbis* 28:1 (1984) 109-20.

—, ed. *Yugoslavia in the 1980's.* Boulder, CO: Westview Press, 1985.

Ramet, Sabrina Petra. *Balkan Babel: The Disintegration of Yugoslavia from the Death of Tito to Ethnic War.* 2nd ed. Boulder, CO: Westview, 1996.

Remington, Robin Alison. "The Federal Dilemma in Yugoslavia." *Current History* 89 (Dec. 1990) 405-08, 429-31.

Roberts, W. R. *Tito, Mihailović and the Allies, 1941-1945.* 2nd ed. Durham: Duke University Press, 1987.

Rusinow, Dennison. "The Yugoslav Concept of All National Defense." American Universities Field Staff Reports, Southeast Europe Series, no. 19. Hanover: Universities Field Staff International, 1982.

—. *The Yugoslav Experiment, 1948-1974.* London: C. Hurst, 1977.

Sabrosky, Alan Ned. "From Bosnia to Sarajevo: A Comparative Discussion of Interstate Crises." *Journal of Conflict Resolution* 19 (1975) 3-24.

Shoup, Paul. *Communism and the Yugoslav National Question*. New York: Columbia University Press, 1968.

Sirc, Ljubo. *Between Hitler and Tito: Nazi Occupation and Communist Oppression*. London: A. Deutsch, 1989.

Steed, Henry Wickham. "United Yugoslavia-European Necessity." *Central European Observer* 20 (Apr. 30, 1943) 139.

Tomasevich, Jozo. *The Chetniks: War and Revolution in Yugoslavia, 1941- 1945*. Stanford: Stanford University Press, 1975.

Vucinich, W., ed. *Contemporary Yugoslavia*. Berkeley: California University Press, 1969.

West, Richard. *Tito and the Rise and Fall of Yugoslavia*. London: Sinclair-Stevenson, 1994.

Wilson, Duncan. *Tito's Yugoslavia*. Cambridge: Cambridge University Press, 1979.

Žerjavić, Vladimir. *Gubici stanovništva Jugoslavije u Drugom svjetskom ratu*. Zagreb: Jugoslavensko viktimološko društvo, 1989.

1992-1995 WAR AND INDEPENDENCE

"The Abdication." *New Republic* (Feb. 12, 1994) 1, 7-9.

Agnes, Mario, ed. *La Crise en yougoslavie: position et action du Saint-Siège (1991-1992)*. Vatican City: Librairie éditrice vaticane, 1992.

Ajami, Fouad. "Beyond Wards: History Rewards the Aggressors." *New Republic* (Aug. 7, 1995) 15-17.

—. "In Europe's Shadows: The Tragedy of Bosnia, and the Long, Troubled History of Islam in the Balkans." *New Republic* (Nov. 21, 1994) 29-37.

Ali, Rabia and Lawrence Lifschultz, eds. *Why Bosnia? Writings on the Balkan War*. Stony Creek, CT: Pamphleteer's Press, 1993.

Allcock, John B. "Yugoslavia: Bosnia and Hercegovina." In Bogdan Szajkowski, ed. *New Political Parties of Eastern Europe and the Soviet Union*. Harlow, Essex, U.K.: Longman, 1991.

Allen, Beverly. *Rape Warfare: The Hidden Genocide in Bosnia-Herzegovina and Croatia.* Minneapolis: University of Minnesota Press, 1996.

Allman, T. D. "Serbia's Blood War." *Vanity Fair* (March, 1993) 97-118.

Almond, Mark. *Europe's Backyard War: The War in the Balkans.* London: Heinemann, 1994.

Amnesty International. *Bosnia-Herzegovina: Gross Abuses of Basic Human Rights.* New York: Amnesty International U.S.A., 1992.

—. *Bosnia-Herzegovina: Rana u Duši: A Wound to the Soul.* New York: Amnesty International U.S.A., 1993.

—. *Bosnia-Herzegovina: Rape and Sexual Abuse by Armed Forces.* New York: Amnesty International U.S.A., 1993.

—. *Yugoslavia: Further Reports of Torture and Deliberate and Arbitrary Killings in War Zones.* New York: Amnesty International U.S.A., 1992.

—. Yugoslavia: *Torture and Deliberate and Arbitrary Killings in War Zones.* New York: Amnesty International U.S.A., 1991.

Arday, L. "The Historical Background of the Crisis in Former Yugoslavia." *Aussen Politik* 44:3 (1993) 253-60.

Armed Conflict in the Balkans and European Security. An international conference April 20-22, 1993. Ljubljana: Center for Strategic Studies, Ministry of Defence, June 1993.

Ash, Timothy Garton. "Bosnia in Our Future." *The New York Review of Books* (Dec. 21, 1995) 27-31.

Atlagić, David, ed. *Bosna i Hercegovina: Ogledalo Razuma.* (an insert). Belgrade: Borba, 1992.

Babić, Marko. *Owen-Stoltenbergovo međunarodno diplomatsko legaliziranje srpske okupacije i zločina u bosanskoj Posavini.* Vidovice, Zagreb: Croatan, 1994.

Bacevich, A. J. "Wilsonian Dream, Bosnian Reality." *First Things* 56 (Oct. 1995) 18-20.

Bächler, Günther. *Bosnien-Herzegowina: Friedliche Streitbeilegung zwischen Realität und konkreter Utopie.* Zurich: Forschungsstelle für Sicherheitspolitik und Konfliktanalyse. 1993.

Bair, Andrew. "Which End-Game in Bosnia?" *Strategic Forum* 16 (Jan. 1995) 1-4.

Balkan War Report. Bulletins of the Institute for War and Peace Reporting, London.

Banac, Ivo. "The Fearful Asymmetry of War: The Causes and Consequences of Yugoslavia's Demise." *Daedalus* 121 (1992) 141-72.

—. "How to Stop Serbia." *National Review* (Sep. 14, 1992) 18.

—. "Misreading the Balkans." *Foreign Policy* 93 (Winter 1993/94) 173-82.

—. "Political Change and National Diversity." *Daedalus* 119 (1990) 141-59.

—. "Shotgun Wedding in the Balkans." *Nation* (Oct. 23, 1995) 466-68.

Bassiouni, M. Cherif. *Sexual Violence: An Invisible Weapon of War in the Former Yugoslavia.* Chicago: International Human Rights Law Institute, DePaul University College of Law, 1996.

Bebler, A. "Yugoslavia's Variety of Communist Federalism and Her Demise." *Communist and Post-Communist Studies* 26:1 (1993) 72-76.

Bebles, Anton. "The Military and the Yugoslav Crisis." *Südosteuropa* 40 (1991) 127-44.

Bell, Martin. *In Harm's Way.* London: Hamish Hamilton, 1995.

Bennett, Christopher. *Yugoslavia's Bloody Collapse.* Washington Square, NY: New York University Press, 1995.

Bianchini, Stefano and Paul Shoup. *The Yugoslav War, Europe and the Balkans: How to Achieve Security?* Ravenna, Italy: Europa and the Balkans, 1995.

Biberaj, Elez. "Yugoslavia: A Continuing Crisis?" *Conflict Studies* 225 (1989) 1-22.

Biden, Joseph. *To Stand against Aggression: Milosevic, the Bosnian Republic, and the Conscience of the West.* A Report to the Committee on Foreign Relations, U.S. Senate, by Senator Joseph R. Biden, Jr. Washington, U.S. GPO, 1993.

Billing, Peter. *Der Bürgerkrieg in Jugoslawien: Ursachen, Hintergründe, Perspektiven.* Frankfurt: Hessische Stiftung Friedens und Konfliktforschung, 1992.

— et al. *Der Krieg in Bosnien und das hilflose Europa: Plädoyer für eine militärische UN-Intervention.* Frankfurt: Hessische Stiftung Friedens und Konfliktforschung, 1993.

Binder, David. "Anatomy of a Massacre." *Foreign Policy* 3:97 (1994-95) 70-78.

Biserko, Sonja, ed. *Yugoslavia: Collapse, War, Crimes.* Belgrade: Centre for Anti-War Action, 1993.

Blaskovich, Jerry. "A Heroine of the Killing Fields of Bosnia." *American Croatian Review* 2:3&4 (1995) 31-32.

—. "A Medical Odyssey to Dante's Inferno." *International Journal of Dermatology* 34:12 (1995) 883-84.

Block, Robert. "The Madness of General Mladic." *New York Review of Books* (Oct. 5, 1995) 7-9.

Bogosavljević, Srđan et al. *Bosna i Hercegovina izmedju rata i mira.* Belgrade: Institut društvenih nauka, 1992.

Borden, Anthony. "Moving Dayton to Bosnia." *Nation* (Mar. 25, 1996) 18-22.

—, Slavenka Drakulic, and George Kenny. "Bosnia's Democratic Charade." *Nation* (Sep. 23, 1996) 14-18.

—, Ben Cohen, Marisa Crevatin, and Davorka Zmiarević, eds. *Breakdown: War and Reconstruction in Yugoslavia.* London: Institute for War and Peace Reporting, 1992.

Bosnia-Herzegovina Achilles Heel of Western "Civilization." Articles from *News and Letters* on the Crisis in Bosnia. Chicago: News & Letters, 1993.

"Bosnia's Trials." *Nation* (Dec. 4, 1995) 691-92.

Bouchet, P. ed. *Le Livre noir de l'ex-Yugoslavie: purification ethnique et crimes de guerre: Documents rassemblés par le Nouvel Observateur et Reporters sans frontières.* Paris: Arléa, 1993.

Boyd, Charles G. "Making Peace with the Guilty: The Truth about Bosnia." *Foreign Affairs* 74:5 (1995) 22-38.

Boyle, Francis Anthony. *The Bosnian People Charge Genocide: Proceedings at the International Court of Justice Concerning Bosnia v. Serbia on the Prevention and Punishment of the Crime of Genocide.* Intro. by Marshall Harris; Foreword by Frank McCloskey. Northampton, MA: Aletheia, 1994.

Brenner, Michael. "The EC in Yugoslavia: A Debut Performance." *Security Studies* 1:4 (1992) 586-608.

Brock, Peter. "Dateline Yugoslavia: The Partisan Press." *Foreign Policy* 93:9 (1993-94) 152-72.

Brown, Michael. "Yugoslavia's Armed Forces Order of Battle." *Jane's Intelligence Review* 3:8 (1991) 366-73.

Brzezinski, Zbigniew. "After Srebrenica:The Speech Clinton Never Gave." *New Republic* (Aug. 7, 1995) 20-21.

Bugajski, Janusz. "Bosnian Blunders." *The World and I* (Nov. 1, 1992) 68-75.

Burg, Steven L. "Why Yugoslavia Fell Apart." *Current History* 92 (1993) 357-63.

Calic, Marie-Janine. *Der Krieg in Bosnia-Hercegovina: Ursachen-Konfliktstrukturen-Internationale Lösungsversuche.* Frankfurt: Suhrkamp, 1995.

Carter, Hodding. "Punishing Serbia." *Foreign Policy* 96 (Fall 1994) 49-56.

Cataldi, Anna. *Letters from Sarajevo.* Tr. Avril Bardoni. Rockport, MD: Element Press, 1993.

Ceh, Nick and Jeff Harder, eds. *The Golden Apple: War and Democracy in Croatia and Bosnia.* Boulder: East Europe Monographs; New York: Distributed by Columbia University Press, 1996.

Charles, R. Patrick. "Tactics of the Serbian and Bosnian-Serb Armies and Territorial Militias." *The Journal of Slavic Military Studies* 7:1 (1994) 16-43.

Cherly, Benard. "Rape As Terror: The Case of Bosnia." *Terrorism and Political Violence* 6:1 (1994) 29-43.

Cigar, Norman. *Genocide in Bosnia: The Policy of "Ethnic Cleansing."* College Station, TX: Texas A&M University Press, 1995

—."How Wars End: War Termination and Serbian Decisionmaking in the Case of Bosnia." *South East European Monitor* 3:1 (1996) 3-47.

—. *The Right to Defence: Thoughts on the Bosnian Arms Embargo.* Institute for European Defence and Strategic Studies. Occasional Paper 63. London: Alliance Publishers, 1995.

—. "The Serbo-Croatian War of 1991: Political and Military Dimensions." *Journal of Strategic Studies* 16:3 (1993) 297-338.

Clark, Jonathan. "Rhetoric Before Reality: Loose Lips Sink Ships." *Foreign Affairs* 74:5 (1995) 2-7.

Clark, Roger and Madeleine Sann, eds. *The Prosecution of International Crimes: A Critical Study of the International Tribunal for the Former Yugoslavia.* New Brunswick: Transaction, 1996.

Cohen, Ben and George Stamkoski, eds. *With No Peace to Keep: United Nations Peacekeeping and the War in the Former Yugoslavia.* London: Grainpress, 1995.

Cohen, Lenard J. "Bosnia and Herzegovina: Fragile Peace in a Segmented State." *Current History* 95:599 (1996) 103-12.

—. *Broken Bonds - The Disintegration of Yugoslavia.* Boulder, CO: Westview Press, 1993.

—. "The Disintegration of Yugoslavia." *Current History* 91:568 (1992) 369-75.

Cohen, Roger. "Peace in His Time." *New Republic* (Mar. 11, 1996) 34-40.

Commission on Security and Cooperation in Europe. *The Referendum on Independence in Bosnia and Hercegovina: February 29-March 1, 1992.* Washington, DC: CSCE, March 12, 1992.

Corry, John. "The Hidden Balkan War." *American Spectator* (Oct. 1995) 22-25.

Cot, Jean, ed. *Dernière guerre balkanique? Ex-Yougoslavie, témoignages, analyses, perspectives.* Paris: L'Harmattan, 1996.

Coulson, Meg. "Looking Behind the Violent Break-up of Yugoslavia." *Feminist Review* 45 (1993) 86-101.

Crnobrnja, Mihailo. *The Yugoslav Drama.* Montreal and Kingston: McGill-Queen's University Press, 1994.

Cushman, Thomas and Stjepan G. Meštrović, eds. *This Time We Knew: Western Response to Genocide in Bosnia.* New York: New York University Press, 1996.

Čuvalo, Ante. "Bosnian Pax Americana: Does Bosnia-Herzegovina Have a Chance?" *American Croatian Review* 3:1 (1996) 1-4.

—. "Federation of Bosnia-Herzegovina: Can a Marriage of Convenience Work?" *American Croatian Review* 2:2 (1995) 5-8.

—. "The Making or Breaking of Bosnia-Herzegovina." *American Croatian Review* 2:3&4 (1995) 1-2.

—. "Serbian Aggression and the West." *American Croatian Review* 2:2 (1995) 24-25.

—. "War in Bosnia-Hercegovina and Croatia: Old and New Myths." *American Croatian Review* 1:1 (1994) 4-5.

Cvetkovski, Cvetan. "The Constitutional Status of Bosnia and Hercegovina in Accordance with the Dayton Documents." *Balkan Forum* 4:2 (1996) 111-28.

Cviic, Christopher. "A Culture of Humiliation." *National Interest* 32 (Summer 1993) 79-82.

—. "Running Late: But Is Dayton Still on Track?" *World Today* 52:6 (1996) 144-46.

Damiani, Sandro. *Jugoslavia: Genesi di una mattanza annunciata.* Pistoia: Sette giorni, 1993.

De Sarajevo à Sarajevo: L'échec yougoslave. (Sous la direction de Jacques Rupnik). Brussels: Editions complexe, 1992.

Dean, Jonathan. *Ending Europe's Wars: The Continuing Search for Peace and Security.* New York: Twentieth Century Fund Press, 1994.

Denitch, Bogdan. *Ethnic Nationalism: The Tragic Death of Yugoslavia.* Minneapolis: University of Minnesota Press, 1994.

—. "Reform and Conflict in Yugoslavia." *Dissent* 37:20 (1990) 151-53.

— and T. Nairn. "Not All Bosnians Yet." *Dissent* 41:1 (1994) 124-26.

Department of State. *Country Reports on Human Rights Practices for 1992.* Washington, DC: U.S. GPO, February 1993.

Dizdarević, Zlatko. *Portraits of Sarajevo.* Trans. Midhat Ridjanović; ed. Ammiel Alcalay. New York: Fromm International, 1995.

—. *Sarajevo: A War Journal.* Preface by Joseph Brodsky. Introduction by Robert Jay Lifton. New York: Fromm International, 1933.

Doder, Dusko. "Yugoslavia: New War, Old Hatreds." *Foreign Affairs* 91 (1993) 3-23.

Doherty, Carroll J. "The Arms Embargo Dilemma: Questions and Answers." (Interview) *Congressional Quarterly Weekly Report* 53:27 (1995) 2008-10.

Dole, Bob. "The Diplomacy of Denial: U.S. Policy in the Former Yugoslavia." *Harvard International Review* 16:2 (1994) 38-39.

Donia, Robert J. and John V.A. Fine, Jr. *Bosnia and Hercegovina: A Tradition Betrayed.* New York: Columbia University Press, 1994.

Drakulić, Slavenka. *The Balkan Express: Fragments from the Other Side of War.* New York: Norton, 1993.

—. "Bosnia: Guilt by Dissociation?" *Partisan Review* 61:1 (1994) 60-79.

—. "Women Hide behind a Wall of Silence." *Nation* (Mar. 1, 1993) 253-54.

Erdelitsch, Walter et al. *Krieg auf dem Balkan: Wie Fernsehreporter den Zusammenbruch Jugoslawiens erlebten.* Vienna: Jugend und Volk, 1992.

Ethnic Cleansing of Croats in Bosnia and Herzegovina 1991-1993. Mostar: n.p. August 1993 and Akron, OH: Akro Printing, 1993.

Evancevich, Michael S. "Danger in the Balkans." *Military Intelligence* 19:2 (1993) 10-15, 51.

Eyal, Jonathan. *Europe and Yugoslavia: Lessons from a Failure.* London: Royal United Services Institute for Defence Studies, 1993.

The FAMA Collective. *Sarajevo: Survival Guide.* Sarajevo, 1993.

Fenske, John. "The West and 'The Problem from Hell.'" *Current History* 92 (1993) 353-56.

Fernández Arribas, Javier. *Casco azul, soldado español.* Madrid: Ediciones temas de hoy, 1994.

Filipović, Zlata. *Zlata's Diary: A Child's Life in Sarajevo.* Trans. Christian Pribichevich-Zoric. New York: Viking Press, 1994.

Flint, David. *Bosnia: Can There Ever Be Peace?* Austin, TX: Raintree Steck-Vaughn, 1996.

Fogelquist, Alan F. *The Breakup of Yugoslavia, International Policy, and the War in Bosnia-Hercegovina.* Los Angeles: Institute of South Central Europe and Balkan Affairs, 1993.

Forest, Jim. "Bosnia's Unhealed Wounds." *Sojourners* 24 (Nov./Dec. 1995) 13.

Free Press and the Serbian Regime: Implementation of the Helsinki Accords. Briefing of the Commission on Security and Cooperation in Europe, May 5, 1995. Washington, DC: U.S. GPO, 1995.

Freedman, Lawrence. "Why the West Failed." *Foreign Policy* 97 (1994-95) 53-69.

Frei, M. "The Bully of the Balkans." *Spectator* (Aug. 17, 1991) 11-13.

Frelick, Bill. *Yugoslavia Torn Asunder: Lessons for Protecting Refugees from Civil War.* Washington, DC: U.S. Committee for Refugees, 1992.

Gagnon, V. P., Jr. "Ethnic Nationalism and International Conflict: The Case of Serbia." *International Security* 19 (Winter 1994/95) 130-66.

—. "Serbia's Road to War." In Larry Diamond and Marc F. Plattner, eds. *Nationalism, Ethnic Conflict, and Democracy*, 117-31. Baltimore: Johns Hopkins University Press, 1994, and in *Journal of Democracy* 5:2 (Apr. 1994) 117-31.

Ganeri, Anita. *I Remember Bosnia.* Austin, TX: Raintree Steck-Vaughn, 1994.

Gati, Charles. "From Sarajevo to Sarajevo." *Foreign Affairs* 71:4 (1992) 64-78.

Gelhard, Susanne. *Ab heute ist Krieg: Der blutige Konflikt im ehemaligen Jugoslawien.* Frankfurt: Fischer Taschenbuch Verlag, 1992.

Genocide, Ethnic Cleansing in Northern Bosnia. Zagreb: Croatian Information Center, 1993.

Gianzero, Gina. "Bosnia in the Balance: The History behind the Bloodshed." *Europe* (Jun. 1994) 14-17.

Gjelten, Tom. *Sarajevo Daily: A City and Its Newspaper under Siege.* New York: HarperCollins Publishers, 1995.

Glenny, Misha. "Bosnia R.I.P." *Nation* (Jul. 12, 1993) 52-53.

—. "Bosnia: The Last Chance?" *New York Review of Books* (Jan. 28, 1993) 5-6+.

—. "Bosnia: The Tragic Prospect." *New York Review of Books* (Nov. 4, 1993) 38+.

—. *The Fall of Yugoslavia: The Third Balkan War.* London: Penguin Books, 1992.

—. "The Godfather of Bihac." *New York Review of Books* (Aug. 12, 1993) 18-19.

—. "Hope for Bosnia?" *New York Review of Books* (Apr. 7, 1994) 6-8.

—. "Perverse Alliance." *Nation* (Sep. 5, 1994) 220.

—. "The Return of the Great Powers." *New Left Review* 205 (1994) 125-30.

—. "What Is to Be Done?" *New York Review of Books* (May 27, 1993) 14-16.

—. "Yugoslavia: The Great Fall." *New York Review of Books* (Mar. 23, 1995) 56-65.

—. "Yugoslavia: The Revenger's Tragedy." *New York Review of Books* (Aug. 13, 1992) 37-43.

Glynn, Patrick. "See no Evil." *New Republic* (Oct. 25, 1993) 23, 26-29.

Golubic, G., S. E. Campbell, and T. S. Golubic. *The Crisis in Bosnia-Hercegovina: Is an Ethnic Division of Bosnia-Hercegovina Desirable or Possible?* Boston: Center for the Study of Small States, Boston University, June 1992.

Gompert, David. "How to Defeat Serbia." *Foreign Affairs* 73:4 (1994) 30-47.

Goodby, James E. "Peacekeeping in the New Europe." *Washington Quarterly* (Spring 1992) 153-71.

Gow, James. "Arms Sales and Embargoes: The Yugoslav Example." *Bulletin of Arms Control* 3 (Aug. 1991) 2-7.

—. "Belgrade and Bosnia: An Assessment of the Yugoslav military." *Jane's Intelligence Review* 5:6 (1993) 243-46.

—. "Bosnia I: Stepping Up the Peace?" *World Today* 51 (Jul. 1995) 126-28.

—. "Deconstructing Yugoslavia." *Survival* 33 (1991) 291-311.

—. *Legitimacy and the Military: The Yugoslav Crisis.* London: St. Martin's Press, 1992.

—. "The Remains of the Yugoslav People's Army." *Jane's Intelligence Review* 4:8 (1992) 359-63.

—. "Serbian Nationalism and the Hissssing Ssssnake in the International Order: Whose Sovereignty? Which Nation?" *Slavonic and East European Review* 72 (Jul. 1994) 457-76.

—. "Towards a Settlement in Bosnia: The Military Dimension." *World Today* 50 (May 1994) 96-99.

—. "The Use of Coercion in the Yugoslav Crisis." *World Today* 48 (Nov. 1992) 198-202.

—. *Yugoslav Endgames: Civil Strife and Inter-State Conflict.* London: Brassey's for the Center for Defence Studies, 1991.

Goytisolo, Juan. *Cuaderno de Sarajevo: Anotaciones de un viaje a la barbarie.* Madrid: El País/Aguilar, 1993.

Graham, Franklin. *Miracle in a Shoe Box: A Christmas Gift of Wonder.* Nashville: Thomas Nelson, 1995.

Granjon, Philippe and Pascal Deloche. "RapeAas a Weapon of War." UN High Commissioner for Refugees. *Refugees* (Oct. 1993) 42-44.

Grmek, Mirko, Marc Gjidara, and Neven Šimac. *Le nettoyage ethnique. Documents historiques sur une idéologie serbe.* Paris: Fayard, 1993.

Grzimek, Martin. *Mostar: Skizzen und Splitter: Ein literarische Tagebuch von 12. bis 26. November 1994.* Heidelberg: HVA, 1995.

Guicherd, Catharine. *L'heure de l'Europe: Les premières leçons du conflit yugoslave.* Paris: CREST-Ecole polytechnique, 1993.

Gutman, Roy. *A Witness to Genocide.* New York: Macmillan, 1993.

Hagman, Hans-Christian. "The Balkan Conflicts: Prevention Is Better Than Cure." *Global Affairs* 8:3 (1993) 18-37.

Hall, Brian. *The Impossible Country: A Journey through the Last Days of Yugoslavia.* Boston: David R. Godine, 1994.

Hammel, E. A. *The Yugoslav Labyrinth.* Berkeley: Institute of International Studies, University of California at Berkeley and Anthropology of East Europe Review, 1992.

Harris, Paul. *Cry Bosnia.* New York: Interlink Books, 1996.

Harrison, Thomas. "Appeasement and War Porn." *Nation* (Apr. 8, 1996) 37-40.

Heuvel van den, M. and J. G. Siccama, eds. *The Disintegration of Yugoslavia.* Amsterdam: Rodopi, 1992.

Heuven van, Marten. "Rehabilitating Serbia." *Foreign Policy* 96 (Fall 1994) 38-56.

Hidovic Harper, Indijana. "Personal Reactions of a Bosnian Woman to the War in Bosnia." *Feminist Review* 45 (1993) 102-07.

Hitchens, Christopher. "Minority Report." *Nation* (Nov. 20, 1995) 599.

—. "Minority Report." *Nation* (Dec. 18, 1995) 776.

Hoare, Attila. "Triumph and Treachery: Will U.S. Diplomacy Strangle Bosnia in Its Hour of Victory?" *Against the Current* (Nov./Dec., 1995) 7-9.

Hodge, Carole. "Hurd Mentality: Britain's Architect of Disaster." *New Republic* (Aug. 7, 1995) 18-19.

Hogan, John. "Hard Road to Sarajevo." *Soldier of Fortune* (Nov., 1995) 40-44, 64-69.

Honig, Jan W. and Norberth Both. *Srebrenica: Record of a War Crime*. New York: Penguin, 1997.

Hukanović, Rezak. "The Evil at Omarska." *New Republic* (Feb. 12, 1996) 24-29.

—. *The Tenth Circle of Hell: A Memoir of Life in the Death Camps in Bosnia*. New York: Basic Books, 1996.

Human Rights Watch. *Abuses by Bosnian Croat and Muslim Forces in Central and Southwestern Bosnia-Hercegovina*. New York: Human Rights Watch, 1993.

—. *Abuses Continue in the Former Yugoslavia: Serbia, Montenegro and Bosnia-Hercegovina*. New York: Human Rights Watch, 1993.

—. *Human Rights in a Dissolving Yugoslavia*. New York: Human Rights Watch, 1991.

—. *Procedural and Evidentiary Issues for the Yugoslav War Crimes Tribunal: Resource Allocation, Evidentiary Questions and Protection of Witnesses*. New York: Human Rights Watch, 1993.

—. *Prosecute Now! Helsinki Watch Releases 8 Cases for War Crimes Tribunal on Former Yugoslavia*. New York: Human Rights Watch, 1993.

—. *War Crimes in Bosnia-Hercegovina*. Vol. 1. New York: Human Rights Watch, 1992.

—. *War Crimes in Bosnia-Hercegovina.* Vol. 2. New York: Human Rights Watch, 1993.

—. *War Crimes in Bosnia-Hercegovina: Bosanski Samac.* New York: Human Rights Watch, 1994.

—. *War Crimes in Bosnia-Hercegovina: U.N. Cease-Fire Won't Help Banja Luka.* New York: Human Rights Watch, 1994.

—. *The War Crimes Tribunal: One Year Later.* New York: Human Rights Watch, 1994.

Husarska, Anna. "Rocky-Road Warrior." *New Republic* (Dec. 4, 1995) 16-17.

Hussein, Mahmoud. NATO's First Mission: Defending Muslims in Europe?" *New Perspectives Quarterly* 13:1 (1996) 48-50.

I Dream of Peace. Preface by James P. Grant, executive director of UNICEF. New York: HarperCollins, 1994.

Ignatieff, Michael. "Homage to Bosnia." *New York Review of Books* (Apr. 21, 1994) 3-6.

—. "The Missed Chance in Bosnia." *New York Review of Books* (Feb. 29, 1996) 8-10.

—. "The Politics of Self-Destruction." *New York Review of Books* (Nov. 2, 1995) 17-19.

Isby, David. "Yugoslavia 1991: Armed Forces in Conflict." *Jane's Intelligence Review* 3:9 (1991) 394-403.

Isaac, John. *Bosnia: Civil War in Europe.* Photos by John Isaac; text by Keith Greenberg. Woodbridge, CT: Blackbirch Press, 1997.

Iugoslavskii krizis i Rossiia: Dokumenty, fakty, kommentarri, 1990-1993. Moscow: Fond slavianskikh issledovanii i strudnichestva "Slavianskaia letopis," 1993.

Jacobsen, C. G. "Myths, Politics and the Not-So-New World Order." *Journal of Peace Research* 30:3 (1993) 241-50.

Kajan, Ibrahim. *Muslimanski danak u krvi: Svjedočanstva zločina nad Muslimanima 1992.* Zagreb: Preporod, 1992.

Kaldor, Mary. "Bosnia: The Problem for Peace Activists." *Progressive* (Sep. 1995) 18-21.

—. "Protect Bosnia." *Nation* (Mar. 22, 1993) 364-65.

—. "Sarajevo's Reproach." *Progressive* (Sep. 1993) 21-23.

—. "Sarajevo: A Glimmer of Hope." *Progressive* (Apr. 1994) 24-26+.

Karahasan, Dževad. *Exodus of a City.* Trans Slobodan Drakulić. Afterword by Slavenka Drakulić. New York: Kodansha International, 1994.

Karaosmanoglu, Ali L. *Crisis in the Balkans.* New York: United Nations, 1993.

Keith, Tom. *Carole Wiley, an Everyday Housewife: One Woman's Response to the War in Bosnia.* Carrigaline, Co. Cork, Eire: Miribride Publications, 1994.

Kelly, Mary Pat. *"Good to Go": The Rescue of Scott O'Grady from Bosnia.* Annapolis, MD: Naval Institute Press, 1996.

Kelly, Michael. "The Negotiator." *New Yorker* (Nov. 6, 1995) 81-92.

Khalilzad, Zalmay M., ed. *Lessons from Bosnia.* Santa Monica, CA: RAND, 1993.

King, Christian. *Krieg auf dem Balkan: Der jugoslawishe Brudersteit: Geschichte, Hintergründe, Motive.* Zurich: Neue Zürcher Zeitung, 1994.

Klare, Michael T. "Bosnia: We Must Support Military Action." *Progressive* (Sep. 1995) 20.

—. "The Guns of Bosnia." *Nation* (Jan. 22, 1996) 23-24.

Korpivaara, Ari, ed. *Dear Unknown Friend: Children's Letters from Sarajevo.* New York: Open Society Fund, 1994.

Kovačević, Anto. *Posavski koridor smrti.* Zagreb: Meditor, 1995.

Kurspahić, Kemal. "Bosnia's Beacon of Hope." *Journal of Democracy* 5:1 (1994) 134-39.

Laber, Jeri and Ivana Nizich. "The War Crimes Tribunal for the Former Yugoslavia: Problems and Prospects." *Fletcher Forum of World Affairs* 18:2 (1994) 7-16.

Lane, Charles. "The Fall of Srebrenica." *New Republic* (Aug. 14, 1995) 14-17.

—. "The Memo: National Insecurity." *New Republic.* (Nov. 20, 1995) 16,18.

—. "Picked Pocket: The Real Story of Bihać. *New Republic* (Dec. 19, 1994) 12-14.

Lane, Charles and Thom Shanker. "Bosnia: What the CIA Didn't Tell Us." *New York Review of Books* (May 9, 1996) 10-15.

Larrabee, F. Stephen. "Long Memories and Short Fuses: Change and Instability in the Balkans." *International Security* 15 (1990-1991) 58-91.

Letters from Sarajevo: Voices of a Besieged City. Compiled, with introduction, by Anna Cataldi; trans. Avril Bardoni. Rockport, MA: Element, 1994.

Lewis, Flora. "Reassembling Yugoslavia." *Foreign Policy* 98 (Spring 1995) 132-44.

Lind, Michale. "Beirut to Bosnia." *New Republic.* (Dec. 18, 1995) 20.

Lučić, Ivo. *Selo moje Ravno: Povijest stradanja Hrvata u Popovu.* Zagreb: HHZ "Herceg Stjepan," 1992.

Lukic, Reneo. "Greater Serbia: A New Reality in the Balkans." *Nationalities Papers* 22:1 (1994) 49-70.

—. "Yugoslavia's: Disintegration through War (Greater Serbia)." *Nationalities Papers* 22:1 (1994) 49-70.

Lupis, Ivan. *War Crimes in Bosnia-Hercegovina: Bosanski Samac: Six War Criminals Named by Victims of "Ethnic Cleansing."* New York: Human Rights Watch/Helsinki, 1994.

Lydall, H. *Yugoslavia in Crisis.* Oxford: Clarendon Press; New York: Oxford University Press, 1989.

Maass, Peter. *Love Thy Neighbor: A Story of War.* New York: Alfred A. Knopf, 1996.

McAdams, Michael C. "Ancient Borders Modern Myths." *American Croatian Review* 2:3&4 (1995) 4-5.

Macdonald, Calum. "Rose-Tinted Spectacles." *New Statesman and Society* 8:339 (1995) 23.

MacKenzie Bob. "SOF Editor's Final." *Soldier of Fortune* (Sep., 1995) 52-55, 73-75.

MacKenzie, Lewis. *Peacekeeper: The Road to Sarajevo.* Vancouver: Douglas and McIntyre, 1993.

Magaš, Branka. *The Destruction of Yugoslavia: Tracking the Break-up 1980-92.* London: Verso, 1993.

—. "From Yugoslavia to Greater Serbia and Greater Croatia: The Rise and Fall of Vance-Owen." *Against Current,* (Jul./Aug., 1993) 13-16.

—. "The Tide of War Turns." *New Statesman and Society* 8:378 (1995) 22-23.

—. "Yugoslavia: The Specter of Balkanization." *New Left Review* 174 (Mar./Apr., 1989) 3-31.

Malcolm, Noel. "Appease With Dishonor: The Truth about the Balkans." *Foreign Affairs* 74 (Nov./Dec., 1995) 148-50.

—. "Bosnia and the West: A Study in Failure." *National Interest* 39 (1995) 3-14.

—. "Furiously in All Directions (NATO and Bosnia)." *National Review* (Mar. 7, 1994) 49-52.

—. "Head in the Sand?" *Wilson Quarterly* 19 (Spring 1995) 132-33.

—. "Is There a Doctor in the House?" *National Review* (Jul. 5, 1993) 39-41.

—. "Seen Ghosts." *National Interest* 32 (Summer 1993) 83-88.

—. "Waiting for a War." *Spectator* (Oct. 19, 1991) 14-15.

—. "The Whole Lot of Them Are Serbs." *Spectator* (Jun. 10, 1995) 14-18.

Martin, J. "Fall from Grace: Progressives' Abandonment of Bosnia." *Socialist Review* 23:4 (1993) 127-40.

Mearcheimer, John J. and Robert A. Pape. "The Answer." *New Republic* (Jun. 14, 1993) 22-28.

Mearcheimer, John J. and Stephen Van Evera. "When Peace Means War: The Partition That Dare Not Speak Its Name." *New Republic* (Dec. 18, 1995) 16-18, 21.

Meron, Theodor. "The Case for War-Crime Trials in Yugoslavia." *Foreign Affairs* 72:3 (1993) 122-35.

Merrill, Christopher. "Beauty and the Beast." *Antioch Review* 52:2 (1994) 209-12.

—. *The Old Bridge: The Third Balkan War and the Age of the Refugee.* Minneapolis, MN: Milweed Editions, 1995.

Meštrović, G. Stjepan, ed. *Genocide after Emotion: The Post-Emotional Balkan War.* New York: Routledge, 1996.

—. "Postemotional Politics in the Balkans." *Society* (Jan./Feb.1995) 69-77.

Milstein, Mark. "Rapid, Willing and Able." *Soldier of Fortune* (Jan. 1996) 36-39, 70.

Miskic, Matt. *Serbian Aggression in Bosnia and Croatia: Or a Civil War.* Walnut Creek, CA: Memory Impact Publishing, 1994.

Mojzes, Paul. *Yugoslavian Inferno: Ethnoreligious Warfare in the Balkans.* New York: Continuum, 1995.

Morillon, Philippe. *Croire et oser: Chronique de Sarajevo.* Paris: B. Grasset, 1993.

Mousavizade, Nader, ed. *The Black Book of Bosnia: The Consequences of Appeasement.* New York: Basic Books/A New Republic Book, 1996.

Nairn, T. "All Bosnians Now." *Dissent* 40:4 (1993) 403-04.

Neller, M. "The International Response to the Dissolution of the SFRJ." *American Journal of International Law* 86:3 (1992) 569-607.

Nelson, Daniel N. *Balkan Imbroglio: Politics and Security in Southeastern Europe.* Boulder, CO: Westview Press, 1991.

Newhouse, John. "The Diplomatic Round: Dodging the Problem." *New Yorker* (Aug. 24, 1992) 60-71.

Novakovich, Josip. "Shrapnel in the Liver: The Third Balkan War." *Massachusetts Review* 34 (1993) 144-60.

Nowak, Manfred. "Beyond 'Bookkeeping':Bringing Human Rights to Bosnia." *World Today* 52:4 (1996) 102-05.

O'Ballance, Edgar. *Civil War in Bosnia 1992-94.* New York: St. Martin's Press, 1995.

O'Grady, Scott. *Return with Honor.* New York: Doubleday, 1995.

Owen, David. *Balkan Odyssey.* New York: Harcourt, Brace, 1995.

—. "Interview with David Owen on the Balkans." Foreign Affairs 72:2 (1993) 1-9.

Pajić, Zoran. *Violation of Fundamental Rights in the Former Yugoslavia.* London: David Davies Memorial Institute of International Studies, 1993.

Palaich, Michael. "Man or Monster: Confessions of a Serb War Criminal." *Soldier of Fortune* (Aug. 1993) 62-64.

Palau, Joseph and Radha Kumar, eds. *Ex-Yugoslavia: From War to Peace: Citizen's Conference for the Peaceful and Democratic Integration of the Balkans into Europe.* Valencia, 4-6 September, 1992. Valencia: Generalitat Valenciana Pub. Dept., 1993.

Parin, P. *Es ist Krieg und wir gehen hin: Bei den jugoslawischen Partisanen.* Berlin: Rowohlt, 1991.

Parlement Européen. *La crise dans l'ex-Yougoslavie.* Série Politique 18. Luxembourg: Direction Générale des Études, 1993.

Pavelić, Dragan. *Bosanski ljetopis: 1992-1993.* Zagreb: Alfa, 1994.

Peress, Gilles. *Farewell to Bosnia.* New York: Scalo Publishers, 1994.

Perry, William J. "Determining Appropriate Use of Force in Bosnia." (Speech on March 10, 1994). *Defense Issues* 9:20 (1994).

—. "'Doing something' about Bosnia." (Remarks made on February 10, 1994). *Defense Issues* 9:4 (1994).

—. "United States Military Objectives" *Vital Speeches* 60:12 (1994) 363-65.

Pflüger, Tobias. *Krieg in Jugoslawien: Seine Ursachen — offene Grenzen für Waffen — aber nicht für Flüchtlinge: Pazifistische Handlungsperspektiven.* Tübingen: M. Jung Verlag, 1993.

Power, Samantha. "Greater Serbs: Sarajevo Postcard." *New Republic* (Aug. 7, 1995) 12-14.

—. "River Phoenix? Mostar Postcard." *New Republic* (Feb. 26, 1996) 11-12.

Ramet, Sabrina P. "The Bosnian War and the Diplomacy of Accommodation." *Current History* 93 (1994) 380-85.

—. "The Breakup of Yugoslavia." Global Affairs 6:2 (1991) 93-110.

—. "Serbia's Slobodan Milošević: A Profile." *Orbis* (Winter 1991) 93-105.

—. "War in the Balkans." *Foreign Affairs* 71:4 (1992) 79-98.

Rat u Bosni i Hercegovini : Uzroci, posljedice, perspektive. Zbornik radova. Samobor: Franjevačka teologija-Sarajevo, 1994.

Rathfelder, Erich, ed. *Krieg auf dem Balkan: Die europäische Verantwortung.* Reinbek bei Hamburg: Rowoholt, 1992.

Ratni zločini muslimanskih vojnih postrojbi nad Hrvatima u sjevernom dijelu Hercegovine. Sarajevo: CPD, 1996.

Ratni zločini muslimanskih vojnih postrojbi nad Hrvatima u središnjem dijelu Bosne i Hercegovine. Sarajevo: CPD, 1996.

Rauch, Jonathan. "A Civil War." *New Republic* (Dec. 19, 1994) 7.

Razun, Miron. *Europe and War in the Balkans: Toward a New Yugoslav Identity.* Westport, CT: Praeger, 1995.

"Recognition of the Yugoslav Successor States." Position Paper of the German Foreign Ministry, Bonn, March 10, 1993. *Statements and Speeches* 16:10 (1993) 2-6.

Reger, James P. *The Rebuilding of Bosnia.* San Diego, CA: Lucent, 1997.

Reissmüller, Johann Georg. *Die bosnishe Tragödie.* Stuttgart: Deutsche Verlags-Anstalt, 1993.

—. *Der Krieg vor unserer Haustür.* Stuttgart: Deutsche Verlags-Anstalt, 1992.

Remington, Robin Alison. "Bosnia: The Tangled Web." *Current History* 92 (1993) 364-69.

Renner, Michael. *Critical Juncture: The Future of Peacekeeping.* Washington, DC: Worldwatch Institute, 1993.

Report on the International Tribunal to Adjudicate War Crimes Committed in the Former Yugoslavia. Washington, DC: Section of International Law and Practice, American Bar Association, 1993.

Report on the Proposed Rules of Procedure and Evidence of the International Tribunal to Adjudicate War Crimes in the Former Yugoslavia. Chicago: American Bar Association; Washington, DC: Section of International Law and Practice, 1995.

Ricchiardi, Sherry. *Bosnia: The Struggle for Peace.* Brookfield, CT: Millbrook Press, 1996.

—. "Covering Carnage in the Balkans." *WJR* 14 (Nov. 1992) 18-23.

—. "Exposing Genocide: For What?" *American Journalism Review* 15 (Jun. 1993) 32-6.

—. "Kill the Reporters." *WJR* 14 (Jan./Feb. 1992) 33-35.

—. "Under the Gun." *American Journalism Review* 16 (Jul./Aug. 1994) 18-25.

—. "Women on War." *American Journalism Review* 16 (Mar. 1994) 16-22.

Ricciuti, Edward R. *War in Yugoslavia: The Breakup of a Nation.* Brookfield, CT: Millbrook Press, 1993.

Rice, Jim. "Into Bosnia." *Sojourners* 25 (Jan./Feb. 1996) 14.

Rieff, David. "The Institution That Saw No Evil." *New Republic* (Feb. 12, 1996) 19-24.

—. "Original Virtue, Original Sin." *New Yorker* (Nov. 23, 1992) 82-95.

—. *Slaughterhouse: Bosnia and the Failure of the West.* New York: Simon & Schuster, 1995.

Rohde, David. Endgame: *The Betrayal and Fall of Srebrenica: Europe's Worst Massacre since World War II.* New York: Farrar, Straus, and Giroux, 1997.

Rojo, A. *Yugoslavia: Holocausto en los Balcanes: La agonia de un estado y por qué se matan entre si sus habitantes.* Barcelona: Planeta, 1992.

Rusinow, Dennison. "Yugoslavia: Balkan Breakup?" *Foreign Policy* 83 (1991) 143-59.

Sacral Institutions on Target: Croatia and Bosnia-Herzegovina. Zagreb: Croatian Information Centre, 1993.

Sahara, Tetsuya. "The Islamic World and the Bosnian Crisis." *Current History* 93 (1994) 386-89.

Sarajevo: A portrait of the siege. Produced by Matthew Naythons; picture selection and design by Alex Castro; text edited by Rebecca Buffum Taylor. New York: Warner Books, 1994.

Savarin, Julian Jay. *MacAllister's Run.* (Fiction). New York: Harper Paperbacks, 1995.

Schaaf, R.W. "United Nations Peacekeeping in Yugoslavia." *Government Publications Review* 19:5 (1992) 537-43.

Scharf, Michael P. *Balkan Justice: The Story behind the First International War Crimes Tribunal since Nuremberg.* Durham, NC: Carolina Academic Press, 1997.

Schear, James A. "Bosnia's Post-Dayton Traumas." *Foreign Policy* 104 (Fall 1996) 86-101.

Schiffer, Daniel S. *Requiem pour l'Europe: Zagreb, Belgrade, Sarajevo.* Lausanne: L'Age d'homme, 1993.

Sekelj, Laslo. *Yugoslavia: The process of disintegration.* Boulder, CO: Social Science Monographs, 1993.

Seroka, Jim and Vukašin Pavlović, eds. *The Tragedy of Yugoslavia: The Failure of Democratic Transformation.* Armonk, NY: M.E. Sharpe, 1992.

Serotta, Edward. *Survival in Sarajevo: How A Jewish Community Came to the Aid of Its City.* Vienna: Edition Christian Brandstatter, 1994.

Sharp, J. M. O. *Bankrupt in the Balkans: British Policy in Bosnia.* London: Institute for Public Policy Research, 1993.

Silber, Laura and Allen Little. *Yugoslavia: Death of a Nation.* London: Penguin Books, TV Books; Distributed by Penguin USA, 1995.

Softić, Elma. *Sarajevo Nights, Sarajevo Days.* Saint Paul, MN: Hungry Mind Press, 1996.

Soric, Susan Alaine. "The Debate on Genocidal Rape in Croatia and Bosnia and Hercegovina." M.T.S. thesis, Garrett Evangelical Theological Seminary, 1995.

Šošić, Stipo. *Do pakla i natrag: U logorima strave i užasa-Keraterm, Omarska, Manjača.* Đakovo: UPT, 1994.

Spotlight on Human Rights Violations in Times of Armed Conflict. Belgrade: Humanitarian Law Center, 1995.

Štefanac, Vladimir. *Iz Kostajnice na Manjaču.* Zagreb: Matica Hrvatska, 1994.

Stefanov, Nenad and Michael Werz, ed. *Bosnian und Europa: die Ethnisierung der Gesellschaft.* Frankfurt: Fischer, 1994.

Stewart, Bob. *Broken Lives: A Personal View of the Bosnian Conflict.* London: HarperCollins, 1993.

Stiglmayer, Alexandra, ed. *Mass Rape: The War against Women in Bosnia-Herzegovina.* Transl. from German by Marion Faber. Foreword by Roy Gutman. Lincoln: University of Nebraska Press, 1994.

Stokes, Gale. *The Walls Came Tumbling Down.* Oxford: Oxford University Press, 1993.

Strautz-Hupé, Robert. "Again, Rendezvous with History at Sarajevo." *Global Affairs* 8:2 (1993) 49-57.

Sugarman, Martin A. *God Be With You: War in Croatia and Bosnia-Herzegovina: Photographs.* Malibu, CA: Sugarman Productions, 1993.

Tašić, Predrag. *Kako je ubijena druga Jugoslavia.* Skopje: self-published, 1994.

Tauran, Jean-Louis. "The Holy See and World Peace: The Case of Former Yugoslavia." *World Today* 50:7 (1994)125-27.

Thompson, Mark. *A Paper House: The Ending of Yugoslavia.* New York: Pantheon Books, 1992.

Thornberry, Cedric. "Saving the War Crimes Tribunal." *Foreign Policy* 104 (Fall 1996) 72-85.

Tindemans, Leo et al. *Unfinished Peace: Report of the International Commission on the Balkans.* Berlin: Aspen Institute; Washington, DC: Carnegie Endowment, 1996.

Tomac, Zdravko. *Tko je ubio Bosnu?* Zagreb: Birotisak, 1944.

Tomić, M. Ivan. *Whose Is Bosnia-Hercegovina?* London, 1990.

Trnka, Kasim. "The Bosnian Case." *New York Review of Books* (Sept. 23, 1993) 65-66.

Tromp, Hylke. "Clash of Paradigms: The Fall of Srebrenica and its Aftermath." *Balkan Forum* 4:1 (1996) 167-88.

Tunjić, Andrija. *Boja smrti: Bosanska ratna zbilja.* Zagreb: AGM, 1994.

The United Nations and the Situation in the Former Yugoslavia. New York: UN Dept. of Public Information, 1993.

U.S. Committee for Refugees. *World Refugee Survey 1993.* Washington, DC: American Council for Nationalities Service, 1993.

U.S. Congress. Commission on Security and Cooperation in Europe. *Development in Bosnia-Herzegovina.* Hearing, Jan. 31, 1995. Washington, DC: U.S. GPO, 1955.

—. *Genocide in Bosnia-Herzegovina.* Hearing, April 4, 1995. Washington, DC: U.S. GPO, 1995.

—. *The Latest Crisis in Bosnia-Herzegovina.* Hearing, June 8, 1995. Washington, DC: U.S. GPO, 1955.

—. *Mass Graves and other Atrocities in Bosnia.* Hearing, Dec. 6, 1995. Washington, DC: U.S. GPO, 1996.

U.S. Congress. House. Committee on International Relations. *Bosnia Elections: A Postmortem.* Hearing, Sep. 19, 1996. Washington, DC: U.S. GPO, 1997.

Bosnian Refugees. Hearing, Sep. 28, 1995. Washington, DC: U.S. GPO, 1996.

—. *Human Rights, Refugees, and War Crimes: The Prospects for Peace in Bosnia.* Hearing, Nov. 15, 1995. Washington, DC: U.S. GPO, 1996.

—. *Prospects for Peace with Justice in Bosnia* (microform). Hearing, Feb.1, 1996. Washington, DC: U.S. GPO, 1996.

—. *U.S. Policy towards Bosnia.* Hearing, Nov. 30, 1995. Washington, DC: U.S. GPO, 1996.

—. *U.S. Policy Toward Bosnia.* Private Witnesses. Hearing, Dec. 6, 1995. Washington, DC: U.S. GPO, 1996.

U.S. Congress. Senate. Committee on Armed Services. *Situation in Bosnia and Appropriate U.S. and Western Responses.* Hearing, Aug. 11, 1992. Washington, DC: U.S. GPO, 1992.

—. *Briefing on the F-16 shootdown in Bosnia and Current Operations.* Hearing, July 13, 1995. Washington, DC: U.S. GPO, 1996.

—. *Joint Chiefs of Staff Briefing on Current Military Operations in Somalia, Iraq, and Yugoslavia.* Hearing, Jan. 29, 1993. Washington, DC: U.S. GPO, 1993.

U.S. Congress. Senate. Committee on Foreign Relations. *The Peace Process in the Former Yugoslavia.* Hearing. Oct. 17 and Dec. 1, 1995. Washington, DC: U.S. GPO, 1996.

—. *Staff Report: The Ethnic Cleansing of Bosnia-Hercegovina.* Aug. 15, 1992. Washington, DC: U.S. GPO, 1992.

—. Subcommittee on European Affairs of the Committee on Foreign Relations. *American policy in Bosnia.* Hearing, Feb. 18, 1993. Washington, DC: U.S. GPO, 1993.

U.S. Department of Commerce. *Building Peace and Stability in Bosnia and Croatia.* Washington, DC: U.S. Dept. of Commerce, 1996.

U.S. Department of State. *Material Relating to the London Conference (August 26-27, 1992) and the Crisis in the Former Yugoslavia.* Bureau of Public Affairs, Dispatch Supplement, September 1992, vol. 3, supplement no. 7.

—. *Submission of Information to the United Nations Security Council in Accordance with Paragraph 5 of Resolution 771* (1992) *and Paragraph 1 of Resolution 780* (1992).

U.S. Department of State Dispatch. "Bosnia after Dayton." (Anthony Lake, Asst. to the President for National Security Affairs). (Transcript). (June 24, 1996) 330-32.

—. "Progress and Next Step in the Balkan Peace Process." (Warren Christopher, Sec. Of State). (Transcript). (June 10, 1996) 301-04.

U.S. General Accounting Office. *Bosnia: Costs Are Exceeding DOD's Estimate.* Washington, DC: The Office, 1996.

—. *Humanitarian Intervention: Effectiveness of U.N. Operations in Bosnia: Brief Report to the Honorable Robert S. Dole, U.S. Senator.* Washington, DC: The Office, 1994.

—. *Peace operations: Update on the Situation in the Former Yugoslavia: Briefing Report to the Majority Leader, U.S. Senate.* Washington, DC: The Office, 1995.

—. *Serbia-Montenegro: Implementation of UN Economic Sanctions.* Washington, DC: The Office, 1993.

Valenta, Anto. *Podjela Bosne i borba za cjelovitost.* Vitez: Napredak, 1991.

Vego, Milan. "The Army of Bosnia and Hercegovina." *Jane's Intelligence Review* 5:2 (1993) 63-67.

—. "The Croatian Forces in Bosnia and Herzegovina." *Jane's Intelligence Review* 5:3 (1993) 99-103.

—. "Federal Army Deployment in Bosnia and Herzegovina." *Jane's Intelligence Review* 4:10 (1992) 445-49.

—. "The Yugoslav Ground Forces." *Jane's Intelligence Review* 5:6 (1993) 247-53.

Veremis, Thanos. "Scholarly Predictions on Balkan Affairs." *European History Quarterly* 24 (1994) 563-68.

Volcic, Demetrio. *Sarajevo: Quando la storia uccide.* Rome: Nuovo ERI; Milan: Arnoldo Mondadori editore, 1993.

Volle, Angelika and Wolfgang Wagner, eds. *Der Krieg auf dem Balkan: Die Hilflosigkeit der Staatenwelt: Beiträge und Dokumente aus dem Europa-Archiv.* Bonn: Verlag für Internationale Politik, 1994.

Vollmer, Johannes. *"Das wir in Bosnien zur Welt Gehören": Für ein multikulturelles Zusammenleben.* Solothurn: Benziger, 1995.

Vranić, Seada. *Pred zidom šutnje.* Zagreb: Antibarbarus, 1996.

Vrcan, Srdjan. "War in Bosnia and Hercegovina." *Balkan Forum* 4:2 (1996) 83-109.

Vulliamy, Ed. *Seasons in Hell: Understanding Bosnia's War.* New York: St. Martin's Press, 1994.

Wagenlehner, Günther. *Konflikt, Konfliktlösung und Friedenssicherung in Südosteuropa.* Munich: Südosteuropa-Gesellschaft, 1994.

Walking, Sarah. "Balkan Arms Control Efforts Focus on Transparency, Arms Limitations." *Arms Control Today* 26:1 (1996) 26.

Weingärtner, Erich, ed. *The Tragedy of Bosnia: Confronting the New World Disorder.* Geneva: World Council of Churches, 1994.

Weller, Marc. "The International Response to the Dissolution of the Socialist Federal Republic of Yugoslavia." *American Journal of International Law* 86 (1992) 569-607.

Welser von, Maria. *Am Ende wünschst du nur noch den Tod: Die Massenvergewaltigungen im Krieg auf dem Balkan.* Munich: Knaur, 1993.

Wigger, Raimar. *Verraten im Herzen Europas: Schicksale im Balkankrieg.* Frankfurt: Eichborn, 1995.

Williams, Paul and Norman Cigar. *War Crimes and Individual Responsibility: A Prima Facie Case for the Indictment of Slobodan Milosevic.* Washington, DC: The Balkan Institute, 1996.

Wohlstetter, Albert. "Creating a Greater Serbia." *New Republic* (August 1, 1994) 22-27.

Wolfgang, Libal. *Das Ende Jugoslawiens: Chronik einer Selbstzerstörung.* Vienna: Europaverlag, 1991.

Woodward, Susan L. *Balkan Tragedy: Chaos and Dissolution after the Cold War.* Washington, DC: Brookings Institution, 1995.

—. "Conflict in Former Yugoslavia: Quest for Solutions." *Great Decisions* (1994) 3-14.

Yancey, Diane. *Life in War-Torn Bosnia.* San Diego, CA: Lucent Books, 1996.

Zametica, John. "The Yugoslav Conflict." *Adelphi Paper 270.* London: International Institute for Strategic Studies, Summer 1992.

Zimmermann, Warren. "The Captive Mind." *New York Review of Books* (Feb. 2, 1995) 3-6.

—."The Last Ambassador: A Memoir of the Collapse of Yugoslavia." *Foreign Affairs* 74:2 (1995) 2-20.

—. *Origins of a Catastrophe: Yugoslavia and Its Destroyers.* New York: Times Books, 1996.

Zülch, Tilman. *Ethnische Säuberung — Völkermord für Grossserbien: eine Dokumentation der Gesellschaft für bedrohte Völker.* Hamburg: Luchterhand, 1993.

Zulfikarpašić, A. et al. *Okovana Bosna: Razgovor*. Zurich: Bošnjački Institut, 1995.

8. ECONOMY

"The Agrarian Revolution in Bosnia and Herzegovina." *Edinburgh Review* 234 (1921) 111-21.

Auty, Phyllis. "Yugoslavia." In Doreen Warriner, ed. *Contrasts in Emerging Societies: Readings in the Social and Economic History of South-Eastern Europe in the Nineteenth Century.* 282-387. Bloomington: Indiana University Press, 1965.

Berend, Tibor Ivan and Gyorgy Ranki. *Economic Development in East-Central Europe in the 19th and 20th Centuries.* New York: Columbia University Press, 1974.

Bosnia and Herzegovina: Toward Economic Recovery. Washington, DC: World Bank, 1996.

Božić, J.D. *Bosansko-Hercegovačko agrarno pitanje i povlastice dane bosanskim Franjevcima od pojedinih sultana.* Senj, 1866.

Brashich, Ranko M. *Land Reform and Ownership in Jugoslavia 1919-1953.* New York: Mid-European Studies Center, Free Europe Committee, 1954.

Bresloff, Leon M. "Economic Adaptation and Development of Family Types in a Bosnian Town." In William G. Lockwood, ed. *Essays in Balkan Ethnology,* 35-53. Special Publications, no. 1. [Berkeley, CA: Kroeber Anthropological Society], 1967.

Burger, Willem. *Yugoslavia's Economic Crisis: The Price of Overexpansion.* The Hague: Institute of Social Studies, 1984.

Čurčić, Vejsil. "Die volkstümliche Fischerei in Bosnien und der Herzegowina." *Wissenschaftliche Mitteilungen aus Bosnien und der Herzegowina* 12 (1912) 490-589.

Duker, David A. *Yugoslavia: Socialism, Development, and Debt.* London: Routledge, 1990.

Faroghi, Suraiya. *Peasants, Dervishes and Traders in the Ottoman Empire.* London: Variorum Reprint, 1986.

Feifalik, Anton. *Ein neuer aktueller Weg zur Lösung der bosnischen Agrarfrage.* Vienna: Franz Deuticke, 1916.
Gonsalves, Priscilla Tapley. "The Austrian Reforms and the Serbian Peasants in Bosanska Krajina, 1878-1914." Ph.D. dissertation, Stanford University, 1981.
—. "A Study of the Habsburg Agricultural Programmes in Bosanska Krajina, 1878-1914." *Slavic and East European Review* 63 (1985) 349-71.
Grünberg, Karl. *Die Agrarverfassung und das Grundentlastungsproblem in Bosnien und der Herzegowina.* Leipzig: Duncker und Humblot, 1911.
—. "Bosnia-Hercegovina: The Land Question, 1878-1910." In D. Warriner, ed. *Contrasts in Emerging Societies,* 374-87. Bloomington: Indiana University Press, 1965.
Hofmann, K. *Entwicklung des Forstwesen in Bosnien u. der Herzegovina.* Vienna, 1894.
Hollmann, Anton H. *Die Bauernbefreiung und Agrarreform in Bosnia und der Herzegowina.* Berlin: Paul Parey, 1929.
Irby, Adelina Paulina. "Bosnia and Its Land Tenure." *Contemporary Review* 56 (1889) 28-40.
J. R. J. "Resources of Servia and Bosnia." *Nature* 14 (1876) 277-78.
Janković, Dvina. *Privredni razvoj Bosne i Hercegovine sa posebnim osvrtom na nacionalni dohodak.* Sarajevo: Svjetlost, 1977.
Jireček, K. *Die Handelsstrassen und Bergwerke von Serbien und Bosnien während des Mittelalters: Historisch-geographische Studien.* Prague, 1878.
Juzbašić, Dževad. *Izgradnja željeznica u Bosni i Hercegovini u svijetlu austrougarske politike od okupacije do kraja Kállayeve ere.* Sarajevo: ANUBiH, 1974.
Kann, Robert A. "Trends toward Colonialism in the Habsburg Empire, 1878-1918: The Case of Bosnia-Hercegovina, 1878-1914." In Don Karl Rowney and G. Edward Orchard, eds. *Russian and Slavic History,* 164-80. Columbus, OH: Slavica, 1977.
Kapidžić, Hamdija, ed. *Agrarni odnosi u Bosni i Hercegovini, 1878-1918.* Sarajevo: Arhiv Bosne i Hercegovine, 1969.
Kosier, Ljubomir Stefan. *Bosna i Hercegovina: Ekonomski fragmenti i konture.* Zagreb, 1926.

Kreševljaković, Hamdija. *Esnafi i obrti u Bosni i Hercegovini.* Sarajevo: Naučno društvo NR Bosne i Hercegovine, 1961.

Laird, W. E. "The Industrialization of Bosnia-Hercegovina: The Relevance of Comparative Advantage." *Florida State University Slavic Papers* 3 (1969) 54-59.

Lampe, John R. and Marvin R. Jackson. *Balkan Economic History 1550-1950: From Imperial Borderlands to Developing Nations.* Bloomington: Indiana University Press, 1982.

Lockwood, William G. *European Moslems: Economy and Ethnicity in Western Bosnia.* New York: Academic Press, 1975.

Lovrenović, Stjepan. *Bosna i Hercegovina u spoljnoj trgovini Jugoslavije.* Sarajevo: ANUBiH, 1985.

Matley, Ian Murray. "Transhumance in Bosnia and Herzegovina." *Geographical Review* 58 (1968): 231-61.

McGowan, B. *Economic Life in Ottoman Europe: Taxation, Trade and the Struggle for Land, 1600-1800.* Cambridge: Cambridge University Press, 1981.

Palairet, Michael. "The Habsburg Industrial Achievements in Bosnia-Hercegovina, 1878-1914: An Economic Spurt That Succeeded?" *Austrian History Yearbook* 24 (1993) 133-88.

Pleština, D. *Regional Development in Communist Yugoslavia: Success, Failure, and Consequences.* Boulder: Westview Press, 1992.

Popović, Vasilj. *Agrarno pitanje u Bosni i turski neredi za vreme reformnog režima Abdul Medžida.* Belgrade: Srpska Akademija Nauka, 1949.

Reuning, W. "The Sanjak Railroad: A Reply to Italian Economic Penetration." *Susquehanna University Studies* 9 (1973) 149-76.

Sućeska, Avdo. "The Eighteenth-Century Austro-Ottoman Wars' Economic Impact on the Population of Bosnia." In Gunther E. Rothenberg, Bela K. Kiraly, and Peter F. Suger, eds. *East Central European Society and War in the Pre-Revolutionary Eighteenth Century,* 339-50. Boulder, CO: Social Science Monographs, 1982.

Suger, Peter F. *Industrialization of Bosnia-Hercegovina 1878-1918.* Seattle: University of Washington Press, 1963.

Tihi, Boris. "The Possibilities for Economic Reconstruction of Bosnia-Hercegovina." *Balkan Forum* 4:1 (1996) 189-207.

Tomasevich, Jozo. *Peasants, Politics, and Economic Change in Yugoslavia*. Stanford: Stanford University Press, 1955.
Truhelka, Ćiro. *Geschichtliche Grundlage der bosnischen Agrarfrage*. Germany, 1909.
Vacalopoulos, C. "Tendances caractéristiques du commerce de la Bosnie et le rôle économique des commerçants grecs au début du XIXe siècle." *Balkan Studies* 20 (1979) 91-110.
Woodward, Susan L. *Socialist Unemployment: The Political Economy of Yugoslavia, 1945-1990*. Princeton: Princeton University Press, 1995.
Zurunić, Th. P. *Die bosnische Pflaume*. Vienna, 1895

9. RELIGION AND RELIGIOUS INSTITUTIONS

GENERAL

Benković, Ambrozije. *Tuzlansko područje negda i sad s posebnim obzirom na vjerske prilike*. Županja-Đakovo, 1971.
Dartel von, Geert. "The Nations and the Churches in Yugoslavia." *Religion, State, and Society* 20:3-4 (1992) 275-88.
Davis, G. Scott, ed. *Religion and Justice in the War over Bosnia*. New York: Routledge, 1996.
Deschner, Karlheinz and Milan Popovic. *Weltkrieg der Religionen: der ewige Kreuzzug auf dem Balkan*. Stuttgart: Weitbrecht, 1995.
Dizdar, M. *Muslimani i kršćani pod turskom vlašću u Bosni i Hercegovini*. Sarajevo, 1944.
Hasluck, F. W. *Christianity and Islam under the Sultan*. Ed. M. M. Hasluck. Oxford: Clarendon, 1929.
Mandić, Dominik. *Državna i vjerska pripadnost Bosne i Hercegovine*. Chicago, Rome: ZIRAL, 1978.
Petrovich, M. B. "Yugoslavia: Religion and the Tension of a Multinational State." *East European Quarterly*, 6:1 (1972) 118-35.
Ramet, Pedro, ed. *Religion and Nationalism in Soviet and Eastern European Politics*. Durham, NC: Duke University Press, 1989.

Sells, Michael A. "Bosnia: Some Religious Dimensions of Genocide." *Religious Studies News* 9:2 (1994) 4-5.

—. *The Bridge Betrayed: Religion and Genocide in Bosnia.* Berkeley: University of California Press, 1996.

Škobalj, Ante. *Obredne gomile.* Čiovo: Sv. Križ, 1970.

Solovjev. A. "Le Tatouage symbolique en Bosnie." *Cahiers d'études cathares* 5:19 (1954) 157-62.

Spinka, Matthew. *A History of Christianity in the Balkans: A Study in the Spread of Byzantine Culture among the Slavs.* [Hamden, CT]: Archon Books, 1968.

Šuffly, Milan. "Zaratrušta u Crvenoj Hrvatskoj." *Croatia Sacra* 1 (1931) 109-14.

Vukšić, Tomo. *Međusobni odnosi katolika i pravoslavaca u Bosni i Hercegovini (1878.-1903.) : Povijesno-teološki prikaz.* Mostar: Teološki institut, 1994.

Wenzel, Marian. "A Medieval Mystery Cult in Bosnia and Herzegovina." *Journal of the Warburg and Courtauld Institutes* 24 (1961) 89-107.

BOSNIAN CHURCH

Babić, Anto. *Bosanski heretici.* Sarajevo, Svjetlost, 1963.

—. "Noviji pogledi u nauci o pitanju srednjovjekovne crkve bosanske." *Pregled* 2 (1954) 101-07.

Bihalji-Merin, Oto and Alojz Benac. *The Bogomils.* London: Thames and Hudson, 1962.

Brockett, Linus Pierpont. *The Bogomils of Bulgaria and Bosnia.* Philadelphia: American Baptist Publ. Society, [1879].

Ćirković, Sima M. "Die bosnische Kirche." In *L'Oriente cristiano nella storia della civiltà,* 547-75. Rome: Accademia nazionale dei Lincei, 1964.

Dragojlović, D. *Krstjani i jeretička crkva bosanska.* Beograd: SANU: Balkonološki institut, 1987.

Džaja, Srećko M. *Die "bosnische Kirche" und das Islamisierungsproblem Bosniens und der Herzegowina in den Forschungen nach dem zweiten Weltkrieg.* Munich: R. Trofenik, 1978.

Fine, John Van Antwerp, Jr. "Aristodios and Rastudije: A Re-examination of the Question." *Godišnjak društva istoričara Bosne i Hercegovine* 16 (1965) 223-29.

—. *The Bosnian Church: A New Interpretation*. Boulder, CO: East European Monographs; Distributed by Columbia University Press, New York, 1975.

—. "Mid-Fifteenth Century Sources on the Bosnian Church: Their Problems and Significance." *Medievalia et Humanistica* 12 (1984) 17-32.

Glušac, Vaso. "Problem Bogomilstva." *Godišnjak istorijskog društva Bosne i Hercegovine* 5 (1953) 105-38.

—. "Srednjovekovna 'bosanska crkva.'" *Prilozi za književnost, jezik, istoriju i folklor* 4 (1924) 1-55.

Gray, Lilian F. "The Bogomils of Yugoslavia." *Hibbert Journal* 39 (1941) 179-87.

Hadžijahić, Muhamed. "Zemljišni posjed 'Crkve Bosanske.'" *Historijski Zbornik* 25-6 (1972-73): 461-80.

Jelenić, Julianus. *De Patarenis Bosnae*. Sarajevo: Typis Vogler, 1908.

Kamber, Dragutin. "Kardinal Torquemada i tri bosanska bogomila (1461)." *Croatia Sacra* 2 (1932) 27-93.

Kniewald, D. "Hierarchie und kultus bosnischer Christen." In *L'Oriente cristiano nella storia della civiltà*, 579-605. Rome: Accademia nazionale dei Lincei, 1964.

—. "Vjerodostojnost latinskih izvora o bosanskim krstjanima." In *Rad jugoslavenske akademije znanosti i umjetnosti* 270 (1949) 115-276.

Lambert, M.D. *Medieval Heresy: Popular Movements from Bogomil to Hus*. New York: Holmes and Meier, 1977.

Loos, Milan. *Dualist Heresy in the Middle Ages*. Prague. Academia, 1974.

—. "L'"Église Bsnienne" dans le contexte du mouvement hérétique européen." *Balcania* 4 (1973) 145-161.

Mandić, Dominik. *Bogomilska crkva bosanskih krstjana*. 2nd ed. Chicago: ZIRAL, 1979.

Matasović, J. "Tri humanista o patarenima." *Godišnjak Skopskog filozofskog fakulteta* 1 (1930) 235-51.

Miletić, Maja. *I 'Krstjani' di Bosnia alla luce dei loro monumenti di pietra.* Rome: Institutum Orientalium Studiorum, 1957.

Obolensky, Dimitri. *The Bogomils: A Study in Balkan Neo-Manichaeism.* Cambridge: Cambridge University Press, 1948. Reprinted New York: AMS Press, 1978.

Okiç, M. Tayyib. "Les Kristians (Bogomils Parfaits) de Bosnie d'après des documents turcs inédits." *Südost Forschungen* 19 (1960) 108-33.

Petranović, B. *Bogomili, cr'kva bosan'ska i kr'stjani.* Zadar, 1867.

Petrović, Leo. *Kršćani bosanske crkve.* Sarajevo: Dobri Pastir, 1953.

Pilar, Ivo. *Bogomilstvo kao religiozno-povijesni te kao socialni i politički problem.* Zagreb, 1927.

Rački, F. *Bogomili i patareni.* Belgrade: Srpska kraljevska akademija, 1931.

Runciman, Steven. *The Medieval Manichee: A study of the Christian Dualist Heresy.* Cambridge: University Press, 1947.

Šanjek, Franjo. *Bosansko humski (hercegovački) krstjani.* Zagreb: Kršćanska Sadašnjost, 1975.

—. *Les chrétiens bosniaques et le mouvement cathare, XIIe-Xve siècles.* Brussels: Nauwelaerts; Paris: diffusion, Vander-Oyez, 1976.

Šidak, Jaroslav. *Crkva bosanska i problem bogumilstva u Bosni.* Zagreb: Matica Hrvatska, 1940.

—. "Pitanje 'crkve bosanske' u novijoj literaturi." *Godišnjak istorijskog društva Bosne i Hercegovine* 5 (1953) 139-60.

—. "Problem 'bosanske crkve' u našoj historiografiji od Petranovića do Glušca." *Rad jugoslavenske akademije znanosi i umjetnosti* 259 (1937) 147-67.

—. *Studije o 'crkvi bosanskoj' i bogumilstvu.* Zagreb: Liber, 1975.

Solovjev, A. "Nastanak bogumilstva i islamizacija Bosne." *Godišnjak istorijskog društva Bosne i Hercegovine* 1 (1949) 42-79.

—. "Simbolika srednjovekovnih spomenika u Bosni i Hercegovini." *Godišnjak istorijskog društva Bosne i Hercegovine* 8 (1956) 5-65.

—. "Svedočanstva pravoslavnih izvora o bogomilstvu na Balkanu." *Godišnjak istorijskog društva Bosne i Hercegovine* 5 (1953) 1-103.

enje bosanske crkve." *Pregled* 3 (1948) 195-205.
_nage de Paul Rycaut sur les restes des Bogomiles en Bosnie." *Byzantion* 23 (1953) 73-86.

Torquemada de, J. *Symbolum pro informatione manichaeorum (El Bogomilismo en Bosnia)*, ed. N. López Martínez and V. Proaño Gil. Publicationes del seminario metropolitana de Burgos, series B, vol. 3. Burgos, 1958.

Truhelka, Ćiro. "Testament Gosta Radian." *Glasnik zemaljskog muzeja* 23 (1911) 355-76.

CATHOLICISM

Batinić, M.V. *Djelovanje franjevaca u Bosni i Hercegovini za prvih šest viekova njihova boravka.* 3 vols. Zagreb: Dionička tiskara, 1881-87.

Bax, Mart. *Medjugorje: Religion, Politics, and Violence in Rural Bosnia.* Amsterdam: Utigverij, 1995.

Benković, Ambrozije. *Katoličke župe BiH i njihove filijale od XII. vijeka do danas.* Đakovo: n.p., 1966.

Bogdanović, Marijan. *Ljetopis Kreševskog samostana, 1765-1817: Izvještaj o pohodu bosanskog vikarijata 1768.* Sarajevo: Veselin Masleša, 1984.

Cheston, Sharon E., ed. *Mary the Mother of All: Protestant Perspectives and Experiences of Medjugorje.* Chicago: Loyola University Press, 1994.

Craig, M. *Spark from Heaven: The Mystery of the Madonna of Medjugorje.* London: Hodder & Stoughton, 1988.

Draganović, Krunoslav. "Izvješće apostolskog vizitatora Petra Masarechija o prilikama katoličkog naroda u Bugarskoj, Srbiji, Srijemu, Slavoniji i Bosni g. 1623 i 1624." *Starine* 39 (1938) 1-48.

—. "Katolička Crkva u Bosni i Hercegovini nekad i danas." *Croatia Sacra* 4 (1934) 175-216.

—. *Masovni prijelazi katolika na pravoslavlje.* Mostar: Crkva na Kamenu, 1991.

Džaja, Srećko M. *Katolici u Bosni i zapadnoj Hercegovini na prijelazu iz 18. u 19. stoljeć.* Zagreb: Kršćanska sadašnjost, 1971.

Džambo, Jozo. *Die Franziskaner im mittelalterlichen Bosnien.* Werl/Westf.: Dietrich-Coelde-Verlag, 1991.

Fine, John Van Antwerp, Jr. "Mysteries about the Newly Discovered Srebrenica-Visoko Bishopric in Bosnia (1434-1441)." *East European Quarterly* 8 (1974) 29-41.

Franolić, Branko. "The Missal of Hrvoje." *BC [British-Croatian] Review* 2:4 (1975) 6-8.

Gavranović, B. *Uspostava redovite katoličke hijerarhije u Bosni i Hercegovini 1881 godine.* Belgrade: Filozofski fakultet, 1935.

Horvat, Rudolf. *Katolici u Bosni i Hercegovini.* Zagreb, 1929.

Ilić, Žarko. *Hercegovina u crkvi.* Duvno: Sveta Baština, 1974.

Ivandić, Ljudevit A. *Pučko praznovjerje kod Hrvata katolika u Bosni.* Madrid: Domovina, 1965.

Jurišić, Karlo. *Katolička crkva na Biokovsko-neretvanskom području u doba turske vladavine.* Zagreb: K. Sadašnjost, 1972.

Katoličanstvo u Bosni i Hercegovini. Sarajevo: Napredak, 1993.

Kemura, (Sarajlija) Sejfudin F. *Bilješke iz prošlosti bosanskih katolika i njihovih bogomolja po turskim dokumentima.* Sarajevo, 1916.

Kraljević, Svetozar. *Apparitions of Our Lady at Medjugorje 1981-1983: An Historical Account with Interviews.* Ed. Michael Scanlan. Chicago: Franciscan Herald Pres, 1984.

Lasić, D. *De vita et operibus S. Iacobi de Marchia: Studium et recensio quorundam textuum.* Ancona: Biblioteca francescana, 1974.

Lavrin, Janko. "The Bogomils and Bogomilism." *Slavic Review* 8 (1929) 269-83.

Luburić, Ante, ed. *Za pravedan mir: Biskupski ordinarijat Mostar u ratnoj drami 1990.-1994.* Mostar: Biskupski ordinarijat, 1995.

Mandić, Dominik. *Croati catholici Bosnae et Hercegovinae in descriptionibus annis 1743 et 1768.* Rome: Hrvatski povijesni institut, 1962.

—. *Franjevačka Bosna: Razvoj i uprava bosanske vikarije i provincije 1340-1735.* Rome: Hrvatski povijesni institut, 1968.

—. *Hercegovački spomenici franjevačkog reda iz turskog doba.* Vol. 1 (1463-1699). Mostar: Povjesno društvo za proučavanje prošlosti jugoslavenskih franjevaca, 1934.

—. "Katolička crkva u Bosni i Hercegovini za turskih vremena." *Novi Život* 2:5-6 (1963) 216-33.

Manuel, David. *Medjugorje under Siege.* Orleans, MA: Paraclete Press, 1992.

Matasović, Josip. *Regesta Fojnicensia.* Belgrade, 1930.

Nikić, Andrija. *Franjevci u Hercegovini u doba fra Matije Divkovića (1563.-1631.).* Mostar: Zavičajna knjižnica, 1985.

—. *Specifičnost crkvenih prilika u Hercegovini u 17. st.* Mostar: Zavičajna knjižnica, 1988.

Pandžić, Bazilije. *Bosna argentina: Studien zur Geschichte des Franziskanerordens in Bosnien und der Herzegowina.* Cologne: Böhlau Verlag, 1995.

Puljić, Vinko. *Suffering with Hope.* Sarajevo: Napredak, 1995.

Rubin, Elizabeth. "Souvenir Miracles: Going to See the Virgin in western Herzegovina." *Harper's Magazine* (Feb. 1995) 63-70.

Truhelka, Ćiro. "Die Tatowirung bei der Katholiken Bosniens und der Hercegovina." *Wissenschaftliche Mitteilungen aus Bosnien und der Herzegowina* 4 (1896) 493-508.

Vrankić, Petar. *La Chiesa cattolica nella Bosnia ed Erzegovina al tempo del vescovo fra Raffaele Barisic, 1832-1862.* Rome: Università Gregoriana, 1984.

Weible, Wayne. *Medjugorje: The Mission.* Orleans, MA: Paraclete Press, 1994.

Zindars-Swartz, Sandra L. *Encountering Mary: From La Salette to Medjugorje.* Princeton, NJ: Princeton University Press, 1991.

ISLAM

Algar, Hamid. "Some Notes on the Naqshbandi Tariqat in Bosnia." *Studies in Comparative Religion* 9:2 (1975) 69-96.

Babinger, Franz. "Der Islam in Südosteuropa." In *Völker und Kulturen Südosteuropas. Kulturhistorische Beiträge,* 211-17. Munich: Südosteuropa-Verlagsgesellschaft, 1959.

Balić, Smail. "Der bosnische-herzegowinische Islam." *Der Islam* 44 (1968) 115-37.

—. "Islam in Bosnia and Herzegovina." *Islamic Review* 37 (1949) 44-46.

—. "Der Islam in Bosnien: Ein Beitrag zu seiner Entstehungsgeschihte." *Österreichische Osthefte* 6:6 (1964) 470-76.

—. "Der Islam zwischen Donau und Adria: *Anatolica. Annuaire internationale pour les civilisations de l'Asie antérieure* 1 (1967) 93-104.

Bringa, Tone. *Being Muslim the Bosnian Way: Identity and Community in a Central Bosnian Village.* Princeton, NJ: Princeton University Press, 1995.

Čančar, Nusret and Enes Karić, eds. *Islamski fundamentalizam: Što je to?* Sarajevo: Mešihat Islamske zajednice u Bosni i Hercegovini, 1990.

Ćehajić, Džemal. *Derviški redovi u Jugoslavenskim Zemljama sa posebnim osvrtom na Bosnu i Hercegovinu.* Sarajevo: Orijentalni Institut, 1986.

Cigar, Norman. "Serbia's Orientalists and Islam: Making Genocide Intellectually Respectable." *Islamic Quarterly* 38:3 (1994) 147-70.

Ebied, R. Y. and M. J. L. Young. "An Exposition of the Islamic Doctrine of Christ's Second Coming as Presented by a Bosnian Muslim Scholar." *Orientalia Lovaniensia Periodica* 5 (1974) 127-38.

Filipović, Nedim. "A Contribution to the Problem of Islamization of the Balkans under Ottoman Rule." In *Ottoman Rule in Middle Europe and Balkan[sic] in the 16th and 17th Centuries,* 305-405. (Papers presented at the 9th Joint Conference of the Czechoslovak-Yugoslav Historical Committee). Prague: Czechoslovak Academy of Sciences, 1978.

Gazić, Lejla, ed. *Vakufname iz Bosne i Hercegovine (XV i XVI vijeka).* Sarajevo: Orijentalni institut u Sarajevu, 1985.

Hadžijahić, Muhamed, Mahmud Traljić, and Nijaz Šurkić. *Islam i Muslimani u Bosni i Hercegovini.* Sarajevo: Starješinstvo Islamske Zajednice, 1977.

Hauptmann, Ferdo, ed. *Borba Muslimana Bosne i Hercegovine za vjersku i vakufsko-mearifsku autonomiju.* Sarajevo: Svjetlost, 1962.

Heyer, Ingomar. *Beiträge zur Kenntnis des Islam in Bosnien und Hercegovina.* Tübingen: Albert Becht, 1940.

Hussein, A. "Communist Yugoslavia's Fear of Islam." *Issues in the Islamic Movement* 4 (1983-84) 34-35.

Irwin, Zachary T. "The Islamic Revival and the Muslims of Bosnia-Herzegovina." *East European Quarterly* 17 (1984) 437-58.

"Islam in Yugoslavia." *Moslem World* 28 (1938) 309-10.

Izetbegovic, Àlija Àli. *Islam between East and West.* 2nd ed. Indianapolis, IN: American Trust Publications, 1989.

Kamber, Charles. *Islam u hrvatskim zemljama.* Winnipeg: n.p., 1957.

Klen, D. "Pokrštavanje 'turske' djece u Rijeci u XVI i XVII stoljeću." *Historijski zbornik — Šidakov zbornik* 29-30 (1976-77) 203-07.

Kornrumpf, Hans-Jürgen. "Scheriat und christlicher Staat: Die Muslime in Bosnien und in den europäischen Nachfolgestaaten des osmanischen Reiches." *Saeculum* 35 (1984) 17-30.

Mažuranić, V. *Südslaven im Dienste des Islams (vom X. bis XVI. Jahrhundert): Ein Forschungsbericht.* Ed. and tr. C. Lucerna. Zagreb, 1928.

"Mixed Motives: Islam, Nationalism and Mevluds in an Unstable Yugoslavia." In Camilla Fawzi El-Solh and Judy Mabro, eds. *Muslim Women's Choices: Religious Belief and Social Reality,* 108-27. Oxford: Berg Publishers, 1994.

Mladenović, Miloš. "The Osmanli Conquest and the Islamization of Bosnia." *Slavic and East European Studies* 3 (1958-59) 219-26.

Mulahalilović, Enver. *Vjerski običaji Muslimana u Bosni i Hercegovini.* Sarajevo: Starješinstvo Islamske Zajednice, 1988.

Niškanović, Miroslav. *Ilindanski dernek kod turbeta Djerzelez Alije u Gerzovu.* Novi Pazar, n.p., 1978.

Norris, H. T. *Islam in the Balkans: Religion and Society between Europe and the Arab World.* Columbia, SC: University of South Carolina Press, 1993.

Popović, Alexandre. "The Contemporary Situation of the Muslim Mystic Orders in Yugoslavia." In Ernest Gellner, ed. *Islamic Dilemmas: Reformers, Nationalists and Industrialization: The*

Southern Shores of the Mediterranean, 240-54. Berlin: Mouton, 1985.

—. *L'Islam balkanique. Les musulmans du Sud-est Européen dans la période post-Ottomane.* Wiesbaden: Harrassowitz, 1986.

—. "L'Islam dans les états du Sud-est européen depuis leur indépendance." In Hans G. Mjer, ed. *Die Staaten Südosteuropas und die Osmanen*, 309-17. Munich: Selbstverlag, 1989.

—. "Les musulmans du Sud-est Européen dans la période post-Ottomane: Problèmes d'approche." *Journal asiatique* 263 (1975) 317-60.

—. *Les Musulmans yougoslaves, 1945-1989: Médiateurs et métaphores.* Lausanne: L'Age d'homme, 1990.

—. "Les Musulmans yougoslaves: Un problème." *Revue des études slaves* 56 (1984) 401-11.

Šamić, Jasna. "La Mystique Musulmane des Ecrivains Yougoslaves (de Bosnie)." *Quaderini di Studi Arabi* 5-6 (1987-88) 690-98.

Šehić, Nusret. *Autonomni pokret Muslimana za vrijeme austrougarske uprave u Bosni i Hercegovini.* Sarajevo: Svjetlost, 1980.

Sijerčić, Irfan. "The Activities of the 'Young Moslems' at the End of the War 1944-1945." *South Slav Journal* 8(1985) 23-28.

Smajlović, Ahmed. *Islam i Muslimani u Bosni i Hercegovini.* Sarajevo: Svjetlost, 1977.

—. "Muslims in Yugoslavia." *Journal of the Institute of Muslim Minority Affairs* 1:1 (1979) 132-44.

Sorabji, Cornelia. "Islamic Revival and Marriage in Bosnia." *Journal, Institute of Muslim Minority Affairs* 9 (1988) 331-37.

—. "Muslim Identity and Islamic Faith in Socialist Sarajevo." Ph.D. thesis, University of Cambridge, 1989.

"Statuto della comunità musulmana della ex Jugoslavia (24 ottobre 1936." *Oreinte moderno* 22 (1936) 44-45.

"The Trial of Moslem Intellectuals in Sarajevo: The Islamic Declaration." *South Slav Journal* 6:1 (1983) 55-89.

Trhulj, Sead. *Mladi Muslimani.* Zagreb: Globus, 1991.

Vucinich, Wayne S. "Yugoslavs of the Moslem Faith." In Robert J. Kerner, ed. *Yugoslavia*, 261-78. Berkeley: University of California Press, 1949.

Željazkova, Antonina. *The Spread of Islam in the Western Balkan Lands under Ottoman Rule (15th-18th Centuries).* Sofia: Bulgarian Academy of Sciences, 1990.

ORTHODOXY

Davidović, Sv. *Srpska pravoslavna crkva u Bosni i Hercegovini (od 960-1930 god).* Sarajevo: "Obod," J. Karić, 1931.

Nilević, Boris. *Srpska Pravoslavna Crkva u Bosni i Hercegovini do obnove Pećke patrijaršije 1557. godine.* Sarajevo: Veselin Masleša, 1990.

Skarić, Vladislav. *Srpski pravoslavni narod i crkva u Sarajevu u 17. i 18. vijeku.* Sarajevo: Državna štamparija, 1928.

Slijepčević, Đoko. *Istorija Srpske Pravoslavne Crkve.* Vol. 1: *Od pokrstavanja Srba do kraja XVII veka.* Munich, 1962. Vol. 2: *Od pocetka XIX veka do kraja Drugog svetskog rata.* Munich, 1966. Vol. 3: *Za vreme Drugog svetskog rata i posle njega.* Cologne: n. p., 1986.

JEWS

Roth, Cecil, ed. *Sarajevo Haggadah.* Belgrade: Jugoslavija, 1973.

10. SOCIETY IN GENERAL

Anderson, Scott. "Bosnia's Lost Generation." *New York Times Magazine* Sep. 8, 1996, 48-53, 64, 84, 92.

Balić, Smail. "Der ethnische Habitus der patriarchalischen Bosniaken." *Anatolica. Annuaire internationale pour les civilisations de l'Asie antérieure* 3 (1969/70) 213-35.

Bertsch, Gary K. *Values and Community in Multi-National Yugoslavia.* Boulder: East European Quarterly, 1976.

Bićanić, Rudolf. *How the People Live: Life in Passive Regions: (Peasant Life in Southwestern Croatia, Bosnia, and Hercegovina: Yugoslavia in 1935.)* Research Report, 21. Amherst, MA: Department of Anthropology, University of Massachusetts, 1981.

Cohen, Leonard. *Political Cohesion in a Fragile Mosaic: The Yugoslav Experience.* Boulder, CO: Westview, 1983.

Čurčić, Vejsil. *Rezente Pfahlbauten von Donja dolina.* Vienna: Verlag des Vereines für öster. Volkskunde, 1913.

Danopoulos, Constantine P. and Daniel Zirker, eds. *Civil-Military Relations in the Soviet and Yugoslav Successor States.* Boulder, CO: Westview Press, 1996.

Hranić, Vojislav (Jozo Markušić). *Kmetsko pitanje u Bosni i Hercegovini.* Sarajevo, 1911.

Lockwood, William G. "Bride Theft and Social Maneuverability in Western Bosnia." *Anthropological Quarterly* 47:3 (1974) 253-69.

—. "Selo and Carsija: The Peasant Market Place As a Mechanism of Social Integration in Western Bosnia." Ph.D. dissertation, University of California, Berkeley, 1970.

—. "Social Status and Cultural Changes in a Bosnian Moslem Village." *East European Quarterly* 9:2 (1975) 123-35.

Lodge, O. *Peasant Life in Yugoslavia.* London: Seely, 1941.

Markovski, Venko. *Goli Otok: The Island of Death: A Diary in Letters.* Boulder, CO: Social Science Monographs, 1984.

Ramet, Sabrina P. *Social Currents in Eastern Europe: The Sources and Meaning of the Great Transformation.* Durham, NC: Duke University Press, 1991.

Vucinich, Alexander S. "Petar Kocic and Bosnian Peasantry." *Slavia* 14 (1939) 22-26.

Vucinich, Wayne S. "The Nature of Balkan Society Under Ottoman Rule." *Slavic Review* 21:4 (1962) 597-616.

—. *A Study in Social Survival: The Katun in Bileća Rudine.* Denver: University of Denver, Graduate School of International Studies, 1975.

Zlatar, B. "O nekim muslimanskim feudalnim porodicama u Bosni." *Prilozi Instituta za istoriju* 14-15 (1978) 81-139.

11. ETHNICITY AND NATIONALISM

GENERAL

Alaupović, Tugomir. *Razvijanje narodne misli u Bosni.* Zagreb: Hrvatska njiva, 1918.

Beck, S. and J. W. Cole, eds. *Ethnicity and Nationalism in Southeastern Europe.* Amsterdam: University of Amsterdam Press, 1981.

Bowman, G., ed. *Antagonism and Identity in the National Idiom: The Case of Former Yugoslavia.* Oxford: Berg, 1994.

Bringa, T. R. "National Categories, National Identification and Identity-Formation in 'Multinational' Bosnia." *Anthropology of Eastern Europe Review* 11:1-2 (1993) 69-77.

Bugajski, Janusz. *Ethnic Politics in Eastern Europe: A Guide to Nationality Politics, Organizations, and Parties.* Armonk, NY: M.E. Sharpe, 1994.

Burg, Steven L. "Nationalism and Democratization in Yugoslavia." *Washington Quarterly* 14:4 (1991) 5-19.

Cozic, P. Charles, ed. *Nationalism and Ethnic Conflict.* San Diego: Greenhaven Press, 1994.

Džaja, Srećko M. *Konfessionalität und Nationalität Bosniens und der Herzegowina: Voremanzipatorische Phase, 1463-1804.* Munich: R. Oldenbourg, 1984.

Filipović, Milenko S. *Prilozi etnološkom poznavanju severoistočne Bosne.* Sarajevo: Akademija nauka i umjetnosti Bosne i Hercegovine, 1969.

Flere, Sergej. "Explaining Ethnic Antagonism in Yugoslavia." *European Sociological Review* 7:3 (1991) 183-93.

Griffiths, Stephen Iwan. *Nationalism and Ethnic Conflict: Threats to European Security.* Oxford: Oxford University Press, 1993.

Halperin, Morton H. and David J. Scheffer with Patricia L. Small. *Self-Determination in the New World Order.* Washington, DC: Carnegie Endowment for International Peace, 1992.

Job, Cvijeto. "Yugoslavia's Ethnic Furies." *Foreign Policy* 92 (1993) 52-74.

Karpat, Kemal. *An Inquiry into the Social Foundations of Nationalism in the Ottoman State: From Social Estates to*

Classes, from Millets to Nations. Princeton: Princeton University Press, 1973.

King, Robert R. *Minorities under Communism: Nationalities As a Source of Tension among Balkan Communist States.* Cambridge, MA: Harvard University Press, 1973.

Klein, George and Patricia V. Klein. "Nationalism vs. Ideology: The Pivot of Yugoslav Politics." In Roman Szporluk, ed. *Communism and Nationalism: Karl Marx versus Friedrich List,* 247-79. Oxford: Oxford University Press, 1988.

Lederer, Ivo J. "Nationalism and the Yugoslavs." In Ivo J. Lederer and Peter F. Suger, eds. *Nationalism in Eastern Europe,* 396-439. Seattle: University of Washington Press, 1969.

Lockwood, William G. "Religion and Language As Criteria of Ethnic Identity: An Exploratory Comparison." In S. Beck and J. W. Cole, eds. *Ethnicity and Nationalism in Southeastern Europe,* 85-98. Amsterdam: University of Amsterdam Press, 1981.

Malbaša, Ante. *Hrvatski i srpski nacionalni problem u Bosni za vrijeme režima Benjamina Kállaya.* Osijek: Gradska tiskara, [1940].

Mandić, Dominik. "The Ethnic and Religious History of Bosnia and Herzegovina." In F. H. Eterovich and C. Spalatin, eds. *Croatia: Land, People, Culture,* vol. 2, 362-93. Toronto: University of Toronto Press, 1970.

Michener, Roger. ed. *Nationality, Patriotism and Nationalism in Liberal Democratic Societies.* St. Paul, MN: Paragon House, 1993.

Milojković-Djurić, Jelena. *Panslavism and National Identity in Russia and in the Balkans, 1830-1880: Images of the Self and Others.* Boulder, CO: East European Monographs; Distributed by Columbia University Press, New York, 1994.

Murray Seymour, Jack. "The Yugoslav Idea: Will It Die with Yugoslavia?" *History of European Ideas* 18:2 (1994) 199-213.

Napotnik, Mihael. *Kratek pregled bosanskega slavstva.* Maribor: Janez Leon, 1884.

Perović, Blažo M. *Jugoslovenstvo i nacional-feudalizm.* Belgrade: Gardoš, 1988.

Pešić, Vesna. "The Cruel Face of Nationalism." In Larry Diamond and Marc F. Plattner, eds. *Nationalism, Ethnic Conflict, and Democracy*, 132-135. Baltimore: Johns Hopkins University Press, 1994.

Poulton, Hugh. *The Balkans: Minorities and States in Conflict.* London: Minority Rights Publication, 1991.

—. *Minorities in the Balkans.* London: Minority Rights Group, 1989.

Pozderac, Hamdija. *Nacionalni odnosi i socijalističko zajedništvo.* Sarajevo: Svjetlost, 1978.

—. "The National Question and the Formation of the Yugoslav Federation." *Socialist Thought and Practice* 23 (1983) 31-47.

Redžić, Enver. *Nacionalni odnosi u Bosni i Hercegovini 1941-1945. u analizama jugoslavenske istoriografije.* Sarajevo: ANUBiH, 1989.

Schöpflin, George. "Nationalism, Politics and the European Experience." *Survey* 28 (1984) 67-86.

—. "Nationality in the Fabric of Yugoslav Politics." *Survey* 25 (1980) 1-19.

—. "Power, Ethnicity and Communism in Yugoslavia." *New Hungarian Quarterly* 33:128 (1992) 3-32.

Seroka, Jim. "Nationalism and the New Political Compact in Yugoslavia." *History of European Ideas* 15:4-6 (1992) 577-81.

Seton-Watson, Hugh. "Unsatisfied Nationalisms." *Journal of Contemporary History* 6 (1971) 3-14.

Udovicki, Jasminka and James Ridgeway, eds. *Yugoslavia's Ethnic Nightmare: The Inside Story of Europe's Unfolding Order.* New York: Lawrence Hill Books, 1995.

"Uneasy Co-existence in Bosnia." *Impact International* 8 (1978) 6-7.

Vasić, M. "Etnićka kretanja u bosanskoj krajini u XVI vijeku." *Godišnjak istorijskog društva Bosne i Hercegovine* 11 (1960) 233-49.

Walker, Tim. *War in Yugoslavia: The Return of Nationalism.* Alexandria, VA: Close Up Publications, 1993.

BOSNIAN MUSLIMS (BOSNIACS)

Babuna, Aydin. "The Emergence of the First Muslim Party in Bosnia-Hercegovina." *East European Quarterly* 30:2 (1996) 131-51.

Balagija, Abduselam. *Les Musulmans Yougoslavs*: Étude Sociologique. Publications de l'Institut d'études orientales IX, Faculté des Letters d'Alger. Algiers: La maison des livres, 1940.

Balić, Smail. "Die Muslims in Bosnia-Herzegowina." *Wissenschaftlicher Dienst Südosteuropas* 12 (1963) 158-61.

—. "Muslims in Eastern and South-Eastern Europe." *Journal, Institute of Muslim Minority Affairs* 6 (1985) 361-74.

—. "The Present Position of the Muslims of Bosnia and Hercegovina." *Islamic Review* 37 (1949) 22-25.

—. *Das unbekannte Bosnien: Europas Brücke zur islamischen Welt.* Cologne: Böhlau Verlag, 1992.

Begović, Mehmed. *Muslimani u Bosni i Hercegovini.* Belgrade: Soko, 1938.

Burg, Steven L. "Muslim Cadres and Soviet Political Development: Reflections from a Comparative Perspective [compared with Yugoslavia]." *World Politics* 37 (1984) 24-47.

—. *The Political Integration of Yugoslavia's Muslims: Determinants of Success and Failure.* Pittsburgh: Russian and East European Studies Program, University of Pittsburgh, 1983.

Canape, Marie-Paule. "L'islam et la question des nationalités en Yougoslavie." In O. Carré and P. Dumont, eds. *Radicalismes islamiques.* Vol. 2, 100-61. Paris: L'Harmattan, 1986.

Ćerić, Salim. *Muslimani srpskohrvatskog jezika.* Sarajevo: Svjetlost, 1968.

Ćimić, Esad. "Osobinosti nacionalnog formiranja Muslimana." *Pregled* 4 (1974) 389-407.

Čubrilović, V. "Poreklo muslimanskog plemstva u Bosni i Hercegovini." *Jugoslovenski istoriski časopis* 1 (1935) 386-403.

Cviic, K.F. "Yugoslavia's Moslem Problem." *World Today* 36:3 (1980) 108-12.

Dedic, Abdullah. "The Muslim Predicament in Yugoslavia: An Impression." *Journal, Institute of Muslim Minority Affairs* 8 (1987): 121-31.

Dizdarević, A. *Bosansko-hercegovački muslimani Hrvati*. Zagreb, 1936.

Dizdarević, Nijaz, ed. *Moslems in Yugoslavia*. Belgrade: Review of International Affairs, 1985.

—. "Stellung der Moslems in Jugoslawien." *Internationale Politik* 36:842 (1985) 7-9.

Donia, R. and W. Lockwood. "The Bosnian Muslims: Class, Ethnicity and Political Behavior." In Suad Joseph and Barbara L.K. Pillsbury, eds. *Muslim-Christian Conflicts: Economic, Political and Social Origins*, 185-207. Boulder: Westview Press, 1978.

Duraković, Asaf. *Mjesto muslimana u hrvatskoj narodnoj zajednici*. Toronto: n.p., 1972.

—. *Od Bleiburga do muslimanske nacije*. Toronto: n.p., 1974.

Duraković, Nijaz. *Prokletstvo Muslimana*. Sarajevo: Oslobođenje, 1993.

Dyker, David A. "The Ethnic Muslims of Bosnia: Some Basic Socio-Economic Data." *Slavonic and East European Review* 50 (1972) 238-56.

Džafčić, Ibrahim. *Fragmenti iz političke istorije bosansko-hercegovačkih muslimana*. Sarajevo, 1925.

Filipović, Milenko S. "Die serbokroatischen Mohammedaner." *Tribus NS* 9 (1960) 55-60.

Fišer, Joseph. "Ethnies ou groupes importants d'origine religieuse? Vers leur coexistence (De la genèse de la République socialiste plurinationale 'islamique' de Bosnie-Herzégovine)." *Review d'ètudes comparatives Est-Ouest* 11:3 (1980) 101-20.

Friedman, Francine. "Bosnian Moslem Nationalism." *Canadian Review of Studies in Nationalism, Bibliography* 8 (1981) 70-76.

—. *The Bosnian Muslims: Denial of a Nation*. Boulder: Westview, 1966.

Gesemann, Gerhard. "Eine jugoslavische Minderheit in Jugoslavien." *Slavische Rundschau* 2 (1930) 764-67.

—. "Jugoslavische Mohammedaner." *Slavische Rundschau* 4 (1932) 391-404.

Hadžijahić, Muhamed. *Od tradicije do identiteta: Geneza nacionalnog pitanja bosanskih Muslimana*. Sarajevo: Svjetlost, 1974.

—. *Porijeklo bosanskih Muslimana*. Sarajevo: Bosna, 1990.

Hadžiselimović, Omer. *Na vratima Istoka*. Sarajevo: Veselin Masleša, 1989.

Handžić, Mehmed. *Islamizacija Bosne i Hercegovine i porijeklo bosansko-hercegovačkih muslimana*. Sarajevo: Islamska dionička štamparija, 1940.

Hasan, K. S. "Communist Yugoslavia and its Muslims." *Pakistan Horizon* 5:4 (1972) 171-87.

Höpken, W. "Die jugoslawischen Kommunisten und die bosnischen Muslime." In A. Kappeler, G. Simon and G. Brunner, eds. *Die Muslime in der Sowjetunion und in Jugoslawien: Identität, Politik, Widerstand*, 181-210. Cologne: Markus, 1989.

Kajan, Ibrahim. *Zavođenje muslimana: (Budi svoj!)*. Zagreb: n.p., 1992.

Kállay, Béni. *Die Lage der Mohammedaner in Bosnia, von einem Ungarn*. Vienna: Holzhausen, 1900.

Kappeler, A. G. Simon, and G. Brunner, eds. *Die Muslime in der Sowjetunion und in Jugoslawien: Identität, Politik, Widerstand*. Cologne: Markus, 1989.

Kohl von, Christina. "Islamic Nationalism in Yugoslavia." *Swiss Review of World Affairs* 33 (1983): 14-15.

Konjhodzich, Alija. "Serbians of the Moslem Faith in Chetnik Ranks." In *Draža Mihailović Memorial Book*. Chicago: Organization of Serbian Chetniks "Ravna Gora," 1981.

Kulišić, Š. "Razmatranja o porijeklu Muslimana u Bosni i Hercegovni." *Glasnik zemaljskog muzeja u Sarajevu* 8 (1953) 145-58.

Kuzmany, N. "Notes on Moslems of Bosnia." *The Muslim World* 15 (1925) 177-81.

Lapčević, D. *O našim Muslimanima*. Belgrade: Geca Kon, 1925.

Lavrencic, Karl. "Still among the Least Known." *Impact International* 9 (1976) 28-33.

Lockwood, William G. "Bosnians." In Richard V. Weekes, ed. *Muslim Peoples: A World Ethnographic Survey*, 111-15. Westport, CT: Greenwood Press, 1978.

—. "Converts and Consanguinity: The Social Organization of Moslem Slavs in Western Bosnia." *Ethnology* 11:1 (1972) 55-79.

—. "Living Legacy of the Ottoman Empire: The Serbo-Croatian Speaking Moslems of Bosnia-Herzegovina." In A. Ascher, T. Halasi-Kun, and B. K. Kiraly, eds. *The Mutual Effects of the Islamic and the Judeo-Christian Worlds: The East European Pattern*, 209-25. New York: Brooklyn College Press, 1979.

Lopasic, Alexander. "Bosnian Muslims: A Search for Identity." British Society for Middle East Studies. *Bulletin* 8 (1981) 115-25.

—. "The 'Turks' of Bosnia." *Research Papers: Muslims in Europe* 16 (1982) 12-23.

Mitrinović, Čedomil. *Naši muslimani: Studija za orientaciju pitanja bosansko-hercegovačkih muslimana*. Belgrade; Društvo, 1926.

Mladenović, Miloš. "Family Names of Osmanli Origin in Bosnia and Herzegovina." In Donald P. Little, ed. *Essays on Islamic Civilization Presented to Niyazi Berkes*, 244-59. Leiden: Brill, 1978.

"The Moslem Challenge." *Economist* 21:5 (1983) 67-68.

Murvar, Vatro. *Nation and Religion in Central Europe and the Western Balkans: The Muslims in Bosnia, Hercegovina, and Sandžak: A Sociological Analysis*. Brookfield, WI: n.p., 1989.

"Muslims in Yugoslavia: Adaption and Accommodation." *Impact International* 7 (1977) 14.

Neville-Bagot, G. H. "The Muslims of Bosnia and the Other Autonomous States of Yugoslavia." *Islamic Review* 48 (Jun. 1960) 31-34.

Nielsen, Jørgen S. "Les musulmans en Europe: Une vue d'ensemble d'une communauté de vingt-trois millions de personnes." *Hommes et migrations* 33:1035 (1982) 3-36.

Parker, Mushtak. *Muslims in Yugoslavia: The Quest for Justice*. Toronto: Croatian Islamic Center, 1986.

Petković, Ranko, ed. *Moslems in Yugoslavia*. Studies. Belgrade: Review of International Affairs, 1985.

Pinson, Mark, ed. *The Muslims of Bosnia-Herzegovina: Their Historic Development from the Middle Ages to the Dissolution of Yugoslavia.* Cambridge, MA: Center for Middle Eastern Studies of Harvard University, 1994.

Popović, Alexander. "Islamische Bewegungen in Jugoslawien." In A. Kappeler, G. Simon, and G. Brunner, eds. *Die Muslime in der Sowjetunion und in Jugoslawien: Identität, Politik, Widerstand,* 273-86. Cologne: Markus, 1989.

—. *Jugoslovenski muslimani.* Belgrade: Akvarius, 1990.

Purivatra, Atif. *Nacionalni i politički razvitak Muslimana.* 3rd ed. Sarajevo: Svjetlost, 1970.

—. "The National Phenomenon of the Moslems of Bosnia-Herzegovina." In Nada Dragić, ed. *Nations and Nationalities of Yugoslavia,* 305-27. Belgrade: Međunarodna Politika, 1974.

Ramet, Pedro. "Die Muslime Bosniens als Nation." In A. Kappeler, G. Simon, and G. Brunner, eds. *Die Muslime in der Sowjetunion und in Jugoslawien: Identität, Politik, Widerstand,* 107-14. Cologne: Markus, 1989.

—. "Primordial Ethnicity of Modern Nationalism: The Case of Yugoslavia's Muslims." *Nationalities Papers* 13:2 (1985) 165-87.

Ramet, Sabrina P. "Primordial Ethnicity or Modern Nationalism: The Case of Yugoslavia's Muslims Reconsidered." *South Slav Journal* 13:1-2 (1990) 1-20.

Redžić, Enver. *Muslimansko autonomaštvo i 13. SS divizija: Autonomija Bosne i Hercegovine i Hitlerov Treći Rajh.* Sarajevo: Svjetlost, 1987.

Reuter-Hendrichs, Irena. "Jugoslawiens Muslime." *Südost Europa Mitteilungen* 29:2 (1989) 105-15.

Rossi, Ettore. "I Musulmani della ex-Jugoslavia." *Oriente Moderno* 22:2 (1942) 39-42.

Rusinow, Dennison. *Yugoslavia's Muslim Nation.* UFSI Reports, 8. Hanover, NH: Universities Field Staff International, 1982.

Salihagić, S. *Bosansko hercegovački muslimani u krilu jugoslavenske zajednice.* Banja Luka: Zvonimir Jović, 1940.

Saltaga, Fuad. *Muslimanska nacija u Jugoslaviji: Porijeklo, Islam, kultura, povijest, politika.* Sarajevo: Institut za proučavanje nacionalnih odnosa, 1991.

Šarac, Petar and Miljenko Primorac, eds. *Hrvatsko podrijetlo bosansko-hercegovačkih muslimana.* Zagreb: HHZ "Herceg Stjepan," 1992.

Sarac, Zajim et al. *Yugoslav Muslims' Message to India.* Bombay: People's Publishing House, 1947.

Sarajevski proces: Suđenje muslimanskim intelektualcima 1983 g. Zurich: Bosanski institut, 1987.

Satric, Hazim. "The Muslims in Yugoslavia." *Islamic Review* 41:4 (1953) 13-18.

Sućeska, Avdo. "Istorijske osnove nacionalne posebnosti bosansko-hercegovačkih Muslimana." *Jugoslovenski istorijski časopis* 4 (1969) 47-54.

Suljević, Kasim. *Nacionalnost Muslimana: Izmedju teorije i politike.* Rijeka: "Otokar Keršovani," 1981.

Tomašić, Dinko Antun. "The Problem of National Consciousness of the Moslems in Bosnia and Hercegovina." *Studies in Comparative Religion* 2 (1961) 174-80.

Wiles, J. W. "Moslem Women in Yugoslavia." *Moslem World* 18 (1928) 61-65.

Yelavitch, L. "Les Musulmans de Bosnie-Herzégovine." *Revue du monde musulman* 39 (1920) 119-33.

Zulfikarpašić, A. *Bosanski Muslimani: Čimbenik mira izmedju Srba i Hrvata.* Zurich: Bošnjački institut, 1986.

OTHERS

Bracewell, Wendy. "Nationalist Histories and National Identities among the Serbs and Croats." In Mary Fulbrook, ed. *National Histories and European History*, 141-61. London: UCL Press, 1993.

Brkić, Milenko, ed. *Prinosi Hrvatstvu Bosne i Hercegovine.* Studenci: PCC Međugorje, 1995.

Čović, Bože et al., eds *Izvori velikosrpske agresije: Rasprave, dokumenti, kartografski prikazi.* Zagreb: August Cesarec and Školska knjiga, 1991.

Čuvalo, Ante. "Serbian National Ideology, Politics, and Warfare: Historical Tendencies." *American Croatian Review* 2:3&4 (1995) 6-10.

Filipescu, T. *Coloniile române din Bosnia: Studiu etnografic şi antropogeografic.* Bucharest, 1906.

Freidenreich, Harriet P. *The Jews of Yugoslavia: A Quest for Community.* Philadelphia: Jewish Publication Society of America, 1979.

Đaković, Luka. *Političke organizacije bosanskohercegovačkih katolika Hrvata.* Zagreb: Globus, 1985.

Glück, L. "Zur physischen Anthropologie der Zigeuner in Bosnien und der Hercegovina." *Wissenschaftliche Mitteilungen aus Bosnien und der Herzegowina* 5 (1897) 403-33.

Goldstein, Slavko, ed. *Jews in Yugoslavia.* Zagreb: Museum Gallery Center, 1988.

Hehn, Paul N. "The Origins of Modern Pan-Serbism: The 1844 Načertanije of Ilija Garašanin: An Analysis and Translation." *East European Quarterly* 9:2 (1975) 153-71.

Hrvati u Bosni i Hercegovini: Ciljevi i mogućnosti. 2nd ed. Toronto: Hrvatski put, 1997.

Krmpotich, M.D. *Croatia, Bosnia and Hercegovina and the Serbian Claims.* Kansas City: n.p., 1916.

Levy, M. *Die Sephardim in Bosnien: Ein Beitrag zur Geschichte der Juden auf der Balkanhalbinsel.* Sarajevo: D.A. Kajon, 1911.

Maier, Hans. *Die deutschen Siedlungen in Bosnia.* Stuttgart: Ausland und Verlags-Aktiengesellschaft, 1924.

Maurer, Franz. "Mitteilungen aus Bosnien. Die spanischen Juden." *Das Ausland* 42:49-50 (1869) 1161-64, 1183-85.

Pinto, Avram. *Jevreji Sarajeva i Bosne i Hercegovine.* Sarajevo: Veselin Maslesa, 1987.

Ramet, Sabrina Petra. "Nationalism and the 'Idiocy' of the Countryside: The Case of Serbia." *Ethnic and Racial Studies* 19:1 (1996) 70-87.

Schwartz, Stephen. "Yo soy una rosa: I Am a Rose - Bosnian Jewry's Present and Past." *Journal of Croatian Studies* 31 (1990) 151-57."

12. CULTURE

GENERAL

Anđelić, P. "Periodi u kulturnoj historiji Bosne i Hercegovine u srednjem vijeku." *Glasnik zemaljskog muzeja Bosne i Hercegovine u Sarajevu* 25 (1970) 119-212.

Andrić, Ivo. *Bosnian Chronicle.* Trans. Joseph G. Hitrec. New York: Knopf, 1963.

—. *Bosnian Story.* Trans. Kenneth Johnstone. London: Lincolns-Prager, 1961.

—. *Bridge on the Drina.* Trans. L. F. Edwards. London: Allen & Unwin, 1959.

—. *The Development of Spiritual Life in Bosnia under the Influence of Turkish Rule.* Trans. Zelimir B. Juricic and John F. Loud. Durham, NC: Duke University Press, 1990.

—. *Devil's Yard.* Trans. Kenneth Johnstone. New York: Grove Press, 1962.

—. *The Vezir's Elephant.* Trans. Drenka Willen. New York: Harcourt, 1962.

—. *The Woman from Sarajevo.* Trans. J. G. Hitrec. London: Calder and Boyars; New York: A.A. Knopf, 1966.

Balić, Smail. "Cultural Achievements of Bosnia-Hercegovinian Muslims." In F. H. Eterovich and C. Spalatin, eds. *Croatia: Land, People, Culture,* vol. 2, 299-361. Toronto: University of Toronto Press, 1970.

—. *Die Kultur der Bosniaken: Supplement.* Vienna: S. Balić, 1978.

—. *Kultura Bošnjaka: Muslimanska komponenta.* Vienna: n.p., 1973.

Basler, Đuro. "Iz kulturne istorije naroda Bosne i Hercegovine." *Pregled* 2-3 (1973) 297-304.

Benac, Alojz et al. *Kulturna istorija Bosne i Hercegovine od najstarijih vremena do pada ovih zemalja pod osmansku vlast.* 2nd ed. Sarajevo: Veselin Masleša, 1984.

Besarović, Risto, ed. *Kultura i umjetnost u Bosni i Hercegovini pod austrougarskom upravom.* Sarajevo: Arhiv Bosne i Hercegovine, 1968.

Bollage, B. "Rebuilding Bosnia's Library." *Chronicle of Higher Education* (Jan. 13, 1995) A35-A37.

La Bosnie-Herzégovine à l'Exposition de Paris 1900. Vienna: Adolphe Holzhausen, 1900.

Dautbegović, Almaz, ed. *Spomenica stogodišnjice rada Zemaljskog Muzeja Bosne i Hercegovine, 1888-1988.* Sarajevo: Zemaljski Muzej BiH, 1988.

Džaja, Srećko M. *Bosnien-Herzegowina in der österreich-ungarische Epoche (1878-1918): Die Intellgentsia zwischen Tradition und Ideologie.* Munich: R. Oldenbourg, 1994.

Džambo, Jozo. *Buchwesen in Bosnia und der Herzegowina (1800-1878): Zum Problem der Lesersoziologie.* Frankfurt; New York: P. Lang, 1985.

Jelenić, Julian. *Kultura i bosanski Franjevci.* Sarajevo: Kramarić and M. Raguz, vol. 1, 1912; vol. 2, 1915.

Kučukalić, Zija. *The Development of Musical Culture in Bosnia and Hercegovina.* Trans. Branka Bokonjić. Sarajevo: Association of Composers of Bosnia and Hercegovina, 1967.

Laštrić, Filip (1700-1783). *Epitome Vetustatem Provinciae Bosnnensis: Pregled starina Bosanske provincije.* Venice, 1765. Foreword and commentary by Andrija Zirdum; trans. Šimun Šimić and Ignacije Gavran. Sarajevo: Veselin Masleša, 1977.

Nametak, Alija. *Islamski kulturni spomenici: Turskog perioda u Bosni i Hercegovini.* Sarajevo: Državna štamparija, 1939.

Nickels, Sylvie. "Where East Meets West: The Republic of Bosnia and Hercegovina, Yugoslavia." *Country Living* (Oct. 17, 1974) 1142-43.

Riedlmayer, A. *Killing Memory: Bosnia's Cultural Heritage and Its Destruction.* Haverford: Community of Bosnia Foundation, 1994.

Smailović, Ismet. *Muslimanska imena orijentalnog porijekla u Bosni i Hercegovini.* Sarajevo: Institut za jezik i književnost, 1977.

Truhelka, Ćiro. *Gazi Husrevbeg, njegov život i njegovo doba.* Sarajevo, 1912.

Zimmerman, William. *Politics and Culture in Yugoslavia.* Ann Arbor, MI: Center for Political Studies, Institute for Social Research, University of Michigan, 1987.

ART AND ARCHITECTURE

Bešlagić, Šefik. *Kamene stolice srednjovjekovne Bosne i Hercegovine.* Sarajevo: Akademija nauka i umjetnosti Bosne i Hercegovine, 1985.

—. "Nevesinjski stećci." *Naše starine* 13 (1972) 97-122.

—. "Novopronađeni natpisi na stećcima." *Naše starine* 12 (1969) 133-48.

—. *Popovo: Srednjovjekovni nadgrobni spomenici.* Sarajevo: Zavod za zaštitu spomenika kulture Bosne i Hercegovine, 1966.

—. *Stećci centralne Bosne.* Sarajevo: Zavod za zaštitu spomenika kulture Bosne i Hercegovine, 1967.

—. *Stećci, kataloško-topografski pregled.* Sarajevo: Veselin Masleša, 1971.

—. *Stećci-kultura i umjetnost.* Sarajevo: Veselin Masleša, 1982.

—. "Stećci okoline Kladnja." *Naše starine* 12 (1969) 155-76.

Bihalji-Merin, Oto and Alojz Benac. *Bogomil Sculpture.* New York: Harcourt, Brace, and World, 1963.

Čelić, Džemal and Mehmed Mujezinović. *Stari mostovi u Bosni i Hercegovini.* Sarajevo: Veselin Masleša, 1969.

Filipović, Mirza, ed. *The Art in Bosnia-Herzegovina.* Sarajevo: Svjetlost, 1987.

Gambrell, Jamey. "Sarajevo: Art in *Extremis.*" *Art in America* 82 (May 1994) 100-103+.

Grabrijan, Dušan. *The Bosnian Oriental Architecture in Sarajevo: With Special Reference to the Contemporary One.* Ljubljana: Univerzum, 1984.

Markotić, Vladimir. "The Medieval Tombstones in Bosnia and Hercegovina: The Kinships and the Professions." In Marc Thompson et al., eds. *Status, Structure and Stratification: Current Archaeological Reconstructions,* 153-57. Calgary: University of Calgary Archaeological Association, 1985.

—. "The Medieval Tombstones of Bosnia and Hercegovina." In Michael Wilson et al. *Megaliths to Medicine Wheels: Boulder Structures in Archeology,* 397-417. Calgary: University of Calgary Archaeological Association, 1981.

Mazalić, Đoka. *Slikarska umjetnost u Bosni i Hercegovini u tursko doba, 1500-1878.* Sarajevo: Veselin Masleša, 1965.

Palavestra, Veljko and Mario Petrić. *Srednjovjekovni nadgrobni spomenici u Žepi.* Sarajevo: Naučnog društva Bosne i Hercegovine. Knjiga 24, Odjel istorijko-filoloških nauka, knjiga 8, 1964.

Radojčić, S. "Reljefi bosanskih i hercegovačkih stećaka." *Letopis Matice Srpske* 137:287 (1961) 1-15.

Redžić, Husref. *Studije o islamskoj arhitektonskoj baštini.* Sarajevo: Veselin Masleša, 1983.

Ressel, Svetlana. *Orientalisch-Osmanische Element im balkanslavische Volksmärchen.* Münster: Aschendorff, 1981.

Sontag, Susan. "Godot Comes to Sarajevo." *New York Review of Books* (Oct. 21, 1993) 52-59.

Stix, Edmund. *Das Bauwesen in Bosnien und der Hercegovina vom Beginn der Occupation durch die österreichisch-ungarische Monarchie bis in das Jahr 1887. Eine technisch-statistische Studie, nach amtlichen Quellen zusammengestellt von Baudepartment der Landesregierung unter der Leitung von Edm. Stix, ed. Landesregierung für Bosnien und die Hercegovina.* Vienna: Hölder, 1887.

Wenzel, Marian. "Bosnian and Herzegovinian Tombstones: Who Made Them and Why?" *Südost-Forschungen* 21 (1962) 102-43.

—. *Ukrasni motivi na stećcima.* Sarajevo: Veselin Masleša, 1965.

FOLK LIFE AND CULTURE

Ackerly, Frederick G. "Five tales from Bosnia." *Journal of the Gypsy Lore Society* 23:3/4 (1944) 97-106.

Beljkašić-Hadžidedić, Ljiljana. *The National Folk Art of Bosnia and Hercegovina.* Sarajevo: Svjetlost, 1983.

Bjelskositche, L. G. and N.W. Thomas. "Animal Folklore from the Herzegovina." *Man* 4 (1904) 132-36.

Bordeaux, Albert F. J. *La Bosnie populaire: Paysages, moeurs et coutumes, légendes, chants populaires, mines.* Paris: Plon, 1904.

Buconjić, Nikola. *Život i običaji Hrvata katoličke vjere u Bosni i Hercegovini.* Sarajevo: A. Kajon, 1908.

Buturović, Đenana. "The Folk Epic Tradition of the Moslems of Bosnia and Herzegovina from the Beginning of the 16th

Century until the Publication of Hörmann's Collection (1888)." *Wissenschafttliche Mitteilungen des bosnisch-herzegowinischen Landesmuseums* 3:B (1980) 5-110.

Capus, M. G. "Tatouages en Bosnie-Hercégovine." *Bulletins de la Société d'anthropologie de Paris.* 4 série, 5 (1894) 625-33.

Colonna, Mathilde. *Contes de la Bosnie, orné de 34 illustrations originales de Léopold Braun.* Paris: Delagrave, 1918.

Ćorović, Svetozar. *Bosna i Hercegovina u hrvatskoj pripovjedci.* Novi Sad: Letopis Matice Srpske, 1901.

Čurčić, Vejsil. "Die volkstümliche Fischerei in Bosnien und der Herzegowina." *Wissenschaftliche Mitteilungen aus Bosnien und der Herzegowina* 12 (1912) 490-589.

Etnografska gradja: Janj, Sarajevo, Livanjsko polje, Visoko, Donji Birač. Urednik Cvijetko Rihtman. Sarajevo: Akademija nauka i umjetnosti Bosne i Hercegovine, 1976.

Hangi, Anton. *Die Moslims in Bosnien-Hercegovina: Ihre Lebensweise, Sitten und Gebräuchen.* Autorisierte Übersetzung von Hermann Tausk. Sarajevo: Kajon, 1907.

—. *Život i običaji muslimana.* Sarajevo: Svjetlost, [1906] 1990.

Lockwood, Yvonne R. *Text and Context: Folksongs in a Bosnian Muslim Village.* Columbus, OH: Slavica Publishers, 1983.

Maners, Lynn D. "The Social Lives of Dances: The Transformation and Recontextualization of Expressive Behavior in Bosnia and Hercegovina." Ph. D. dissertation, University of California, Los Angeles, 1993.

Michel, Robert. *Halbmond über Narenta: Bosnische Erzählungen.* Vienna: Wiener Verlagsgesellschaft, 1940.

—. *Halbmond über der Narenta: Erzälungen aus Bosnien und der Herzegovina.* Neue Auflage. Vienna: Wiener Verlag, 1947.

Preindlsberger-Mrazović, Milena. *Bosnische Volksmärchen.* Innsbruck: Edlinger, 1905.

Sivrić, Ivo. *The Peasant Culture of Bosnia and Herzegovina.* Chicago: Franciscan Herald Press, 1982.

Truhelka, Ćiro. "Die Heilkunde nach volksthümlicher Überlieferung mit Auszügen aus einer alten Handschrift." In *Wissenschaftliche Mitteilungen aus Bosnien und der Hercegovina* 2 (1894) 375-91.

—. "Die phrygische Mütz in Bosnien." In *Wissenschaftliche Mitteilungen aus Bosnien und der Hercegovina* 4 (1896) 509-15.

—. "Volksleben." In *Die österr.-ung. Monarchie in Wort und Bild.* vol. 22: *Bosnien und Hercegovina.* Vienna: Kaiserl.-königl. Hof- und Staatsdruckerei, 1901.

Zovko, Ivan. *Hrvatsko ime u narodnoj predaji i običajima Bosne i Hercegovine.* Ivan Alilović, ed. Zagreb: HKD Sv. Ćiril i Metod, 1990.

13. URBAN DWELLING

Anđelić, Pavao. *Srednjovjekovni gradovi u Neretvi.* Sarajevo: GZM, 1958.

Babinger von, F. "Sarayevo." In the *Encyclopedia of Islam.* "Die Gründung von Elbasan" 94-103. Berlin: Ostasiatische Studien, 1931.

Ćirković, Sima. "Unfulfilled Autonomy: Urban Society in Serbia and Bosnia." In Bariša Krekić, ed. *Urban Society of Eastern Europe in Premodern Times,* 158-84. Berkeley: University of California Press, 1987.

Kreševljaković, Hamdija. *Sarajevo za vrijeme Austro-Ugarske uprave.* Sarajevo: Arhiv grada, 1969.

—. *Stari bosanski gradovi.* Sarajevo: Naše starine, 1953.

Michel, Robert. *Mostar.* Prague, 1909.

Palavestra, Vlajko. *Legends of Old Sarajevo.* Trans. Mario Suško and William Tribe. Sarajevo: International Literary Manifestations Sarajevo Poetry Days, 1987.

Pašalić, E. and R. Mišević, eds. *Sarajevo.* Sarajevo, 1954.

Peez, Carl. *Mostar und sein Kulturkreis.* Leipzig: Brockhaus, 1891.

Peixotto, Mary H. "Mostar: A Herzegovinian Sketch." *Scribner's* 32 (1902) 317-29.

Pelletier, René. *La Chanson d'amour à Sarajevo.* Besançon, 1938.

Skarić, Vladislav. "Postanak Sarajeva u XV i XVI stoljeću." *Glasnik Zemaljskog Muzeja.* Sarajevo, 1929.

—. *Sarajevo i njegova okolina od najstarijih vremena do austro-ugarske okupacije.* Sarajevo: Izdanje opštine, 1937.

Sućeska, Avdo. "Die Rechtsstellung der Bevölkerung in den Städten Bosniens und der Herzegowina unter den Osmanen (1463-1878)." In *Die Stadt in Südosteuropa: Struktur und Geschichte,* 84-99. Munich: Trofenik, 1968.

Vego, Marko. *Naselja bosanske srednjovjekovne države.* Sarajevo: Svjetlost, 1957.

14. EDUCATION

Bogićević, Vojislav. *Istorija razvitka osnovnih škola u Bosni i Hercegovini od 1463-1918.* Sarajevo: Zavod za izdavanje udžbenika, 1965.

—. *Pismenost u Bosni i Hercegovini od pojave slovenske pismenosti u XI v. do kraja austro-ugarske vladavine u Bosni i Hercegovini 1918 godine.* Sarajevo: Veselin Masleša, 1975.

Ćurić, Hajrudin. *Muslimansko školstvo u Bosni i Hercegovini do 1918. godine.* Sarajevo: Veselin Masleša, 1983.

—. *Osnovne škole milosrdnih sestara u Bosni i Hercegovini za vrijeme Turske (1871-1878).* Sarajevo: Naša škola, 1953.

—. *Školske prilike muslimana u Bosni i Hercegovini 1800-1878.* Belgrade: Naučno delo, 1965.

Kapidžić, Hamdija, ed. *Naučne ustanove u Bosni i Hercegovini za vrijeme austrougarske uprave.* Sarajevo: Arhiv Bosne i Hercegovine, 1973.

Papić, Mitar. *Hrvatsko školstvo u Bosni i Hercegovini do 1918. godine.* Sarajevo: Veselin Masleša, 1982.

—. *Istorija srpskih škola u Bosni i Hercegovini.* Sarajevo: Veselin Masleša, 1978.

—. *Školstvo u Bosni i Hercegovini za vrijeme austrougarske okupacije (1878-1918).* Sarajevo: Veselin Masleša, 1972.

15. LITERATURE

Bašagić, Safvetbeg. *Bošnjaci i Hercegovci u islamskoj književnosti.* Sarajevo: Glasnik zemaljskog muzeja, 1912.

Blau, Ernst Otto. *Bosnische-Türkische Sprachdenkmäler gesammelt.* Leipzig: Brockhaus, 1868.

Dobrača, Kasim. *Gazi Husrev-Begova Biblioteka: Katalog arapskih, turskih i perzijskih rukopisa.* Sarajevo, 1963.

Grubišić, Vinko. *Grafija hrvatske lapidarne ćirilice.* Munich-Barcelona: Hrvatska Revija, 1978.

Hadžijahić, Muhamed. *Hrvatska muslimanska književnost prije 1878.* Sarajevo: Štamparija Omer Šehić, 1938.

Hadžiosmanović, L. and S. Trako. *Tragom poezije Bosanskohercegovačkih muslimana na turskom jeziku.* Sarajevo: Gazi Husrevbegova biblioteka u Sarajevu, 1985.

Handžić, Mehmed. *Književni rad bosansko-hercegovačkih muslimana.* Sarajevo, 1934.

Hawkesworth, Celia. *Ivo Andrić: Bridge between East and West.* Dover, NH: Athlone Press, 1984.

Huković, Muhamed. *Alhamijado književnost i njeni stvaraoci.* Sarajevo: Svjetlost, 1986.

Lehfeldt, W. *Das serbokroatische Aljamiado-Schriftum der bosnisch-hercegovinische Muslime: Transkriptionsprobleme.* Munich: R. Trofenik, 1969.

Rizvić, Muhsin. *Behar: Književnoistorijska monografija.* Sarajevo: Svjetlost, 1971.

—. *Književno stvaranje muslimanskih pisaca u Bosni i Hercegovini u doba austrougarske vladavine.* Sarajevo: ANUBiH, 1973.

—. *Pregled književnosti naroda Bosne i Hercegovine.* Sarajevo: Veselin Masleša, 1985.

—. *Tokovi i stvaraoci iz književne Bosne.* Tuzla: Univerzal, 1986.

Škaljić, Abdulah. *Turcizmi u srpskohrvatskom-hrvatskosrpskom jeziku.* Sarajevo: Svjetlost, 1985.

Tandarić, J. "Glagoljska pismenost u srednjovjekovnoj Bosni." In J. Turćinović, ed. *Povijesno-teološki simpozij u povodu 500. obljetnice smrti bosanske kraljice Katarine,* 47-51. Sarajevo: Kršćanska sadašnjost, 1979.

Truhelka, Ćiro. "Bosančica." *Glasnik zemaljskog muzeja* 1 (1889) 65-83.

16. MASS MEDIA

Dennis, Everett E. and Jon Vanden Heuvel. *Emerging Voices: East European Media in Transition: A Report of the Gannett Foundation Task Force on Press Freedom in Eastern Europe.* New York: Gannett Center for Media Studies, Columbia University, 1990.

Emery, Walter Byron. "Five European Broadcasting Systems." *Journalism Monographs* 1 (August 1966).

Micovic, Vojislav. *The Information System in Yugoslavia.* Studies. Belgrade: Jugoslovenska stvarnost, 1980.

Paulu, Burton. *Radio and Television Broadcasting in Eastern Europe.* Minneapolis: University of Minnesota Press, 1974.

Thompson, Mark. *Forging War: The Media in Serbia, Croatia and Bosnia-Hercegovina.* London: Article 19. The International Center against Censorship, 1994.

17. HERALDRY

Petrinić, Mirko. *Fojnica crest-collection.* Sarajevo: Oslobodjenje, 1972.

18. VIDEOS

Bosnia! (117 min.) Un film de Gilles Herzog et Bernard-Henri Levy; réalisé par Alain Ferrari et Bernard-Henri Levy; une coproduction, Les Films du Lendemain, Radio Télévision de Bosnie-Herzégovine, France 2 Cinema. New York: Zeitgeist Films, 1994.

Bosnia: We Are All Neighbors (50 min.) Grenada TV, 1994. Stunning documentary follows individual families as first tensions then war break up an ethnically -mixed community in central Bosnia in 1992-93. Won an Emmy for best documentary.

Bosnian Arms Embargo. (86 min.) U.S. Senate. C-SPAN, 1994.

Beyond the News: Hope for Bosnia. (30 min.) Produced by Mennonite Media Productions; field producer, D. Michael

Hostetter; post producer, Jerry L. Holsopple. Harrisonburg, VA: Mennonite Media Productions, 1993.

Events in Bosnia. (21 min.) House Foreign Affairs Committee Chairman, Representative Lee Hamilton. July 30, 1993. C-SPAN, 1993.

Peacekeepers: How the UN Failed. (50 min.) *Nightline* special report on the role of the UN in Bosnia. New York: ABC News, 1995.

The Refugee Crisis and War Crimes in Former Yugoslavia. (122 min.) Directed by Jerry Echols, U.S. Commission for Security and Cooperation in Europe. C-SPAN, 1993.

Relief Efforts in the Balkans. (38 min.) National Press Club; Catholic Relief Services Speaker. C-SPAN, 1993.

Riedlayer, Andras. *Killing Memory: Bosnia's Cultural Heritage and Its Destruction.* (45 min.) Haverford, PA: DUTV, 1994.

Situation in Bosnia. (44 min.) Directed by Brad Speare, Carnegie Endowment for International Peace. Host William Magnes. C-SPAN, 1992.

Sixty Minutes, "Exercise in Hypocrisy?" (15 min.) CBS Video, 1994.

United Nations Policy toward Bosnia. (45 min.) Produced by Evans Pierre and Mark Farkas; directed by Maurice Haynes; Guest Host, ed. Maddox; Guest Speaker, U.N. Major-General Lewis MacKenzie. C-SPAN, 1993.

Urbicide: A Sarajevo Diary. (50 min.) Bill Tribe; W.O.W. Productions in Association with Channel 4 Television Co., U.K. New York: First Run/ICARUS Films, 1993.

U.S. Policy in Bosnia. (51 min.) C-SPAN, 1993.

U.S. Policy toward Bosnia. (152 min.) Directed by Gary Ellenwood; Senate Foreign Relations Subcommittee Chairman and Moderator, Sen. Joseph Biden, Jr.. C-SPAN, 1993.

U.S./Europe Security Interests. (92 min.) Atlantic Council. Host, General Andrew Goodpaster. Speaker, Stephen Oxman (U.S. State Department). C-SPAN, 1993.

We Are All Neighbours: Bosnia. (52 min.) Granada Television. London: Films Incorporated Video, 1993.

While America Watched: The Bosnia Tragedy. ABC News. Oak Forest, IL: MPI Video, 1991.

19. SOUND RECORDING

Jordanova, Victoria. *Requiem for Bosnia.* Four Preludes for harp; *Once Upon a Time*; Variations for Harp. CD 673. New York: CRI, 1994.

ABOUT THE AUTHOR

ANTE ČUVALO is of Croatian background. He was born in Bosnia- Herzegovina and has been living in the United States since the 1960s. He received a bachelor's degree in philosophy from St. Francis College, Burlington, Wisconsin; a master's degree in history from John Carroll University, Cleveland, Ohio; and a doctorate in history from Ohio State University, Columbus, Ohio. He has taught at OSU and presently is teaching at Joliet Jr. College, Joliet, Illinois. He has written many articles dealing with Bosnia and Herzegovina, Croatia, and the former Yugoslavia. He is the author of *The Croatian National Movement 1966-1972* (1990), a book dealing with the Croatian Spring, and is coauthor and editor of *Croatia and the Croatians* (1991), a survey book on Croatian past and present. He is a regular contributor and associate editor of *American Croatian Review*, a quarterly journal published in the United States.